Level I

Paradigm
PUBLISHING

Microsoft®

Word 2007

BENCHMARK SERIES

Nita Rutkosky
Pierce College at Puyallup
Puyallup, Washington

Audrey Rutkosky Roggenkamp
Pierce College at Puyallup
Puyallup, Washington

Managing Editor	Sonja Brown
Production Editor	Donna Mears
Cover and Text Designer	Leslie Anderson
Copy Editor	Susan Capecchi
Desktop Production	John Valo, Desktop Solutions
Proofreader	Laura Nelson
Indexer	Nancy Fulton

Acknowledgments: The authors and editors wish to thank the following individuals for their technical and academic contributions.

- Catherine Caldwell, a technical writer and consultant from Memphis, Tennessee, tested the instruction and exercises for accuracy.
- Madlyn Huber, Instructor, Bridgerland Applied Technology College, Logan, Utah, tested exercises for accuracy and prepared annotated model answers.
- Pamela J. Silvers, Chairperson, Business Computer Technologies, Asheville-Buncombe Technical Community College, Asheville, North Carolina, tested the instruction and exercises for accuracy.

Care has been taken to verify the accuracy of information presented in this book. However, the authors, editors, and publisher cannot accept responsibility for Web, e-mail, newsgroup, or chat room subject matter or content, or for consequences from application of the information in this book, and make no warranty, expressed or implied, with respect to its content.

Photo Credits: Introduction page 1 (clockwise from top), Lexmark International, Inc., courtesy of Dell Inc., all rights Hewlett-Packard Company, Logitech, Micron Technology, Inc.; Word Level 1 page 3, Asia Images Group/AsiaPix/Getty Images, page 4, © Corbis; photos in Student Resources CD, courtesy of Kelly Rutkosky and Michael Rutkosky.

We have made every effort to trace the ownership of all copyrighted material and to secure permission from copyright holders. In the event of any question arising as to the use of any material, we will be pleased to make the necessary corrections in future printings. Thanks are due to the aforementioned authors, publishers, and agents for permission to use the materials indicated.

ISBN 978-0-76382-984-1 (Text)
ISBN 978-0-76383-000-7 (Text + CD)

© 2008 by Paradigm Publishing, Inc.
875 Montreal Way
St. Paul, MN 55102
E-mail: educate@emcp.com
Web site: www.emcp.com

Printed in the United States of America

16 15 14 13 12 11 10   4 5 6 7 8 9 10

CONTENTS

Benchmark Microsoft Word 2007 is designed for students who want to learn how to use this powerful word processing program to create professional-looking documents for workplace, school, and personal communication needs. No prior knowledge of word processing is required. After successfully completing a course using this textbook, students will be able to

- Create and edit memos, letters, and reports of varying complexity
- Apply appropriate formatting elements and styles to a range of document types
- Add graphics and other visual elements to enhance written communication
- Plan, research, write, revise, and publish documents to meet specific information needs
- Given a workplace scenario requiring a written solution, assess the communication purpose and then prepare the materials that achieve the goal efficiently and effectively

In addition to mastering Word skills, students will learn the essential features and functions of computer hardware, the Windows XP operating system, and Internet Explorer 7.0. Upon completing the text, they can expect to be proficient in using Word to organize, analyze, and present information.

Achieving Proficiency in Word 2007

Since its inception several Office versions ago, the Benchmark Series has served as a standard of excellence in software instruction. Elements of the book function individually and collectively to create an inviting, comprehensive learning environment that produces successful computer users.

MODULE OPENERS highlight key features of Word 2007 within the context of organizing, analyzing, and presenting information.

UNIT OPENERS display the unit's four chapter titles. Each level has two units, which conclude with a comprehensive unit performance assessment.

CHAPTER OPENERS present the Performance Objectives and an overview of the skills taught.

CD icon identifies a folder of data files to be copied to the student's storage medium.

The SNAP icon alerts students to corresponding SNAP tutorial titles.

New! PROJECT APPROACH organizes instruction and practice into projects that focus on related program features.

Project overview identifies tasks to accomplish and the features to use in completing the work.

Content shown within the figure:

Level 1

Microsoft®

word

Unit 2: Enhancing and Customizing Documents

➤ Applying Formatting and Inserting Objects
➤ Maintaining Documents
➤ Creating Tables and SmartArt
➤ Merging Documents

CHAPTER 5

Word

Applying Formatting and Inserting Objects

PERFORMANCE OBJECTIVES

Upon successful completion of Chapter 5, you will be able to:

- Insert section breaks
- Create and format text in columns
- Hyphenate words automatically and manually
- Create a drop cap
- Insert symbols, special characters, and the date and time
- Use the Click and Type feature
- Vertically align text
- Insert, format, and customize pictures, clip art images, text boxes, shapes, and WordArt

word Chapter 5

SNAP

Tutorial 5.1
Creating Presentable Documents
Tutorial 5.2
Using Additional Features

To apply page or document formatting to only a portion of the document, insert a section break. You can insert a continuous section break or a section break that begins a new page. A section break is useful when formatting text in columns. The hyphenation feature hyphenates words at the end of lines, creating a less ragged margin. Use buttons in the Text and Symbols groups in the Insert tab to insert symbols, special characters, and the date and time. With the Click and Type feature, you can position the insertion point at various locations in the document and change the paragraph alignment. Use the *Vertical alignment* option at the Page Setup dialog box with the Layout tab selected to align text vertically on the page. Along with these features, you will also learn how to increase the visual appeal of a document by inserting and customizing images such as pictures, clip art, text boxes, shapes, and WordArt.

Note: Before beginning computer projects, copy to your storage medium the Word2007L1C5 subfolder from the Word2007L1 folder on the CD that accompanies this textbook and then make Word2007L1C5 the active folder.

Project 1 Format a Document on Computer Input Devices

You will format into columns text in a document on computer input devices, improve the readability of the document by hyphenating long words, and improve the visual appeal by inserting a drop cap.

word Level 1
Applying Formatting and Inserting Objects 153

PROJECT APPROACH: Builds Skill Mastery within Realistic Context

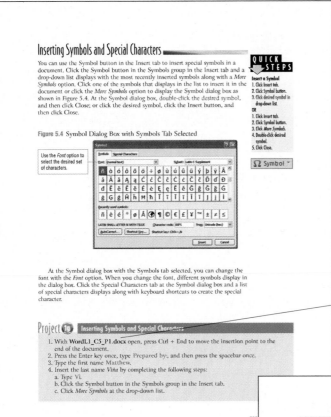

Following each project part, the text presents instruction on the features and skills necessary to accomplish the next section of the project.

Typically, a file remains open throughout all parts of the project. Students save their work incrementally.

Each project exercise guides students step by step to a successful conclusion. Screen captures illustrate what the screen should look like at key points.

Text in magenta identifies material to type.

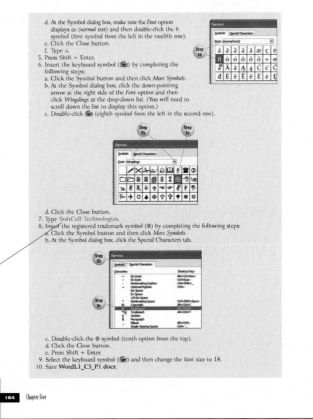

At the end of the project, students print their work. Locked, watermarked model answers in PDF format on the Student Resources CD allow students to check their work. This option rewards careful effort and ensures software mastery.

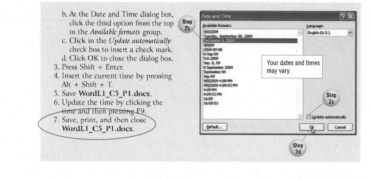

b. At the Date and Time dialog box, click the third option from the top in the *Available formats* group.
c. Click in the *Update automatically* check box to insert a check mark.
d. Click OK to close the dialog box.
3. Press Shift + Enter.
4. Insert the current time by pressing Alt + Shift + T.
5. Save **WordL1_C5_P1.docx**.
6. Update the time by clicking the time and then pressing F9.
7. Save, print, and then close **WordL1_C5_P1.docx**.

Your dates and times may vary.

Step 2b
Step 2c
Step 2d

Project 2 Create an Announcement about Supervisory Training

You will create an announcement about upcoming supervisory training and use the click and type feature to center and right align text. You will vertically center the text on the page and insert and format a picture to add visual appeal to the announcement.

Using the Click and Type Feature

Word contains a click and type feature you can use to position the insertion point at a specific location and alignment in the document. This feature allows you to position one or more lines of text as you write (type), rather than typing the text and then selecting and reformatting the text, which requires multiple steps.

To use click and type, make sure the document displays in Print Layout view and then hover the mouse pointer at the location where you want the insertion point positioned. As you move the mouse pointer, you will notice that the pointer displays with varying horizontal lines representing the alignment. Double-click the mouse button and the insertion point is positioned at the location of the mouse pointer. Turn off the click and type feature by clicking the Office button and then clicking Word Options. Click the Advanced option in the left pane, click the *Enable click and type* check box to remove the check mark, and then click OK.

QUICK STEPS

Use Click and Type
1. Hover mouse at left margin, between left and right margin, or at right margin.
2. Double-click left mouse button.

QUICK STEPS provide feature summaries for reference and review.

QUICK STEPS

Use Click and Type
1. Hover mouse at left margin, between left and right margin, or at right margin.
2. Double-click left mouse button.

CHAPTER REVIEW ACTIVITIES: A Hierarchy of Learning Assessments

CHAPTER summary

- Insert a section break in a document to apply formatting to a portion of a document. You can insert a continuous section break or a section break that begins a new page. View a section break in Draft view since section breaks are not visible in Print Layout view.
- Set text in columns to improve readability of documents such as newsletters or reports. Format text in columns using the Columns button in the Page Setup group in the Page Layout tab or with options at the Columns dialog box.
- Remove column formatting with the Columns button in the Page Layout tab or at the Columns dialog box. Balance column text on the last page of a document by inserting a continuous section break at the end of the text.
- Improve the display of text lines by hyphenating long words that fall at the end of the line. You can automatically or manually hyphenate words in a document.
- To enhance the appearance of text, use drop caps to identify the beginning of major sections or parts of a paragraph. Create drop caps with the Drop Cap button in the Text group in the Insert tab.
- Insert symbols with options at the Symbol dialog box with the Symbols tab selected and insert special characters with options at the Symbol dialog box with the Special Characters
- Click the Date & Time b the Date and Time dialog dialog box or with keyboar update the field with the
- Use the click and type fea
- Vertically align text in a d Setup dialog box with the
- Insert an image such as a group in the Insert tab.
- Customize and format an Format tab. Size an image Picture Tools Format tab c selected image.
- Move an image with optio in the Picture Tools Forma moving the image by drag
- To insert a picture, click t desired folder at the Insert
- To insert a clip art image, then click the desired imag
- Insert a pull quote in a do tab, clicking the Text Box box at the drop-down list.

186   Chapter Five

CHAPTER SUMMARY captures the purpose and execution of key features.

COMMANDS review

FEATURE	RIBBON TAB, GROUP	BUTTON	OPTION	KEYBOARD SHORTCUT
Continuous section break	Page Layout, Page Setup	Breaks	Continuous	
Columns dialog box	Page Layout, Page Setup	Columns	More Columns	
Columns	Page Layout, Page Setup	Columns		
Hyphenate words automatically	Page Layout, Page Setup	Hyphenation	Automatic	
Manual Hyphenation dialog box	Page Layout, Page Setup	Hyphenation	Manual	
Drop cap	Insert, Text	Drop Cap		
Symbol dialog box	Insert, Symbols	Symbol		
Date and Time dialog box	Insert, Text	Date & Time		
Insert date				Alt + Shift + D
Insert time				
Update field				
Page Setup dialog box	Page Layout, Page Setup			
Insert Picture dialog box	Insert, Illustrations			
Clip Art task pane	Insert, Illustrations			
Pull quote (Built-in text box)	Insert, Text			
Shapes	Insert, Illustrations			
Text box	Insert, Text			
Link text box	Text Box Tools Format, Text			
Select objects	Home, Editing			
WordArt	Insert, Text			

188   Chapter Five

COMMANDS REVIEW summarizes visually the major features and alternative methods of access.

CONCEPTS check

Test Your Knowledge

Completion: On a blank sheet of paper, indicate the correct term, symbol, or command for each item.

1. View a section break in this view.

2. Format text into columns with the Columns button located in this group in the Page Layout tab.

3. Balance column text on the last page of a document by inserting this type of break at the end of the text.

4. The first letter of the first word of a paragraph that is set into a paragraph is called this.

5. The Symbol button is located in this tab.

6. This is the keyboard shortcut to insert the current date.

7. Use this feature to position the insertion point at a specific location and alignment in a document.

8. Vertically align text with the *Vertical alignment* option at the Page Setup dialog box with this tab selected.

9. Insert an image in a document with buttons in this group in the Insert tab.

10. Customize and format an image with options and buttons in this tab.

11. Size an image with the sizing handles that display around the selected image or with these boxes in the Picture Tools Format tab.

12. Click the Picture button in the Insert tab and this dialog box displays.

13. Click the Clip Art button in the Insert tab and this displays at the right side of the screen.

14. This is the term for a quote that is enlarged and positioned in an attractive location on the page.

15. Format text boxes with options and buttons in this tab.

16. The Shapes button is located in this tab.

word Level 1
Applying Formatting and Inserting Objects   189

CONCEPTS CHECK questions assess knowledge recall.

17. To copy a selected shape, hold down this key while dragging the shape.

18. Link text boxes using this button in the Text group.

19. To select multiple objects in a document, click the Select button in the Editing group in the Home tab and then click this option.

20. Use this feature to distort or modify text to conform to a variety of shapes.

SKILLS check
Demonstrate Your Proficiency

Assessment

1 ADD VISUAL APPEAL TO A REPORT ON THE FUTURE OF THE INTERNET

1. Open **WordReport02.docx** and then save the document and name it **WordL1_C5_A1**.
2. Remove the first line indent by selecting text from the beginning of the first paragraph of text to the end of the document and then dragging the First Line Indent marker on the horizontal ruler to the 0″ mark.
3. Apply the Heading 1 style to the title of the report and apply the Heading 2 style to the headings in the report.
4. Change the Quick Styles set to *Formal*.
5. Format the text from the first paragraph to the end of the document into two columns with 0.4 inches between columns.
6. Select the title *FUTURE OF THE INTERNET* and then change the font size to 16 points, increase the spacing after the title to 12 points and, if necessary center-align the title.
7. Balance the text on the second page.
8. Insert a clip art image related to *satellite*. (Choose the clip art image that is available with Word and does not require downloading. This clip art image is blue and black and contains a satellite and a person holding a telephone and a briefcase.)
9. Make the following customizations to the clip art image:
   a. Change the height to 1.3″.
   b. Apply tight text wrapping.
   c. Recolor the clip art image to Accent color 6 Dark.
   d. Change the brightness to +10%.
   e. Drag the image so it is positioned at the left margin in the *Satellite Internet Connections* section.
10. Insert the *Alphabet Quote* built-in text box and then make the following customizations:
    a. Type the following text in the text box: "A remedy for the traffic clogging the information highway is Internet2."

> SKILLS CHECK exercises ask students to create a variety of documents using multiple features without how-to directions.

CASE study
Apply Your Skills

Part 1
You work for Honoré Financial Services and have been asked by the office manager, Jason Monroe, to prepare an information newsletter. Mr. Monroe has asked you open the document named **WordBudget.docx** and then format it into columns. You determine the number of columns and any additional enhancements to the columns. He also wants you to proofread the document and correct any spelling and grammatical errors. Save the completed newsletter and name it **WordL1_C5_CS_P1** and then print the newsletter. When Mr. Monroe reviews the newsletter, he decides that it needs additional visual appeal. He wants you to insert visual elements in the newsletter such as WordArt, clip art, a built-in text box, and/or a drop cap. Save **WordL1_C5_CS_P1.docx** and then print and close the document.

Part 2
Honoré Financial Services will be offering a free workshop on Planning for Financial Success. Mr. Monroe has asked you to prepare an announcement containing information on the workshop. You determine what to include in the announcement such as the date, time, location, and so forth. Enhance the announcement by inserting a picture or clip art and by applying formatting such as font, paragraph alignment, and borders. Save the completed document and name it **WordL1_C5_CS_P2**. Print and then close the document.

Part 3
Honoré Financial Services has adopted a new slogan and Mr. Monroe has asked you to create a shape with the new slogan inside. Experiment with the shadow and 3-D effects available at the Text Box Tools Format tab and then create a shape and enhance the shape with shadow and/or 3-D effects. Insert the new Honoré Financial Services slogan "Retirement Planning Made Easy" in the shape. Include any additional enhancements to improve the visual appeal of the shape and slogan. Save the completed document and name it **WordL1_C5_CS_P3**. Print and then close the document.

Part 4

Mr. Monroe has asked you to prepare a document containing information on teaching children how to budget. Use the Internet to find Web sites and articles that provide information on how to teach children to budget their money. Write a synopsis of the information you find and include at least four suggestions on how to teach children to manage their money. Format the text in the document into newspaper columns. Add additional enhancements to improve the appearance of the document. Save the completed newsletter and name it **WordL1_C5_CS_P4**. Print and then close the document.

> The chapter CASE STUDY requires planning and executing multi-part workplace projects.

> Students search the Web and/or use the program's Help feature to locate information.

UNIT PERFORMANCE ASSESSMENT: Cross-Disciplinary, Comprehensive Evaluation

Unit 2
Enhancing and Customizing Documents

ASSESSING proficiency

In this unit, you have learned to format text into columns; insert, format, and customize objects to enhance the visual appeal of a document; manage files, print envelopes and labels, and create documents using templates; create and edit tables; visually represent data in SmartArt diagrams and organizational charts; and use Mail Merge to create letters, envelopes, labels, and directions.

Note: Before beginning unit assessments, delete the Word2007L1C8 folder from your storage medium. Next, copy to your storage medium the Word2007L1U2 subfolder from the Word2007L1 on the CD that accompanies this textbook and then make Word2007L1U2 the active folder.

Assessment 1 Format a Technology Occupations Document

1. Open **WordReport09.docx** and then save the document and name it **WordL1_U2_A1**.
2. Move the insertion point to the beginning of the heading *Telecommuting* and then insert the file named **WordDocument19.docx**.
3. Apply the Heading 1 style to the title and the Heading 2 style to the headings in the document.
4. Change the Quick Styles set to *Formal*.
5. Insert a continuous section break at the beginning of the first paragraph of text (the paragraph that begins *The march of computer technology . . .*).
6. Format the text below the section break into two newspaper columns.
7. Balance the columns on the second page.
8. Insert a pull quote of your choosing on the first page of the document that includes the text *"As the future of wireless unfolds, many new jobs will emerge as well."*
9. Create a drop cap with the first letter of the first word *The* that begins the first paragraph of text and make the drop cap two lines in height.
10. Manually hyphenate words in the document.
11. Insert page numbering that prints at the bottom of each page (you determine the page number formatting).
12. Save, print, and then close **WordL1_U2_A1.docx**.

Assessment 2 Create a Workshop Flyer

1. Create the flyer shown in Figure U2.1 with the following specifications:
   a. Insert the WordArt shape with WordArt style 15 and then customize the WordArt by changing the shadow effect to Shadow Style 1, the shape to Deflate Bottom, and increasing the width of the WordArt to 6.5" and the height to 1".

ASSESSING PROFICIENCY checks mastery of features.

WRITING ACTIVITIES involve applying program skills in a communication context.

WRITING activities

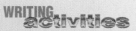

The following activities give you the opportunity to practice your writing skills along with demonstrating an understanding of some of the important Word features you have mastered in this unit. Use correct grammar, appropriate word choices, and clear sentence constructions.

Activity 1 Compose a Letter to Volunteers

You are an employee for the City of Greenwater and are responsible for coordinating volunteers for the city's Safe Night program. Compose a letter to the volunteers listed below and include the following information in the letter:
- Safe Night event scheduled for Saturday, June 19, 2010.
- Volunteer orientation scheduled for Thursday, May 20, 2010, at 7:30 p.m. At the orientation, participants will learn about the types of volunteer positions available and the work schedule.

Include any additional information in the letter, including a thank you to the volunteers. Use the Mail Merge feature to create a data source with the names ...ain document, which is the letter to the ...**WordL1_U2_Act01** and then print the

Mr. Matthew Klein
7408 Ryan Road
Greenwater, OR 99034

Mr. Brian McDonald
8980 Union Street
Greenwater, OR 99034

Mrs. Nola Alverez
598 McBride Street
Greenwater, OR 99034

...head
...d shipping business and need letterhead ...company in a header and/or footer. Use ...ating a header that only displays and prints ...in a header that displays and prints only on ...r the following: a clip art image, a picture, a ...de the following information in the header:

...e it **WordL1_U2_Act02**. Print and then

INTERNET RESEARCH project reinforces research, writing, and word processing skills.

INTERNET research

Create a Flyer on an Incentive Program

The owner of Evergreen Travel is offering an incentive to motivate travel consultants to increase travel bookings. The incentive is a sales contest with a grand prize of a one-week paid vacation to Cancun, Mexico. The owner has asked you to create a flyer that will be posted on the office bulletin board that includes information about the incentive program and some information about Cancun. Create this flyer using information about Cancun that you find on the Internet. Include a photo you find on a Web site (make sure it is not copyrighted) or include a clip art image representing travel. Include any other information or object to add visual appeal to the flyer. Save the completed flyer and name it **WordL1_U2_InternetResearch**. Print and then close the document.

JOB study

Develop Recycling Program Communications

The Chief Operating Officer of Harrington Engineering has just approved your draft of the company's new recycling policy (see the file named **WordRecyclingPolicy.docx** located in the Word2007L1U2 folder) with a note that you need to add some statistics on national average costs of recycling, which you can locate on the Internet. Edit the draft and prepare a final copy of the policy along with a memorandum to all employees describing the new guidelines. To support the company's energy resources conservation effort, you will send hard copies of the new policy to the Somerset Recycling Program president and to directors of Somerset Chamber of Commerce.

Using the concepts and techniques you learned in this unit, prepare the following documents:
- Format the recycling policy manual, including a cover page, appropriate headers and footers, and page numbers. Add at least one graphic and one diagram where appropriate. Format the document using a Quick Styles set and styles. Save the manual and name it **WordL1_U2_JobStudyManual**. Print the manual.
- Download a memo template from the Microsoft Online Web site and then create a memo from Susan Gerhardt, Chief Operating Officer of Harrington Engineering to all employees introducing the new recycling program. Copy the *Procedure* section of the recycling policy manual into the memo where appropriate. Include a table listing five employees who will act as Recycling Coordinators at Harrington Engineering (make up the names). Add columns for the employees' department names and their telephone extensions. Save the memo and name it **WordL1_U2_JobStudyMemo**. Print the memo.
- Write a letter to the President of the Somerset Recycling Program, William Elizondo, enclosing a copy of the recycling policy manual. Add a notation

JOB STUDY presents a capstone assessment requiring critical thinking and problem solving.

Student Courseware

Student Resources CD Each Benchmark Series textbook is packaged with a Student Resources CD containing the data files required for completing the projects and assessments. A CD icon and folder name displayed on the opening page of chapters reminds students to copy a folder of files from the CD to the desired storage medium before beginning the project exercises. Directions for copying folders are printed on the inside back cover. The Student Resources CD also contains the model answers in PDF format for the project exercises within chapters. Files are locked and watermarked, but students can compare their completed documents with the PDF files, either on screen or in hard copy (printed) format.

Internet Resource Center Additional learning tools and reference materials are available at the book-specific Web site at www.emcp.net/BenchmarkWord07XP. Students can access the same resources that are on the Student Resources CD along with study aids, Web links, and tips for using computers effectively in academic and workplace settings.

SNAP Training and Assessment SNAP is a Web-based program that provides hands-on instruction, practice, and testing for learning Microsoft Office 2007 and Windows. SNAP course work simulates operations of Office 2007. The program is comprised of a Web-based learning management system, multimedia tutorials, performance skill items, a concept test bank, and online grade book and course planning tools. A CD-based set of tutorials teaching the basics of Office and Windows is also available for additional practice not requiring Internet access.

Class Connections Available for both WebCT and Blackboard e-learning platforms, Paradigm's Class Connection provides self-quizzes and study aids and facilitates communication among students and instructors via e-mail and e-discussion.

Instructor Resources

Curriculum Planner and Resources Instructor support for the Benchmark Series has been expanded to include a *Curriculum Planner and Resources* binder with CD. This all-in-one print resource includes planning resources such as Lesson Blueprints and sample course syllabi; presentation resources such as teaching hints and handouts; and assessment resources including an overview of assessment venues, model answers for intrachapter projects, and annotated model answers for end-of-chapter and end-of-unit assessments. Contents of the *Curriculum Planner and Resources* binder are also available on the Instructor's CD and on the password-protected Instructor's section of the Internet Resource Center for this title at www.emcp.com.

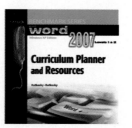

Computerized Test Generator Instructors can use ExamView test generating software and the provided bank of multiple-choice items to create customized Web-based or print tests.

System Requirements

This text is designed for the student to complete projects and assessments on a computer running a standard installation of Microsoft Office 2007, Professional Edition, and the Microsoft Windows XP operating system with Service Pack 2 or later. To effectively run this suite and operating system, your computer should be outfitted with the following:

- 500 MHz processor or higher; 256 MB RAM or higher
- DVD drive
- 2 GB of available hard-disk space
- CD-ROM drive
- 800 by 600 minimum monitor resolution; 1024 by 768 recommended
  Note: Screen captures in this book were created using 1024 by 768 resolution; screens with higher resolution may look different.
- Computer mouse or compatible pointing device

About the Authors

Nita Rutkosky began teaching business education courses at Pierce College in Puyallup, Washington, in 1978. Since then she has taught a variety of software applications to students in postsecondary Information Technology certificate and degree programs. In addition to co-authoring texts in the *Benchmark Office 2007 Series*, she has co-authored *Signature Word 2007*, *Marquee Office 2007*, and *Using Computers in the Medical Office: Microsoft Word, Excel, and PowerPoint 2003*. Other textbooks she has written for Paradigm Publishing include books on previous versions of Microsoft Office along with WordPerfect, desktop publishing, keyboarding, and voice recognition.

Audrey Rutkosky Roggenkamp has been teaching courses in the Business Information Technology department at Pierce College in Puyallup including keyboarding, skill building, and Microsoft Office programs. In addition to titles in the *Benchmark Office 2007 Series*, she has co-authored *Using Computers in the Medical Office*, *Marquee Office 2007*, and *Signature Word 2007*.

Getting Started in Office 2007

In this textbook, you will learn to operate several computer application programs that combine to make an application "suite." This suite of programs is called Microsoft Office 2007. The programs you will learn to operate are the software, which includes instructions telling the computer what to do. Some of the application programs in the suite include a word processing program named Word, a spreadsheet program named Excel, a database program named Access, and a presentation program named PowerPoint.

Identifying Computer Hardware

The computer equipment you will use to operate the suite of programs is referred to as hardware. You will need access to a microcomputer system that should consist of the CPU, monitor, keyboard, printer, drives, and mouse. If you are not sure what equipment you will be operating, check with your instructor. The computer system shown in Figure G.1 consists of six components. Each component is discussed separately in the material that follows.

Figure G.1 Microcomputer System

CPU

CPU stands for Central Processing Unit and it is the intelligence of the computer. All the processing occurs in the CPU. Silicon chips, which contain miniaturized circuitry, are placed on boards that are plugged into slots within the CPU. Whenever an instruction is given to the computer, that instruction is processed through circuitry in the CPU.

Monitor

The monitor is a piece of equipment that looks like a television screen. It displays the information of a program and the text being input at the keyboard. The quality of display for monitors varies depending on the type of monitor and the level of resolution. Monitors can also vary in size—generally from 14-inch size up to 21-inch size or larger.

Keyboard

The keyboard is used to input information into the computer. Keyboards for microcomputers vary in the number and location of the keys. Microcomputers have the alphabetic and numeric keys in the same location as the keys on a typewriter. The symbol keys, however, may be placed in a variety of locations, depending on the manufacturer. In addition to letters, numbers, and symbols, most microcomputer keyboards contain function keys, arrow keys, and a numeric keypad. Figure G.2 shows an enhanced keyboard.

Figure G.2 Keyboard

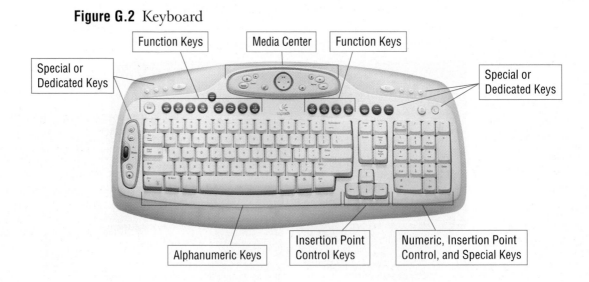

The 12 keys at the top of the keyboard, labeled with the letter F followed by a number, are called *function keys*. Use these keys to perform functions within each of the suite programs. To the right of the regular keys is a group of *special* or *dedicated keys*. These keys are labeled with specific functions that will be performed when you press the key. Below the special keys are arrow keys. Use these keys to move the insertion point in the document screen.

A keyboard generally includes three mode indicator lights. When you select certain modes, a light appears on the keyboard. For example, if you press the Caps Lock key, which disables the lowercase alphabet, a light appears next to Caps Lock. Similarly, pressing the Num Lock key will disable the special functions on the numeric keypad, which is located at the right side of the keyboard.

Disk Drives

Depending on the computer system you are using, Microsoft Office 2007 is installed on a hard drive or as part of a network system. Whether you are using Office on a hard drive or network system, you will need to have available a DVD or CD drive and a USB drive or other storage medium. You will insert the CD (compact disc) that accompanies this textbook in the DVD or CD drive and then copy folders from the CD to your storage medium. You will also save documents you complete at the computer to folders on your storage medium.

Printer

A document you create in Word is considered soft copy. If you want a hard copy of a document, you need to print it. To print documents you will need to access a printer, which will probably be either a laser printer or an ink-jet printer. A laser printer uses a laser beam combined with heat and pressure to print documents, while an ink-jet printer prints a document by spraying a fine mist of ink on the page.

Mouse

Many functions in the suite of programs are designed to operate more efficiently with a mouse. A mouse is an input device that sits on a flat surface next to the computer. You can operate a mouse with the left or the right hand. Moving the mouse on the flat surface causes a corresponding mouse pointer to move on the screen. Figure G.1 shows an illustration of a mouse.

Using the Mouse

The programs in the Microsoft Office suite can be operated using a keyboard or they can be operated with the keyboard and a mouse. The mouse may have two or three buttons on top, which are tapped to execute specific functions and commands. To use the mouse, rest it on a flat surface or a mouse pad. Put your hand over it with your palm resting on top of the mouse and your wrist resting on the table surface. As you move the mouse on the flat surface, a corresponding pointer moves on the screen.

When using the mouse, you should understand four terms—point, click, double-click, and drag. When operating the mouse, you may need to point to a specific command, button, or icon. Point means to position the mouse pointer on the desired item. With the mouse pointer positioned on the desired item, you may need to click a button on the mouse. Click means quickly tapping a button on the mouse once. To complete two steps at one time, such as choosing and then executing a function, double-click a mouse button. Double-click means to tap the left mouse button twice in quick succession. The term drag means to press and hold the left mouse button, move the mouse pointer to a specific location, and then release the button.

Using the Mouse Pointer

The mouse pointer will change appearance depending on the function being performed or where the pointer is positioned. The mouse pointer may appear as one of the following images:

- The mouse pointer appears as an I-beam (called the I-beam pointer) in the document screen and can be used to move the insertion point or select text.

- The mouse pointer appears as an arrow pointing up and to the left (called the arrow pointer) when it is moved to the Title bar, Quick Access toolbar, ribbon, or an option in a dialog box. For example, to open a new document with the mouse, position the I-beam pointer on the Office button located in the upper left corner of the screen until the pointer turns into an arrow pointer and then click the left mouse button. At the drop-down list that displays, make a selection by positioning the arrow pointer on the desired option and then clicking the left mouse button.

- The mouse pointer becomes a double-headed arrow (either pointing left and right, pointing up and down, or pointing diagonally) when performing certain functions such as changing the size of an object.

- In certain situations, such as moving an object or image, the mouse pointer becomes a four-headed arrow. The four-headed arrow means that you can move the object left, right, up, or down.

- When a request is being processed or when a program is being loaded, the mouse pointer may appear with an hourglass beside it. The hourglass image means "please wait." When the process is completed, the hourglass image is removed.

- The mouse pointer displays as a hand with a pointing index finger in certain functions such as Help and indicates that more information is available about the item.

Choosing Commands

Once a program is open, you can use several methods in the program to choose commands. A command is an instruction that tells the program to do something. You can choose a command using the mouse or the keyboard. When a program such as Word or PowerPoint is open, the ribbon contains buttons for completing tasks and contains tabs you click to display additional buttons. To choose a button on the Quick Access toolbar or in the ribbon, position the tip of the mouse arrow pointer on a button and then click the left mouse button.

The Office suite provides access keys you can press to use a command in a program. Press the Alt key on the keyboard to display KeyTips that identify the access key you need to press to execute a command. For example, press the Alt key in a Word document and KeyTips display as shown in Figure G.3. Continue pressing access keys until you execute the desired command. For example, if you want to begin spell checking a document, you would press the Alt key, press the R key on the keyboard to display the Review tab, and then press the letter S on the keyboard.

Figure G.3 Word KeyTips

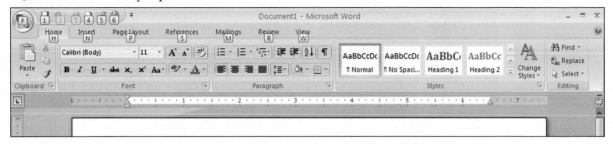

Choosing Commands from Drop-Down Lists

To choose a command from a drop-down list with the mouse, position the mouse pointer on the desired option and then click the left mouse button. To make a selection from a drop-down list with the keyboard, type the underlined letter in the desired option.

Some options at a drop-down list may be gray-shaded (dimmed), indicating that the option is currently unavailable. If an option at a drop-down list displays preceded by a check mark, that indicates that the option is currently active. If an option at a drop-down list displays followed by an ellipsis (...), a dialog box will display when that option is chosen.

Choosing Options from a Dialog Box

A dialog box contains options for applying formatting to a file or data within a file. Some dialog boxes display with tabs along the top providing additional options. For example, the Font dialog box shown in Figure G.4 contains two tabs—the Font tab and the Character Spacing tab. The tab that displays in the front is the

Figure G.4 Word Font Dialog Box

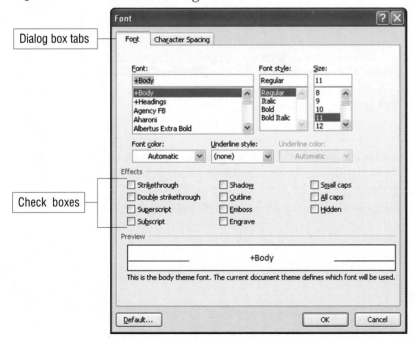

active tab. To make a tab active using the mouse, position the arrow pointer on the desired tab and then click the left mouse button. If you are using the keyboard, press Ctrl + Tab or press Alt + the underlined letter on the desired tab.

To choose options from a dialog box with the mouse, position the arrow pointer on the desired option and then click the left mouse button. If you are using the keyboard, press the Tab key to move the insertion point forward from option to option. Press Shift + Tab to move the insertion point backward from option to option. You can also hold down the Alt key and then press the underlined letter of the desired option. When an option is selected, it displays with a blue background or surrounded by a dashed box called a marquee. A dialog box contains one or more of the following elements: text boxes, list boxes, check boxes, option buttons, spin boxes, and command buttons.

Text Boxes

Some options in a dialog box require you to enter text. For example, the boxes below the *Find what* and *Replace with* options at the Excel Find and Replace dialog box shown in Figure G.5 are text boxes. In a text box, you type text or edit existing text. Edit text in a text box in the same manner as normal text. Use the Left and Right Arrow keys on the keyboard to move the insertion point without deleting text and use the Delete key or Backspace key to delete text.

Figure G.5 Excel Find and Replace Dialog Box

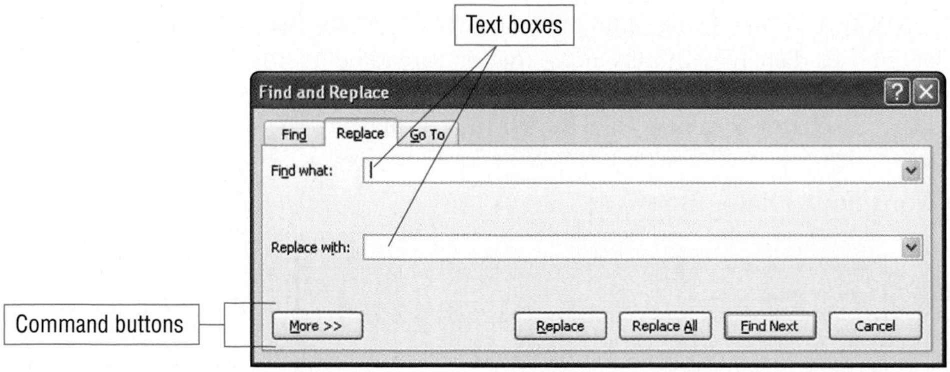

List Boxes

Some dialog boxes such as the Word Open dialog box shown in Figure G.6 may contain a list box. The list of files below the *Look in* option is contained in a list box. To make a selection from a list box with the mouse, move the arrow pointer to the desired option and then click the left mouse button.

Figure G.6 Word Open Dialog Box

Some list boxes may contain a scroll bar. This scroll bar will display at the right side of the list box (a vertical scroll bar) or at the bottom of the list box (a horizontal scroll bar). You can use a vertical scroll bar or a horizontal scroll bar to move through the list if the list is longer than the box. To move down through a list on a vertical scroll bar, position the arrow pointer on the down-pointing arrow and hold down the left mouse button. To scroll up through the list in a vertical scroll bar, position the arrow pointer on the up-pointing arrow and hold down the left mouse button. You can also move the arrow pointer above the scroll box and click the left mouse button to scroll up the list or move the arrow pointer below the scroll box and click the left mouse button to move down the list. To move through a list with a horizontal scroll bar, click the left-pointing arrow to scroll to the left of the list or click the right-pointing arrow to scroll to the right of the list.

To make a selection from a list using the keyboard, move the insertion point into the box by holding down the Alt key and pressing the underlined letter of the desired option. Press the Up and/or Down Arrow keys on the keyboard to move through the list.

In some dialog boxes where enough room is not available for a list box, lists of options are inserted in a drop-down list box. Options that contain a drop-down list box display with a down-pointing arrow. For example, the *Underline style* option at the Word Font dialog box shown in Figure G.4 contains a drop-down list. To display the list, click the down-pointing arrow to the right of the *Underline style* option box. If you are using the keyboard, press Alt + U.

Check Boxes

Some dialog boxes contain options preceded by a box. A check mark may or may not appear in the box. The Word Font dialog box shown in Figure G.4 displays a variety of check boxes within the *Effects* section. If a check mark appears in the box, the option is active (turned on). If the check box does not contain a check mark, the option is inactive (turned off). Any number of check boxes can be active. For example, in the Word Font dialog box, you can insert a check mark in any or all of the boxes in the *Effects* section and these options will be active.

To make a check box active or inactive with the mouse, position the tip of the arrow pointer in the check box and then click the left mouse button. If you are using the keyboard, press Alt + the underlined letter of the desired option.

Option Buttons

The Word Print dialog box shown in Figure G.7 contains options in the *Print range* section preceded by option buttons. Only one option button can be selected at any time. When an option button is selected, a green circle displays in the button. To select an option button with the mouse, position the tip of the arrow pointer inside the option button and then click the left mouse button. To make a selection with the keyboard, hold down the Alt key and then press the underlined letter of the desired option.

Figure G.7 Word Print Dialog Box

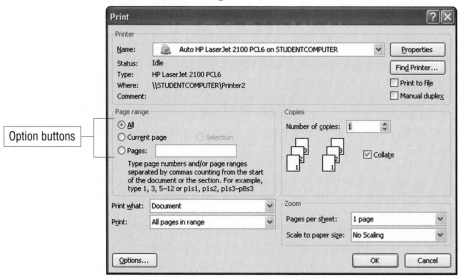

Option buttons

Spin Boxes

Some options in a dialog box contain measurements or numbers you can increase or decrease. These options are generally located in a spin box. For example, the Word Paragraph dialog box shown in Figure G.8 contains spin boxes located after the *Left*, *Right*, *Before*, and *After* options. To increase a number in a spin box, position the tip of the arrow pointer on the up-pointing arrow to the right of the desired option and then click the left mouse button. To decrease the number, click the down-pointing arrow. If you are using the keyboard, press Alt + the underlined letter of the desired option and then press the Up Arrow key to increase the number or the Down Arrow key to decrease the number.

Figure G.8 Word Paragraph Dialog Box

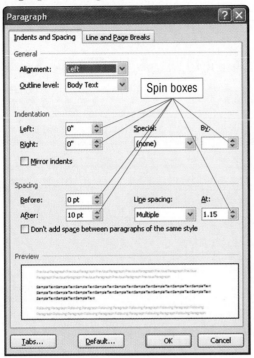

Command Buttons

In the Excel Find and Replace dialog box shown in Figure G.5, the boxes along the bottom of the dialog box are called command buttons. Use a command button to execute or cancel a command. Some command buttons display with an ellipsis (...). A command button that displays with an ellipsis will open another dialog box. To choose a command button with the mouse, position the arrow pointer on the desired button and then click the left mouse button. To choose a command button with the keyboard, press the Tab key until the desired command button contains the marquee and then press the Enter key.

Choosing Commands with Keyboard Shortcuts

Applications in the Office suite offer a variety of keyboard shortcuts you can use to executive specific commands. Keyboard shortcuts generally require two or more keys. For example, the keyboard shortcut to display the Open dialog box in an application is Ctrl + O. To use this keyboard shortcut, hold down the Ctrl key, type the letter O on the keyboard, and then release the Ctrl key. For a list of keyboard shortcuts, refer to the Help files.

Choosing Commands with Shortcut Menus

The software programs in the suite include menus that contain commands related to the item with which you are working. A shortcut menu appears in the file in the location where you are working. To display a shortcut menu, click the right mouse button or press Shift + F10. For example, if the insertion point is positioned in a paragraph of text in a Word document, clicking the right mouse button or pressing Shift + F10 will cause the shortcut menu shown in Figure G.9 to display in the document screen.

Figure G.9 Word Shortcut Menu

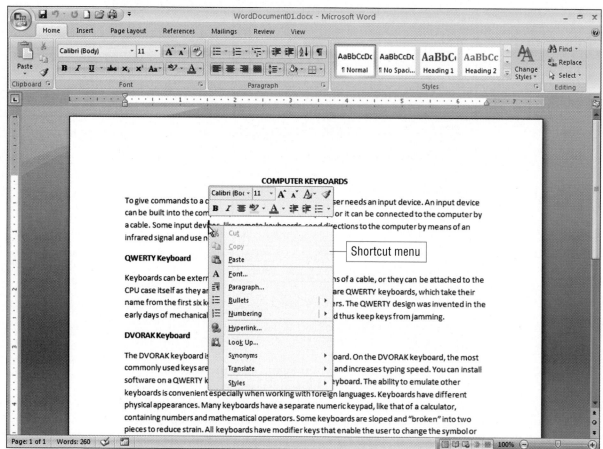

To select an option from a shortcut menu with the mouse, click the desired option. If you are using the keyboard, press the Up or Down Arrow key until the desired option is selected and then press the Enter key. To close a shortcut menu without choosing an option, click anywhere outside the shortcut menu or press the Esc key.

Working with Multiple Programs

As you learn the various programs in the Microsoft Office suite, you will notice how executing commands in each is very similar. For example, the steps to save, close, and print are virtually the same whether you are working in Word, Excel, or PowerPoint. This consistency between programs greatly enhances a user's ability to transfer knowledge learned in one program to another within the suite. Another appeal of Microsoft Office is the ability to have more than one program open at the same time. For example, you can open Word, create a document, and then open Excel, create a spreadsheet, and copy the spreadsheet into Word.

When you open a program, the name of the program displays in the Taskbar. If you open a file within the program, the file name follows the program name on the button on the Taskbar. If you open another program, the program name displays on a button positioned to the right of the first program button. Figure G.10 shows the Taskbar with Word, Excel, and PowerPoint open. To move from one program to another, click the button on the Taskbar representing the desired program file.

Figure G.10 Taskbar with Word, Excel, and PowerPoint Open

Completing Computer Projects

Some computer projects in this textbook require that you open an existing file. Project files are saved on the Student CD that accompanies this textbook. The files you need for each chapter are saved in individual folders. Before beginning a chapter, copy the necessary folder from the CD to your storage medium. After completing projects in a chapter, delete the chapter folder before copying the next chapter folder. (Check with your instructor before deleting a folder.)

The Student CD also contains model answers in PDF format for the project exercises within (but not at the end of) each chapter so you can check your work. To access the PDF files, you will need to have Adobe Acrobat Reader installed on your computer's hard drive. A free download of Adobe Reader is available at Adobe Systems' Web site at www.adobe.com.

Copying a Folder

As you begin working in a chapter, copy the chapter folder from the CD to your storage medium using the My Computer window by completing the following steps:

1. Insert the CD that accompanies this textbook in the CD drive.
2. Insert your storage medium in the appropriate drive.
3. At the Windows XP desktop, open the My Computer window by clicking the Start button and then clicking *My Computer* at the Start menu.
4. Double-click the CD drive in the contents pane (probably displays as *Office2007_Bench* or *Word2007, Excel 2007*, etc. followed by the drive letter).
5. Double-click the *StudentDataFiles* folder in the contents pane.
6. Double-click the desired folder name in the contents pane. (For example, if you are copying a folder for a Word Level 1 chapter, double-click the *Word2007L1* folder.)
7. Click once on the desired chapter subfolder name to select it.
8. Click the <u>Copy this folder</u> hyperlink in the *File and Folder Tasks* section of the task pane.
9. At the Copy Items dialog box, click the drive where your storage medium is located and then click the Copy button.
10. After the folder is copied to your storage medium, close the My Computer window by clicking the Close button (white X on red background) that displays in the upper right corner of the window.

Deleting a Folder

Before copying a chapter folder onto your storage medium, you may need to delete any previous chapter folders. Do this in the My Computer window by completing the following steps:

1. Insert your storage medium in the appropriate drive.
2. At the Windows XP desktop, open the My Computer window by clicking the Start button and then clicking *My Computer* at the Start menu.
3. Double-click the drive where you storage medium is located in the contents pane.
4. Click the chapter folder in the list box.
5. Click the <u>Delete this folder</u> hyperlink in the *File and Folder Tasks* section of the task pane.
6. At the message asking if you want to remove the folder and all its contents, click the Yes button.
7. If a message displays asking if you want to delete a read-only file, click the Yes to All button.
8. Close the My Computer window by clicking the Close button (white X on red background) that displays in the upper right corner of the window.

Viewing or Printing the Project Model Answers

If you want to access the PDF model answer files, first make sure that Adobe Acrobat Reader is installed on your hard drive. Double-click the folder, double-click the desired chapter subfolder name, and double-click the appropriate file name to open the file. You can view and/or print the file to compare it with your own completed exercise file.

Customizing the Quick Access Toolbar

The four applications in the Office 2007 suite—Word, Excel, PowerPoint, and Access—each contain a Quick Access toolbar that displays at the top of the screen. By default, this toolbar contains three buttons: Save, Undo, and Redo. Before beginning chapters in this textbook, customize the Quick Access toolbar by adding three additional buttons: New, Open, and Quick Print. To add these three buttons to the Word Quick Access toolbar, complete the following steps:

1. Open Word.
2. Click the Customize Quick Access Toolbar button that displays at the right side of the toolbar.
3. At the drop-down list, click *New*. (This adds the New button to the toolbar.)
4. Click the Customize Quick Access Toolbar button and then click *Open* at the drop-down list. (This adds the Open button to the toolbar.)
5. Click the Customize Quick Access Toolbar button and then click *Quick Print* at the drop-down list. (This adds the Quick Print button to the toolbar.)

Complete the same steps for Excel, Access, and PowerPoint. You will only need to add the buttons once to the Quick Access toolbar. These buttons will remain on the toolbar even when you exit and then reopen the application.

Using Windows XP

A computer requires an operating system to provide necessary instructions on a multitude of processes including loading programs, managing data, directing the flow of information to peripheral equipment, and displaying information. Windows XP Professional is an operating system that provides functions of this type (along with much more) in a graphical environment. Windows is referred to as a *graphical user interface* (GUI—pronounced *gooey*) that provides a visual display of information with features such as icons (pictures) and buttons. In this introduction, you will learn the basic features of Windows XP:

Tutorial WXP1
Exploring Windows XP
Tutorial WXP2
Working with Files and Folders
Tutorial WXP3
Customizing Windows
Tutorial WXP4
Using Applications

- Use desktop icons and the Taskbar to launch programs and open files or folders
- Organize and manage data, including copying, moving, creating, and deleting files and folders
- Customize the desktop by changing the theme, background, colors, and settings, and adding a screen saver
- Use the Help and Support Center features
- Customize monitor settings

Historically, Microsoft has produced two editions of Windows—one edition for individual users (on desktop and laptop computers) and another edition for servers (on computers that provide service over networks). Windows XP is an upgrade and a merging of these two Windows editions and is available in two versions. The Windows XP Home Edition is designed for home use and Windows XP Professional is designed for small office and workstation use. Whether you are using Windows XP Home Edition or Windows XP Professional, you will be able to complete the steps in the projects in this introduction.

Before using one of the software programs in the Microsoft Office suite, you will need to start the Windows XP operating system. To do this, turn on the computer. Depending on your computer equipment configuration, you may also need to turn on the monitor and printer. If you are using a computer that is part of a network system or if your computer is set up for multiple users, a screen will display showing the user accounts defined for your computer system. At this screen, click your user account name and, if necessary, type your password and then press the Enter key. The Windows XP operating system will start and, after a few moments, the desktop will display as shown in Figure W.1. (Your desktop may vary from what you see in Figure W.1.)

Figure W.1 Windows XP Desktop

icon

Taskbar

Exploring the Desktop

When Windows XP is loaded, the main portion of the screen is called the **desktop**. Think of the desktop in Windows as the top of a desk in an office. A business person places necessary tools—such as pencils, pens, paper, files, calculator—on the desktop to perform functions. Like the tools that are located on a desk, the desktop contains tools for operating the computer. These tools are logically grouped and placed in dialog boxes or panels that you can display using icons on the desktop. The desktop contains a variety of features for using your computer and software programs installed on the computer. The features available on the desktop are represented by icons and buttons.

Using Icons

Icons are visual symbols that represent programs, files, or folders. Figure W.1 identifies the *Recycle Bin* icon located on the Windows XP desktop. The Windows XP desktop on your computer may contain additional icons. Programs that have been installed on your computer may be represented by an icon on the desktop. Also, icons may display on your desktop representing files or folders. Double-click an icon and the program, file, or folder it represents opens on the desktop.

Using the Taskbar

The bar that displays at the bottom of the desktop (see Figure W.1) is called the Taskbar. The Taskbar, shown in Figure W.2, contains the Start button, a section that displays task buttons representing open programs, and the notification area.

Figure W.2 Windows XP Taskbar

Start button   Task button area   Notification area

Click the Start button, located at the left side of the Taskbar, and the Start menu displays as shown in Figure W.3 (your Start menu may vary). You can also display the Start menu by pressing the Windows key on your keyboard or by pressing Ctrl + Esc. The left column of the Start menu contains *pinned programs*, which are programs that always appear in that particular location on the Start menu, and links to the most recently and frequently used programs. The right column contains links to folders, the Control Panel, online help, and the search feature.

Figure W.3 Start Menu

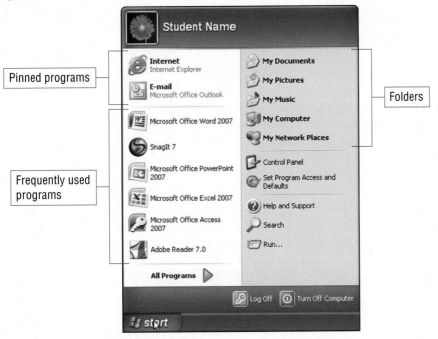

To choose an option from the Start menu, drag the arrow pointer to the desired option (referred to as *pointing*) and then click the left mouse button. Pointing to options at the Start menu that are followed by a right-pointing arrow will cause a side menu to display with additional options. When a program is open, a task button representing the program appears on the Taskbar. If multiple programs are open, each program will appear as a task button on the Taskbar (a few specialized tools may not).

Project 1 — Opening Programs and Switching between Programs

1. Open Windows XP. (To do this, turn on the computer and, if necessary, turn on the monitor and/or printer. If you are using a computer that is part of a network system or if your computer is set up for multiple users, you may need to click your user account name and, if necessary, type your password and then press the Enter key. Check with your instructor to determine if you need to complete any additional steps.)
2. When the Windows XP desktop displays, open Microsoft Word by completing the following steps:
   a. Position the arrow pointer on the Start button on the Taskbar and then click the left mouse button.
   b. At the Start menu, point to *All Programs* (a side menu displays) and then point to *Microsoft Office* (another side menu displays).
   c. Drag the arrow pointer to *Microsoft Office Word 2007* in the side menu and then click the left mouse button.
   d. When the Microsoft Word program is open, notice that a task button representing Word displays on the Taskbar.

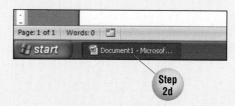

Step
2d

3. Open Microsoft Excel by completing the following steps:
   a. Position the arrow pointer on the Start button on the Taskbar and then click the left mouse button.
   b. At the Start menu, point to *All Programs* and then point to *Microsoft Office*.
   c. Drag the arrow pointer to *Microsoft Office Excel 2007* in the side menu and then click the left mouse button.
   d. When the Microsoft Excel program is open, notice that a task button representing Excel displays on the Taskbar to the right of the task button representing Word.
4. Switch to the Word program by clicking the task button on the Taskbar representing Word.

Step
4

Step
6

5. Switch to the Excel program by clicking the task button on the Taskbar representing Excel.
6. Exit Excel by clicking the Close button that displays in the upper right corner of the Excel window.
7. Exit Word by clicking the Close button that displays in the upper right corner of the Word window.

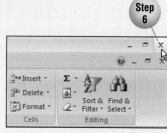

Exploring the Notification Area

The notification area is located at the right side of the Taskbar and contains the system clock along with small icons representing specialized programs that run in the background. Position the arrow pointer over the current time in the notification area of the Taskbar and today's date displays in a small yellow box above the time. Double-click the current time displayed on the Taskbar and the Date and Time Properties dialog box displays as shown in Figure W.4.

Figure W.4 Date and Time Properties Box

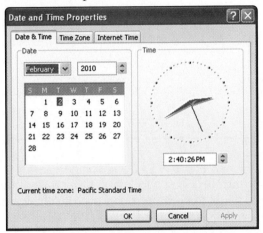

Change the date with options in the *Date* section of the dialog box. For example, to change the month, click the down-pointing arrow at the right side of the option box containing the current month and then click the desired month at the drop-down list. Change the year by clicking the up- or down-pointing arrow at the right side of the option box containing the current year until the desired year displays. To change the day, click the desired day in the monthly calendar that displays in the dialog box. To change the time, double-click either the hour, minute, or seconds and then type the appropriate time or use the up- and down-pointing arrows to adjust the time.

Some programs, when installed, will add an icon to the notification area of the Taskbar. Display the name of the icon by positioning the mouse pointer on the icon and, after approximately one second, the icon label displays in a small yellow box. Some icons may display information in the yellow box rather than the icon label. If more icons have been inserted in the notification area than can be viewed at one time, a left-pointing arrow button displays at the left side of the notification area. Click this left-pointing arrow button and the remaining icons display.

Setting Taskbar Properties

By default, the Taskbar is locked in its current position and size. You can change this default setting, along with other default settings, with options at the Taskbar and Start Menu Properties dialog box, shown in Figure W.5. To display this dialog box, position the arrow pointer on any empty spot on the Taskbar and then click the right mouse button. At the shortcut menu that displays, click *Properties*.

Figure W.5 Taskbar and Start Menu Properties Box

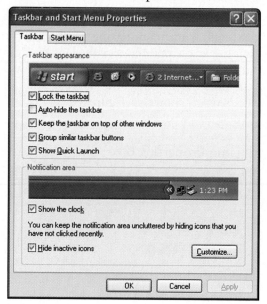

Each property is controlled by a check box. Property options containing a check mark are active. Click the option to remove the check mark and make the option inactive. If an option is inactive, clicking the option will insert a check mark in the check box and turn on the option (make it active).

Project ② Changing Taskbar Properties

1. Make sure Windows XP is open and the desktop displays.
2. Hide the Taskbar and remove the display of the clock by completing the following steps:
   a. Position the arrow pointer on any empty area on the Taskbar and then click the right mouse button.
   b. At the shortcut menu that displays, click *Properties*.
   c. At the Taskbar and Start Menu Properties dialog box, click *Auto-hide the taskbar*. (This inserts a check mark in the check box.)
   d. Click *Show the clock*. (This removes the check mark from the check box.)
   e. Click the Apply button.
   f. Click OK to close the dialog box.

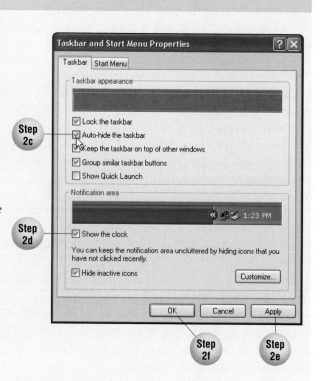

3. Display the Taskbar by positioning the mouse pointer at the bottom of the screen. When the Taskbar displays, notice that the time no longer displays at the right side of the Taskbar.
4. Return to the default settings for the Taskbar by completing the following steps:
   a. With the Taskbar displayed (if it does not display, position the mouse pointer at the bottom of the desktop), position the arrow pointer on any empty area on the Taskbar and then click the right mouse button.
   b. At the shortcut menu that displays, click *Properties*.
   c. At the Taskbar and Start Menu Properties dialog box, click *Auto-hide the taskbar*. (This removes the check mark from the check box.)
   d. Click *Show the clock*. (This inserts a check mark in the check box.)
   e. Click the Apply button.
   f. Click OK to close the dialog box.

Turning Off the Computer

When you are finished working with your computer, you can choose to shut down the computer completely, shut down and then restart the computer, put the computer on standby, or tell the computer to hibernate. Do not turn off your computer until your screen goes blank. Important data is stored in memory while Windows XP is running and this data needs to be written to the hard drive before turning off the computer.

To shut down your computer, click the Start button on the Taskbar and then click *Turn Off Computer* at the Start menu. At the Turn off computer window, shown in Figure W.6, click the *Stand By* option and the computer switches to a low power state causing some devices such as the monitor and hard drives to turn off. With these devices off, the computer uses less power. Stand By is particularly useful for saving battery power for portable computers. Tell the computer to "hibernate" by holding down the Shift key while clicking the *Stand By* option. In hibernate mode, the computer saves everything in memory, turns off the monitor and hard drive, and then turns off the computer. Click the *Turn Off* option if you want to shut down Windows XP and turn off all power to the computer. Click the *Restart* option if you want to restart the computer and restore the desktop exactly as you left it. You can generally restore your desktop from either standby or hibernate by pressing once on the computer's power button. Usually, bringing a computer out of hibernation takes a little longer than bringing a computer out of standby.

Figure W.6 Turn Off Computer Window

Managing Files and Folders

As you begin working with programs in Windows XP, you will create files in which data (information) is saved. A file might contain a Word document, an Excel workbook, or a PowerPoint presentation. As you begin creating files, consider creating folders into which those files will be stored. You can complete file management tasks such as creating a folder and copying and moving files and folders at the My Computer window. To display the My Computer window shown in Figure W.7, click the Start button on the Taskbar and then click My Computer. The various components of the My Computer window are identified in Figure W.7.

Figure W.7 My Computer Window

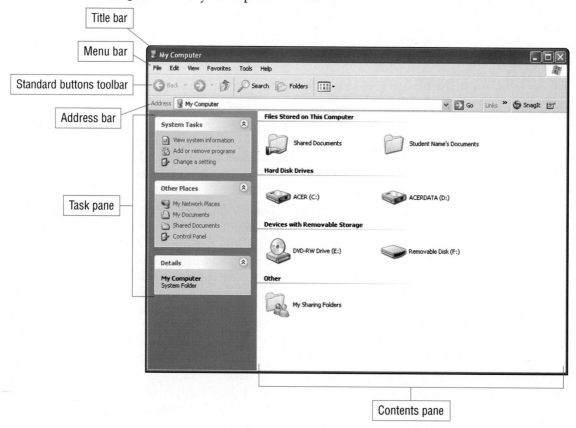

Copying, Moving, and Deleting Files/Folders

File and folder management activities might include copying and moving files or folders from one folder or drive to another, or deleting files or folders. The My Computer window offers a variety of methods for copying, moving, and deleting files/folders. You can use options in the task pane, drop-down menu options, or shortcut menu options. This section will provide you with the steps for copying, moving, and deleting files/folders using options in the task pane.

To copy a file/folder to another folder or drive, first display the file in the contents pane by identifying the location of the file. If the file is located in the My Documents folder, click the My Documents hyperlink in the *Other Places* section of the task pane. If the file is located on the hard drive, double-click the desired drive in the contents pane; if the file is located on a USB drive, DVD, or CD, double-click the desired drive letter. Next, click the folder or file name in the contents pane that you want to copy. This changes the options in the task pane to include management options such as renaming, moving, copying, and deleting folders or files. Click the Copy this folder (or Copy this file) hyperlink in the task pane and the Copy Items dialog box displays as shown in Figure W.8. At the Copy Items dialog box, click the desired folder or drive and then click the Copy button.

Figure W.8 Copy Items Dialog Box

To move adjacent files/folders, click the first file or folder, hold down the Shift key, and then click the last file or folder. This selects and highlights all files/folders from the first file/folder you clicked to the last file/folder you clicked. With the adjacent files/folders selected, click the Move the selected items hyperlink in the File and Folder Tasks section of the task pane and then specify the desired location at the Move Items dialog box. To select nonadjacent files/folders, click the first file/folder to select it, hold down the Ctrl key, and then click any other files/folders you want to move or copy.

You can easily remove (delete) a file or folder from the My Computer window. To delete a file or folder, click the file or folder in the contents pane, and then click the Delete this folder (or Delete this file) hyperlink in the task pane. At the dialog box asking you to confirm the deletion, click Yes. A deleted file or folder is sent to the Recycle Bin. You will learn more about the Recycle Bin in the next section.

In Project 3, you will insert the CD that accompanies this book into the DVD or CD drive. When the CD is inserted, the drive may automatically activate and a dialog box may display on the screen telling you that the disk or device contains more than one type of content and asking what you want Windows to do. If this dialog box displays, click Cancel to remove the dialog box.

Project ③ Copying a File and Folder and Deleting a File

1. At the Windows XP desktop, insert the CD that accompanies this textbook into the appropriate drive. If a dialog box displays telling you that the disk or device contains more than one type of content and asking what you want Windows to do, click Cancel.
2. At the Windows XP desktop, open the My Computer window by clicking the Start button on the Taskbar and then clicking *My Computer* at the Start menu.
3. Copy a file from the CD that accompanies this textbook to the drive containing your storage medium by completing the following steps:
   a. Insert your storage medium in the appropriate drive.
   b. In the contents pane, double-click the drive containing the CD (probably displays as *Office2007_Bench* followed by a drive letter). (Make sure you double-click the mouse button because you want the contents of the CD to display in the contents pane.)
   c. Double-click the *StudentDataFiles* folder.
   d. Double-click the *WindowsXP* folder in the contents pane.
   e. Click **WordDocument01.docx** in the contents pane to select it.
   f. Click the <u>Copy this file</u> hyperlink located in the *File and Folder Tasks* section of the task pane.

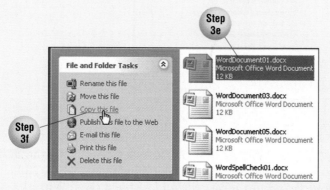

   g. At the Copy Items dialog box, click in the list box the drive containing your storage medium.
   h. Click the Copy button.

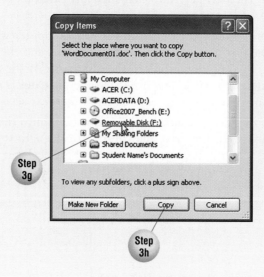

4. Delete **WordDocument01.docx** from your storage medium by completing the following steps:

   a. Click the <u>My Computer</u> hyperlink located in the *Other Places* section of the task pane.

   b. Double-click in the contents pane the drive containing your storage medium.

   c. Click ***WordDocument01.docx***.

   d. Click the <u>Delete this file</u> hyperlink in the *File and Folder Tasks* section of the task pane.

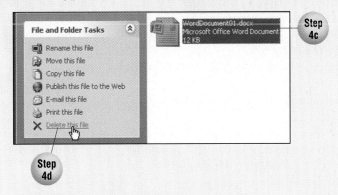

   e. At the message asking you to confirm the deletion, click Yes.

5. Copy the WindowsXP folder from the CD drive to the drive containing your storage medium by completing the following steps:

   a. Click the My Computer hyperlink in the *Other Places* section of the task pane.

   b. In the contents pane, double-click the drive containing the CD (probably displays as *Office2007_Bench* followed by a drive letter).

   c. Double-click the *StudentDataFiles* folder.

   d. Click the *WindowsXP* folder in the contents pane to select it.

   e. Click the <u>Copy this folder</u> hyperlink in the *File and Folder Tasks* section of the task pane.

   f. At the Copy Items dialog box, click the drive containing your storage medium.

   g. Click the Copy button.

6. Close the window by clicking the Close button (contains a white *X* on a red background) located in the upper right corner of the window. (You can also close the window by clicking File on the Menu bar and then clicking *Close* at the drop-down list.)

Selecting Files/Folders

You can move, copy, or delete more than one file or folder at the same time. Before moving, copying, or deleting files/folders, select the desired files or folders. Selecting files/folders is easier when you change the display in the contents pane to List or Details. To change the display, open the My Computer window and then click the Views button on the Standard Buttons toolbar. At the drop-down list that displays, click the *List* option or the *Details* option.

To move adjacent files/folders, click the first file or folder, hold down the Shift key, and click the last file or folder. This selects and highlights all files/folders from the first file/folder you clicked to the last file/folder you clicked. With the adjacent files/folders selected, click the <u>Move the selected items</u> hyperlink in the *File and Folder Tasks* section of the task pane and then specify the desired location at the Move Items dialog box. To select nonadjacent files/folders, click the first file/folder to select it, hold down the Ctrl key, and then click any other files/folders you want to move or copy.

Project ④   Copying and Deleting Files

1. At the Windows XP desktop, open the My Computer window by clicking the Start button and then clicking *My Computer* at the Start menu.
2. Copy files from the CD that accompanies this textbook to the drive containing your storage medium by completing the following steps:
   a. Make sure the CD that accompanies this textbook and your storage medium are inserted in the appropriate drives.
   b. Double-click the CD drive in the contents pane (probably displays as *Office2007_Bench* followed by the drive letter).
   c. Double-click the *StudentDataFiles* folder in the contents pane.
   d. Double-click the *WindowsXP* folder in the contents pane.
   e. Change the display to Details by clicking the Views button on the Standard Buttons toolbar and then clicking *Details* at the drop-down list.

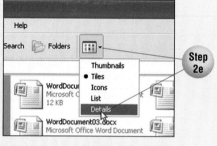

   f. Position the arrow pointer on **WordDocument01.docx** in the contents pane and then click the left mouse button.
   g. Hold down the Shift key, click **WordDocument05.docx**, and then release the Shift key. (This selects **WordDocument01.docx**, **WordDocument02.docx**, **WordDocument03.docx**, **WordDocument04.docx**, and **WordDocument05.docx**.)
   h. Click the <u>Copy the selected items</u> hyperlink in the *File and Folder Tasks* section of the task pane.

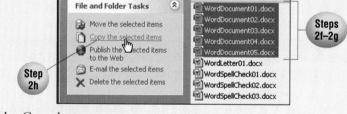

   i. At the Copy Items dialog box, click the drive containing your storage medium and then click the Copy button.
3. Display the files and folder saved on your storage medium by completing the following steps:
   a. Click the <u>My Computer</u> hyperlink in the *Other Places* section of the task pane.
   b. Double-click the drive containing your storage medium.
4. Delete the files from your storage medium that you just copied by completing the following steps:
   a. Change the view by clicking the Views button on the Standard Buttons toolbar and then clicking *List* at the drop-down list.
   b. Click **WordDocument01.docx** in the contents pane.
   c. Hold down the Shift key, click **WordDocument05.docx**, and then release the Shift key. (This selects **WordDocument01.docx**, **WordDocument02.docx**, **WordDocument03.docx**, **WordDocument04.docx**, and **WordDocument05.docx**.)
   d. Click the <u>Delete the selected items</u> hyperlink in the *File and Folder Tasks* section of the task pane.
   e. At the message asking you to confirm the deletion, click Yes.

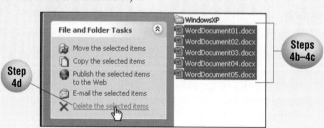

5. Close the window by clicking the Close button (white *X* on red background) that displays in the upper right corner of the window.

Manipulating and Creating Folders

As you begin working with and creating a number of files, consider creating folders in which you can logically group the files. To create a folder, display the My Computer window and then display in the contents pane the drive where you want to create the folder. Click File on the Menu bar, point to *New*, and then click *Folder* at the side menu. This inserts a folder icon in the contents pane and names the folder *New Folder*. Type the desired name for the new folder and then press Enter.

Project ⑤ Creating a New Folder

1. At the Windows XP desktop, open the My Computer window.
2. Create a new folder by completing the following steps:
   a. Double-click in the contents pane the drive that contains your storage medium.
   b. Double-click the *WindowsXP* folder in the contents pane. (This opens the folder.)
   c. Click File on the Menu bar, point to *New*, and then click *Folder*.

Step 2c

   d. Type **SpellCheckFiles** and then press Enter. (This changes the name from *New Folder* to *SpellCheckFiles*.)
3. Copy **WordSpellCheck01.docx**, **WordSpellCheck02.docx**, and **WordSpellCheck03.docx** into the SpellCheckFiles folder you just created by completing the following steps:
   a. Click the Views button on the Standard Buttons toolbar and then click *List* at the drop-down list.
   b. Click once on the file named *WordSpellCheck01.docx* located in the contents pane.

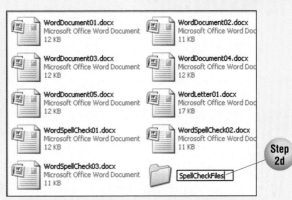

Step 2d

   c. Hold down the Shift key, click once on the file named *WordSpellCheck03.docx*, and then release the Shift key. (This selects **WordSpellCheck01.docx**, **WordSpellCheck02.docx**, and **WordSpellCheck03.docx**.)
   d. Click the Copy the selected items hyperlink in the *File and Folder Tasks* section of the task pane.
   e. At the Copy Items dialog box, click in the list box the drive containing your storage medium.
   f. Click *WindowsXP* in the list box.
   g. Click *SpellCheckFiles* in the list box.
   h. Click the Copy button.
4. Display the files you just copied by double-clicking the *SpellCheckFiles* folder in the contents pane.

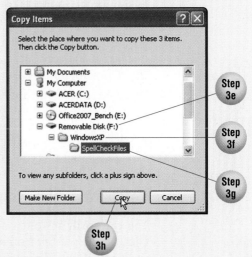

Step 3e

Step 3f

Step 3g

Step 3h

5. Delete the SpellCheckFiles folder and its contents by completing the following steps:
   a. Click the Up button on the Standard Buttons toolbar. (This displays the contents of the WindowsXP folder which is up one folder from the SpellCheckFiles folders.)
   b. Click the *SpellCheckFiles* folder in the contents pane to select it.
   c. Click the <u>Delete this folder</u> hyperlink in the *File and Folder Tasks* section of the task pane.
   d. At the message asking you to confirm the deletion, click Yes.
6. Close the window by clicking the Close button located in the upper right corner of the window.

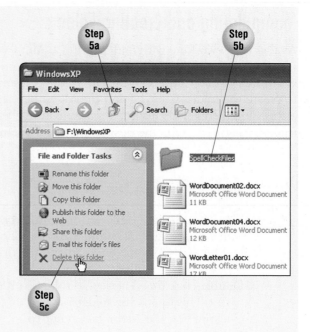

Using the Recycle Bin

Deleting the wrong file can be a disaster but Windows XP helps protect your work with the Recycle Bin. The Recycle Bin acts just like an office wastepaper basket; you can "throw away" (delete) unwanted files, but you can "reach in" to the Recycle Bin and take out (restore) a file if you threw it away by accident.

Deleting Files to the Recycle Bin

A file/folder or selected files/folders deleted from the hard drive are sent automatically to the Recycle Bin. Files/folders deleted from a disk are deleted permanently. (Recovery programs are available, however, that will help you recover deleted text. If you accidentally delete a file/folder from a disk, do not do anything more with the disk until you can run a recovery program.)

One method for deleting files is to display the My Computer window and then display in the contents pane the file(s) and/or folder(s) you want deleted. Click the file or folder or select multiple files or folders and then click the appropriate delete option in the task pane. At the message asking you to confirm the deletion, click Yes. Another method for deleting a file is to drag the file to the *Recycle Bin* icon on the desktop. Drag a file icon to the Recycle Bin until the *Recycle Bin* icon is selected (displays with a blue background) and then release the mouse button. This drops the file you are dragging into the Recycle Bin.

Recovering Files from the Recycle Bin

You can easily restore a deleted file from the Recycle Bin. To restore a file, double-click the *Recycle Bin* icon on the desktop. This opens the Recycle Bin window shown in Figure W.9. (The contents of the Recycle Bin will vary.) To restore a file, click the file you want restored, and then click the <u>Restore this item</u> hyperlink in the *Recycle Bin Tasks* section of the task pane. This removes the file from the Recycle Bin and returns it to its original location. You can also restore a file by positioning the arrow pointer on the file, clicking the right mouse button, and then clicking *Restore* at the shortcut menu.

Figure W.9 Recycle Bin Window

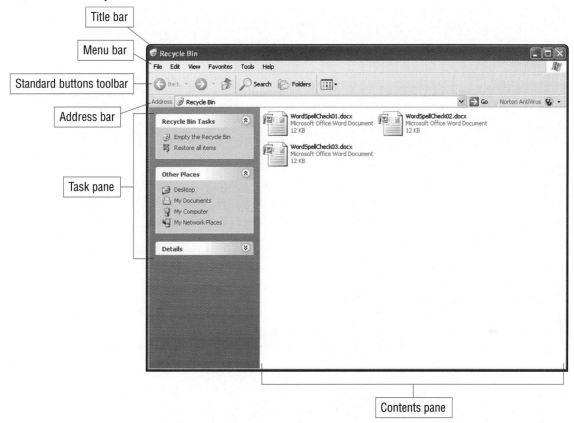

Title bar
Menu bar
Standard buttons toolbar
Address bar
Task pane
Contents pane

Project ⑥   Deleting Files to and Recovering Files from the Recycle Bin

Before beginning this project, check with your instructor to determine if you can copy files to the hard drive.

1. At the Windows XP desktop, open the My Computer window.
2. Copy files from your storage medium to the My Documents folder on your hard drive by completing the following steps:
   a. Double-click in the contents pane the drive containing your storage medium.
   b. Double-click the *WindowsXP* folder in the contents pane.
   c. Click the Views button on the Standard Buttons toolbar and then click *List* at the drop-down list.
   d. Position the arrow pointer on **WordSpellCheck01.docx** and then click the left mouse button.
   e. Hold down the Shift key, click *WordSpellCheck03.docx*, and then release the Shift key.

Step
2g

    f. Click the Copy the selected items hyperlink in the *File and Folder Tasks* section of the task pane.

    g. At the Copy Items dialog box, click *My Documents* in the list box.

    h. Click the Copy button.

3. Click the <u>My Documents</u> hyperlink in the *Other Places* section of the task pane. (The files you copied, **WordSpellCheck01.docx** through **WordSpellCheck03.docx**, will display in the contents pane in alphabetical order.)

4. Delete **WordSpellCheck01.docx** through **WordSpellCheck03.docx** from the My Documents folder and send them to the Recycle Bin by completing the following steps:

    a. Select **WordSpellCheck01.docx** through **WordSpellCheck03.docx** in the contents pane. (If these files are not visible, you will need to scroll down the list of files.)

    b. Click the <u>Delete the selected items</u> hyperlink in the *File and Folder Tasks* section of the task pane.

    c. At the message asking you to confirm the deletion to the Recycle Bin, click Yes.

5. Click the Close button to close the window.

6. At the desktop, display the contents of the Recycle Bin by double-clicking the *Recycle Bin* icon.

7. At the Recycle Bin window, restore **WordSpellCheck01.docx** through **WordSpellCheck03.docx** to the My Documents folder by completing the following steps:

    a. Select **WordSpellCheck01.docx** through **WordSpellCheck03.docx** in the contents pane of the Recycle Bin window. (If these files are not visible, you will need to scroll down the list of files.)

    b. With the files selected, click the <u>Restore the selected items</u> hyperlink in the *Recycle Bin Tasks* section of the task pane.

8. Close the Recycle Bin window by clicking the Close button located in the upper right corner of the window.

9. Display the My Computer window.

10. Click the <u>My Documents</u> hyperlink in the *Other Places* section of the task pane.

11. Delete the files you restored by completing the following steps:

    a. Select **WordSpellCheck01.docx** through **WordSpellCheck03.docx** in the contents pane. (If these files are not visible, you will need to scroll down the list of files. These are the files you recovered from the Recycle Bin.)

    b. Click the <u>Delete the selected items</u> hyperlink in the *File and Folder Tasks* section of the task pane.

    c. At the message asking you to confirm the deletion, click Yes.

12. Close the window.

Emptying the Recycle Bin

Just like a wastepaper basket, the Recycle Bin can get full. To empty the Recycle Bin, position the arrow pointer on the *Recycle Bin* icon on the desktop and then click the right mouse button. At the shortcut menu that displays, click *Empty Recycle Bin*. At the message asking you to confirm the deletion, click Yes. You can also empty the Recycle Bin by double-clicking the *Recycle Bin* icon. At the Recycle Bin window, click the <u>Empty the Recycle Bin</u> hyperlink in the *Recycle Bin Tasks* section of the task pane. At the message asking you to confirm the deletion, click Yes. (You can also empty the Recycle Bin by clicking File on the Menu bar and then clicking *Empty Recycle Bin* at the drop-down menu.)

Emptying the Recycle Bin deletes all files/folders. You can delete a specific file/folder from the Recycle Bin (rather than all files/folders). To do this, double-click the *Recycle Bin* icon on the desktop. At the Recycle Bin window, select the file/folder or files/folders you want to delete. Click File on the Menu bar and then click *Delete* at the drop-down menu. (You can also right-click a selected file/folder and then click *Delete* at the shortcut menu.) At the message asking you to confirm the deletion, click Yes.

Project ⑦ Emptying the Recycle Bin

Before beginning this project, check with your instructor to determine if you can delete files/folders from the Recycle Bin.

1. At the Windows XP desktop, double-click the *Recycle Bin* icon.
2. At the Recycle Bin window, empty the contents of the Recycle Bin by completing the following steps:
   a. Click the <u>Empty the Recycle Bin</u> hyperlink in the *Recycle Bin Tasks* section of the task pane.

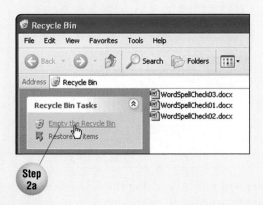

   b. At the message asking you to confirm the deletion, click Yes.
3. Close the Recycle Bin window by clicking the Close button located in the upper right corner of the window.

When you empty the Recycle Bin, the files cannot be recovered by the Recycle Bin or by Windows XP. If you have to recover a file, you will need to use a file recovery program such as Norton Utilities. These utilities are separate programs, but might be worth their cost if you ever need them.

Creating a Shortcut

If you use a file or program on a consistent basis, consider creating a shortcut to the file or program. A shortcut is a specialized icon that represents very small files that point the operating system to the actual item, whether it is a file, a folder, or an application. If you create a shortcut to a Word document, the shortcut icon is not the actual document but a path to the document. Double-click the shortcut icon and Windows XP opens the document in Word.

One method for creating a shortcut is to display the My Computer window and then display the drive or folder where the file is located. Right-click the desired file, point to *Send To*, and then click *Desktop (create shortcut)*. You can easily delete a shortcut icon from the desktop by dragging the shortcut icon to the Recycle Bin icon. This deletes the shortcut icon but does not delete the file to which the shortcut pointed.

Project ⑧ Creating a Shortcut

1. At the Windows XP desktop, display the My Computer window.
2. Double-click the drive containing your storage medium.
3. Double-click the *WindowsXP* folder in the contents pane.
4. Change the display of files to a list by clicking the Views button on the Standard Buttons toolbar and then clicking *List* at the drop-down list.
5. Create a shortcut to the file named **WordLetter01.docx** by right-clicking on **WordLetter01.docx**, pointing to *Send To*, and then clicking *Desktop (create shortcut)*.

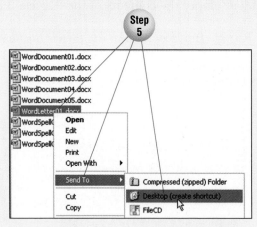

Step 5

Step 7

6. Close the My Computer window by clicking the Close button located in the upper right corner of the window.
7. Open Word and the file named **WordLetter01.docx** by double-clicking the *WordLetter01.docx* shortcut icon on the desktop.
8. After viewing the file in Word, exit Word by clicking the Close button that displays in the upper right corner of the window.
9. Delete the *WordLetter01.docx* shortcut icon by completing the following steps:
   a. At the desktop, position the mouse pointer on the *WordLetter01.docx* shortcut icon.
   b. Hold down the left mouse button, drag the icon on top of the *Recycle Bin* icon, and then release the mouse button.

Customizing the Desktop

You can customize the Windows XP desktop to fit your particular needs and preferences. For example, you can choose a different theme, change the desktop background, add a screen saver, and apply a different appearance to windows, dialog boxes, and menus. To customize the desktop, position the arrow pointer on any empty location on the desktop and then click the right mouse button. At the shortcut menu that displays, click *Properties*. This displays the Display Properties dialog box with the Themes tab selected as shown in Figure W.10.

Figure W.10 Display Properties Dialog Box

Changing the Theme

A Windows XP theme specifies a variety of formatting such as fonts, sounds, icons, colors, mouse pointers, background, and screen saver. Windows XP contains two themes—Windows XP (the default) and Windows Classic (which appears like earlier versions of Windows). Other themes are available as downloads from the Microsoft Web site. Change the theme with the *Theme* option at the Display Properties dialog box with the Themes tab selected.

Changing the Desktop

With options at the Display Properties dialog box with the Desktop tab selected, as shown in Figure W.11, you can choose a different desktop background and customize the desktop. Click any option in the *Background* list box and preview the results in the preview screen. With the *Position* option, you can specify that the background image is centered, tiled, or stretched on the desktop. Use the *Color* option to change the background color and click the Browse button to choose a background image from another location or Web site.

Figure W.11 Display Properties Dialog Box with Desktop Tab Selected

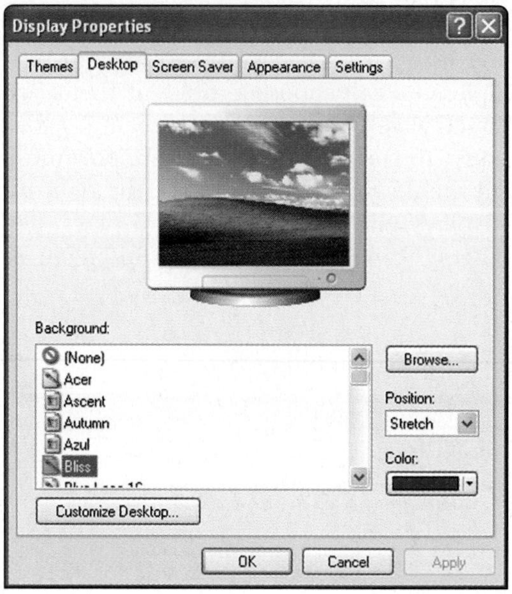

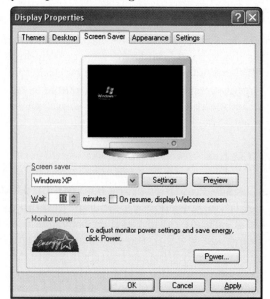

Adding a Screen Saver

If your computer sits idle for periods of time, consider adding a screen saver. A screen saver is a pattern that changes constantly, thus eliminating the problem of an image staying on the screen too long. To add a screen saver, display the Display Properties dialog box and then click the Screen Saver tab. This displays the dialog box as shown in Figure W.12.

Figure W.12 Display Properties Dialog Box with Screen Saver Tab Selected

Click the down-pointing arrow at the right side of the *Screen saver* option box to display a list of installed screen savers. Click a screen saver and a preview displays in the monitor located toward the top of the dialog box. Click the Preview button and the dialog box is hidden and the screen saver displays on your monitor. Move the mouse or click a button on the mouse and the dialog box will reappear. Click the Power button in the *Monitor power* section and a dialog box displays with options for choosing a power scheme appropriate to the way you use your computer. The dialog box also includes options for specifying how long the computer can be left unused before the monitor and hard disk are turned off and the system goes to standby or hibernate mode.

Changing Colors

Click the Appearance tab at the Display Properties dialog box and the dialog box displays as shown in Figure W.13. At this dialog box, you can change the desktop scheme. Schemes are predefined collections of colors used in windows, menus, title bars, and system fonts. Windows XP loads with the Windows XP style color scheme. Choose a different scheme with the Windows and buttons option and choose a specific color with the Color scheme option.

Figure W.13 Display Properties Dialog Box with Appearance Tab Selected

Changing Settings

Click the Settings tab at the Display Properties dialog box and the dialog box displays as shown in Figure W.14. At this dialog box, you can set color and screen resolution. The *Color quality* option determines how many colors your monitor displays. The more colors that are shown, the more realistic the images will appear. However, a lot of computer memory is required to show thousands of colors. Your exact choice is determined by the specific hardware you are using. The *Screen resolution* slide bar sets the screen's resolution. The higher the number, the more you can fit onto your screen. Again, your actual values depend on your particular hardware.

Figure W.14 Display Properties Dialog Box with Settings Tab Selected

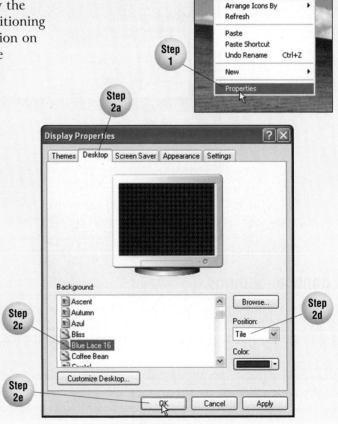

Project ⑨ Customizing the Desktop

Before beginning this project, check with your instructor to determine if you can customize the desktop.

1. At the Windows XP desktop, display the Display Properties dialog box by positioning the arrow pointer on an empty location on the desktop, clicking the right mouse button, and then clicking *Properties* at the shortcut menu.

2. At the Display Properties dialog box, change the desktop background by completing the following steps:
   a. Click the Desktop tab.
   b. If a background is selected in the *Background* list box (other than the *(None)* option), make a note of this background name.
   c. Click *Blue Lace 16* in the *Background* list box. (If this option is not available, choose another background.)
   d. Make sure *Tile* is selected in the *Position* list box.
   e. Click OK to close the dialog box.

3. After viewing the desktop with the Blue Lace 16 background, remove the background image and change the background color by completing the following steps:

   a. Display the Display Properties dialog box.
   b. At the Display Properties dialog box, click the Desktop tab.
   c. Click *(None)* in the *Background* list box.
   d. Click the down-pointing arrow at the right side of the *Color* option and then click the dark red option at the color palette.
   e. Click OK to close the Display Properties dialog box.

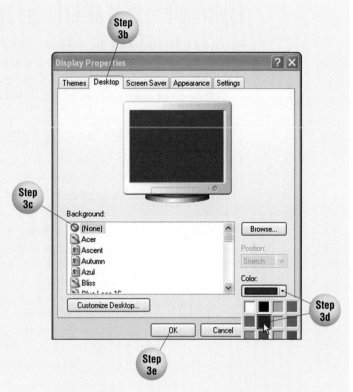

4. After viewing the desktop with the dark red background color, add a screen saver and change the wait time by completing the following steps:

   a. Display the Display Properties dialog box.
   b. At the Display Properties dialog box, click the Screen Saver tab. (If a screen saver is already selected in the *Screen saver* option box, make a note of this screen saver name.)
   c. Click the down-pointing arrow at the right side of the *Screen saver* option box.
   d. At the drop-down list that displays, click a screen saver that interests you. (A preview of the screen saver displays in the screen located toward the top of the dialog box.)
   e. Click a few other screen savers to see how they will display on the monitor.
   f. Click OK to close the Display Properties dialog box.

5. Return all settings back to the default by completing the following steps:

   a. Display the Display Properties dialog box.
   b. Click the Desktop tab.
   c. If a background and color were selected when you began this project, click that background name in the *Background* list box and change the color back to the original color.
   d. Click the Screen Saver tab.
   e. At the Display Properties dialog box with the Screen Saver tab selected, click the down-pointing arrow at the right side of the *Screen saver* option box, and then click *(None)*. (If a screen saver was selected before completing this project, return to that screen saver.)
   f. Click OK to close the Display Properties dialog box.

Exploring Windows XP Help and Support

Windows XP includes an on-screen reference guide providing information, explanations, and interactive help on learning Windows features. The on-screen reference guide contains complex files with hypertext used to access additional information by clicking a word or phrase.

Using the Help and Support Center Window

Display the Help and Support Center window shown in Figure W.15 by clicking the Start button on the Taskbar and then clicking *Help and Support* at the Start menu. The appearance of your Help and Support Center window may vary slightly from what you see in Figure W.15.

If you want to learn about a topic listed in the *Pick a Help topic* section of the window, click the desired topic and information about the topic displays in the window. Use the other options in the Help and Support Center window to get assistance or support from a remote computer or Windows XP newsgroups, pick a specific task, or learn about the additional help features. If you want help on a specific topic and do not see that topic listed in the *Pick a Help topic* section of the window, click inside the *Search* text box (generally located toward the top of the window), type the desired topic, and then press Enter or click the Start searching button (white arrow on a green background).

Figure W.15 Help and Support Center Window

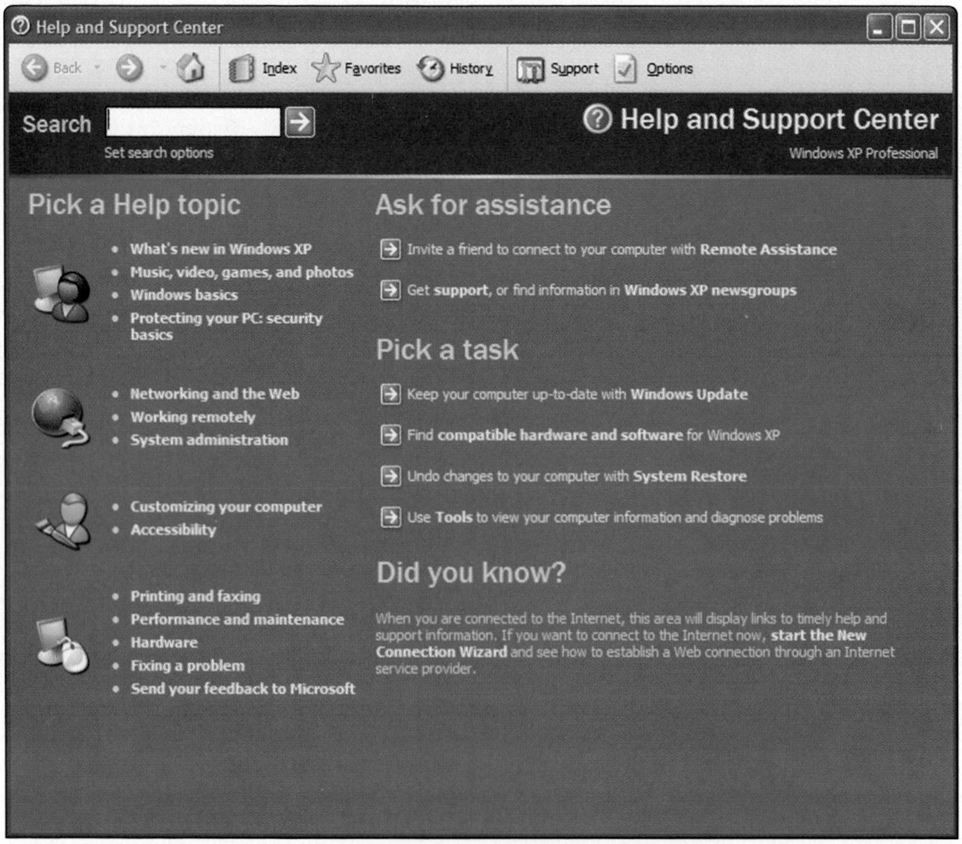

Project ⑩ Using the Help and Support Center

1. At the Windows XP desktop, use the Help and Support feature to learn about new Windows XP features by completing the following steps:
    a. Click the Start button on the Taskbar and then click *Help and Support* at the Start menu.
    b. At the Help and Support Center window, click the <u>What's new in Windows XP</u> hyperlink located in the *Pick a Help topic* section of the window.

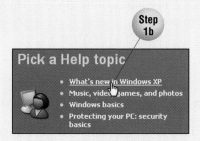

Step 1b

    c. Click the <u>What's new</u> hyperlink located in the *What's new in Windows XP* section of the window. (This displays a list of Help options at the right side of the window.)
    d. Click the <u>What's new in Windows XP</u> hyperlink located at the right side of the window below the subheading *Overviews, Articles, and Tutorials*.

    e. Read the information about Windows XP that displays at the right side of the window.
    f. Print the information by completing the following steps:
        1) Click the Print button located on the toolbar that displays above the information titled *What's new in Windows XP Professional*.

Step 1d

Step 1f1

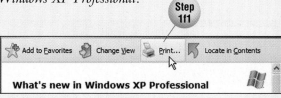

        2) At the Print dialog box, make sure the correct printer is selected and then click the Print button.
2. Return to the opening Help and Support Center window by clicking the Home button located on the Help and Support Center toolbar.
3. Use the *Search* text box to search for information on deleting files by completing the following steps:
    a. Click in the *Search* text box located toward the top of the Help and Support Center window.
    b. Type deleting files and then press Enter.
    c. Click the <u>Delete a file or folder</u> hyperlink that displays in the *Search Results* section of the window (below the *Pick a task* subheading).

Step 3b

Step 3c

d. Read the information about deleting a file or folder that displays at the right side of the window and then print the information by clicking the Print button on the toolbar and then clicking the Print button at the Print dialog box.

e. Click the <u>Delete or restore files in the Recycle Bin</u> hyperlink that displays in the *Search Results* section of the window.

f. Read the information that displays at the right side of the window about deleting and restoring files in the Recycle Bin and then print the information.

4. Close the Help and Support Center window by clicking the Close button located in the upper right corner of the window.

Displaying an Index of Help and Support Topics

Display a list of help topics available by clicking the Index button on the Help and Support Center window toolbar. This displays an index of help topics at the left side of the window as shown in Figure W.16. Scroll through this list until the desired topic displays and then double-click the topic. Information about the selected topic displays at the right side of the window. If you are looking for a specific topic or keyword, click in the *Type in the keyword to find* text box, type the desired topic or keyword, and then press Enter.

Figure W.16 Help and Support Center Window with Index Displayed

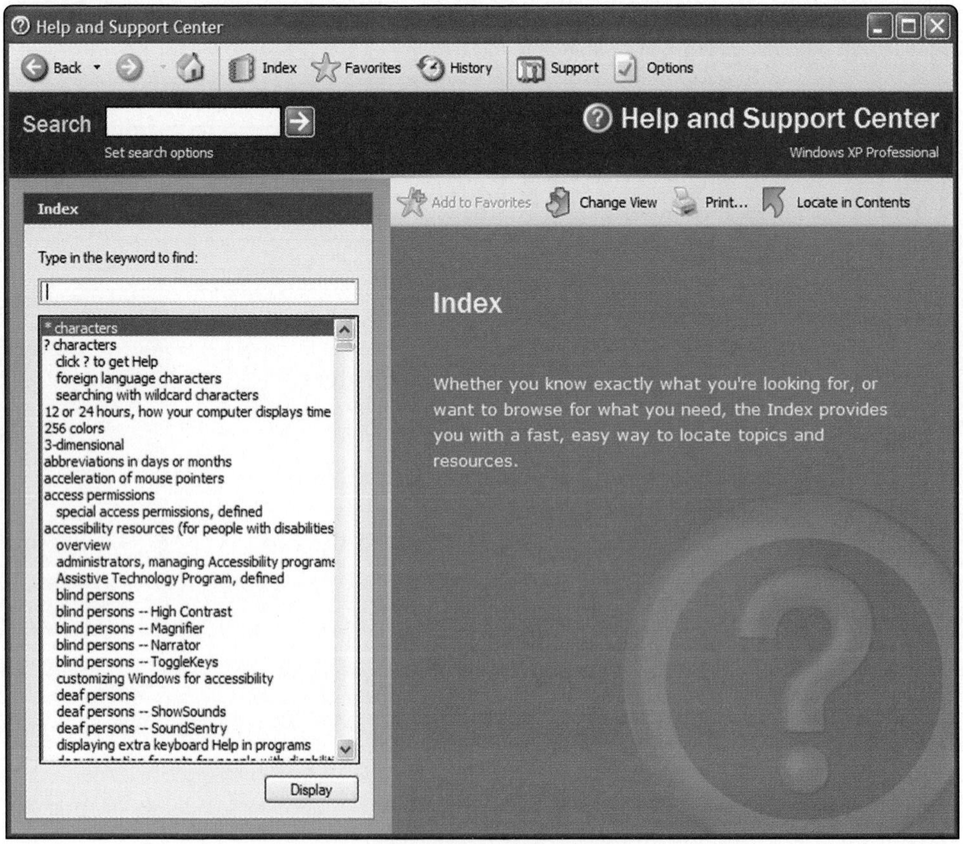

Project 11 Using the Index to Search for Information

1. At the Windows XP desktop, use the Index to display information on accessing programs by completing the following steps:
   a. Click the Start button on the Taskbar and then click *Help and Support* at the Start menu.
   b. Click the Index button on the Help and Support Center window toolbar.
   c. Scroll down the list of Index topics until *accessing programs* is visible and then double-click the subheading *overview* that displays below *accessing programs*.

Step 1c

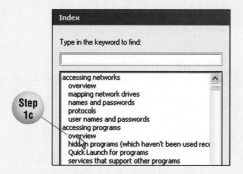

   d. Read the information that displays at the right side of the window and then print the information.
2. Find information on adding a shortcut to the desktop by completing the following steps:
   a. Select and delete the text *overview* that displays in the *Type in the keyword to find* text box and then type **shortcuts**.
   b. Double-click the subheading *for specific programs* that displays below the *shortcuts* heading.

Step 2a

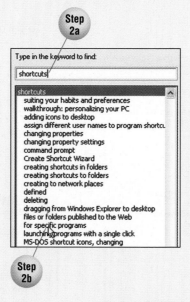

Step 2b

   c. Read the information that displays at the right side of the window and then print the information.
3. Close the Help and Support Center window by clicking the Close button located in the upper right corner of the window.

Customizing Settings

Before beginning computer projects in this textbook, you may need to customize the monitor settings and turn on the display of file extensions. Projects in the chapters in this textbook assume that the monitor display is set to 1024 by 768 pixels and that the display of file extensions is turned on. To change the monitor display to 1024 by 768, complete the following steps:

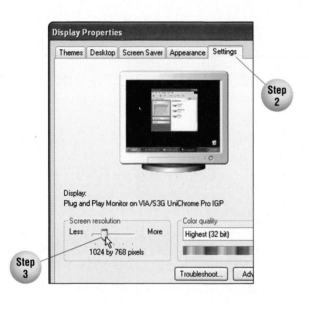

1. At the Windows XP desktop, right-click on any empty location on the desktop and then click *Properties* at the shortcut menu.
2. At the Display Properties dialog box, click the Settings tab.
3. Using the mouse, drag the slide bar button in the *Screen resolution* section to the left or right until *1024 by 768* displays below the slider bar.
4. Click the Apply button.
5. Click the OK button.

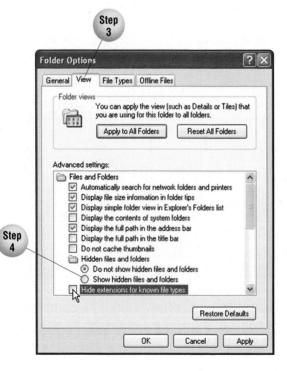

To turn on the display of file extensions, complete the following steps:

1. At the Windows XP desktop, click the Start button and then click *My Computer*.
2. At the My Computer window, click Tools on the Menu bar and then click *Folder Options* at the drop-down list.

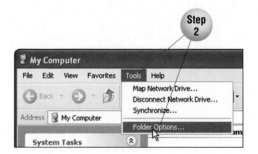

3. At the Folder Options dialog box, click the View tab.
4. Click the *Hide extentions for known file types* check box to remove the check mark.
5. Click the Apply button.
6. Click the OK button.

Browsing the Internet Using Internet Explorer 7.0

Microsoft Internet Explorer 7.0 is a Web browser program with options and features for displaying sites as well as navigating and searching for information on the Internet. The *Internet* is a network of computers connected around the world. Users access the Internet for several purposes: to communicate using instant messaging and/or e-mail, to subscribe to newsgroups, to transfer files, to socialize with other users around the globe in "chat" rooms, and also to access virtually any kind of information imaginable.

Tutorial IE1
Browsing the Internet with
   Internet Explorer 7.0
Tutorial IE2
Gathering and Downloading
   Information and Files

Using the Internet, people can find a phenomenal amount of information for private or public use. To use the Internet, three things are generally required: an Internet Service Provider (ISP), a program to browse the Web (called a *Web browser*), and a *search engine*. In this section, you will learn how to:

- Navigate the Internet using URLs and hyperlinks
- Use search engines to locate information
- Download Web pages and images

Browsing the Internet

You will use the Microsoft Internet Explorer Web browser to locate information on the Internet. Uniform Resource Locators, referred to as URLs, are the method used to identify locations on the Internet. The steps for browsing the Internet vary but generally include: opening Internet Explorer, typing the URL for the desired site, navigating the various pages of the site, navigating to other sites using links, and then closing Internet Explorer.

To launch Internet Explorer 7.0, double-click the *Internet Explorer* icon on the Windows desktop. Figure IE.1 identifies the elements of the Internet Explorer, version 7.0, window. The Web page that displays in your Internet Explorer window may vary from what you see in Figure IE.1.

Figure IE.1 Internet Explorer Window

Title bar

Navigation bar

Address bar

Instant search box

Toolbar

Tabbed browsing—display multiple Web pages by inserting new tabs

Status bar

Change zoom level

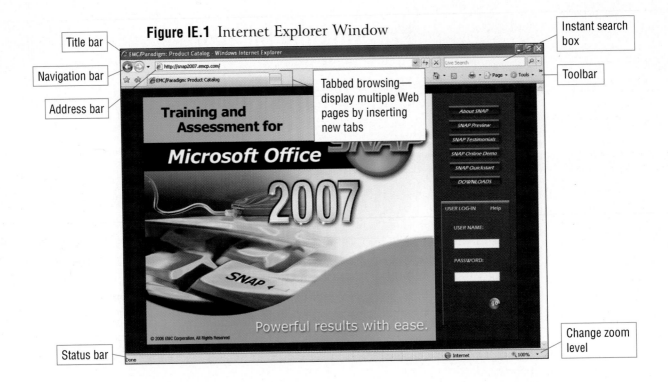

If you know the URL for the desired Web site, click in the Address bar, type the URL, and then press Enter. The Web site's home page displays in a tab within the Internet Explorer window. URLs (Uniform Resource Locators) are the method used to identify locations on the Internet. The format of a URL is *http://server-name.path*. The first part of the URL, *http*, stands for HyperText Transfer Protocol, which is the protocol or language used to transfer data within the World Wide Web. The colon and slashes separate the protocol from the server name. The server name is the second component of the URL. For example, in the URL http://www.microsoft.com, the server name is *microsoft*. The last part of the URL specifies the domain to which the server belongs. For example, *.com* refers to "commercial" and establishes that the URL is a commercial company. Other examples of domains include *.edu* for "educational," *.gov* for "government," and *.mil* for "military."

Project ① Browsing the Internet Using URLs

1. Make sure you are connected to the Internet through an Internet Service Provider and that the Windows desktop displays. (Check with your instructor to determine if you need to complete steps for accessing the Internet such as typing a user name and password to log on.)
2. Launch Microsoft Internet Explorer by double-clicking the *Internet Explorer* icon located on the Windows desktop.
3. At the Internet Explorer window, explore the Web site for Yosemite National Park by completing the following steps:
   a. Click in the Address bar, type **www.nps.gov/yose**, and then press Enter.

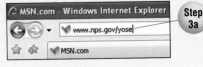

Step 3a

b. Scroll down the home page for Yosemite National Park by clicking the down-pointing arrow on the vertical scroll bar located at the right side of the Internet Explorer window.

Step 3c

Step 3b

c. Print the home page by clicking the Print button located on the Internet Explorer toolbar.

4. Explore the Web site for Glacier National Park by completing the following steps:

a. Click in the Address bar, type www.nps.gov/glac, and then press Enter.

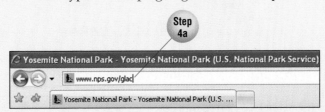

Step 4a

b. Print the home page by clicking the Print button located on the Internet Explorer toolbar.

5. Close Internet Explorer by clicking the Close button (contains an X) located in the upper right corner of the Internet Explorer window.

Navigating Using Hyperlinks

Most Web pages contain "hyperlinks" that you click to connect to another page within the Web site or to another site on the Internet. Hyperlinks may display in a Web page as underlined text in a specific color or as images or icons. To use a hyperlink, position the mouse pointer on the desired hyperlink until the mouse pointer turns into a hand, and then click the left mouse button. Use hyperlinks to navigate within and between sites on the Internet. The navigation bar in the Internet Explorer window contains a Back button that, when clicked, takes you to the previous Web page viewed. If you click the Back button and then want to return to the previous page, click the Forward button. You can continue clicking the Back button to back your way out of several linked pages in reverse order since Internet Explorer maintains a history of the Web sites you visit.

Project ② Navigating Using Hyperlinks

1. Make sure you are connected to the Internet and then double-click the *Internet Explorer* icon on the Windows desktop.

2. At the Internet Explorer window, display the White House Web page and navigate in the page by completing the following steps:

a. Click in the Address bar, type whitehouse.gov, and then press Enter.

b. At the White House home page, position the mouse pointer on a hyperlink that interests you until the pointer turns into a hand, and then click the left mouse button.

c. At the linked Web page, click the Back button. (This returns you to the White House home page.)

Step 2c

d. At the White House home page, click the Forward button to return to the previous Web page viewed.

e. Print the Web page by clicking the Print button on the Internet Explorer toolbar.

3. Display the Web site for Amazon.com and navigate in the site by completing the following steps:

a. Click in the Address bar, type www.amazon.com, and then press Enter.

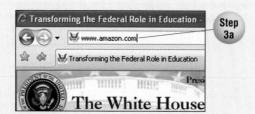

Step 3a

b. At the Amazon.com home page, click a hyperlink related to books.

c. When a book Web page displays, click the Print button on the Internet Explorer toolbar.

4. Close Internet Explorer by clicking the Close button (contains an X) located in the upper right corner of the Internet Explorer window.

Searching for Specific Sites

If you do not know the URL for a specific site or you want to find information on the Internet but do not know what site to visit, complete a search with a search engine. A search engine is a software program created to search quickly and easily for desired information. A variety of search engines are available on the Internet, each offering the opportunity to search for specific information. One method for searching for information is to click in the *Instant Search* box (displays the text *Live Search*) located at the right end of the navigation bar, type a keyword or phrase related to your search, and then click the Search button or press Enter. Another method for completing a search is to visit the Web site for a search engine and use options at the site.

Project ③ Searching for Information by Topic

1. Start Internet Explorer.

2. At the Internet Explorer window, search for sites on bluegrass music by completing the following steps:

a. Click in the *Instant Search* box (may display with *Live Search*) located at the right end of the of the navigation bar.

b. Type bluegrass music and then press Enter.

c. When a list of sites displays in the Live Search tab, click a site that interests you.

d. When the page displays, click the Print button.

Step 2b

3. Use the Yahoo! search engine to find sites on bluegrass music by completing the following steps:
   a. Click in the Address bar, type www.yahoo.com, and then press Enter.
   b. At the Yahoo! Web site, with the insertion point positioned in the *Search* text box, type **bluegrass music** and then press Enter. (Notice that the sites displayed vary from sites displayed in the earlier search.)

   c. Click hyperlinks until a Web site displays that interests you.
   d. Print the page.
4. Use the Google search engine to find sites on jazz music by completing the following steps:
   a. Click in the Address bar, type www.google.com, and then press Enter.
   b. At the Google Web site, with the insertion point positioned in the search text box, type **jazz music** and then press Enter.

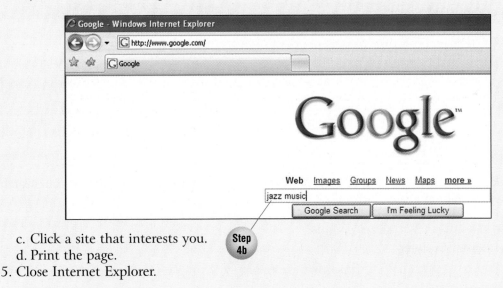

   c. Click a site that interests you.
   d. Print the page.
5. Close Internet Explorer.

Completing Advanced Searches for Specific Sites

The Internet contains an enormous amount of information. Depending on what you are searching for on the Internet and the search engine you use, some searches can result in several thousand "hits" (sites). Wading through a large number of sites can be very time-consuming and counterproductive. Narrowing a search to very specific criteria can greatly reduce the number of hits for a search. To narrow a search, use the advanced search options offered by the search engine.

Web Search

Project ④ Narrowing a Search

1. Start Internet Explorer.
2. Search for sites on skydiving in Oregon by completing the following steps:
   a. Click in the Address bar and then type www.yahoo.com.
   b. At the Yahoo! Web site, click the Web Search button next to the Search text box and then click the Advanced Search hyperlink.

c. At the Advanced Web Search page, click in the search text box next to *all of these words*.
d. Type **skydiving Oregon tandem static line**. (This limits the search to Web pages containing all of the words typed in the search text box.)

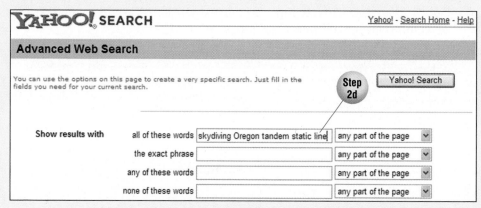

e. Choose any other options at the Advanced Web Search page that will narrow your search.
   f. Click the Yahoo! Search button.
   g. When the list of Web sites displays, click a hyperlink that interests you.
   h. Print the page.
3. Close Internet Explorer.

Downloading Images, Text, and Web Pages from the Internet

The image(s) and/or text that display when you open a Web page as well as the Web page itself can be saved as a separate file. This separate file can be viewed, printed, or inserted in another file. The information you want to save in a separate file is downloaded from the Internet by Internet Explorer and saved in a folder of your choosing with the name you specify. Copyright laws protect much of the information on the Internet. Before using information downloaded from the Internet, check the site for restrictions. If you do use information, make sure you properly cite the source.

Project 5 Downloading Images and Web Pages

1. Start Internet Explorer.
2. Download a Web page and image from Banff National Park by completing the following steps:
   a. Search for sites on the Internet for Banff National Park.
   b. From the list of sites that displays, choose a site that contains information about Banff National Park and at least one image of the park.
   c. Save the Web page as a separate file by clicking the Page button on the Internet Explorer toolbar, and then clicking *Save As* at the drop-down list.
   d. At the Save Webpage dialog box, click the down-pointing arrow at the right side of the *Save in* option and then click the drive you are using as your storage medium at the drop-down list.
   e. Select the text in the *File name* text box, type **BanffWebPage**, and then press Enter.

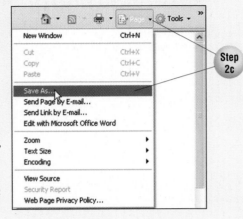

Step 2c

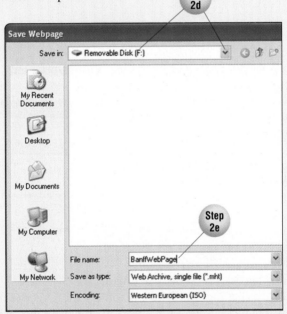

Step 2d

Step 2e

3. Save an image file by completing the following steps:
   a. Right-click an image that displays on the Web site. (The image that displays may vary from what you see below.)
   b. At the shortcut menu that displays, click *Save Picture As*.

Step 3b

c. At the Save Picture dialog box, change the *Save in* option to your storage medium.

d. Select the text in the *File name* text box, type **BanffImage**, and then press Enter.

4. Close Internet Explorer.

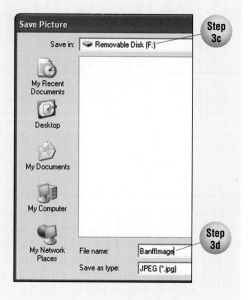

Step 3c

Step 3d

OPTIONAL

Project Opening the Saved Web Page and Image in a Word Document

1. Open Microsoft Word by clicking the Start button on the Taskbar, pointing to *All Programs*, pointing to *Microsoft Office*, and then clicking *Microsoft Office Word 2007*.

2. With Microsoft Word open, insert the image in a document by completing the following steps:

   a. Click the Insert tab and then click the Picture button in the Illustrations group.

   b. At the Insert Picture dialog box, change the *Look in* option to the location where you saved the Banff image and then double-click ***BanffImage.jpg***.

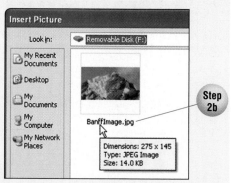

Step 2b

   c. When the image displays in the Word document, print the document by clicking the Print button on the Quick Access toolbar.

   d. Close the document by clicking the Office button and then clicking *Close* at the drop-down menu. At the message asking if you want to save the changes, click No.

3. Open the **BanffWebPage.mht** file by completing the following steps:

   a. Click the Office button and then click *Open* at the drop-down menu.

   b. At the Open dialog box, change the *Look in* option to the location where you saved the Banff Web page and then double-click ***BanffWebPage.mht***.

Step 3b

   c. Print the Web page by clicking the Print button on the Quick Access toolbar.

   d. Close the **BanffWebPage.mht** file by clicking the Office button and then *Close*.

4. Close Word by clicking the Close button (contains an X) that displays in the upper right corner of the screen.

Microsoft®

WORD

Making Word Work for You!

Format text in columns to improve the readability of a document.

COMPUTER INPUT DEVICES

Engineers have been especially creative in designing new ways to get information into computers. Some input methods are highly specialized and unusual, while common devices often undergo redesign to improve their capabilities or their ergonomics, the ways in which they affect people physically. Some common input devices include keyboards, mice, trackballs, and touch pads.

Keyboard

A keyboard can be an external device that is attached by means of a cable, or it can

also have function keys, labeled F1, F2, F3, and so on. These keys allow the user to issue commands by pressing a single key.

Mouse

Graphical operating systems contain many elements that a user can choose by pointing at them. Such elements include buttons, tools, pull-down menus, and icons for file folders, programs, and document files. Often pointing to and clicking on one of these elements is more convenient than using the cursor or arrow keys on the keyboard. This pointing and clicking can be done by using a mouse. The mouse is

Organize text in tables to help readers interpret information more quickly.

TRI-STATE PRODUCTS

Computer Technology Department Microsoft® Office 2007 Training		
Application	**# Enrolled**	**# Completed**
Access 2007	20	15
Excel 2007	62	56
PowerPoint 2007	40	33
Word 2007	80	72
Total	202	176

Communicating and managing information are needs that drive our entire economy. With Microsoft Word 2007, individuals and companies are in a better position than ever before to organize, analyze, and present information using word processing software.

Organizing Information

You can create documents using Word 2007 and then organize the data in documents using a variety of tools such as columns and tables. Improve the readability of text in a document by organizing the text in columns. The shorter line length of column text helps increase the ease with which a person can read the text. Organizing text in tables can help readers interpret complex information much more quickly. For example, which is easier to understand: paragraphs of text identifying various stocks, their type, and their prices—or a table of the same information with columns for stock, stock type, and price? With Word's Table feature, you can create tables or convert existing data into a table.

To help organize personal or company documents, apply a theme to provide a uniform and consistent appearance and help "brand" documents. Apply a Word theme to customize the fonts, colors, and effects applied to data in a document.

Analyzing Information

Word's Spelling and Grammar features provide proofing tools that help you fine-tune your documents. The features mark words as you type so that you can immediately see if a word or sentence needs correction. With the view side-by-side feature, you can compare the contents of two documents to analyze similarities and differences. Use the Reveal Formatting feature to display formatting differences in documents.

In today's global workplace, it is common for two or more people to collaborate on a report or proposal, often with geographical distances between them. Word's ability to save files in different formats, such as PDF (Portable Document Format), allows a person to send files to other collaborators in a common file format. Each person can add comments to the document and return it to the sender for preparing a final version.

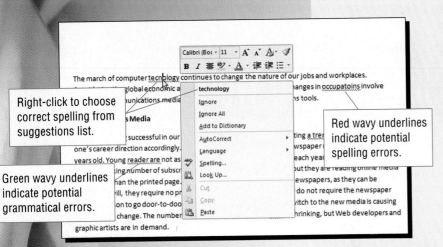

Right-click to choose correct spelling from suggestions list.

Green wavy underlines indicate potential grammatical errors.

Red wavy underlines indicate potential spelling errors.

When sending files to other collaborators, consider saving a document in a universal file format such as PDF.

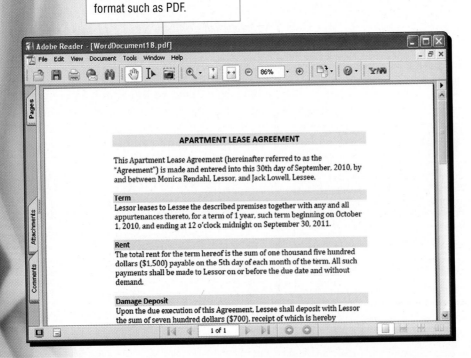

Presenting Information

Word simplifies the task of creating, editing, and formatting text so that you can concentrate on the message rather than the process. Rich text enhancements give you the capability to create visually stimulating documents. Inserting pictures, drawings, and images is just a few mouse clicks away.

Word 2007 includes the SmartArt feature that you can use to create graphic designs and organizational charts. A SmartArt graphic is a visual presentation of information that helps the reader understand and interpret the data. If you need to illustrate visually hierarchical data, consider creating an organizational chart with the SmartArt feature.

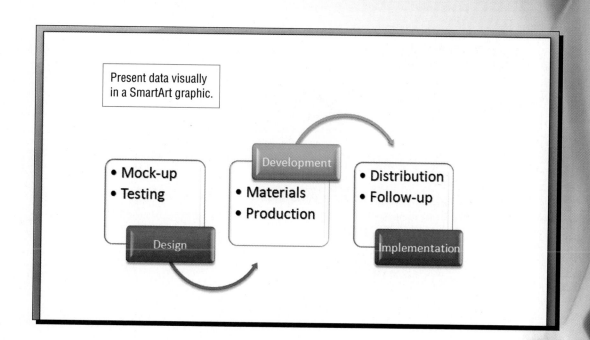

Present data visually in a SmartArt graphic.

When you are nearing the completion of your studies and getting ready to enter the workforce, consider using a resume template to help sell your capabilities to prospective employers. Microsoft provides a number of predesigned resume templates you can download from Microsoft Online. When designing your resume, be sure to note that you are Word 2007 proficient.

Display the New Document dialog box and then browse through the Microsoft Office Online templates. Consider using a cover page template to help you write a cover letter to send with your resume. After the interview, use another template to help you write a thank-you letter. With Word 2007, you can download templates for every imaginable need. Templates provide the formatting and standard text so that all you need to do in most cases is fill in the blanks.

Learning Word is an essential skill for today's employee. Microsoft Word 2007 is an easy-to-use program that will have you creating, editing, and formatting documents in no time—like a pro. You have our word.

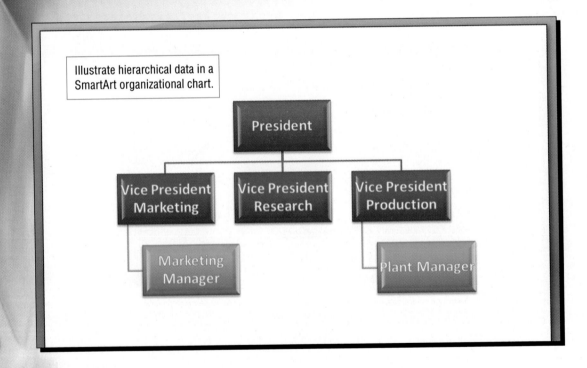

Illustrate hierarchical data in a SmartArt organizational chart.

Microsoft®

word

Unit 1: Editing and Formatting Documents

- ➤ Preparing Documents
- ➤ Formatting Characters and Paragraphs
- ➤ Customizing Paragraphs
- ➤ Formatting Pages

Benchmark Microsoft® Word 2007 Level 1

Microsoft Certified Application Specialist Skills—Unit 1

Reference No.	Skill	Pages
1	**Creating and Customizing Documents**	
1.1	Create and format documents	
1.1.2	Apply styles from a Quick Styles set	45-46
1.1.3	Apply themes to documents	47-48
1.1.4	Modify themes	47-48
1.1.5	Format page backgrounds	125-128
1.1.6	Add a blank page or a cover page	115-118, 116-118
1.2	Lay out documents	
1.2.1	Change page format	103-139, 109-118
1.2.2	Insert and edit headers and footers	
	(not using Quick Parts)	120-125, 124, 125
2	**Formatting Content**	
2.1	Format text and paragraphs	
2.1.1	Format with Format Painter	57-58
2.1.3	Change typestyles, fonts, and font effects	36-44
2.1.4	Customize paragraph formats	48-56, 69-97
2.1.5	Manipulate tabs	82-85
2.2	Manipulate text	
2.2.1	Cut, move, copy, and paste text	88-93
2.2.2	Use Find and Replace	129-136
2.3	Control pagination	
2.3.1	Insert and remove page breaks	114-115
3	**Working with Visual Content**	
3.2	Format illustrations	
3.2.3	Use Quick Styles	45-46
5	**Reviewing Documents**	
5.1	Navigate documents	106-108
5.1.1	Locate and move to locations in a document; use Find and Go To	17-19
5.1.2	Switch to a different window view	104-109

Note: The Level 1 and Level 2 texts each address approximately half of the Microsoft Certified Application Specialist skills. Complete coverage of the skills is offered in the combined Level 1 and Level 2 text titled *Benchmark Series Microsoft® Word 2007: Levels 1 and 2,* which has been approved as certified courseware and which displays the Microsoft Certified Application Specialist logo on the cover.

Preparing Documents

PERFORMANCE OBJECTIVES

Upon successful completion of Chapter 1, you will be able to:

- **Open Microsoft Word**
- **Create, save, name, print, open, and close a Word document**
- **Exit Word and Windows**
- **Edit a document**
- **Move the insertion point within a document**
- **Scroll within a document**
- **Select text in a document**
- **Use the Undo and Redo buttons**
- **Check spelling and grammar in a document**
- **Use the Help feature**

Tutorial 1.1
Creating a Document

In this chapter, you will learn to create, save, name, print, open, close, and edit a Word document as well as complete a spelling and grammar check. You will also learn about the Help feature, which is an on-screen reference manual providing information on features and commands for each program in the Office suite. Before continuing, make sure you read the *Getting Started* section presented at the beginning of this book. This section contains information about computer hardware and software, using the mouse, executing commands, and exploring Help files.

Note: Before beginning computer projects, copy to your storage medium the Word2007L1C1 subfolder from the Word2007L1 folder on the CD that accompanies this textbook. Steps on how to copy a folder are presented on the inside of the back cover of this textbook. Do this every time you start a chapter's projects.

roject **1** **Prepare a Word Document**

You will create a short document containing information on computers and then save, print, and close the document.

Opening Microsoft Word

QUICK STEPS

Open Word
1. Click Start button.
2. Point to *All Programs, Microsoft Office.*
3. Click *Microsoft Office Word 2007.*

Microsoft Office 2007 contains a word processing program named Word that you can use to create, save, edit, and print documents. The steps to open Word may vary depending on your system setup. Generally, to open Word, you would click the Start button on the Taskbar at the Windows desktop, point to *All Programs,* point to *Microsoft Office,* and then click *Microsoft Office Word 2007.*

Creating, Saving, Printing, and Closing a Document

HINT

To avoid opening the same program twice, use the Taskbar to see which programs are open.

start

When Microsoft Word is open, a blank document displays as shown in Figure 1.1. The features of the document screen are described in Table 1.1.

At a blank document, type information to create a document. A document is any information you choose—for instance, a letter, report, term paper, table, and so on. Some things to consider when typing text are:

- **Word Wrap:** As you type text to create a document, you do not need to press the Enter key at the end of each line because Word wraps text to the next line. A word is wrapped to the next line if it begins before the right margin and continues past the right margin. The only times you need to press Enter are to end a paragraph, create a blank line, or end a short line.

Figure 1.1 Blank Document

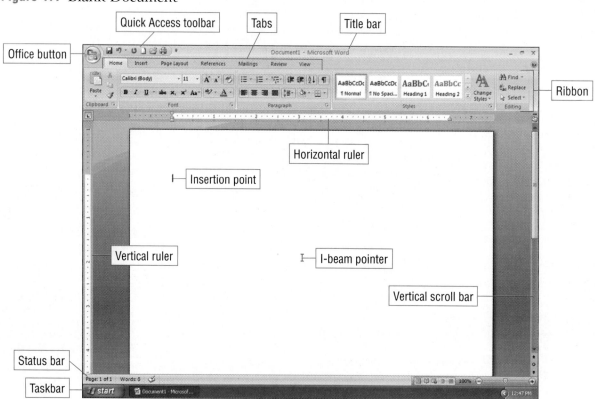

Table 1.1 Microsoft Word Screen Features

Feature	Description
Office button	Displays as a Microsoft Office logo and, when clicked, displays a list of options along with the most recently opened documents
Quick Access toolbar	Contains buttons for commonly used commands
Title bar	Displays document name followed by program name
Tabs	Contains commands and features organized into groups
Ribbon	Area containing the tabs and commands divided into groups
Horizontal ruler	Used to set margins, indents, and tabs
Vertical ruler	Used to set top and bottom margins
I-beam pointer	Used to move the insertion point or to select text
Insertion point	Indicates location of next character entered at the keyboard
Vertical scroll bar	Used to view various parts of the document
Status bar	Displays number of pages and words, View buttons, and the Zoom slider bar

- **AutoCorrect:** Word contains a feature that automatically corrects certain words as you type them. For example, if you type the word *adn* instead of *and*, Word automatically corrects it when you press the spacebar after the word. AutoCorrect will also superscript the letters that follow an ordinal number. For example, if you type *2nd* and then press the spacebar or Enter key, Word will convert this ordinal number to 2nd.

- **Automatic Spell Checker:** By default, Word will automatically insert a red wavy line below words that are not contained in the Spelling dictionary or automatically corrected by AutoCorrect. This may include misspelled words, proper names, some terminology, and some foreign words. If you type a word not recognized by the Spelling dictionary, leave it as written if the word is correct. However, if the word is incorrect, you have two choices—you can delete the word and then type it correctly, or you can position the I-beam pointer on the word, click the right mouse button, and then click the correct spelling in the pop-up list.

- **Automatic Grammar Checker:** Word includes an automatic grammar checker. If the grammar checker detects a sentence containing a grammatical error, a green wavy line is inserted below the sentence. You can leave the sentence as written or position the mouse I-beam pointer on the sentence, click the *right* mouse button, and a pop-up list will display with possible corrections.

- **Spacing Punctuation:** Typically, Word uses Calibri as the default typeface, which is a proportional typeface. (You will learn more about typefaces in Chapter 2.) When typing text in a proportional typeface, space once (rather than twice) after end-of-sentence punctuation such as a period, question mark, or exclamation

HINT

A book icon displays in the Status bar. A check mark on the book indicates no spelling errors detected in the document by the spell checker, while an X in the book indicates errors. Double-click the book icon to move to the next error. If the book icon is not visible, right-click the Status bar and then click the *Spelling and Grammar Check* option at the pop-up list.

point, and after a colon. Proportional typeface is set closer together, and extra white space at the end of a sentence or after a colon is not needed.

- **Option Buttons:** As you insert and edit text in a document, you may notice an option button popping up in your text. The name and appearance of this option button varies depending on the action. If a word you type is corrected by AutoCorrect, if you create an automatic list, or if autoformatting is applied to text, the AutoCorrect Options button appears. Click this button to undo the specific automatic action. If you paste text in a document, the Paste Options button appears near the text. Click this button to display options for controlling how the pasted text is formatted.

- **AutoComplete:** Microsoft Word and other Office applications include an AutoComplete feature that inserts an entire item when you type a few identifying characters. For example, type the letters *Mond* and *Monday* displays in a ScreenTip above the letters. Press the Enter key or press F3 and Word inserts *Monday* in the document.

Using the New Line Command

A Word document is based on a template that applies default formatting. Some basic formatting includes 1.15 line spacing and 10 points of spacing after a paragraph. Each time you press the Enter key, a new paragraph begins and 10 points of spacing is inserted after the paragraph. If you want to move the insertion point down to the next line without including the additional 10 points of spacing, use the New Line command, Shift + Enter.

Project **1a**   Creating a Document

1. Follow the instructions in this chapter to open Microsoft Word or check with your instructor for specific instructions.
2. At a blank document, type the information shown in Figure 1.2 with the following specifications:
   a. Correct any errors highlighted by the spell checker as they occur.
   b. Space once after end-of-sentence punctuation.
   c. After typing *Created:* press Shift + Enter to move the insertion point to the next line without adding 10 points of additional spacing.
   d. To insert the word *Thursday* located towards the end of the document, type Thur and then press F3. (This is an example of the AutoComplete feature.)
   e. To insert the word *December*, type Dece and then press the Enter key. (This is another example of the AutoComplete feature.)
   f. Press Shift + Enter after typing *December 9, 2010*.
   g. When typing the last line (the line containing the ordinal numbers), type the ordinal number text and AutoCorrect will automatically convert the letters in the ordinal numbers to superscript.
3. When you are finished typing the text, press the Enter key once.

The first large computers made use of the decimal number system, in which numbers are indicated by the symbols 0 through 9. Engineers soon hit upon a much simpler system known as machine language for representing data with numbers.

Machine language uses binary numbers ("bi" means two), which are constructed solely of the symbols 0 and 1. The bit (0 or 1) is the smallest unit of data in the binary system. By itself, a bit is not very meaningful. However, a group of eight bits, or a byte, is significant because a byte contains enough possible combinations of zeros and ones to represent 256 separate characters.

Created:
Thursday, December 9, 2010
Note: The two paragraphs will become the 2nd and 3rd paragraphs of the 5th section.

Saving a Document

Save a document if you want to use it in the future. You can use a variety of methods to save a document such as clicking the Save button on the Quick Access toolbar, clicking the Office button and then clicking *Save As* at the drop-down menu, or using the keyboard shortcut Ctrl + S. To save a document, click the Save button on the Quick Access toolbar. At the Save As dialog box shown in Figure 1.3, type the name of the document and then press Enter or click the Save button located in the lower right corner of the dialog box.

QUICK STEPS

Save a Document
1. Click Save button.
2. Type document name.
3. Click Save button.

HINT
Save a document approximately every 15 minutes or when interrupted.

Save

Figure 1.3 Save As Dialog Box

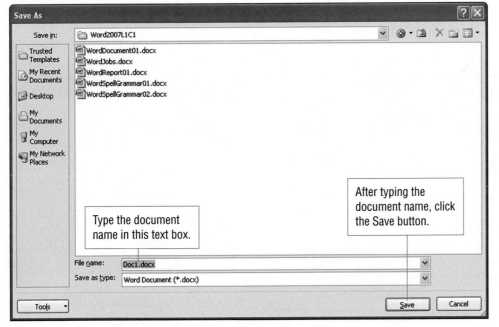

Type the document name in this text box.

After typing the document name, click the Save button.

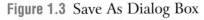

Office button

Naming a Document

Document names created in Word and other applications in the Office suite can be up to 255 characters in length, including drive letter and any folder names, and may include spaces. File names cannot include any of the following characters:

forward slash (/)
backslash (\)
greater than sign (>)
less than sign (<)
asterisk (*)

question mark (?)
quotation mark (")
colon (:)
semicolon (;)
pipe symbol (|)

Quick Print

Printing a Document

Many of the computer exercises you will be creating will need to be printed. A printing of a document on paper is referred to as ***hard copy*** and a document displayed in the screen is referred to as ***soft copy***. Send a document to the printer by clicking the Quick Print button on the Quick Access toolbar. This sends the document immediately to the printer. (If the Quick Print button does not display on the Quick Access toolbar, click the Customize Quick Access Toolbar button that displays at the right side of the toolbar and then click *Quick Print* at the drop-down list.) You can also print by clicking the Office button and then clicking *Print* at the drop-down list or by pressing the keyboard shortcut, Ctrl + P. This displays the Print dialog box. At this dialog box, click OK to send the document to the printer.

Closing a Document

When you save a document it is saved on your storage medium and remains in the document screen. To remove the document from the screen, click the Office button and then click *Close* at the drop-down list or use the keyboard shortcut, Ctrl + F4. When you close a document, the document is removed and a blank screen displays. At this screen, you can open a previously saved document, create a new document, or exit the Word program.

Project **1b**   Saving, Printing, and Closing a Document

1. Save the document you created for Project 1a and name it **WordL1_C1_P1** (for Word Level 1, Chapter 1, Project 1) by completing the following steps:
   a. Click the Save button on the Quick Access toolbar.

Step 1a

b. At the Save As dialog box, type WordL1_C1_P1 and then press Enter.
2. Print the document by clicking the Quick Print button on the Quick Access toolbar.
3. Close the document by clicking the Office button and then clicking *Close* at the drop-down list.

Step 2

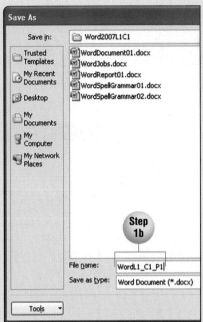

Step 1b

P roject ❷ **Save and Edit a Word Document**

You will open a document located in the Word2007L1C1 folder on your storage medium, add text to the document, and then save the document with a new name.

Creating a New Document

When you close a document, a blank screen displays. If you want to create a new document, display a blank document. To do this, click the New button on the Quick Access toolbar or click the Office button and then click *New*. (If the New button does not display on the Quick Access toolbar, click the Customize Quick Access Toolbar button that displays at the right side of the toolbar and then click *New* at the drop-down list.) At the New Document dialog box, double-click the *Blank document* option. You can also open a new document using the keyboard shortcut, Ctrl + N.

New

Opening a Document

After you save and close a document, you can open it at the Open dialog box shown in Figure 1.4. To display this dialog box, click the Open button on the Quick Access toolbar, click the Office button and then click *Open*, or use the keyboard shortcut, Ctrl + O. (If the Open button does not display on the Quick Access toolbar, click

Open a Document
1. Click Office button.
2. Click *Open*.
3. Double-click document name.

Open

the Customize Quick Access Toolbar button that displays at the right side of the toolbar and then click *Open* at the drop-down list.) At the Open dialog box, double-click the document name. The most recently opened documents display in a list at the right side of the Office button drop-down menu. Click a document in the list to open the document.

Figure 1.4 Open Dialog Box

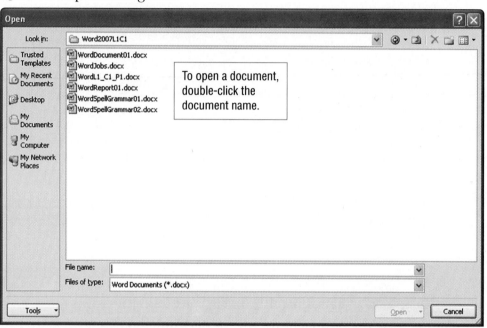

To open a document, double-click the document name.

Project 2a   **Opening a Document**

1. Open the **WordJobs.docx** document by completing the following steps:
   a. Click the Open button on the Quick Access toolbar.
   b. At the Open dialog box, make sure the Word2007L1C1 folder on your storage medium is the active folder.
   c. Double-click *WordJobs.docx*.
2. With the insertion point positioned at the beginning of the document, type the text shown in Figure 1.5.

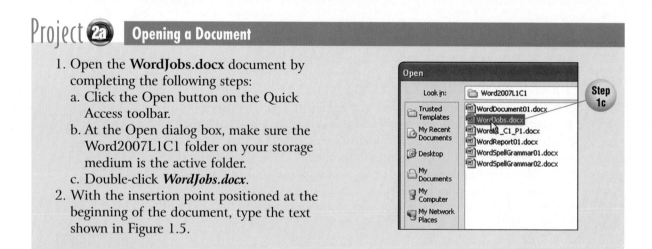

Step 1c

Figure 1.5 Project 2a

The majority of new jobs being created in the United States today involve daily work with computers. Computer-related careers include technical support jobs, sales and training, programming and applications development, network and database administration, and computer engineering.

Saving a Document with Save As

If you open a previously saved document and want to give it a new name, use the *Save As* option from the Office button drop-down list rather than the *Save* option. When you click *Save As*, the Save As dialog box displays. At this dialog box, type the new name for the document and then press Enter.

Exiting Word

When you are finished working with Word and have saved all necessary information, exit Word by clicking the Office button and then clicking the Exit Word button (located at the bottom right side of the drop-down list). You can also exit the Word program by clicking the Close button located in the upper right corner of the screen.

QUICK STEPS

Save a Document with Save As
1. Click Office button.
2. Click *Save As*.
3. Navigate to desired folder.
4. Type document name.
5. Click Save button.

Exit Word
1. Click Office button.
2. Click Exit Word.
OR
Click Close button.

HINT
Save any open documents before exiting Word.

X Exit Word

Project **2b** **Saving a Document with Save As**

1. With **WordJobs.docx** open, save the document with a new name by completing the following steps:
   a. Click the Office button and then click *Save As*.
   b. At the Save As dialog box, type WordL1_C1_P2.
   c. Press Enter.
2. Print the document by clicking the Quick Print button on the Quick Access toolbar.
3. Close the document by pressing Ctrl + F4.

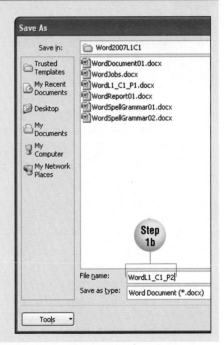

Project 3 Scroll and Browse in a Document

You will open a previously created document, save it with a new name, and then use scrolling and browsing techniques to move the insertion point to specific locations in the document.

Editing a Document

When editing a document, you may decide to insert or delete text. To edit a document, use the mouse, the keyboard, or the mouse combined with the keyboard to move the insertion point to specific locations in the document. To move the insertion point using the mouse, position the I-beam pointer where you want the insertion point located and then click the left mouse button.

You can also scroll in a document, which changes the text display but does not move the insertion point. Use the mouse with the *vertical scroll bar*, located at the right side of the screen, to scroll through text in a document. Click the up scroll arrow at the top of the vertical scroll bar to scroll up through the document and click the down scroll arrow to scroll down through the document. The scroll bar contains a scroll box that indicates the location of the text in the document screen in relation to the remainder of the document. To scroll up one screen at a time, position the arrow pointer above the scroll box (but below the up scroll arrow) and then click the left mouse button. Position the arrow pointer below the scroll box and click the left button to scroll down a screen. If you hold down the left mouse button, the action becomes continuous. You can also position the arrow pointer on the scroll box, hold down the left mouse button, and then drag the scroll box along the scroll bar to reposition text in the document screen. As you drag the scroll box along the vertical scroll bar in a longer document, page numbers display in a box at the right side of the document screen.

Project 3a Scrolling in a Document

1. Open **WordReport01.docx** and then press the Enter key once. (This document is located in the Word2007L1C1 folder you copied to your storage medium.)
2. Save the document with Save As and name it **WordL1_C1_P3**.
3. Position the I-beam pointer at the beginning of the first paragraph and then click the left mouse button.
4. Click the down scroll arrow on the vertical scroll bar several times. (This scrolls down lines of text in the document.) With the mouse pointer on the down scroll arrow, hold down the left mouse button and keep it down until the end of the document displays.
5. Position the mouse pointer on the up scroll arrow and hold down the left mouse button until the beginning of the document displays.
6. Position the mouse pointer below the scroll box and then click the left mouse button. Continue clicking the mouse button (with the mouse pointer positioned below the scroll box) until the end of the document displays.

7. Position the mouse pointer on the scroll box in the vertical scroll bar. Hold down the left mouse button, drag the scroll box to the top of the vertical scroll bar, and then release the mouse button. (Notice that the document page numbers display in a box at the right side of the document screen.)
8. Click on the title at the beginning of the document. (This moves the insertion point to the location of the mouse pointer.)

Moving the Insertion Point to a Specific Page

Along with scrolling options, Word also contains navigation buttons for moving the insertion point to specific locations. Navigation buttons display toward the bottom of the vertical scroll bar and include the Previous button, the Select Browse Object button, and the Next button. The full names of and the tasks completed by the Previous and Next buttons vary depending on the last navigation completed. Click the Select Browse Object button and a palette of browsing choices displays. You will learn more about the Select Browse Object button in the next section.

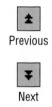

Previous

Next

Word includes a Go To option you can use to move the insertion point to a specific page within a document. To move the insertion point to a specific page, click the Find button arrow located in the Editing group in the Home tab and then click *Go To* at the drop-down list. At the Find and Replace dialog box with the Go To tab selected, type the page number in the *Enter page number* text box and then press Enter. Click the Close button to close the dialog box.

Browsing in a Document

The Select Browse Object button located toward the bottom of the vertical scroll bar contains options for browsing through a document. Click this button and a palette of browsing choices displays. Use the options on the palette to move the insertion point to various features in a Word document. Position the arrow pointer on an option in the palette and the option name displays below the options. The options on the palette and the location of the options vary depending on the last function performed.

Select Browse Object

Moving the Insertion Point with the Keyboard

To move the insertion point with the keyboard, use the arrow keys located to the right of the regular keyboard. You can also use the arrow keys on the numeric keypad. If you use these keys, make sure Num Lock is off. Use the arrow keys together with other keys to move the insertion point to various locations in the document as shown in Table 1.2.

When moving the insertion point, Word considers a word to be any series of characters between spaces. A paragraph is any text that is followed by a stroke of the Enter key. A page is text that is separated by a soft or hard page break. If you open a previously saved document, you can move the insertion point to where the insertion point was last located when the document was closed by pressing Shift + F5.

Table 1.2 Insertion Point Movement Commands

To move insertion point	Press
One character left	Left Arrow
One character right	Right Arrow
One line up	Up Arrow
One line down	Down Arrow
One word to the left	Ctrl + Left Arrow
One word to the right	Ctrl + Right Arrow
To end of a line	End
To beginning of a line	Home
To beginning of current paragraph	Ctrl + Up Arrow
To beginning of next paragraph	Ctrl + Down Arrow
Up one screen	Page Up
Down one screen	Page Down
To top of previous page	Ctrl + Page Up
To top of next page	Ctrl + Page Down
To beginning of document	Ctrl + Home
To end of document	Ctrl + End

Project 3b Moving the Insertion Point and Browsing in a Document

1. With **WordL1_C1_P3.docx** open, move the insertion point to page 3 by completing the following steps:
   a. Click the Find button arrow located in the Editing group in the Home tab and then click *Go To* at the drop-down list.
   b. At the Find and Replace dialog box with the Go To tab selected, type 3 in the *Enter page number* text box and then press Enter.
   c. Click the Close button to close the Find and Replace dialog box.
2. Click the Previous Page button located immediately above the Select Browse Object button on the vertical scroll bar. (This moves the insertion point to page 2.)

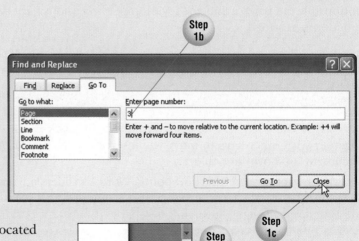

3. Click the Previous Page button again. (This moves the insertion point to page 1.)
4. Click the Next Page button located immediately below the Select Browse Object button on the vertical scroll bar. (This moves the insertion point to the beginning of page 2.)

Step 4

5. Move to the beginning of page 3 by completing the following steps:
   a. Click the Select Browse Object button.
   b. At the palette of browsing choices, click the last choice in the bottom row (*Browse by Page*). (This moves the insertion point to page 3.)

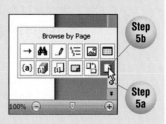

Step 5b

Step 5a

6. Press Ctrl + Home to move the insertion point to the beginning of the document.
7. Practice using the keyboard commands shown in Table 1.2 to move the insertion point within the document.
8. Close **WordL1_C1_P3.docx**.

roject ④ **Insert and Delete Text**

You will open a previously created document, save it with a new name, and then make editing changes to the document. The editing changes include selecting, inserting, and deleting text.

Inserting and Deleting Text

Editing a document may include inserting and/or deleting text. To insert text in a document, position the insertion point in the desired location and then type the text. Existing characters move to the right as you type the text. A number of options are available for deleting text. Some deletion commands are shown in Table 1.3.

Table 1.3 Deletion Commands

To delete	Press
Character right of insertion point	Delete key
Character left of insertion point	Backspace key
Text from insertion point to beginning of word	Ctrl + Backspace
Text from insertion point to end of word	Ctrl + Delete

By default, text you type in a document is inserted in the document and existing text is moved to the right. If you want to type over something, you need to turn on the Overtype mode. With the Overtype mode on, anything you type will replace existing text. To turn on the Overtype mode, click the Office button and then click the Word Options button located toward the bottom of the drop-down list. At the Word Options dialog box, click *Advanced* in the left panel. In the *Advanced options for working with Word.* section, insert a check mark in the *Use Overtype mode* check box if you want the Overtype mode always on in the document. Or, insert a check mark in the *Use the Insert key to control Overtype mode* check box if you want to use the Insert key to turn Overtype mode on and off. After making your selection, click the OK button located in the lower right corner of the dialog box.

Selecting Text

You can use the mouse and/or keyboard to select a specific amount of text. Once selected, you can delete the text or perform other Word functions involving the selected text. When text is selected, it displays with a blue background as shown in Figure 1.6 and the Mini toolbar displays in a dimmed fashion and contains options for common tasks. Move the mouse pointer over the Mini toolbar and it becomes active. (You will learn more about the Mini toolbar in Chapter 2.)

Figure 1.6 Selected Text and Mini Toolbar

Selecting Text with the Mouse

Use the mouse to select a word, line, sentence, paragraph, or the entire document. Table 1.4 indicates the steps to follow to select various amounts of text. To select a specific amount of text such as a line or a paragraph, the instructions in the table tell you to click in the selection bar. The selection bar is the space located toward the left side of the document screen between the left edge of the page and the text. When the mouse pointer is positioned in the selection bar, the pointer turns into an arrow pointing up and to the right (instead of to the left).

To select an amount of text other than a word, sentence, or paragraph, position the I-beam pointer on the first character of the text to be selected, hold down the left mouse button, drag the I-beam pointer to the last character of the text to be selected, and then release the mouse button. You can also select all text between the current insertion point and the I-beam pointer. To do this, position the insertion point where you want the selection to begin, hold down the Shift key, click the I-beam pointer at the end of the selection, and then release the Shift key. To cancel a selection using the mouse, click anywhere in the document screen outside the selected text.

HINT

To select text vertically, hold down the Alt key while dragging the mouse.

Table 1.4 Selecting with the Mouse

To select	Complete these steps using the mouse
A word	Double-click the word.
A line of text	Click in the selection bar to the left of the line.
Multiple lines of text	Drag in the selection bar to the left of the lines.
A sentence	Hold down the Ctrl key, then click anywhere in the sentence.
A paragraph	Double-click in the selection bar next to the paragraph or triple-click anywhere in the paragraph.
Multiple paragraphs	Drag in the selection bar.
An entire document	Triple-click in the selection bar.

Selecting Text with the Keyboard

To select a specific amount of text using the keyboard, turn on the Selection Mode by pressing the F8 function key. With the Selection Mode activated, use the arrow keys to select the desired text. If you want to cancel the selection, press the Esc key and then press any arrow key. You can customize the Status bar to display text indicating that the Selection Mode is activated. To do this, right-click any blank location on the Status bar and then click *Selection Mode* at the pop-up list. When you press F8 to turn on the Selection Mode, the words *Selection Mode* display on the Status bar. You can also select text with the commands shown in Table 1.5.

HINT
If text is selected, any character you type replaces the selected text.

Project 4a **Editing a Document**

1. Open **WordDocument01.docx**. (This document is located in the Word2007L1C1 folder you copied to your storage medium.)
2. Save the document with Save As and name it **WordL1_C1_P4**.
3. Change the word *give* in the first sentence of the first paragraph to *enter*.
4. Change the second *to* in the first sentence to *into*.
5. Delete the words *means of* in the first sentence in the *QWERTY Keyboard* section.

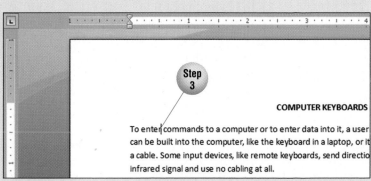

Step 3

COMPUTER KEYBOARDS

To enter commands to a computer or to enter data into it, a user can be built into the computer, like the keyboard in a laptop, or it a cable. Some input devices, like remote keyboards, send directio infrared signal and use no cabling at all.

6. Select the words *and use no cabling at all* and the period that follows located at the end of the last sentence in the first paragraph, and then press the Delete key.
7. Insert a period immediately following the word *signal*.

8. Delete the heading line containing the text *QWERTY Keyboard* using the Selection Mode by completing the following steps:
   a. Position the insertion point immediately before the *Q* in *QWERTY*.
   b. Press F8 to turn on the Selection Mode.
   c. Press the Down Arrow key.
   d. Press the Delete key.
9. Complete steps similar to those in Step 8 to delete the heading line containing the text *DVORAK Keyboard*.
10. Begin a new paragraph with the sentence that reads *Keyboards have different physical appearances.* by completing the following steps:
    a. Position the insertion point immediately left of the *K* in *Keyboards* (the first word of the fifth sentence in the last paragraph).
    b. Press the Enter key.
11. Save **WordL1_C1_P4.docx**.

To enter commands into a computer device can be built into the computer computer by a cable. Some input dev means of an infrared signal.

Steps 8a–8c

QWERTY Keyboard

Keyboards can be external devices tha itself as they are in laptops. Most key the first six keys at the left of the first of mechanical typewriters to slow do

To enter commands into a computer or device can be built into the computer, li computer by a cable. Some input device means of an infrared signal.

Keyboards can be external devices that itself as they are in laptops. Most keybo the first six keys at the left of the first ro of mechanical typewriters to slow down

The DVORAK keyboard is an alternative commonly used keys are placed close to install software on a QWERTY keyboard keyboards is convenient especially whe

Steps 10a–10b

Keyboards have different physical appe that of a calculator, containing number "broken" into two pieces to reduce stra change the symbol or characters entere

Table 1.5 Selecting with the Keyboard

To select	Press
One character to right	Shift + Right Arrow
One character to left	Shift + Left Arrow
To end of word	Ctrl + Shift + Right Arrow
To beginning of word	Ctrl + Shift + Left Arrow
To end of line	Shift + End
To beginning of line	Shift + Home
One line up	Shift + Up Arrow
One line down	Shift + Down Arrow
To beginning of paragraph	Ctrl + Shift + Up Arrow
To end of paragraph	Ctrl + Shift + Down Arrow
One screen up	Shift + Page Up
One screen down	Shift + Page Down
To end of document	Ctrl + Shift + End
To beginning of document	Ctrl + Shift + Home
Entire document	Ctrl + A or click Select button in Editing group and then Select All

Using the Undo and Redo Buttons

If you make a mistake and delete text that you did not intend to, or if you change your mind after deleting text and want to retrieve it, you can use the Undo or Redo buttons on the Quick Access toolbar. For example, if you type text and then click the Undo button, the text will be removed. You can undo text or commands. For example, if you add formatting such as bolding to text and then click the Undo button, the bolding is removed.

If you use the Undo button and then decide you do not want to reverse the original action, click the Redo button. For example, if you select and underline text and then decide to remove underlining, click the Undo button. If you then decide you want the underlining back on, click the Redo button. Many Word actions can be undone or redone. Some actions, however, such as printing and saving, cannot be undone or redone.

Word maintains actions in temporary memory. If you want to undo an action performed earlier, click the Undo button arrow. This causes a drop-down list to display. To make a selection from this drop-down list, click the desired action and the action, along with any actions listed above it in the drop-down list, is undone.

Undo

Redo

Project 4b Undoing and Redoing Deletions

1. With **WordL1_C1_P4.docx** open, delete the last sentence in the last paragraph using the mouse by completing the following steps:
   a. Position the I-beam pointer anywhere in the sentence that begins *All keyboards have modifier keys . . . .*
   b. Hold down the Ctrl key and then click the left mouse button.

> install software on a QWERTY keyboard that emulates a DVORAK keyboard. The ability to emulate other keyboards is convenient especially when working with foreign languages.
>
> Keyboards have different physical appearances. Many keyboards have a separate numeric keypad, like that of a calculator, containing numbers and mathematical operators. Some keyboards are sloped and "broken" into two pieces to reduce strain. All keyboards have modifier keys that enable the user to change the symbol or characters entered when a given key is pressed.

Steps
1a–1b

   c. Press the Delete key.
2. Delete the last paragraph by completing the following steps:
   a. Position the I-beam pointer anywhere in the last paragraph (the paragraph that reads *Keyboards have different physical appearances.*).
   b. Triple-click the left mouse button.
   c. Press the Delete key.
3. Undo the deletion by clicking the Undo button on the Quick Access toolbar.
4. Redo the deletion by clicking the Redo button on the Quick Access toolbar.
5. Select the first sentence in the second paragraph and then delete it.
6. Select the first paragraph in the document and then delete it.

7. Undo the two deletions by completing the following steps:
   a. Click the Undo button arrow.
   b. Click the *second* Clear listed in the drop-down list. (This will redisplay the first sentence in the second paragraph as well as displaying the first paragraph. The sentence will be selected.)
8. Click outside the sentence to deselect it.
9. Save, print, and then close **WordL1_C1_P4.docx**.

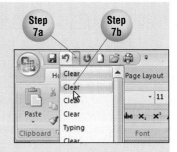

Step 7a

Step 7b

Project **5** **Complete a Spelling and Grammar Check**

You will open a previously created document, save it with a new name, and then check the spelling and grammar in the document.

Checking the Spelling and Grammar in a Document

QUICK STEPS

Check Spelling and Grammar
1. Click Review tab.
2. Click Spelling & Grammar button.
3. Change or ignore error.
4. Click OK.

HINT

Complete a spelling and grammar check on a portion of a document by selecting the text first and then clicking the Spelling & Grammar button.

Spelling & Grammar

Two tools for creating thoughtful and well-written documents include a spelling checker and a grammar checker. The spelling checker finds misspelled words and offers replacement words. It also finds duplicate words and irregular capitalizations. When you spell check a document, the spelling checker compares the words in your document with the words in its dictionary. If the spelling checker finds a match, it passes over the word. If a match is not found for the word, the spelling checker will stop, select the word, and offer replacements.

The grammar checker will search a document for errors in grammar, punctuation, and word usage. The spelling checker and the grammar check can help you create a well-written document, but do not replace the need for proofreading. To complete a spelling and grammar check, click the Review tab and then click the Spelling & Grammar button in the Proofing group. You can also begin spelling and grammar checking by pressing the keyboard shortcut, F7. As the spelling and grammar checker selects text, make a choice from some of the options in the Spelling and Grammar dialog box as shown in Table 1.6.

By default, a spelling and grammar check are both completed on a document. If you want to check only the spelling in a document and not the grammar, remove the check mark from the *Check grammar* check box located in the lower left corner of the Spelling and Grammar dialog box. When spell checking a document, you can temporarily leave the Spelling and Grammar dialog box, make corrections in the document, and then resume spell checking by clicking the Resume button.

Table 1.6 Spelling and Grammar Dialog Box Buttons

Button	Function
Ignore Once	During spell checking, skips that occurrence of the word; in grammar checking, leaves currently selected text as written
Ignore All	During spell checking, skips that occurrence of the word and all other occurrences of the word in the document
Ignore Rule	During grammar checking, leaves currently selected text as written and ignores the current rule for remainder of the grammar check
Add to Dictionary	Adds selected word to the main spelling check dictionary
Change	Replaces selected word in sentence with selected word in *Suggestions* list box
Change All	Replaces selected word in sentence with selected word in *Suggestions* list box and all other occurrences of the word
AutoCorrect	Inserts selected word and correct spelling of word in AutoCorrect dialog box
Explain	During grammar checking, displays grammar rule information about the selected text
Undo	Reverses most recent spelling and grammar action
Next Sentence	Accepts manual changes made to sentence and then continues grammar checking
Options	Displays a dialog box with options for customizing a spelling and grammar check

Project 5 Checking the Spelling and Grammar in a Document

1. Open **WordSpellGrammar01.docx**.
2. Save the document with Save As and name it **WordL1_C1_P5**.
3. Click the Review tab.
4. Click the Spelling & Grammar button in the Proofing group.

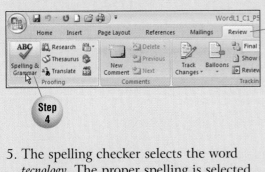

Step 3

Step 4

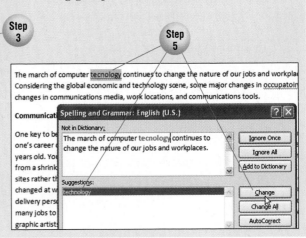

Step 5

5. The spelling checker selects the word *tecnology*. The proper spelling is selected in the *Suggestions* list box, so click the Change button (or Change All button).

6. The spelling checker selects the word *occupatoins*. The proper spelling of the word is selected in the *Suggestions* list box, so click the Change button (or Change All button).

7. The grammar checker selects the sentence that begins *One key to being successful . . .* and displays *trends* and *a trend* in the *Suggestions* list box. Click *a trend* in the *Suggestions* list box and then click the Change button.

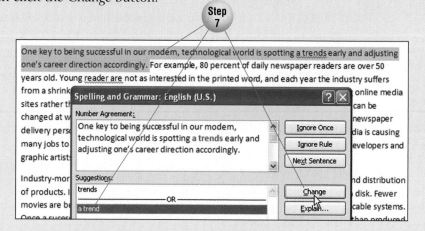

8. The grammar checker selects the sentence that begins *Young reader are not as interested . . .* and displays *reader is* and *readers are* in the *Suggestions* text box. Click the Explain button, read the information about subject-verb agreement that displays in the Word Help window, and then click the Close button located in the upper right corner of the Word Help window.

9. Click *readers are* in the *Suggestions* text box and then click the Change button.

10. The spelling checker selects *excelent*. The proper spelling is selected in the *Suggestions* list box, so click the Change button.

11. The grammar checker selects the sentence that begins *The number of printing and lithography job's is shrinking . . . .* Click the Explain button, read the information about plural or possessive that displays in the Word Help window, and then click the Close button located in the upper right corner of the Word Help window.

12. With *jobs* selected in the *Suggestions* list box, click the Change button.

13. The spelling checker selects the word *sucessful* and offers *successful* in the *Suggestions* text box. Since this word is misspelled in another location in the document, click the Change All button.

14. The spelling checker selects the word *telework*. This word is correct so click the Ingore All button.

15. The spelling checker selects the word *are* that is repeated twice. Click the Delete button to delete the word.

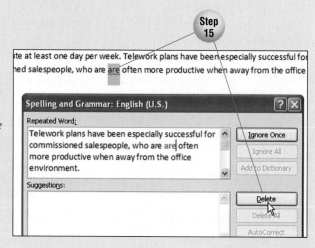

16. When the message displays telling you that the spelling and grammar check is complete, click the OK button.

17. Save, print, and then close **WordL1_C1_P5.docx**.

Project 6 Use the Help Feature

You need to learn more about selecting text and saving a document so you decide to use Help to research these features.

Using Help

Word's Help feature is an on-screen reference manual containing information about all Word features and commands. Word's Help feature is similar to the Windows Help and the Help features in Excel, PowerPoint, and Access. Get help by clicking the Microsoft Office Word Help button located in the upper right corner of the screen (a question mark in a circle) or by pressing the keyboard shortcut, F1. This displays the Word Help window. In this window, type a topic, feature, or question in the *Search* text box and then press Enter. Topics related to the search text display in the Help window. Click a topic that interests you. If the topic window contains a <u>Show All</u> hyperlink in the upper right corner, click this hyperlink and the information expands to show all help information related to the topic. When you click the <u>Show All</u> hyperlink, it becomes the <u>Hide All</u> hyperlink.

QUICK STEPS

Use Help Feature
1. Click Microsoft Office Word Help button.
2. Type topic, feature, or question.
3. Press Enter.
4. Click desired topic.

Help

Project 6a Using the Help Feature

1. At a blank document, click the Microsoft Office Word Help button located in the upper right corner of the screen.
2. At the Word Help window, type selecting text in the *Search* text box.

Step 1

Step 2

3. Press the Enter key.
4. When the list of topics displays, click the <u>Select text</u> hyperlink.

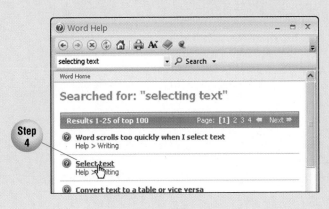

Step 4

5. Click the <u>Show All</u> hyperlink that displays in the upper right corner of the window.
6. Read the information about selecting text.
7. Print the information by clicking the Print button located toward the top of the Word Help window.
8. At the Print dialog box, click the Print button.
9. Click the Close button to close the Word Help window.

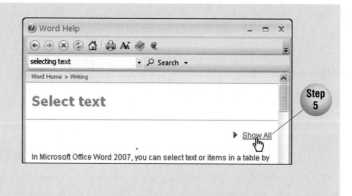

Getting Help in a Dialog Box

Dialog boxes contain a Help button you can click to display the Word Help window that is specific to the dialog box. This button is located in the upper right corner of the dialog box and displays as a question mark inside a square. Click this button and the Word Help window displays with topics related to the dialog box.

Project 6b   **Getting Help in a Dialog Box**

1. At a blank document, click the Office button and then click *Save As* at the drop-down list.
2. At the Save As dialog box, click the Help button located in the upper right corner of the dialog box.
3. At the Word Help window, click the <u>Save As</u> hyperlink.
4. In the Save As list box, click *Microsoft Office Word*.
5. Read the information that displays about saving in Word and then click the Close button to close the Word Help window.
6. Close the Save As dialog box.

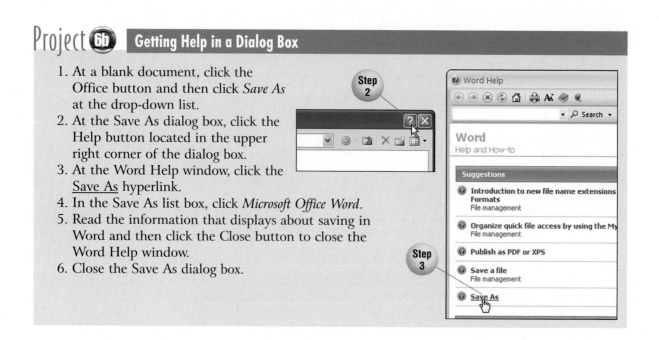

CHAPTER summary

- Open Microsoft Word by clicking the Start button on the Taskbar, pointing to *All Programs*, pointing to *Microsoft Office*, and then clicking *Microsoft Office Word 2007*.
- The Office button displays as a Microsoft Office logo and, when clicked, displays a list of options and most recently opened documents.
- The Quick Access toolbar is located to the right of the Office button and contains buttons for commonly used commands.
- The Title bar is located to the right of the Quick Access toolbar and displays the document name followed by the program name.
- The ribbon area contains tabs with commands and options divided into groups.
- The insertion point displays as a blinking vertical line and indicates the position of the next character to be entered in the document.
- The mouse displays in the screen as an I-beam pointer or as an arrow pointing up and to the left.
- Use the vertical scroll bar to view various parts of the document.
- The Status bar displays the number of pages and words, View buttons, and the Zoom slider bar.
- Word automatically wraps text to the next line as you type information. Press the Enter key only to end a paragraph, create a blank line, or end a short line.
- Word contains a feature named AutoCorrect that automatically corrects certain words as they are typed.
- When typing text, the automatic spell checker feature inserts a red wavy line below words not contained in the Spelling dictionary, and the automatic grammar checker inserts a green wavy line below a sentence containing a grammatical error.
- The AutoComplete feature inserts an entire item when you type a few identifying characters and then press Enter or F3.
- Document names can contain a maximum of 255 characters, including the drive letter and folder names, and may include spaces.
- The insertion point can be moved throughout the document without interfering with text by using the mouse, the keyboard, or the mouse combined with the keyboard.
- You can move the insertion point by character, word, screen, or page, and from the first to the last character in a document. Refer to Table 1.2 for keyboard insertion point movement commands.
- The scroll box on the vertical scroll bar indicates the location of the text in the document in relation to the remainder of the document.
- Click the Select Browse Object button located at the bottom of the vertical scroll bar to display options for browsing through a document.
- You can delete text by character, word, line, several lines, or partial page using specific keys or by selecting text using the mouse or the keyboard.

- You can select a specific amount of text using the mouse or the keyboard. Refer to Table 1.4 for information on selecting with the mouse and refer to Table 1.5 for information on selecting with the keyboard.
- Use the Undo button on the Quick Access toolbar if you change your mind after typing, deleting, or formatting text and want to undo the action. Use the Redo button to redo something that had been undone with the Undo button.
- The spelling checker matches the words in your document with the words in its dictionary. If a match is not found, the word is selected and possible corrections are suggested. The grammar checker searches a document for errors in grammar, style, punctuation, and word usage. When a grammar error is detected, display information about the error by clicking the Explain button at the Spelling & Grammar dialog box.
- Word's Help feature is an on-screen reference manual containing information about all Word features and commands.
- Click the Microsoft Office Word Help button or press F1 to display the Word Help window. At this window, type a topic and then press Enter.
- Dialog boxes contain a Help button you can click to display the Word Help window with information specific to the dialog box.

COMMANDS review

FEATURE	RIBBON TAB, GROUP	BUTTON	QUICK ACCESS TOOLBAR	OFFICE BUTTON DROP-DOWN LIST	KEYBOARD SHORTCUT
Close document				Close	Ctrl + F4
Exit Word		✖		Exit Word	
Find and Replace dialog box with Go To tab selected	Home, Editing	Find ▾, Go To			Ctrl + G
New blank document			🗋	New, Blank document	Ctrl + N
Open dialog box			📂	Open	Ctrl + O
Print dialog box				Print	Ctrl + P
Print document			🖶	Print, Quick Print	
Save document			💾	Save	Ctrl + S
Select document	Home, Editing	Select ▾			Ctrl + A
Spelling and Grammar dialog box	Review, Proofing	ABC ✓			F7
Word Help window		ⓘ			F1

CONCEPTS check

Test Your Knowledge

Completion: In the space provided at the right, indicate the correct term, symbol, or command.

1. This toolbar contains the Save button.

   Quickaccess

2. This button displays in the upper left corner of the screen and displays with the Microsoft logo.

   Office Button

3. This is the area located toward the top of the screen that contains tabs with commands and options divided into groups.

   Ribbon ?, Tabs ?

4. This bar, located toward the bottom of the screen, displays number of pages and words, View buttons, and the Zoom slider bar.

   States Bar

5. This tab is selected by default.

   Home

6. This feature automatically corrects certain words as you type them.

   Spellcheck AutoCorrect

7. This feature inserts an entire item when you type a few identifying characters and then press Enter or F3.

   Auto complete

8. This is the keyboard shortcut to display the Print dialog box.

   Control + O

9. This is the keyboard shortcut to close a document.

   Control + F4

10. This is the keyboard shortcut to display a new blank document.

    Control + N

11. Use this keyboard shortcut to move the insertion point to the beginning of the previous page.

    control + Page Up

12. Use this keyboard shortcut to move the insertion point to the end of the document.

    control + End

13. Press this key on the keyboard to delete the character left of the insertion point.

    Backspace

14. Using the mouse, do this to select one word.

    Double click word

15. To select various amounts of text using the mouse, you can click in this bar.

    selection Bar

16. Click this tab to display the Spelling & Grammar button in the Proofing group.

    Review

17. This is the keyboard shortcut to display the Word Help window.

    F÷1

SKILLS check
Demonstrate Your Proficiency

Assessment

1 TYPE AND EDIT A DOCUMENT ON FUZZY LOGIC

1. Open Word and then type the text in Figure 1.7. Correct any errors highlighted by the spell checker and space once after end-of-sentence punctuation.
2. Make the following changes to the document:
   a. Delete *AI* in the first sentence of the first paragraph and then insert *artificial intelligence*.
   b. Insert the words *for approximations and* between the words *allowing* and *incomplete* located in the first sentence of the first paragraph.
   c. Insert the words *or numerical* between the words *yes/no* and *information* in the second sentence of the first paragraph.
   d. Delete the words *hard to come by* in the last sentence of the first paragraph and replace with the word *rare*.
   e. Insert the letters *SQL* between the words *logic* and *database* in the last sentence of the second paragraph.
   f. Move the insertion point immediately left of the period at the end of the last sentence of the last paragraph, type a comma, and then insert the words *and trade shares on the Tokyo Stock Exchange*. Delete the word *and* before the words *automobile transmissions* in the last sentence.
   g. Join the first and second paragraphs.
   h. Delete the name *Marie Solberg* and then type your first and last names.
3. Save the document and name it **WordL1_C1_A1**.
4. Print and then close **WordL1_C1_A1.docx**.

Assessment

2 CHECK THE SPELLING AND GRAMMAR OF A COMPUTER SOFTWARE DOCUMENT

1. Open **WordSpellGrammar02.docx**.
2. Save the document with Save As and name it **WordL1_C1_A2**.
3. Complete a spelling and grammar check on the document. You determine what to change and what to leave as written.
4. Insert the sentence *Wizards are small programs designed to assist users by automating tasks.* between the third and fourth sentences in the *User-Friendly System Software* section.
5. Move the insertion point to the end of the document, type your first and last names, press Shift + Enter, and then type the current date.
6. Save, print, and then close **WordL1_C1_A2.docx**.

Figure 1.7 Assessment 1

Fuzzy Logic

The fuzzy logic branch of AI attempts to model human reasoning by allowing incomplete input data. Instead of demanding precise yes/no information, fuzzy logic systems allow users to input "fuzzy" data. The terminology used by the system is deliberately vague and includes terms such as very probable, somewhat decreased, reasonable, or very slight. This is an attempt to simulate real-world conditions, where precise answers are hard to come by.

A fuzzy logic system attempts to work more naturally with the user by piecing together an answer in a manner similar to that used by a traditional expert system. Fuzzy logic database queries seem significantly more human than traditional queries.

Fuzzy logic systems are much more common in Japan than they are in the United States, where traditional expert systems and neural networks tend to be favored. In Japan, microprocessors specially designed by Toshiba and Hitachi to use fuzzy logic operate subways, consumer electronics, and automobile transmissions.

Created by Marie Solberg
Monday, September 27, 2010
Note: Please insert this information between the 4th and 5th sections.

3 CREATE A DOCUMENT DESCRIBING KEYBOARD SHORTCUTS

1. Click the Microsoft Office Word Help button, type keyboard shortcuts, and then press Enter.
2. At the Word Help window, click the Keyboard shortcuts for Microsoft Office Word hyperlink.
3. At the keyboard shortcut window, click the Show All hyperlink.
4. Read through the information in the Word Help window.
5. Create a document describing four keyboard shortcuts.
6. Save the document and name it **WordL1_C1_A3**.
7. Print and then close **WordL1_C1_A3.docx**.

CASE study

Apply Your Skills

Part 1

You are the assistant to Paul Brewster, the training coordinator at a medium-sized service-oriented business. You have been asked by Mr. Brewster to prepare a document for Microsoft Word users within the company explaining how to use the Save As command when saving a document rather than the Save command. Save the document and name it **WordL1_C1_CS_P1**. Print and then close the document.

Part 2

Mr. Brewster would like a document containing a brief summary of some basic Word commands for use in Microsoft Word training classes. He has asked you to prepare a document containing the following information:

- A brief explanation on how to move the insertion point to a specific page
- Keyboard shortcuts to move the insertion point to the beginning and end of a text line and beginning and end of a document
- Commands to delete text from the insertion point to the beginning of the word and from the insertion point to the end of the word
- Steps to select a word, a sentence, a paragraph, and an entire document using the mouse.
- Keyboard shortcut to select the entire document

Save the document and name it **WordL1_C1_CS_P2**. Print and then close the document.

Part 3

According to Mr. Brewster, the company is considering updating the Resources Department computers to Microsoft Office 2007. He has asked you to use the Internet to go to the Microsoft home page at www.microsoft.com and then use the search feature to find information on the system requirements for Office Professional Edition 2007. When you find the information, type a document that contains the Office Professional Edition 2007 system requirements for the computer and processor, memory, hard disk space, drives, and operating system. Save the document and name it **WordL1_C1_CS_P3**. Print and then close the document.

CHAPTER 2

Formatting Characters and Paragraphs

PERFORMANCE OBJECTIVES

Upon successful completion of Chapter 2, you will be able to:

- Change the font and font effects
- Format selected text with buttons on the Mini toolbar
- Apply styles from Quick Styles sets
- Apply themes
- Change the alignment of text in paragraphs
- Indent text in paragraphs
- Increase and decrease spacing before and after paragraphs
- Repeat the last action
- Automate formatting with Format Painter
- Change line spacing in a document
- Reveal and compare formatting

Tutorial 2.1
Modifying Text Format
Tutorial 2.2
Other Formatting Features
Tutorial 2.3
Modifying and Comparing Text
Formatting

A Word document is based on a template that applies default formatting. Some of the default formats include 11-point Calibri, line spacing of 1.15, 10 points of spacing after each paragraph, and left-aligned text. The appearance of a document in the document screen and how it looks when printed is called the *format*. In this chapter, you will learn about character formatting that can include such elements as changing the typeface, type size, and typestyle as well as applying font effects such as bolding and italicizing. The Paragraph group in the Home tab includes buttons for applying formatting to paragraphs of text. In Word, a paragraph is any amount of text followed by the press of the Enter key. In this chapter, you will learn to apply paragraph formatting to text such as changing text alignment, indenting text, applying formatting with Format Painter, and changing line spacing.

Note: Before beginning computer projects, copy to your storage medium the Word2007L1C2 subfolder from the Word2007L1 folder on the CD that accompanies this textbook and then make Word2007L1C2 the active folder.

Changing Fonts

The Font group shown in Figure 2.1 contains a number of buttons you can use to apply character formatting to text in a document. The top row contains buttons for changing the font and font size as well as buttons for increasing and decreasing the size of the font. The bottom row contains buttons for applying typestyles such as bold, italics, underlining, superscript, and subscript. You can remove character formatting (as well as paragraph formatting) applied to text by clicking the Clear Formatting button in the Font group. Remove only character formatting from selected text by pressing the keyboard shortcut, Ctrl + spacebar.

Clear Formatting

Figure 2.1 Font Group Buttons

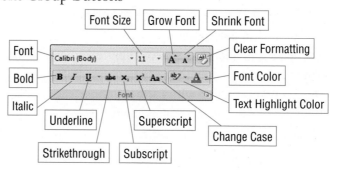

A Word document is based on a template that formats text in 11-point Calibri. You may want to change this default to some other font for such reasons as changing the mood of the document, enhancing the visual appeal, and increasing the readability of the text. A font consists of three elements—typeface, type size, and typestyle.

A typeface is a set of characters with a common design and shape and can be decorative or plain and either monospaced or proportional. Word refers to typeface as *font*. A monospaced typeface allots the same amount of horizontal space for each character while a proportional typeface allots a varying amount of space for each character. Proportional typefaces are divided into two main categories: *serif* and *sans serif*. A serif is a small line at the end of a character stroke. Consider using a serif typeface for text-intensive documents because the serifs help move the reader's eyes across the page. Use a sans serif typeface for headings, headlines, and advertisements.

Microsoft Word 2007 includes six new typefaces designed for extended on-screen reading. These typefaces include the default, Calibri, as well as Cambria, Candara, Consolas, Constantia, and Corbel. Calibri, Candara, and Corbel are sans serif typefaces; Cambria and Constantia are serif typefaces; and Consolas is monospaced. These six typefaces as well as some other popular typefaces are shown in Table 2.1.

Table 2.1 Serif and Sans Serif Typefaces

Serif Typefaces	Sans Serif Typefaces	Monospaced Typefaces
Cambria	Calibri	Consolas
Constantia	Candara	Courier
Times New Roman	Corbel	Letter Gothic
Bookman Old Style	Arial	

Type size is generally set in proportional size. The size of proportional type is measured vertically in units called *points*. A point is approximately ½ of an inch—the higher the point size, the larger the characters. Within a typeface, characters may have a varying style. Type styles are divided into four main categories: regular, bold, italic, and bold italic.

You can use the Font button in the Font group to change the font and the Font Size button to change the size. When you select text and then click the Font button arrow, a drop-down gallery displays of font options. Hover your mouse pointer over a font option and the selected text in the document displays with the font applied. You can continue hovering your mouse pointer over different font options to see how the selected text displays in the specified font. The Font button drop-down gallery is an example of the *live preview* feature, which allows you to see how the font formatting affects your text without having to return to the document. The live preview feature is also available when you click the Font Size button arrow.

Project 1a Changing the Font

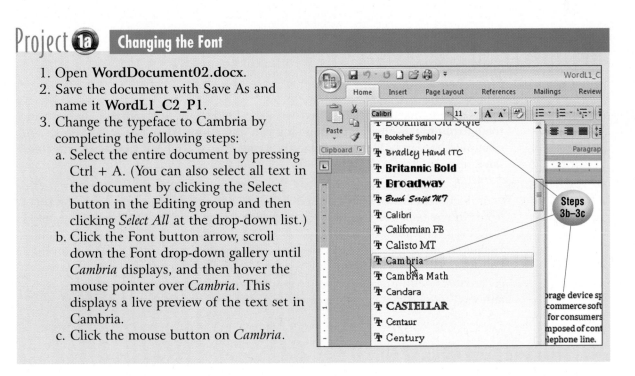

1. Open **WordDocument02.docx**.
2. Save the document with Save As and name it **WordL1_C2_P1**.
3. Change the typeface to Cambria by completing the following steps:
   a. Select the entire document by pressing Ctrl + A. (You can also select all text in the document by clicking the Select button in the Editing group and then clicking *Select All* at the drop-down list.)
   b. Click the Font button arrow, scroll down the Font drop-down gallery until *Cambria* displays, and then hover the mouse pointer over *Cambria*. This displays a live preview of the text set in Cambria.
   c. Click the mouse button on *Cambria*.

4. Change the type size to 14 by completing the following steps:
   a. With the text in the document still selected, click the Font Size button arrow.
   b. At the drop-down gallery that displays, hover the mouse pointer on *14* and look at the live preview of the text with 14 points applied.
   c. Click the left mouse button on *14*.
5. At the document screen, deselect the text by clicking anywhere in the document screen outside the selected text.
6. Change the type size and typeface by completing the following steps:
   a. Press Ctrl + A to select the entire document.
   b. Click three times on the Shrink Font button in the Font group. (This decreases the size to 10 points.)
   c. Click twice on the Grow Font button. (This increases the size of the font to 12 points.)
   d. Click the Font button arrow, scroll down the drop-down gallery, and then click *Constantia*. (The most recently used fonts display at the beginning of the document, followed by a listing of all fonts.)
7. Save **WordL1_C2_P1.docx**.

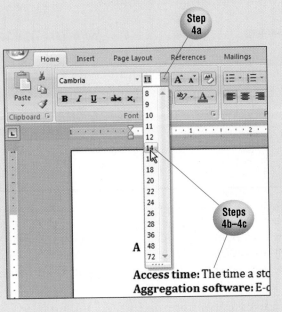

Step 4a

Steps 4b–4c

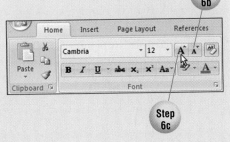

Step 6b

Step 6c

Bold

Italic

Underline

Choosing a Typestyle

Apply a particular typestyle to text with the Bold, Italic, or Underline buttons in the bottom row in the Font group. You can apply more than one style to text. For example, you can bold and italicize the same text or apply all three styles to the same text.

Each of the three styles has traditional uses that you may find appropriate in your documents. Bold is often used to draw the reader's attention to important words to remember. In this text, for example, bold is used for file names in exercises. Italics typically are used to emphasize certain words or phrases within a sentence. In biology texts, they are used for genus and species names. In this text, you may have noticed italics are used to set apart the names of features in drop-down galleries. Underlining also serves to emphasize and set apart words or phrases, although most style manuals recommend using italics instead of underlines.

1. With **WordL1_C2_P1.docx** open, press Ctrl + Home to move the insertion point to the beginning of the document.

2. Type a heading for the document by completing the following steps:

   a. Press the Caps Lock key.

   b. Click the Bold button in the Font group. (This turns on bold.)

   c. Click the Underline button in the Font group. (This turns on underline.)

   d. Type GLOSSARY OF TERMS.

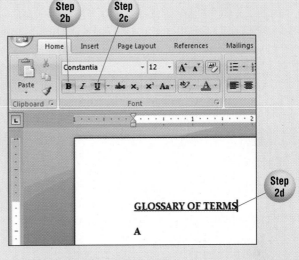

3. Press Ctrl + End to move the insertion point to the end of the document.

4. Type the text shown in Figure 2.2 with the following specifications:

   a. While typing the document, make the appropriate text bold as shown in the figure by completing the following steps:

   1) Click the Bold button in the Font group. (This turns on bold.)

   2) Type the text.

   3) Click the Bold button in the Font group. (This turns off bold.)

   b. While typing the document, italicize the appropriate text as shown in the figure by completing the following steps:

   1) Click the Italic button in the Font group.

   2) Type the text.

   3) Click the Italic button in the Font group.

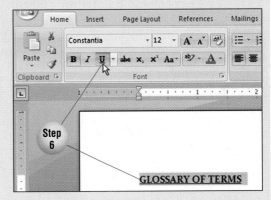

5. After typing the text, press the Enter key twice.

6. Remove underlining from the title by selecting *GLOSSARY OF TERMS* and then clicking the Underline button in the Font group.

7. With the title *GLOSSARY OF TERMS* selected, change the font size to 14 points.

8. Save **WordL1_C2_P1.docx**.

Figure 2.2 Project 1b

C

Chip: A thin wafer of *silicon* containing electronic circuitry that performs various functions, such as mathematical calculations, storage, or controlling computer devices.

Cluster: A group of two or more *sectors* on a disk, which is the smallest unit of storage space used to store data.

Coding: A term used by programmers to refer to the act of writing source code.

Crackers: A term coined by computer hackers for those who intentionally enter (or hack) computer systems to damage them.

Choosing a Font Effect

Strikethrough

Subscript

Superscript

Change Case

Text Highlight Color

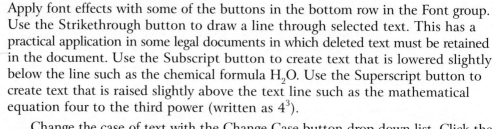
Font Color

Apply font effects with some of the buttons in the bottom row in the Font group. Use the Strikethrough button to draw a line through selected text. This has a practical application in some legal documents in which deleted text must be retained in the document. Use the Subscript button to create text that is lowered slightly below the line such as the chemical formula H_2O. Use the Superscript button to create text that is raised slightly above the text line such as the mathematical equation four to the third power (written as 4^3).

Change the case of text with the Change Case button drop-down list. Click the Change Case button and a drop-down list displays with the options *Sentence case*, *lowercase*, *UPPERCASE*, *Capitalize Each Word*, and *tOGGLE cASE*. You can also change the case of selected text with the keyboard shortcut, Shift + F3. Each time you press Shift + F3, selected text cycles through the case options.

The bottom row in the Font group contains two additional buttons—the Text Highlight Color button and the Font Color button. Use the Text Highlight Color button to highlight specific text in a document and use the Font Color button to change the color of text.

Using Keyboard Shortcuts

Several of the buttons in the Font group have keyboard shortcuts. For example, you can press Ctrl + B to turn on bold or press Ctrl + I to turn on italics. Position the mouse pointer on a button and an enhanced ScreenTip displays with the name of the button; the keyboard shortcut, if any; a description of the action performed by the button; and sometimes access to the Word Help window. Table 2.2 identifies the keyboard shortcuts available for buttons in the Font group.

Table 2.2 Font Button Keyboard Shortcuts

Font Group Button	*Keyboard Shortcut*
Font	Ctrl + Shift + F
Font Size	Ctrl + Shift + P
Grow Font	Ctrl + Shift + >
Shrink Font	Ctrl + Shift + <
Bold	Ctrl + B
Italic	Ctrl + I
Underline	Ctrl + U
Subscript	Ctrl + =
Superscript	Ctrl + Shift + +
Change Case	Shift + F3

Formatting with the Mini Toolbar

When you select text, the Mini toolbar displays in a dimmed fashion above the selected text. Hover the mouse pointer over the Mini toolbar and it becomes active. Click a button on the Mini toolbar to apply formatting to selected text.

Project 1c Applying Font Effects

1. With **WordL1_C2_P1.docx** open, move the insertion point to the beginning of the term *Chip*, press the Enter key, and then press the Up Arrow key. Type the text shown in Figure 2.3. Create the superscript numbers by clicking the Superscript button, typing the number, and then clicking the Superscript button.

2. Change the case of text by completing the following steps:
   a. Select the title *GLOSSARY OF TERMS*.
   b. Click the Change Case button in the Font group and then click *Capitalize Each Word* at the drop-down list.

3. Strike through text by completing the following steps:
   a. Select the words and parentheses *(or hack)* in the *Crackers* definition.
   b. Click the Strikethrough button in the Font group.

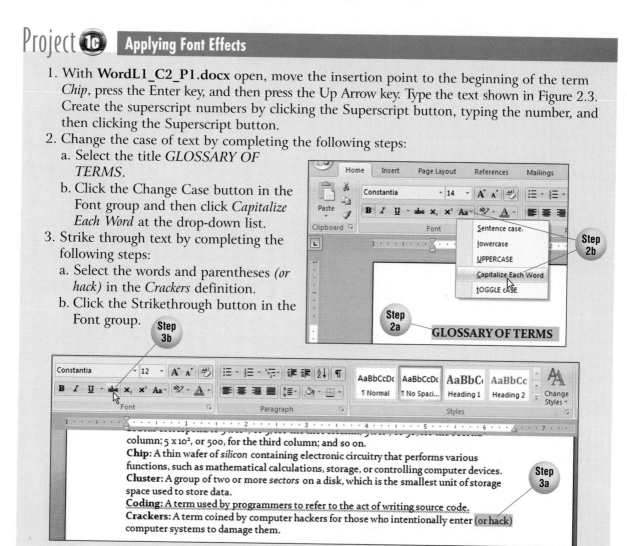

4. Change the font color by completing the following steps:
   a. Press Ctrl + A to select the entire document.
   b. Click the Font Color button arrow.
   c. Click the Dark Blue color (second color from *right* in the *Standard Colors* section) at the drop-down gallery.
   d. Click outside the selected area to deselect text.

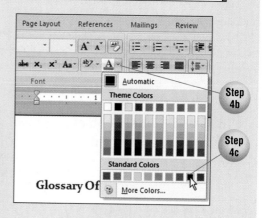

5. Highlight text in the document by completing the following steps:
   a. Click the Text Highlight Color button in the Font group. (This causes the mouse pointer to display as an I-beam pointer with a pen attached.)
   b. Select the term *Beta-testing* and the definition that follows.

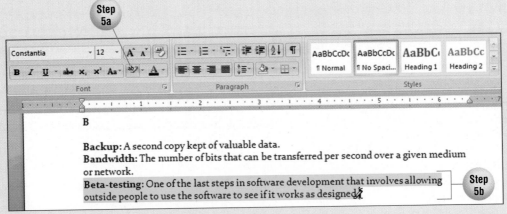

6. Change the case of the title by selecting *Glossary Of Terms* and then pressing Shift + F3. (This changes the case of the title text to uppercase.)
   c. Click the Text Highlight Color button arrow and then click a green color (you decide which green).
   d. Select the term *Cluster* and the definition that follows.
   e. Click the Text Highlight Color button arrow and then click the yellow color that displays in the upper left corner of the drop-down gallery.
   f. Click the Text Highlight Color button to turn off highlighting.
6. Change the case of the title by selecting *Glossary Of Terms* and then pressing Shift + F3. (This changes the case of the title text to uppercase.)
7. Apply italic formatting using the Mini toolbar by completing the following steps:
   a. Select the text *one-stop shopping* located in the definition for the term *Aggregation software*. (When you select the text, the Mini toolbar displays.)
   b. Click the Italic button on the Mini toolbar.
   c. Select the word *bits* located in the definition for the term *Bandwidth* and then click the Italic button on the Mini toolbar.
8. Save **WordL1_C2_P1.docx**.

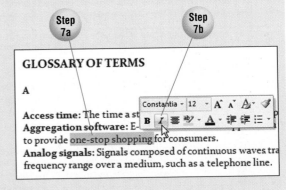

Figure 2.3 Project 1c

Chinese abacus: Pebbles strung on a rod inside a frame. Pebbles in the upper part of an abacus correspond to 5×10^0, or 5, for the first column; 5×10^1, or 50, for the second column; 5×10^2, or 500, for the third column; and so on.

Changing Fonts at the Font Dialog Box

In addition to buttons in the Font group, you can use options at the Font dialog box shown in Figure 2.4 to change the typeface, type size, and typestyle of text as well as apply font effects. Display the Font dialog box by clicking the Font group dialog box launcher. The dialog box launcher is a small square containing a diagonal-pointing arrow that displays in the lower right corner of the Font group.

QUICK STEPS

Change Font and Apply Effects
1. Click Font group dialog box launcher.
2. Choose desired options at dialog box.
3. Click OK.

Figure 2.4 Font Dialog Box

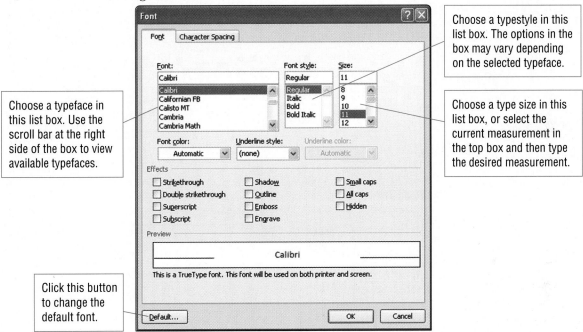

Choose a typestyle in this list box. The options in the box may vary depending on the selected typeface.

Choose a typeface in this list box. Use the scroll bar at the right side of the box to view available typefaces.

Choose a type size in this list box, or select the current measurement in the top box and then type the desired measurement.

Click this button to change the default font.

Project 1d **Changing the Font at the Font Dialog Box**

1. With **WordL1_C2_P1.docx** open, press Ctrl + End to move the insertion point to the end of the document. (Make sure the insertion point is positioned a double space below the last line of text.)
2. Type Created by Susan Ashby and then press the Enter key.
3. Type Wednesday, February 17, 2010.
4. Change the font to 13-point Times New Roman and the color to dark red by completing the following steps:
   a. Press Ctrl + A to select the entire document.
   b. Click the Font group dialog box launcher.

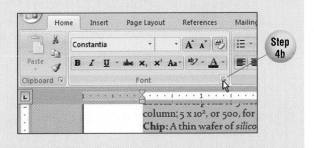

Step 4b

c. At the Font dialog box, click the down-pointing arrow at the right side of the *Font* list box to scroll down the list box and then click *Times New Roman*.

d. Click in the *Size* text box and then type **13**.

e. Click the down-pointing arrow at the right side of the *Font color* list box and then click a dark red color of your choosing at the color gallery.

f. Click OK to close the dialog box.

5. Double underline text by completing the following steps:

a. Select *Wednesday, February 17, 2010*.

b. Click the Font group dialog box launcher.

c. At the Font dialog box, click the down-pointing arrow at the right side of the *Underline style* option box and then click the double-line option at the drop-down list.

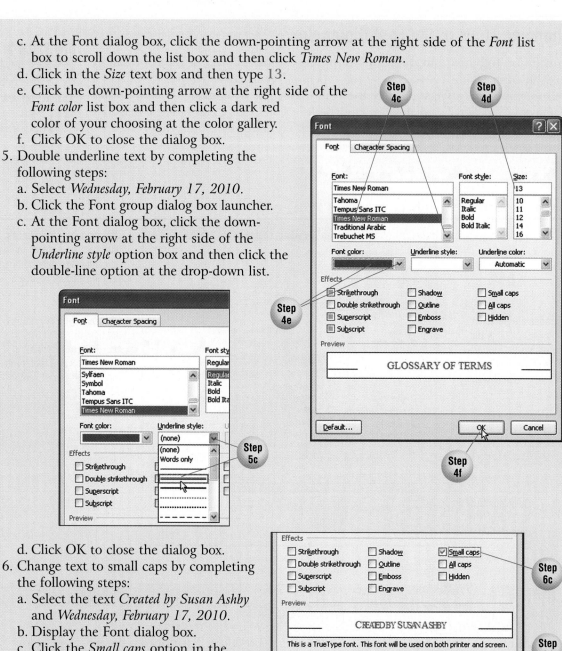

d. Click OK to close the dialog box.

6. Change text to small caps by completing the following steps:

a. Select the text *Created by Susan Ashby* and *Wednesday, February 17, 2010*.

b. Display the Font dialog box.

c. Click the *Small caps* option in the *Effects* section. (This inserts a check mark in the check box.)

d. Click OK to close the dialog box.

7. Save, print, and then close **WordL1_C2_P1.docx**.

P roject ② Apply Styles and Themes

You will open a document containing information on the life cycle of software, apply styles to text, and then change the Quick Styles set. You will also apply a theme and then change the theme colors and fonts.

Applying Styles from a Quick Styles Set

A Word document contains a number of predesigned formats grouped into style sets called Quick Styles. Four of the styles in the default Quick Styles set display in the Styles group in the Home tab. Display additional styles by clicking the More button that displays at the right side of the four styles. This displays a drop-down gallery of style choices. To apply a style, position the insertion point in the paragraph of text to which you want the style applied, click the More button at the right side of the styles in the Styles group, and then click the desired style at the drop-down gallery.

A Word document contains some default formatting including 10 points of spacing after paragraphs and a line spacing of 1.15. (You will learn more about these formatting options later in this chapter.) You can remove this default formatting as well as any character formatting applied to text in your document by applying the No Spacing style to your text. This style is located in the Styles group.

Changing the Quick Styles Set

Word contains a number of Quick Styles sets containing styles you can use to apply formatting to a document. To change to a different Quick Styles set, click the Change Styles button in the Styles group in the Home tab and then point to Style Set. This displays a side menu with Quick Styles sets. Click the desired set and the style formatting changes for the styles in the set.

QUICK STEPS

Apply a Style
1. Position insertion point in paragraph of desired text.
2. Click More button in Styles group.
3. Click desired style.

Change Quick Style Set
1. Click Change Style button.
2. Point to Style Set.
3. Click desired set.

More

Change Styles

Project 2a   Applying Quick Styles

1. Open **WordDocument05.docx**.
2. Save the document with Save As and name it **WordL1_C2_P2**.
3. Remove the 10 points of spacing after paragraphs and change the line spacing to 1 by completing the following steps:
   a. Press Ctrl + A to select the entire document.
   b. Click the No Spacing style in the Styles group in the Home tab.

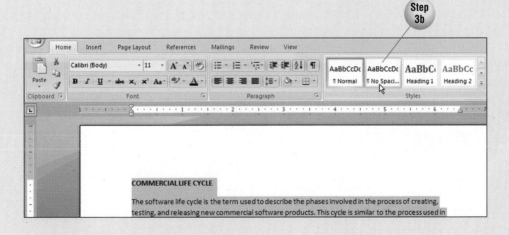

4. Position the insertion point on any character in the title *COMMERCIAL LIFE CYCLE* and then click the Heading 1 style that displays in the Styles group.

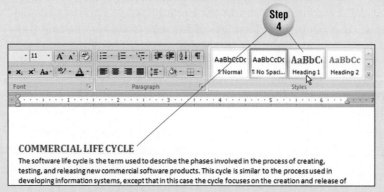

5. Position the insertion point on any character in the heading *Proposal and Planning* and then click the Heading 2 style that displays in the Styles group.

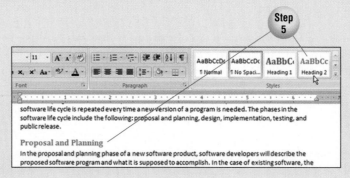

6. Position the insertion point on any character in the heading *Design* and then click the Heading 2 style in the Styles group.
7. Apply the Heading 2 style to the remaining headings (*Implementation*, *Testing*, and *Public Release and Support*).
8. Click the Change Styles button in the Styles group, point to *Style Set*, and then click *Modern*. (Notice how the Heading 1 and Heading 2 formatting changes.)

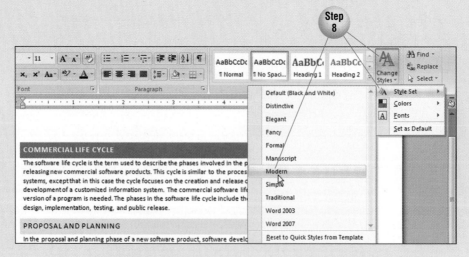

9. Save and then print **WordL1_C2_P2.docx**.

Applying a Theme

Word provides a number of themes you can use to format text in your document. A theme is a set of formatting choices that include a color theme (a set of colors), a font theme (a set of heading and body text fonts), and an effects theme (a set of lines and fill effects). To apply a theme, click the Page Layout tab and then click the Themes button in the Themes group. At the drop-down gallery that displays, click the desired theme. You can hover the mouse pointer over a theme and the live preview feature will display your document with the theme formatting applied. With the live preview feature you can see how the theme formatting affects your document before you make your final choice. Applying a theme is an easy way to give your document a professional look.

QUICK STEPS

Apply a Theme
1. Click Page Layout tab.
2. Click Themes button.
3. Click desired theme.

Project 2b   Applying a Theme to Text in a Document

1. With **WordL1_C2_P2.docx** open, click the Page Layout tab and then click the Themes button in the Themes group.
2. At the drop-down gallery, hover your mouse pointer over each theme and notice how the text formatting changes in your document.
3. Click the *Module* theme.
4. Save and then print **WordL1_C2_P2.docx**.

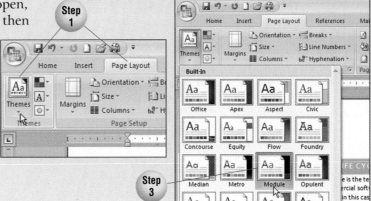

Step 1

Step 3

Changing Themes

You can change a theme with the three buttons that display at the right side of the Themes button. A theme contains specific color formatting, which you can change with options from the Theme Colors button in the Themes group. Click this button and a drop-down gallery displays with named color schemes. The names of the color schemes correspond to the names of the themes. Each theme applies specific fonts, which you can change with options from the Theme Fonts button in the Themes group. Click this button and a drop-down gallery displays with font choices. Each font group in the drop-down gallery contains two choices. The first choice in the group is the font that is applied to headings and the second choice is the font that is applied to body text in the document. If you are formatting a document containing graphics with lines and fills, you can apply a specific theme effect with options at the Theme Effects drop-down gallery.

QUICK STEPS

Change Theme Color
1. Click Page Layout tab.
2. Click Theme Colors button.
3. Click desired theme color.

Change Theme Fonts
1. Click Page Layout tab.
2. Click Theme Fonts button.
3. Click desired theme font.

Theme Colors   Theme Fonts

Theme Effects

1. With **WordL1_C2_P2.docx** open, click the Theme Colors button in the Themes group and then click *Foundry* at the drop-down gallery. (Notice how the colors in the title and headings change.)
2. Click the Theme Fonts button and then click the *Civic* option. (Notice how the document text font changes.)

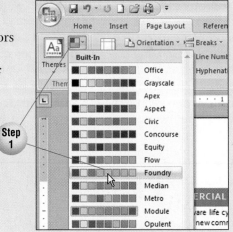

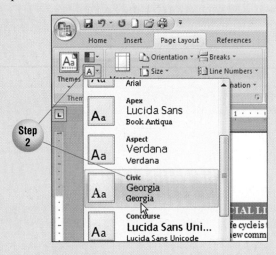

3. Save, print, and then close **WordL1_C2_P2.docx**.

Project ③ Apply Paragraph Formatting and Use Format Painter

You will open a report on intellectual property and fair use issues and then format the report by changing the alignment of text in paragraphs, applying spacing before and after paragraphs of text, and repeating the last formatting action.

Changing Paragraph Alignment

By default, paragraphs in a Word document are aligned at the left margin and ragged at the right margin. Change this default alignment with buttons in the Paragraph group in the Home tab or with keyboard shortcuts as shown in Table 2.3.

You can change the alignment of text in paragraphs before you type the text or you can change the alignment of existing text. If you change the alignment before typing text, the alignment formatting is inserted in the paragraph mark. As you type text and press Enter, the paragraph formatting is continued. For example, if you click the Center button in the Paragraph group, type text for the first paragraph, and then press the Enter key, the center alignment formatting is still active and the insertion point displays centered between the left and right margins. To display the paragraph symbols in a document, click the Show/Hide ¶ button in the Paragraph

Center

Show/Hide

Table 2.3 Paragraph Alignment Buttons and Keyboard Shortcuts

To align text	Paragraph Group Button	Keyboard Shortcut
At the left margin		Ctrl + L
Between margins		Ctrl + E
At the right margin		Ctrl + R
At the left and right margins		Ctrl + J

group. With the Show/Hide ¶ button active (displays with an orange background), nonprinting formatting symbols display such as the paragraph symbol ¶ indicating a press of the Enter key or a dot indicating a press of the spacebar.

To return paragraph alignment to the default (left-aligned), click the Align Text Left button in the Paragraph group. You can also return all paragraph formatting to the default with the keyboard shortcut, Ctrl + Q. This keyboard shortcut removes paragraph formatting from selected text. If you want to remove all formatting from selected text including character and paragraph formatting, click the Clear Formatting button in the Font group.

To change the alignment of existing text in a paragraph, position the insertion point anywhere within the paragraph. You do not need to select the entire paragraph. To change the alignment of several adjacent paragraphs in a document, select a portion of the first paragraph through a portion of the last paragraph. You do not need to select all of the text in the paragraphs.

Align Text Left

HINT

Align text in a document so the message of the document can be followed and the page is attractive.

Project **3a** | **Changing Paragraph Alignment**

1. Open **WordReport03.docx**. (Some of the default formatting in this document has been changed.)
2. Save the document with Save As and name it **WordL1_C2_P3**.
3. Click the Show/Hide ¶ button in the Paragraph group in the Home tab to turn on the display of nonprinting characters.

Step 3

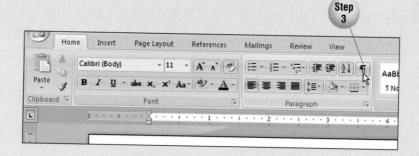

4. Press Ctrl + A to select the entire document and then change the alignment to Justify by clicking the Justify button in the Paragraph group in the Home tab.

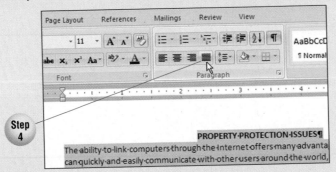

Step 4

5. Press Ctrl + End to move the insertion point to the end of the document.
6. Press the Enter key once.
7. Press Ctrl + E to move the insertion point to the middle of the page.
8. Type Prepared by Clarissa Markham.
9. Press Shift + Enter and then type Edited by Joshua Streeter.

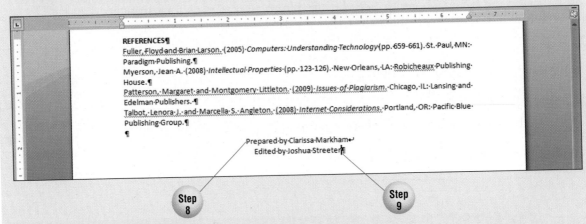

Step 8

Step 9

10. Click the Show/Hide ¶ button in the Paragraph group in the Home tab to turn off the display of nonprinting characters.
11. Save **WordL1_C2_P3.docx**.

QUICK
STEPS

Change Paragraph Alignment
Click desired alignment button in Paragraph group.
OR
1. Click Paragraph group dialog box launcher.
2. Click *Alignment* option down-pointing arrow.
3. Click desired alignment.
4. Click OK.

Changing Alignment at the Paragraph Dialog Box

Along with buttons in the Paragraph group and keyboard shortcuts, you can also change paragraph alignment with the Alignment option at the Paragraph dialog box shown in Figure 2.5. Display this dialog box by clicking the Paragraph group dialog box launcher. At the Paragraph dialog box, click the down-pointing arrow at the right side of the *Alignment* option box. At the drop-down list that displays, click the desired alignment option and then click OK to close the dialog box.

Figure 2.5 Paragraph Dialog Box with Alignment Options

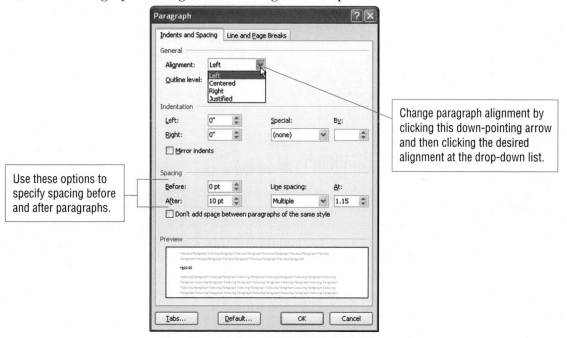

Change paragraph alignment by clicking this down-pointing arrow and then clicking the desired alignment at the drop-down list.

Use these options to specify spacing before and after paragraphs.

Project **3b**   **Changing Paragraph Alignment at the Paragraph Dialog Box**

1. With **WordL1_C2_P3.docx** open, change paragraph alignment by completing the following steps:
   a. Select the entire document.
   b. Click the Paragraph group dialog box launcher.
   c. At the Paragraph dialog box with the Indents and Spacing tab selected, click the down-pointing arrow at the right of the *Alignment* list box and then click *Left*.
   d. Click OK to close the dialog box.
   e. Deselect the text.

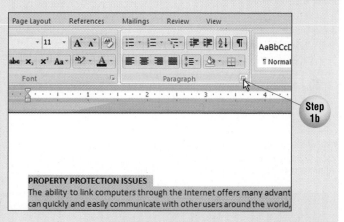

Step 1b

2. Change paragraph alignment by completing the following steps:
   a. Press Ctrl + End to move the insertion point to the end of the document.
   b. Position the insertion point on any character in the text *Prepared by Clarissa Markham*.
   c. Click the Paragraph group dialog box launcher.
   d. At the Paragraph dialog box with the Indents and Spacing tab selected, click the down-pointing arrow at the right of the *Alignment* list box and then click *Right*.

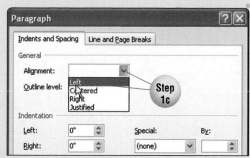

Step 1c

e. Click OK. (The line of text containing the name *Clarissa Markham* and the line of text containing the name *Joshua Streeter* are both aligned at the right since you used the New Line command, Shift + End, to separate the lines of text without creating a new paragraph.)

3. Save and then print **WordL1_C2_P3.docx.**

Indenting Text in Paragraphs

QUICK STEPS

Indent Text in Paragraph
Drag indent marker(s) on Ruler.
OR
Press keyboard shortcut keys.
OR
1. Click Paragraph group dialog box launcher.
2. Insert measurement in *Left, Right,* and/or *By* text box.
3. Click OK.

View Ruler

By now you are familiar with the word wrap feature of Word, which ends lines and wraps the insertion point to the next line. To indent text from the left margin, the right margin, or both, use indent buttons in the Paragraph group, in the Page Layout tab, keyboard shortcuts, options from the Paragraph dialog box, markers on the Ruler, or use the Alignment button on the Ruler. Figure 2.6 identifies indent markers and the Alignment button on the Ruler. Refer to Table 2.4 for methods for indenting text in a document. To display the Ruler, click the View Ruler button located at the top of the vertical scroll bar.

One situation that may call for indented text is the use of a lengthy passage of quoted material. Suppose you are writing a report in which you quote a paragraph of text from a well known expert's book. Rather than using quotation marks to set off the paragraph, consider indenting it from both margins. This option creates a block of text that the reader recognizes instantly as being separate from the body of the report and therefore "new" or "different."

Another type of indent is a negative indent, which is referred to as an "outdent" because it moves the text out into the left margin. A negative indent is an additional option for highlighting, or calling special attention to, a section of writing.

Figure 2.6 Ruler and Indent Markers

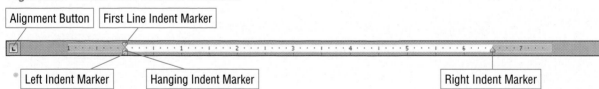

Alignment Button | First Line Indent Marker

Left Indent Marker | Hanging Indent Marker | Right Indent Marker

Table 2.4 Methods for Indenting Text

Indent	Methods for Indenting
First line of paragraph	• Press the Tab key. • Display Paragraph dialog box, click the down-pointing arrow to the right of the *Special* list box, click *First line*, and then click OK. • Drag the First Line Indent marker on the Ruler. • Click the Alignment button located at the left side of the Ruler until the First Line Indent button displays and then click on the Ruler at the desired location.
Text from left margin	• Click the Increase Indent button in the Paragraph group in the Home tab to increase the indent or click the Decrease Indent button to decrease the indent. • Insert a measurement in the *Indent Left* measurement button in the Paragraph group in the Page Layout tab. • Press Ctrl + M to increase the indent or press Ctrl + Shift + M to decrease the indent. • Display the Paragraph dialog box, type the desired indent measurement in the *Left* measurement box, and then click OK. • Drag the left indent marker on the Ruler.
Text from right margin	• Insert a measurement in the *Indent Right* measurement button in the Paragraph group in the Page Layout tab. • Display the Paragraph dialog box, type the desired indent measurement in the *Right* measurement box, and then click OK. • Drag the right indent marker on the Ruler.
All lines of text except the first (called a hanging indent)	• Press Ctrl + T. (Press Ctrl + Shift + T to remove hanging indent.) • Display the Paragraph dialog box, click the down-pointing arrow to the right of the *Special* list box, click *Hanging*, and then click OK. • Click the Alignment button located at the left side of the Ruler until the Hanging Indent button displays and then click on the Ruler at the desired location.
Text from both left and right margins	• Display the Paragraph dialog box, type the desired indent measurement in the *Left* measurement box, type the desired measurement in the *Right* measurement box, and then click OK. • Insert a measurement in the *Indent Right* and *Indent Left* measurement buttons in the Paragraph group in the Page Layout tab. • Drag the left indent marker on the Ruler; then drag the right indent marker on the Ruler.

1. With **WordL1_C2_P3.docx** open, indent the first line of text in paragraphs by completing the following steps:
   a. Select the first two paragraphs of text in the document (the text after the title *PROPERTY PROTECTION ISSUES* and before the heading *Intellectual Property*.
   b. Position the mouse pointer on the First Line Indent marker on the Ruler, hold down the left mouse button, drag the marker to the 0.5-inch mark, and then release the mouse button.

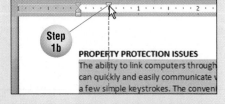

   c. Select the paragraphs of text in the *Intellectual Property* section and then drag the First Line Indent marker on the Ruler to the 0.5-inch mark.
   d. Select the paragraphs of text in the *Fair Use* section, click the Alignment button located at the left side of the Ruler until the First Line Indent button displays, and then click on the Ruler at the 0.5-inch mark.

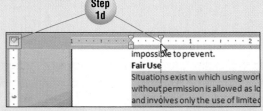

   e. Position the insertion point on any character in the paragraph of text below the *Intellectual Property Protection* heading, make sure the First Line Indent button displays in the Alignment button, and then click at the 0.5-inch mark on the Ruler.
2. Since the text in the second paragraph in the *Fair Use* section is a quote, you need to indent the text from the left and right margins by completing the following steps:
   a. Position the insertion point anywhere within the second paragraph in the *Fair Use* section (the paragraph that begins *[A] copyrighted work, including such . . .*).
   b. Click the Paragraph group dialog box launcher.
   c. At the Paragraph dialog box, with the Indents and Spacing tab selected, select the current measurement in the *Left* measurement box and then type 0.5.
   d. Select the current measurement in the *Right* measurement box and then type 0.5.
   e. Click the down-pointing arrow at the right side of the *Special* list box and then click *(none)* at the drop-down list.
   f. Click OK or press Enter.

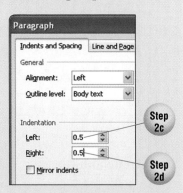

3. Create a hanging indent for the first paragraph in the *REFERENCES* section by positioning the insertion point anywhere in the first paragraph below *REFERENCES* and then pressing Ctrl + T.
4. Create a hanging indent for the second paragraph in the *REFERENCES* section by completing the following steps:
   a. Position the insertion point anywhere in the second paragraph in the *REFERENCES* section.

b. Make sure the Ruler is displayed. (If not, click the View Ruler button located at the top of the vertical scroll bar.)

c. Click the Alignment button located at the left side of the Ruler until the Hanging Indent button displays.

d. Click on the 0.5-inch mark on the Ruler.

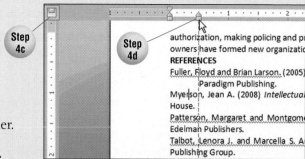

5. Create a hanging indent for the third and fourth paragraphs by completing the following steps:

a. Select a portion of the third and fourth paragraphs.

b. Click the Paragraph group dialog box launcher.

c. At the Paragraph dialog box with the Indents and Spacing tab selected, click the down-pointing arrow at the right side of the *Special* list box and then click *Hanging* at the drop-down list.

d. Click OK or press Enter.

6. Save **WordL1_C2_P3.docx**.

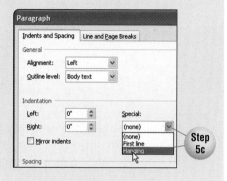

Spacing Before and After Paragraphs

By default, Word applies 10 points of additional spacing after a paragraph. You can remove this spacing, increase or decrease the spacing, and insert spacing above the paragraph. To change spacing before or after a paragraph, use the Spacing Before and Spacing After measurement boxes located in the Paragraph group in the Page Layout tab, or the *Before* and/or *After* options at the Paragraph dialog box with the Indents and Spacing tab selected.

> **HINT**
> Line spacing determines the amount of vertical space between lines while paragraph spacing determines the amount of space above or below paragraphs of text.

Spacing before or after a paragraph is part of the paragraph and will be moved, copied, or deleted with the paragraph. If a paragraph, such as a heading, contains spacing before it, and the paragraph falls at the top of a page, Word ignores the spacing.

Spacing before or after paragraphs is added in points and a vertical inch contains approximately 72 points. To add spacing before or after a paragraph you would click the Page Layout tab, select the current measurement in the *Spacing Before* or the *Spacing After* measurement box, and then type the desired number of points. You can also click the up- or down-pointing arrows at the right side of the *Spacing Before* and *Spacing After* measurement boxes to increase or decrease the amount of spacing.

Repeating the Last Action

If you apply formatting to text and then want to apply the same formatting to other text in the document, consider using the Repeat command. To use this command, apply the desired formatting, move the insertion point to the next location where you want the formatting applied, and then press the F4 function key or press Ctrl + Y.

> **QUICK STEPS**
>
> **Repeat Last Action**
> Press F4
> OR
> Press Ctrl + Y

1. With **WordL1_C2_P3.docx** open, add 6 points of spacing before and after each paragraph in the document by completing the following steps:
   a. Select the entire document.
   b. Click the Page Layout tab.
   c. Click once on the up-pointing arrow at the right side of the *Spacing Before* measurement box in the Paragraph group (this inserts *6 pt* in the box).
   d. Click once on the up-pointing arrow at the right side of the *Spacing After* measurement box in the Paragraph group (this inserts *6 pt* in the text box).

Step 1b   Step 1c   Step 1d

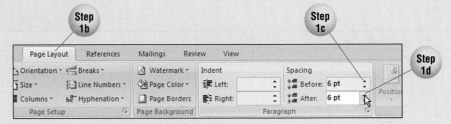

2. Add an additional 6 points of spacing above the headings by completing the following steps:
   a. Position the insertion point on any character in the heading *Intellectual Property* and then click once on the up-pointing arrow at the right side of the *Spacing Before* measurement box (this changes the measurement to *12 pt*).

Step 2a

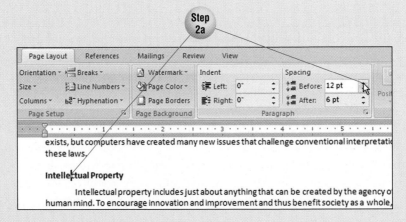

   b. Position the insertion point on any character in the heading *Fair Use* and then press F4 (this is the Repeat command).
   c. Position the insertion point on any character in the heading *Intellectual Property Protection* and then press F4.
   d. Position the insertion point on any character in the heading *REFERENCES* and then press Ctrl + Y (this is also the Repeat command).
3. Save **WordL1_C2_P3.docx**.

Formatting with Format Painter

The Clipboard group in the Home tab contains a button for copying formatting and displays in the Clipboard group as a paintbrush. To use the Format Painter button, position the insertion point on a character containing the desired formatting, click the Format Painter button, and then select text to which you want the formatting applied. When you click the Format Painter button, the mouse I-beam pointer displays with a paintbrush attached. If you want to apply formatting a single time, click the Format Painter button once. If you want to apply the formatting in more than one location in the document, double-click the Format Painter button and then select text to which you want formatting applied. When you are finished, click the Format Painter button to turn it off. You can also turn off Format Painter by pressing the Esc key.

QUICK STEPS

Format with Format Painter
1. Format text.
2. Double-click Format Painter button.
3. Select text.
4. Click Format Painter button.

Format Painter

Project 3e — Formatting Headings with the Format Painter

1. With **WordL1_C2_P3.docx** open, click the Home tab.
2. Select the entire document and then change the font to 12-point Cambria.
3. Select the title *PROPERTY PROTECTION ISSUES*, click the Center button in the Paragraph group, and then change the font to 16-point Candara bold.
4. Apply 16-point Candara bold formatting to the *REFERENCES* heading by completing the following steps:
   a. Click on any character in the title *PROPERTY PROTECTION ISSUES*.
   b. Click once on the Format Painter button in the Clipboard group.

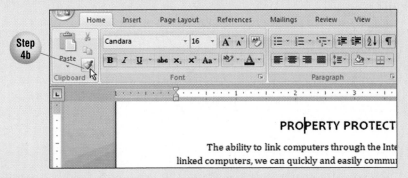

Step 4b

   c. Press Ctrl + End to move the insertion point to the end of the document and then select the heading *REFERENCES*. (This applies the 16-point Candara bold formatting and centers the text.)
5. With the insertion point positioned on any character in the heading *REFERENCES*, add an additional 6 points of spacing before the heading.
6. Select the heading *Intellectual Property* and then change the font to 14-point Candara bold.
7. Use the Format Painter button and apply 14-point Candara bold formatting to the other headings by completing the following steps:
   a. Position the insertion point on any character in the heading *Intellectual Property*.
   b. Double-click the Format Painter button in the Clipboard group.
   c. Using the mouse, select the heading *Fair Use*.

d. Using the mouse, select the heading *Intellectual Property Protection*.

e. Click once on the Format Painter button in the Clipboard group. (This turns off the feature.)

f. Deselect the heading.

8. Save **WordL1_C2_P3.docx**.

QUICK STEPS

Change Line Spacing
Click Line Spacing button in Paragraph group, then click desired option at drop-down list.
OR
Press shortcut command keys.
OR
1. Click Paragraph group dialog box launcher.
2. Click *Line Spacing* option down-pointing arrow.
3. Click desired line spacing option.
4. Click OK.
OR
1. Click Paragraph group dialog box launcher.
2. Type line measurement in *At* text box.
3. Click OK.

Line Spacing

Changing Line Spacing

The default line spacing for a document is 1.15. (The line spacing for the **WordReport03.docx** document, which you opened at the beginning of Project 3, had been changed to single.) In certain situations, Word automatically adjusts the line spacing. For example, if you insert a large character or object such as a graphic, Word increases the line spacing of that specific line. But you also may sometimes encounter a writing situation in which you decide to change the line spacing for a section or for the entire document.

Change line spacing using the Line Spacing button in the Paragraph group in the Home tab, with keyboard shortcuts, or with options from the Paragraph dialog box. Table 2.5 displays the keyboard shortcuts to change line spacing.

Table 2.5 Line Spacing Keyboard Shortcuts

Press	*To change line spacing to*
Ctrl + 1	single spacing
Ctrl + 2	double spacing
Ctrl + 5	1.5 line spacing

You can also change line spacing at the Paragraph dialog box with the *Line spacing* option or the *At* option. If you click the down-pointing arrow at the right side of the *Line spacing* option, a drop-down list displays with a variety of spacing options. For example, to change the line spacing to double you would click *Double* at the drop-down list. You can type a specific line spacing measurement in the *At* text box. For example, to change the line spacing to 1.75, type 1.75 in the *At* text box.

Project 3f   Changing Line Spacing

1. With **WordL1_C2_P3.docx** open, change the line spacing for all paragraphs to double spacing by completing the following steps:
   a. Select the entire document.
   b. Click the Line Spacing button located in the Paragraph group in the Home tab.
   c. Click *2.0* at the drop-down list.

2. With the entire document still selected, press Ctrl + 5. (This changes the line spacing to 1.5 line spacing.)

3. Change the line spacing to 1.3 using the Paragraph dialog box by completing the following steps:
   a. With the document still selected, click the Paragraph group dialog box launcher.
   b. At the Paragraph dialog box, make sure the Indents and Spacing tab is selected, click inside the *At* text box, and then type 1.3. (This text box is located to the right of the *Line spacing* list box.)
   c. Click OK or press Enter.
   d. Deselect the text.

4. Save, print, and then close **WordL1_C2_P3.docx**.

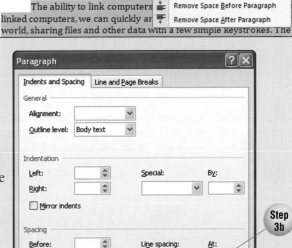

Project 4   Format Quiz Document

You will open a document containing two problems to solve, reveal the formatting, compare the formatting, and make formatting changes.

Revealing Formatting

Display formatting applied to specific text in a document at the Reveal Formatting task pane. The Reveal Formatting task pane displays font, paragraph, and section formatting applied to text where the insertion point is positioned or to selected text. Display the Reveal Formatting task pane with the keyboard shortcut Shift + F1.

Generally, a minus symbol precedes *Font* and *Paragraph* and a plus symbol precedes *Section* in the *Formatting of selected text* section of the Reveal Formatting task pane. Click the minus symbol to hide any items below a heading and click the plus symbol to reveal items. Some of the items below headings in the *Formatting of selected text* section are hyperlinks. Click a hyperlink and a dialog box displays with the specific option.

Figure 2.7 Reveal Formatting Task Pane

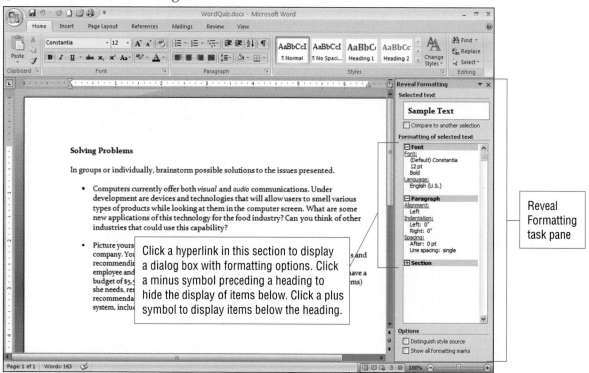

Click a hyperlink in this section to display a dialog box with formatting options. Click a minus symbol preceding a heading to hide the display of items below. Click a plus symbol to display items below the heading.

Reveal Formatting task pane

Project 4a — Revealing Formatting

1. Open **WordQuiz.docx**.
2. Save the document with Save As and name it **WordL1_C2_P4**.
3. Press Shift + F1 to display the Reveal Formatting task pane.
4. Click anywhere in the heading *Solving Problems* and then notice the formatting information that displays in the Reveal Formatting task pane.
5. Click in the bulleted paragraph and notice the formatting information thast displays in the Reveal Formatting task pane.

Comparing Formatting

Along with displaying formatting applied to text, you can use the Reveal Formatting task pane to compare formatting of two text selections to determine what formatting is different. To compare formatting, select the first instance of formatting to be compared, click the *Compare to another selection* check box, and then select the second instance of formatting to compare. Any differences between the two selections display in the *Formatting differences* list box.

Compare Formatting
1. Display Reveal Formatting task pane.
2. Click or select text.
3. Click *Compare to another selection* check box.
4. Click or select text.

Project 4h Comparing Formatting

1. With **WordL1_C2_P4.docx** open, make sure the Reveal Formatting task pane displays. If it does not, turn it on by pressing Shift + F1.
2. Select the first bulleted paragraph (the paragraph that begins *Computers currently offer both . . .*).
3. Click the *Compare to another selection* check box to insert a check mark.
4. Select the second bulleted paragraph (the paragraph that begins *Picture yourself working in the . . .*).
5. Determine the formatting differences by reading the information in the *Formatting differences* list box. (The list box displays *12 pt -> 11 pt* below the Font: hyperlink, indicating that the difference is point size.)
6. Format the second bulleted paragraph so it is set in 12-point size.
7. Click the *Compare to another selection* check box to remove the check mark.
8. Select the word *visual* that displays in the first sentence in the first bulleted paragraph.
9. Click the *Compare to another selection* check box to insert a check mark.
10. Select the word *audio* that displays in the first sentence of the first bulleted paragraph.
11. Determine the formatting differences by reading the information in the *Formatting differences* list box.
12. Format the word *audio* so it matches the formatting of the word *visual*.
13. Click the *Compare to another selection* check box to remove the check mark.
14. Close the Reveal Formatting task pane by clicking the Close button (contains an X) that displays in the upper right corner of the task pane.
15. Save, print, and then close **WordL1_C2_P4.docx**.

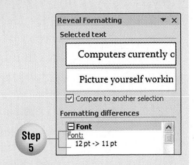

Step 5

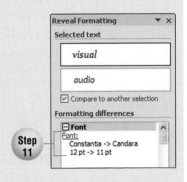

Step 11

CHAPTER summary

- The appearance of a document in the document screen and how it looks when printed is called the format.

- The top row in the Font group in the Home tab contains buttons for changing the font and font size. The bottom row contains buttons for applying typestyles and effects.

- A font consists of three parts: typeface, type size, and typestyle.

- A typeface (font) is a set of characters with a common design and shape. Typefaces are either monospaced, allotting the same amount of horizontal space to each character, or proportional, allotting a varying amount of space for each character. Proportional typefaces are divided into two main categories: serif and sans serif.

- Type size is measured in point size—the higher the point size, the larger the characters.

- A typestyle is a variation of style within a certain typeface. You can apply typestyle formatting with some of the buttons in the Font group.

- With some of the buttons in the Font group, you can apply font effects such as superscript, subscript, and strikethrough.

- Some buttons in the Font group contain keyboard shortcuts. Refer to Table 2.2 for a list of these shortcuts.

- The Mini toolbar automatically displays above selected text. Use buttons on this toolbar to apply formatting to selected text.

- With options at the Font dialog box, you can change the font, font size, and font style and apply specific effects. Display this dialog box by clicking the Font group dialog box launcher.

- A Word document contains a number of predesigned formats grouped into style sets called Quick Styles. Change to a different Quick Styles set by clicking the Change Styles button in the Styles group in the Home tab, pointing to Style Set, and then clicking the desired set.

- Word provides a number of themes, which are a set of formatting choices that include a color theme (a set of colors), a font theme (a set of heading and body text fonts), and an effects theme (a set of lines and fill effects). Apply a theme and change theme colors, fonts, and effects with buttons in the Themes group in the Page Layout tab.

- In Word, a paragraph is any amount of text followed by a paragraph mark (a stroke of the Enter key). Word inserts into the paragraph mark any paragraph formatting that is turned on.

- By default, paragraphs in a Word document are aligned at the left margin and ragged at the right margin. Change this default alignment with buttons in the Paragraph group, at the Paragraph dialog box, or with keyboard shortcuts.

- To turn on or off the display of nonprinting characters such as paragraph marks, click the Show/Hide ¶ button in the Paragraph group.

- Indent text in paragraphs with indent buttons in the Paragraph group in the Home tab, buttons in the Paragraph group in the Page Layout tab, keyboard shortcuts, options from the Paragraph dialog box, markers on the Ruler, or use the Alignment button on the Ruler. Refer to Table 2.4 for a description of the various indenting options.

- Increase and/or decrease spacing before and after paragraphs using the *Spacing Before* and *Spacing After* measurement boxes in the Paragraph group in the Page Layout tab, or using the *Before* and/or *After* options at the Paragraph dialog box.

- Repeat the last action by pressing the F4 function key or pressing Ctrl + Y.

- Use the Format Painter button in the Clipboard group in the Home tab to copy formatting already applied to text to different locations in the document.

- Change line spacing with the Line Spacing button in the Paragraph group in the Home tab, keyboard shortcuts, or options from the Paragraph dialog box.

- Display the Reveal Formatting task pane to display formatting applied to text. Use the *Compare to another selection* option in the task pane to compare formatting of two text selections to determine what formatting is different.

COMMANDS review

FEATURE	RIBBON TAB, GROUP	BUTTON	KEYBOARD SHORTCUT
Bold text	Home, Font	**B**	Ctrl + B
Center-align text	Home, Paragraph	≡	Ctrl + E
Change case of text	Home, Font	Aa ▾	Shift + F3
Change Quick Styles set	Home, Styles	AA	
Clear all formatting	Home, Font	A₃	
Clear character formatting			Ctrl + spacebar
Clear paragraph formatting			Ctrl + Q
Decrease font size	Home, Font	A▾	Ctrl + <
Display nonprinting characters	Home, Paragraph	¶	Ctrl + *
Font	Home, Font	Calibri (Body) ▾	
Font color	Home, Font	A ▾	
Font dialog box	Home, Font	⌐	Ctrl + Shift + F
Format Painter	Home, Clipboard	◢	Ctrl + Shift + C

continued

FEATURE	RIBBON TAB, GROUP	BUTTON	KEYBOARD SHORTCUT
Highlight text	Home, Font		
Increase font size	Home, Font		Ctrl + >
Italicize text	Home, Font		Ctrl + I
Justify-align text	Home, Paragraph		Ctrl + J
Left-align text	Home, Paragraph		Ctrl + L
Line spacing	Home, Paragraph		Ctrl + 1 (single) Ctrl + 2 (double) Ctrl + 5 (1.5)
Paragraph dialog box	Home, Paragraph		
Repeat last action			F4 or Ctrl + Y
Reveal Formatting task pane			Shift + F1
Right-align text	Home, Paragraph		Ctrl + R
Spacing after paragraph	Page Layout, Paragraph	After: 0 pt	
Spacing before paragraph	Page Layout, Paragraph	Before: 0 pt	
Strikethrough text	Home, Font		
Subscript text	Home, Font	x_2	Ctrl + =
Superscript text	Home, Font	x^2	Ctrl + Shift + +
Theme Colors	Page Layout, Themes		
Theme Fonts	Page Layout, Themes		
Themes	Page Layout, Themes		
Underline text	Home, Font		Ctrl + U

CONCEPTS check

Test Your Knowledge

Completion: In the space provided at the right, indicate the correct term, symbol, or command.

1. The Bold button is located in this group in the Home tab. _____

2. Click this button in the Font group to remove all formatting from selected text. _____

3. Proportional typefaces are divided into two main categories, serif and this. _____

4. This is the keyboard shortcut to italicize selected text. _____

5. This term refers to text that is raised slightly above the regular text line. _____

6. This automatically displays above selected text. _____

7. Click this to display the Font dialog box. _____

8. A Word document contains a number of predesigned formats grouped into style sets called this. _____

9. Apply a theme and change theme colors, fonts, and effects with buttons in the Themes group in this tab. _____

10. This is the default paragraph alignment. _____

11. Click this button in the Paragraph group to turn on the display of nonprinting characters. _____

12. Return all paragraph formatting to normal with this keyboard shortcut. _____

13. Click this button in the Paragraph group in the Home tab to align text at the right margin. _____

14. In this type of paragraph, the first line of text remains at the left margin and the remaining lines of text are indented to the first tab. _____

15. Repeat the last action by pressing F4 or with this keyboard shortcut. _____

16. Use this button in the Clipboard group in the Home tab to copy formatting already applied to text to different locations in the document. _____

17. Change line spacing to 1.5 with this keyboard shortcut. _____

18. Press these keys to display the Reveal Formatting task pane. _____

SKILLS check

Demonstrate Your Proficiency

Assessment

1 APPLY CHARACTER FORMATTING TO A LEASE AGREEMENT DOCUMENT

1. Open **WordDocument03.docx**.
2. Save the document with Save As and name it **WordL1_C2_A1**.
3. Press Ctrl + End to move the insertion point to the end of the document and then type the text shown in Figure 2.8. Bold, italicize, and underline text as shown.
4. Select the entire document and then change the font to 12-point Candara.
5. Select and then bold *THIS LEASE AGREEMENT* located in the first paragraph.
6. Select and then bold *DOLLARS* located in the *Rent* section.
7. Select and then bold *DOLLARS* located in the *Damage Deposit* section.
8. Select and then italicize *12 o'clock midnight* in the *Term* section.
9. Select the title *LEASE AGREEMENT* and then change the font to 18-point Corbel and the font color to dark blue. (Make sure the title retains the bold formatting.)
10. Select the heading *Term*, change the font to 14-point Corbel, and apply small caps formatting. (Make sure the heading retains the bold formatting.)
11. Use Format Painter to change the formatting to small caps in 14-point Corbel for the remaining headings (*Rent, Damage Deposit, Use of Premises, Condition of Premises, Alterations and Improvements, Damage to Premises, Inspection of Premises, Default,* and *Late Charge*).
12. Save, print, and then close **WordL1_C2_A1.docx**.

Figure 2.8 Assessment 1

Inspection of Premises

Lessor shall have the right at all reasonable times during the term of this Agreement to exhibit the Premises and to display the usual *for sale*, *for rent*, or *vacancy* signs on the Premises at any time within <u>forty-five</u> days before the expiration of this Lease.

Default

If Lessee fails to pay rent when due and the default continues for <u>seven</u> days thereafter, Lessor may declare the entire balance immediately due and payable and may exercise any and all rights and remedies available to Lessor.

Late Charge

In the event that any payment required to be paid by Lessee is not made by the 10th day of the month, Lessee shall pay to Lessor a *late fee* in the amount of **$50**.

Figure 3.1 Project 1a

Technology Career Questions

1. What is your ideal technical job?
2. Which job suits your personality?
3. Which is your first-choice certificate?
4. How does the technical job market look in your state right now? Is the job market wide open or are the information technology career positions limited?

If you do not want automatic numbering in a document, turn off the feature at the AutoCorrect dialog box with the AutoFormat As You Type tab selected as shown in Figure 3.2. To display this dialog box, click the Office button and then click the Word Options button that displays toward the bottom of the drop-down list. At the Word Options dialog box, click the *Proofing* option located in the left panel and then click the AutoCorrect Options button that displays in the *AutoCorrect options* section of the dialog box. At the AutoCorrect dialog box, click the AutoFormat As You Type tab and then click the *Automatic numbered lists* check box to remove the check mark. Click OK to close the AutoCorrect dialog box and then click OK to close the Word Options dialog box.

Figure 3.2 AutoCorrect Dialog Box with AutoFormat As You Type Tab Selected

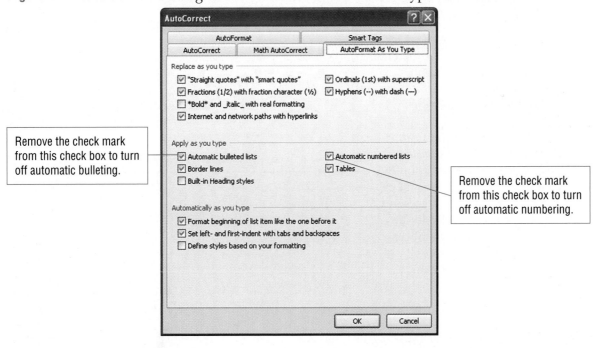

Remove the check mark from this check box to turn off automatic bulleting.

Remove the check mark from this check box to turn off automatic numbering.

You can also automate the creation of numbered paragraphs with the Numbering button in the Paragraph group. To use this button, type the text (do not type the number) for each paragraph to be numbered, select the paragraphs to be numbered, and then click the Numbering button in the Paragraph group. You can insert or delete numbered paragraphs in a document.

Project 1b Inserting Paragraph Numbering

1. With **WordL1_C3_P1.docx** open, apply numbers to paragraphs by completing the following steps:
   a. Select the five paragraphs of text in the *Technology Information Questions* section.
   b. Click the Numbering button in the Paragraph group.
2. Add the paragraph shown in Figure 3.3 between paragraphs 4 and 5 in the *Technology Information Questions* section by completing the following steps:
   a. Position the insertion point immediately to the right of the question mark at the end of the fourth paragraph.
   b. Press Enter.
   c. Type the paragraph shown in Figure 3.3.
3. Delete the second question (paragraph) in the *Technology Information Questions* section by completing the following steps:
   a. Select the text of the second paragraph (you will not be able to select the number).
   b. Press the Delete key.
4. Save **WordL1_C3_P1.docx**.

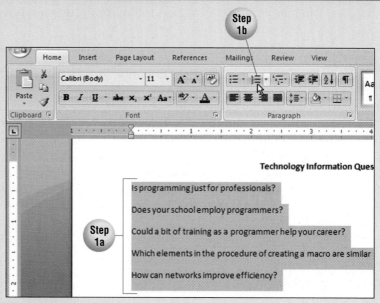

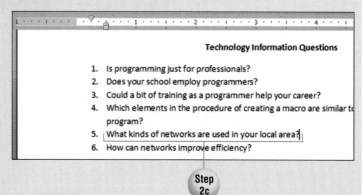

Figure 3.3 Project 1b

What kinds of networks are used in your local area?

Bulleting Paragraphs

In addition to automatically numbering paragraphs, Word's AutoFormat feature will create bulleted paragraphs. You can also create bulleted paragraphs with the Bullets button in the Paragraph group. Figure 3.4 shows an example of bulleted paragraphs. Bulleted lists with hanging indents are automatically created when a paragraph begins with the symbol *, >, or -. Type one of the symbols, press the spacebar, type text, and then press Enter. The AutoFormat feature inserts a bullet approximately 0.25 inch from the left margin and indents the text following the bullet another 0.25 inch. The type of bullet inserted depends on the type of character entered. For example, if you use the asterisk (*) symbol, a round bullet is inserted and an arrow bullet is inserted if you type the greater than symbol (>). Like the numbering feature, you can turn off the automatic bulleting feature at the AutoCorrect dialog box with the AutoFormat As You Type tab selected.

QUICK STEPS

Type Bulleted Paragraphs
1. Type *, >, or - symbol.
2. Press spacebar.
3. Type text.
4. Press Enter.

HINT
Define new bullets by clicking the Bullets button arrow and then clicking Define New Bullet.

Figure 3.4 Bulleted Paragraphs

- This is a paragraph preceded by a bullet. A bullet indicates a list of items or topics.

- This is another paragraph preceded by a bullet. You can easily create bulleted paragraphs by typing certain symbols before the text or with the Bullets button in the Paragraph group.

Project 1C Typing Bulleted Paragraphs

1. With **WordL1_C3_P1.docx** open, press Ctrl + End to move the insertion point to the end of the document and then press the Enter key once.
2. Type the text shown in Figure 3.5. Bold and center the title *Technology Timeline: Computer Design*. Create the bulleted paragraphs by completing the following steps:
   a. With the insertion point positioned at the left margin of the first paragraph to contain a bullet, type the greater than symbol (>).
   b. Press the spacebar once.
   c. Type the text of the first bulleted paragraph.
   d. Press the Enter key once and then continue typing the text after the bullets.
3. After typing the last bulleted paragraph, press the Enter key twice (this turns off bullets).
4. Save **WordL1_C3_P1.docx**.

Figure 3.5 Project 1c

Technology Timeline: Computer Design

➢ 1937: Dr. John Atanasoff and Clifford Berry design and build the first electronic digital computer.

➢ 1958: Jack Kilby, an engineer at Texas Instruments, invents the integrated circuit, thereby laying the foundation for fast computers and large-capacity memory.

➢ 1981: IBM enters the personal computer field by introducing the IBM-PC.

➢ 2004: Wireless computer devices, including keyboards, mice, and wireless home networks, become widely accepted among users.

Create Bulleted Paragraphs
1. Select text.
2. Click Bullets button.

You can also create bulleted paragraphs with the Bullets button in the Paragraph group. To create bulleted paragraphs using the Bullets button, type the text (do not type the bullet) of the paragraphs, select the paragraphs, and then click the Bullets button in the Paragraph group.

Project 1d Inserting Bullets Using the Bullets Button

1. With **WordL1_C3_P1.docx** open, insert bullets before the paragraphs of text in the *Technology Timeline: Computers in the Workplace* section by completing the following steps:
   a. Select the paragraphs of text in the *Technology Timeline: Computers in the Workplace* section.
   b. Click the Bullets button in the Paragraph group. (Word will insert the same arrow bullets that you inserted in Project 1c. Word keeps the same bullet formatting until you choose a different bullet.)

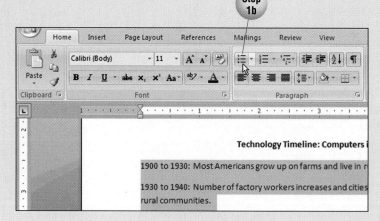

2. Save and then print **WordL1_C3_P1.docx**. (This document will print on two pages.)

Inserting Paragraph Borders and Shading

Every paragraph you create in Word contains an invisible frame. You can apply a border to the frame around the paragraph. You can apply a border to specific sides of the paragraph or to all sides, you can customize the type of border lines, and you can add shading and fill to the border. Add borders and shading to paragraphs in a document using the Borders and Shading buttons in the Paragraph group or options from the Borders and Shading dialog box.

Borders

Shading

Inserting Paragraph Borders

When a border is added to a paragraph of text, the border expands and contracts as text is inserted or deleted from the paragraph. You can create a border around a single paragraph or a border around selected paragraphs. One method for creating a border is to use options from the Borders button in the Paragraph group. Click the Borders button arrow and a drop-down list displays as shown in Figure 3.6.

Figure 3.6 Borders Drop-down List

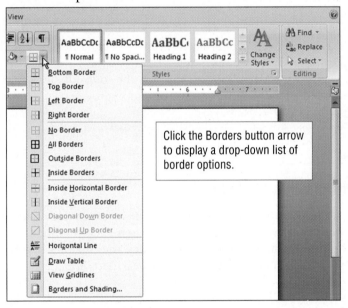

Click the Borders button arrow to display a drop-down list of border options.

At the drop-down list, click the option that will insert the desired border. For example, to insert a border at the bottom of the paragraph, click the *Bottom Border* option. Clicking an option will add the border to the paragraph where the insertion point is located. To add a border to more than one paragraph, select the paragraphs first and then click the desired option.

Apply Border
1. Select text.
2. Click Borders button.

1. With **WordL1_C3_P1.docx** open, select text from the beginning of the title *Technology Timeline: Computer Design* through the four bulleted paragraphs of text below and then press the Delete key.

2. Insert an outside border to specific text by completing the following steps:

   a. Select text from the title *Technology Information Questions* through the five numbered paragraphs of text.

   b. In the Paragraph group, click the Borders button arrow.

   c. At the Borders drop-down list, click the *Outside Borders* option.

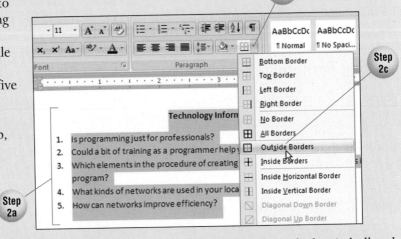

3. Select text from the title *Technology Timeline: Computers in the Workplace* through the six bulleted paragraphs of text and then click the Borders button in the Paragraph group. (The button will apply the border option that was previously selected.)

4. Select text from the title *Technology Career Questions* through the four numbered paragraphs of text below and then click the Borders button in the Paragraph group.

5. Save and then print **WordL1_C3_P1.docx**.

Adding Paragraph Shading

QUICK STEPS

Apply Shading
1. Select text.
2. Click Shading button.

With the Shading button in the Paragraph group you can add shading to text in a document. Select text you want to shade and then click the Shading button. This applies a background color behind the text. Click the Shading button arrow and a Shading drop-down gallery displays as shown in Figure 3.7.

Figure 3.7 Shading Gallery

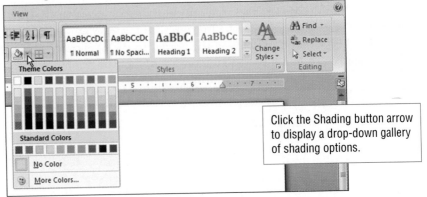

Click the Shading button arrow to display a drop-down gallery of shading options.

Paragraph shading colors display in themes in the drop-down gallery. Use one of the theme colors or click one of the standard colors that displays at the bottom of the gallery. Click the *More Colors* option and the Colors dialog box displays. At the Colors dialog box with the Standard tab selected, click the desired color or click the Custom tab and then specify a custom color.

Project ⑪ Applying Shading to Paragraphs

1. With **WordL1_C3_P1.docx** open, apply paragraph shading and change border lines by completing the following steps:
   a. Position the insertion point on any character in the title *Technology Information Questions*.
   b. Click the Borders button arrow and then click *No Border* at the drop-down list.
   c. Click the Borders button arrow and then click *Bottom Border* at the drop-down list.
   d. Click the Shading button arrow and then click the *Purple, Accent 4, Lighter 60%* option.

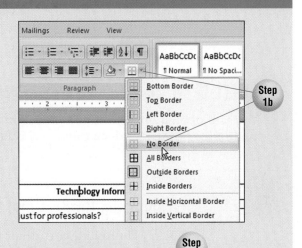

2. Apply the same formatting to the other titles by completing the following steps:
   a. With the insertion point positioned on any character in the title *Technology Information Questions*, double-click the Format Painter button in the Clipboard group.
   b. Select the title *Technology Timeline: Computers in the Workplace*.
   c. Select the title *Technology Career Questions*.
   d. Click the Format Painter button in the Clipboard group.

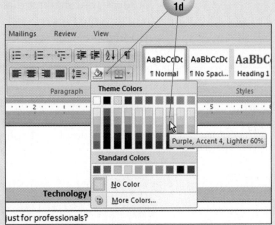

3. Remove the paragraph border and apply shading to paragraphs by completing the following steps:
   a. Select the numbered paragraphs of text below the *Technology Information Questions* title.
   b. Click the Borders button arrow and then click *No Border* at the drop-down list.
   c. Click the Shading button arrow and then click the *Purple, Accent 4, Lighter 80%* option.

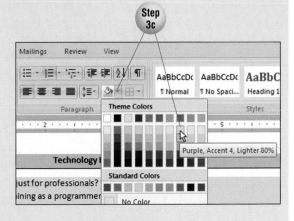

4. Select the bulleted paragraphs of text below the *Technology Timeline: Computers in the Workplace* title, click the Borders button, and then click the Shading button. (Clicking the Borders button will apply the previous border option, which was no border. Clicking the Shading button will apply the previous shading option, which was *Purple, Accent 4, Lighter 80%*.)
5. Select the numbered paragraphs of text below the *Technology Career Questions* title, click the Borders button, and then click the Shading button.
6. Save, print, and then close **WordL1_C3_P1.docx**.

Project ② Customize a Document on Online Shopping

You will open a document containing information on online shopping, apply and customize borders and shading, and then sort text in the document.

Customizing Borders and Shading

If you want to further customize paragraph borders and shading, use options at the Borders and Shading dialog box. Click the Borders tab and options display for customizing the border; click the Shading tab and shading options display. As you learned in a previous section, you can add borders to a paragraph with the Borders button in the Paragraph group. If you want to further customize borders, use options at the Borders and Shading dialog box with the Borders tab selected as shown in Figure 3.8. Display this dialog box by clicking the Borders button arrow and then clicking *Borders and Shading* at the drop-down list. At the Borders and Shading dialog box, specify the desired border, style, color, and width. Click the Shading tab and the dialog box displays with shading options as shown in Figure 3.9.

Figure 3.8 Borders and Shading Dialog Box with the Borders Tab Selected

Click the sides, top, or bottom of this preview area to insert or remove a border.

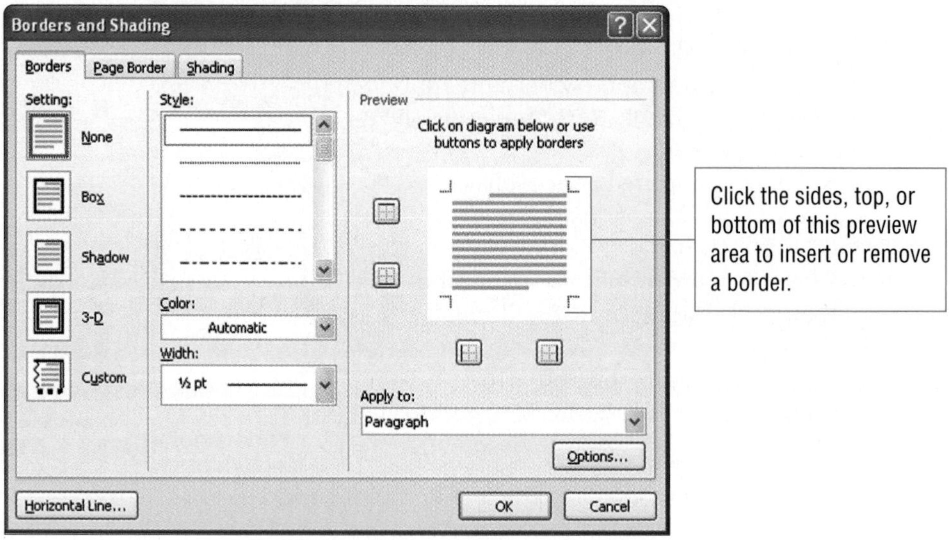

Figure 3.9 Borders and Shading Dialog Box with the Shading Tab Selected

Click this down-pointing arrow to display a drop-down list of shading options.

Project 2a Adding Customized Border and Shading to a Document

1. Open **WordDocument13.docx**.
2. Save the document with Save As and name it **WordL1_C3_P2**.
3. Make the following changes to the document:
   a. Insert 12 points of space before and 6 points of space after the headings *Online Shopping*, *Advantages of Online Shopping*, *Online Shopping Venues*, *Online Shopping Safety Tips*, and *REFERENCES*. (Do this with the *Spacing Before* and *Spacing After* measurement boxes in the Page Layout tab.)
   b. Center the *REFERENCES* title.
4. Insert a custom border and add shading to a heading by completing the following steps:
   a. Move the insertion point to any character in the heading *Online Shopping*.
   b. Click the Borders button arrow and then click *Borders and Shading* at the drop-down list.
   c. At the Borders and Shading dialog box with the Borders tab selected, click the down-pointing arrow at the right side of the *Color* option box and then click the *Dark Blue* color in the *Standard Colors* section.

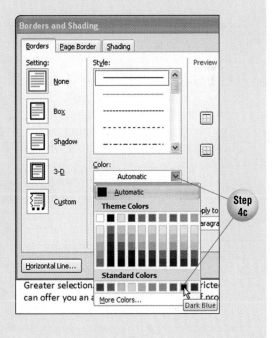

Step 4c

d. Click the down-pointing arrow at the right of the *Width* option box and then click *1 pt* at the drop-down list.

e. Click the top border of the box in the *Preview* section of the dialog box.

f. Click the down scroll arrow in the *Style* list box and then click the first thick/thin line.

g. Click the down-pointing arrow at the right side of the *Color* option box and then click the *Dark Blue* color in the *Standard Colors* section.

h. Click the bottom border of the box in the *Preview* section of the dialog box.

i. Click the Shading tab.

j. Click the down-pointing arrow at the right side of the *Fill* option box and then click *Olive Green, Accent 3, Lighter 60%*.

k. Click OK to close the dialog box.

5. Use Format Painter to apply the same border and shading formatting to the remaining headings by completing the following steps:

a. Position the insertion point on any character in the heading *Online Shopping*.

b. Double-click the Format Painter button in the Clipboard group in the Home tab.

c. Select the heading *Advantages of Online Shopping*.

d. Select the heading *Online Shopping Venues*.

e. Select the heading *Online Shopping Safety Tips*.

f. Click the Format Painter button once.

6. Move the insertion point to any character in the heading *Online Shopping* and then remove the 12 points of spacing above.

7. Save **WordL1_C3_P2.docx**.

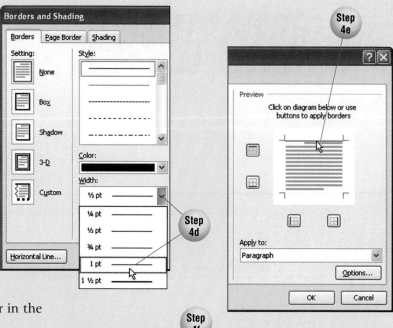

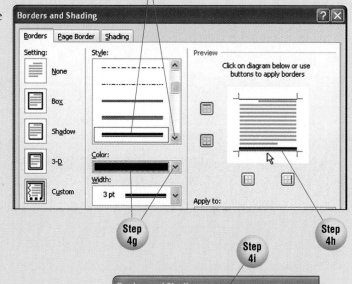

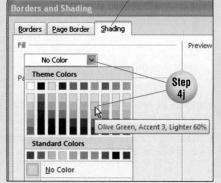

Sorting Text in Paragraphs

You can sort text arranged in paragraphs alphabetically by the first character. This character can be a number, symbol (such as $ or #), or letter. Type paragraphs you want to sort at the left margin or indented to a tab stop. Unless you select specific paragraphs for sorting, Word sorts the entire document.

To sort text in paragraphs, open the document. If the document contains text you do not want sorted, select the specific paragraphs. Click the Sort button in the Paragraph group and the Sort Text dialog box displays as shown in Figure 3.10. At this dialog box, click OK. If you select text and then display the dialog box the *Sort by* option is set at *Paragraph*. If the text you select is numbers, then *Numbers* displays in the Sort Text dialog box.

Figure 3.10 Sort Text Dialog Box

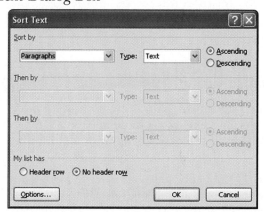

Project Sorting Paragraphs Alphabetically

1. With **WordL1_C3_P2.docx** open, sort the bulleted text alphabetically by completing the following steps:
   a. Select the bulleted paragraphs in the *Advantages of Online Shopping* section.
   b. Click the Sort button in the Paragraph group.
   c. At the Sort Text dialog box, make sure *Paragraphs* displays in the *Sort by* option box and the *Ascending* option is selected.
   d. Click OK.

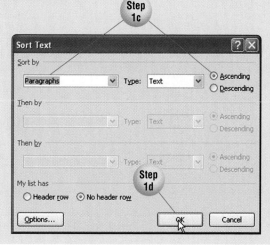

Step 1c

Step 1d

2. Sort the numbered paragraphs by completing the following steps:
   a. Select the numbered paragraphs in the *Online Shopping Safety Tips* section.
   b. Click the Sort button in the Paragraph group.
   c. Click OK at the Sort Text dialog box.
3. Follow steps similar to those in Step 1 or Step 2 to sort alphabetically the three paragraphs of text below the *REFERENCES* title.
4. Save, print, and then close **WordL1_C3_P2.docx**.

roject ③ **Prepare a Document on Workshops and Training Dates**

You will set and move tabs on the Ruler and at the Tabs dialog box and type tabbed text about workshops, training dates, and a table of contents.

Manipulating Tabs on the Ruler

When you work with a document, Word offers a variety of default settings such as margins and line spacing. One of these defaults is a left tab set every 0.5 inch. In some situations, these default tabs are appropriate; in others, you may want to create your own. Two methods exist for setting tabs. Tabs can be set on the Ruler or at the Tabs dialog box.

Use the Ruler to set, move, and delete tabs. If the Ruler is not visible, click the View Ruler button located at the top of the vertical scroll bar. The Ruler displays left tabs set every 0.5 inch. These default tabs are indicated by tiny vertical lines along the bottom of the Ruler. With a left tab, text aligns at the left edge of the tab. The other types of tabs that can be set on the Ruler are center, right, decimal, and bar. Use the Alignment button that displays at the left side of the Ruler to specify tabs. Each time you click the Alignment button, a different tab or paragraph alignment symbol displays. Table 3.1 shows the tab alignment button and what type of tab each will set.

Table 3.1 Tab Alignment Symbols

Alignment Button	*Type of Tab*
⌊	Left tab
⊥	Center tab
⌋	Right tab
⊥.	Decimal tab
∣	Bar tab

Setting Tabs

To set a left tab on the Ruler, make sure the left alignment symbol (see Table 3.1) displays in the Alignment button. Position the arrow pointer just below the tick mark (the marks on the Ruler) where you want the tab symbol to appear and then click the left mouse button. When you set a tab on the Ruler, any default tabs to the left are automatically deleted by Word. Set a center, right, decimal, or bar tab on the Ruler in a similar manner.

Before setting a tab on the Ruler, click the Alignment button at the left side of the Ruler until the appropriate tab symbol displays and then set the tab. If you change the tab symbol in the Alignment button, the symbol remains until you change it again or you exit Word. If you exit and then reenter Word, the tab symbol returns to the default of left tab.

If you want to set a tab at a specific measurement on the Ruler, hold down the Alt key, position the arrow pointer at the desired position, and then hold down the left mouse button. This displays two measurements on the Ruler. The first measurement displays the location of the arrow pointer on the Ruler in relation to the left margin. The second measurement is the distance from the location of the arrow pointer on the Ruler to the right margin. With the left mouse button held down, position the tab symbol at the desired location and then release the mouse button and the Alt key.

If you change tab settings and then create columns of text using the New Line command, Shift + Enter, the tab formatting is stored in the paragraph mark at the end of the columns. If you want to make changes to the tab settings for text in the columns, position the insertion point anywhere within the columns (all of the text in the columns does not have to be selected) and then make the changes.

QUICK STEPS

Set Tabs on Ruler
1. Click Alignment button on Ruler.
2. Click desired location on Ruler.

HINT

When setting tabs on the ruler, a dotted guideline displays to help align tabs.

HINT

Position the insertion point in any paragraph of text, and tabs for the paragraph appear on the Ruler.

Project 3a — Setting Left, Center, and Right Tabs on the Ruler

1. At a new blank document, type **WORKSHOPS** centered and bolded as shown in Figure 3.11.
2. Press the Enter key and then return the paragraph alignment back to left and turn off bold.
3. Set a left tab at the 0.5-inch mark, a center tab at the 3.25-inch mark, and a right tab at the 6-inch mark by completing the following steps:
   a. Click the Show/Hide ¶ button in the Paragraph group in the Home tab to turn on the display of nonprinting characters.
   b. Make sure the Ruler is displayed. (If not, click the View Ruler button located at the top of the vertical scroll bar.)
   c. Make sure the left tab symbol displays in the Alignment button at the left side of the Ruler.
   d. Position the arrow pointer on the 0.5-inch mark on the Ruler and then click the left mouse button.

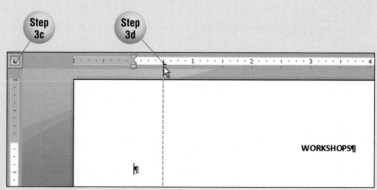

e. Position the arrow pointer on the Alignment button at the left side of the Ruler and then click the left mouse button until the center tab symbol displays (see Table 3.1).

f. Position the arrow pointer below the 3.25-inch mark on the Ruler. Hold down the Alt key and then the left mouse button. Make sure the first measurement on the Ruler displays as *3.25"* and then release the mouse button and the Alt key.

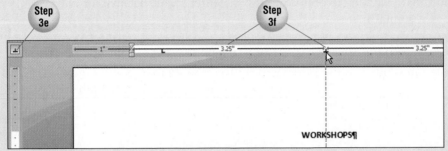

g. Position the arrow pointer on the Alignment button at the left side of the Ruler and then click the left mouse button until the right tab symbol displays (see Table 3.1).

h. Position the arrow pointer below the 6-inch mark on the Ruler. Hold down the Alt key and then the left mouse button. Make sure the first measurement on the Ruler displays as *6"* and then release the mouse button and the Alt key.

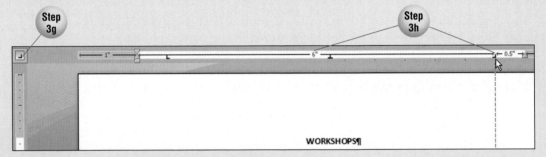

4. Type the text in columns as shown in Figure 3.11. Press the Tab key before typing each column entry and press Shift + Enter after typing the text in the third column.
5. After typing the last column entry, press the Enter key twice.
6. Press Ctrl + Q to remove paragraph formatting (tab settings).
7. Click the Show/Hide ¶ button to turn off the display of nonprinting characters.
8. Save the document and name it **WordL1_C3_P3**.

Figure 3.11 Project 3a

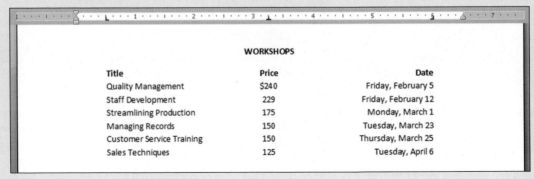

Moving Tabs

After a tab has been set on the Ruler, it can be moved to a new location. To move a tab, position the arrow pointer on the tab symbol on the Ruler, hold down the left mouse button, drag the symbol to the new location on the Ruler, and then release the mouse button.

Deleting Tabs

To delete a tab from the Ruler, position the arrow pointer on the tab symbol you want deleted, hold down the left mouse button, drag the symbol down into the document, and then release the mouse button.

Project **3b** **Moving Tabs**

1. With **WordL1_C3_P3.docx** open, position the insertion point on any character in the first entry in the tabbed text.
2. Position the arrow pointer on the left tab symbol at the 0.5-inch mark, hold down the left mouse button, drag the left tab symbol to the 1-inch mark on the Ruler, and then release the mouse button. *Hint: Use the Alt key to help you precisely position the tab symbol.*

3. Position the arrow pointer on the right tab symbol at the 6-inch mark, hold down the left mouse button, drag the right tab symbol to the 5.5-inch mark on the Ruler, and then release the mouse button. *Hint: Use the Alt key to help you precisely position the tab symbol.*
4. Save **WordL1_C3_P3.docx**.

Manipulating Tabs at the Tabs Dialog Box

Use the Tabs dialog box shown in Figure 3.12 to set tabs at a specific measurement. You can also use the Tabs dialog box to set tabs with preceding leaders and clear one tab or all tabs. To display the Tabs dialog box, click the Paragraph group dialog box launcher. At the Paragraph dialog box, click the Tabs button located in the bottom left corner of the dialog box.

QUICK STEPS

Set Tabs at Tabs Dialog Box
1. Click Paragraph group dialog box launcher.
2. Click Tabs button.
3. Specify tab positions, alignments, and leader options.
4. Click OK.

Figure 3.12 Tabs Dialog Box

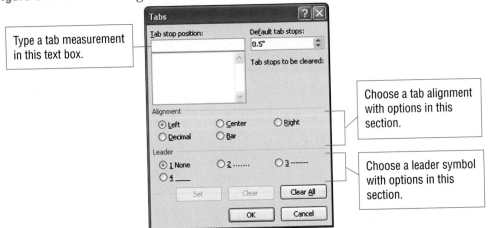

Type a tab measurement in this text box.

Choose a tab alignment with options in this section.

Choose a leader symbol with options in this section.

Clearing Tabs

At the Tabs dialog box, you can clear an individual tab or all tabs. To clear all tabs, click the Clear All button. To clear an individual tab, specify the tab position, and then click the Clear button.

Setting Tabs

At the Tabs dialog box, you can set a left, right, center, or decimal tab as well as a bar. (For an example of a bar tab, refer to Figure 3.13.) You can also set a left, right, center, or decimal tab with preceding leaders. To change the type of tab at the Tabs dialog box, display the dialog box and then click the desired tab in the Alignment section. Type the desired measurement for the tab in the *Tab stop position* text box.

Project **3C** Setting Left Tabs and a Bar Tab at the Tabs Dialog Box

1. With **WordL1_C3_P3.docx** open, press Ctrl + End to move the insertion point to the end of the document.
2. Type the title TRAINING DATES bolded and centered as shown in Figure 3.13, press the Enter key, return the paragraph alignment back to left, and then turn off bold.
3. Display the Tabs dialog box and then set left tabs and a bar tab by completing the following steps:
   a. Click the Paragraph group dialog box launcher.
   b. At the Paragraph dialog box, click the Tabs button located in the lower left corner of the dialog box.
   c. Make sure *Left* is selected in the *Alignment* section of the dialog box.
   d. Type 1.75 in the *Tab stop position* text box.
   e. Click the Set button.
   f. Type 4 in the *Tab stop position* text box and then click the Set button.
   g. Type 3.25 in the *Tab stop position* text box, click *Bar* in the *Alignment* section, and then click the Set button.
   h. Click OK to close the Tabs dialog box.

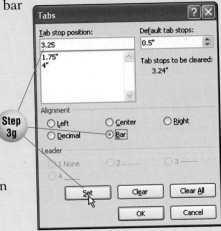

Step 3g

4. Type the text in columns as shown in Figure 3.13. Press the Tab key before typing each column entry and press Shift + Enter to end each line.
5. After typing *February 23*, complete the following steps:
   a. Press the Enter key.
   b. Clear tabs by displaying the Tabs dialog box, clicking the Clear All button, and then clicking OK.
   c. Press the Enter key.
6. Remove the 10 points of spacing after the last entry in the text by completing the following steps:
   a. Position the insertion point on any character in the *January 18* entry.
   b. Click the Page Layout tab.
   c. Click twice on the down-pointing arrow at the right side of the *Spacing After* measurement box. (This changes the measurement to *0 pt.*)
7. Save **WordL1_C3_P3.docx**.

Figure 3.13 Project 3c

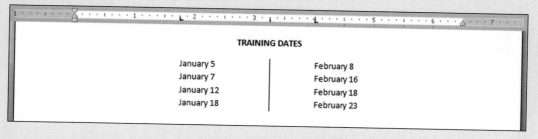

TRAINING DATES

January 5	February 8
January 7	February 16
January 12	February 18
January 18	February 23

Setting Leader Tabs

The four types of tabs can also be set with leaders. Leaders are useful in a table of contents or other material where you want to direct the reader's eyes across the page. Figure 3.14 shows an example of leaders. Leaders can be periods (.), hyphens (-), or underlines (_). To add leaders to a tab, click the type of leader desired in the *Leader* section of the Tabs dialog box.

Project 3d Setting a Left Tab and a Right Tab with Dot Leaders

1. With **WordL1_C3_P3.docx** open, press Ctrl + End to move the insertion point to the end of the document.
2. Type the title TABLE OF CONTENTS bolded and centered as shown in Figure 3.14.
3. Press the Enter key and then return the paragraph alignment back to left and turn off bold.
4. Set a left tab and a right tab with dot leaders by completing the following steps:
   a. Click the Paragraph group dialog box launcher.
   b. Click the Tabs button located in the lower left corner of the Paragraph dialog box.
   c. At the Tabs dialog box, make sure *Left* is selected in the *Alignment* section of the dialog box.
   d. With the insertion point positioned in the *Tab stop position* text box, type 1 and then click the Set button.

e. Type 5.5 in the *Tab stop position* text box.

f. Click *Right* in the *Alignment* section of the dialog box.

g. Click *2 ......* in the *Leader* section of the dialog box and then click the Set button.

h. Click OK to close the dialog box.

5. Type the text in columns as shown in Figure 3.14. Press the Tab key before typing each column entry and press Shift + Enter to end each line.

6. Save, print, and then close **WordL1_C3_P3.docx**.

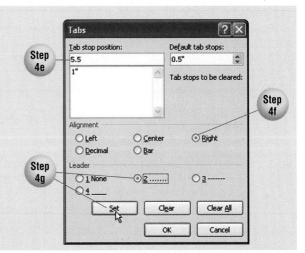

Figure 3.14 Project 3d

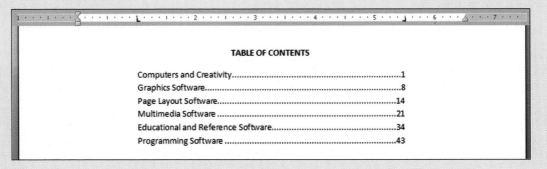

Project 4 Move and Copy Text in a Document on Online Shopping Tips

You will open a document containing information on online shopping safety tips and then cut, copy, and paste text in the document.

Cutting, Copying, and Pasting Text

When editing a document, you may need to delete specific text, move text to a different location in the document, and/or copy text to various locations in the document. You can complete these activities using buttons in the Clipboard group in the Home tab.

Deleting Selected Text

Word offers different methods for deleting text from a document. To delete a single character, you can use either the Delete key or the Backspace key. To delete more than a single character, select the text, and then press the Delete key on the keyboard or click the Cut button in the Clipboard group. If you press the Delete key, the text is deleted permanently. (You can restore deleted text with the Undo button on the Quick Access toolbar.) The Cut button in the Clipboard group will remove the

Cut

selected text from the document and insert it in the ***Clipboard***. Word's Clipboard is a temporary area of memory. The Clipboard holds text while it is being moved or copied to a new location in the document or to a different document.

Cutting and Pasting Text

To move text to a different location in the document, select the text, click the Cut button in the Clipboard group, position the insertion point at the location where you want the text inserted, and then click the Paste button in the Clipboard group.

You can also move selected text with a shortcut menu. To do this, select the text and then position the insertion point inside the selected text until it turns into an arrow pointer. Click the *right* mouse button and then click *Cut* at the shortcut menu. Position the insertion point where you want the text inserted, click the *right* mouse button, and then click *Paste* at the shortcut menu. Keyboard shortcuts are also available for cutting and pasting text. Use Ctrl + X to cut text and Ctrl + V to insert text.

When selected text is cut from a document and inserted in the Clipboard, it stays in the Clipboard until other text is inserted in the Clipboard. For this reason, you can paste text from the Clipboard more than just once. For example, if you cut text to the Clipboard, you can paste this text in different locations within the document or other documents as many times as desired.

H I N T
The Clipboard contents are deleted when the computer is turned off. Text you want to save permanently should be saved as a separate document.

Paste

QUICK STEPS

Move Selected Text
1. Select text.
2. Click Cut button.
3. Move to desired location.
4. Click Paste button.

Project 4a   Moving Selected Text

1. Open **WordDocument10.docx**.
2. Save the document with Save As and name it **WordL1_C3_P4**.
3. Move a paragraph by completing the following steps:
   a. Select the paragraph that begins with *Only buy at secure sites.* including the blank line below the paragraph.
   b. Click the Cut button in the Clipboard group in the Home tab.
   c. Position the insertion point at the beginning of the paragraph that begins with *Look for sites that follow* ... .
   d. Click the Paste button in the Clipboard group. (If the first and second paragraphs are not separated by a blank line, press the Enter key once.)
4. Following steps similar to those in Step 3, move the paragraph that begins with *Never provide your social security number.* so it is positioned before the paragraph that begins *Look for sites that follow privacy* ... and after the paragraph that begins *Only buy at secure sites.*.
5. Save **WordL1_C3_P4.docx**.

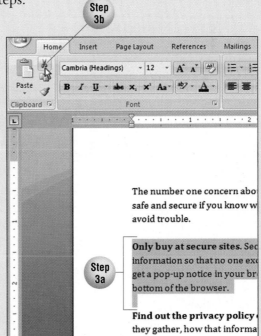

Moving Text by Dragging with the Mouse

You can also use the mouse to move text. To do this, select text to be moved and then position the I-beam pointer inside the selected text until it turns into an arrow pointer. Hold down the left mouse button, drag the arrow pointer (displays with a gray box attached) to the location where you want the selected text inserted, and then release the button. If you drag and then drop selected text in the wrong location, immediately click the Undo button.

Project ④b Moving Text by Dragging with the Mouse

1. With **WordL1_C3_P4.docx** open, use the mouse to select the paragraph that begins with *Keep current with the latest Internet scams.* including the blank line below the paragraph.
2. Move the I-beam pointer inside the selected text until it becomes an arrow pointer.
3. Hold down the left mouse button, drag the arrow pointer (displays with a small gray box attached) so that the insertion point, which displays as a grayed vertical bar, is positioned at the beginning of the paragraph that begins with *Never provide your social security number.*, and then release the mouse button.

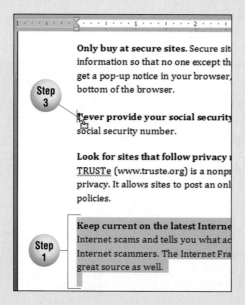

4. Deselect the text.
5. Save **WordL1_C3_P4.docx**.

Using the Paste Options Button

Paste Options

When selected text is pasted, the Paste Options button displays in the lower right corner of the text. Click this button and a drop-down list displays as shown in Figure 3.15. Use options from this drop-down list to specify how you want information pasted in the document. By default, pasted text retains the formatting of the selected text. You can choose to match the formatting of the pasted text with the formatting where the text is pasted, paste only the text without retaining formatting, or apply a style to pasted text.

Figure 3.15 Paste Options Button Drop-down List

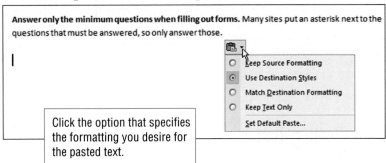

Click the option that specifies the formatting you desire for the pasted text.

Project 4c Using the Paste Options Button

1. With **WordL1_C3_P4.docx** open, open **WordParagraph01.docx**.
2. Select the paragraph of text in the document including the blank line below the paragraph and then click the Copy button in the Clipboard group.
3. Close **WordParagraph01.docx**.
4. Move the insertion point to the end of the document.
5. Click the Paste button in the Clipboard group.
6. Click the Paste Options button that displays at the end of the paragraph and then click the *Match Destination Formatting* option. (This changes the font so it matches the formatting of the other paragraphs in the document.)

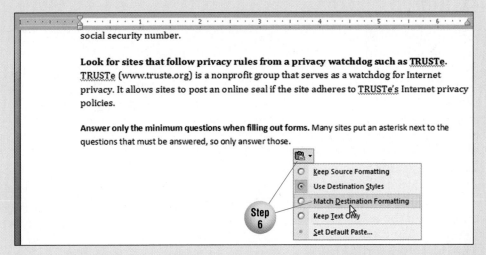

7. Save, print, and then close **WordL1_C3_P4.docx**.

Project 5 Copy Text in a Staff Meeting Announcement

You will copy and paste text in a document announcing a staff meeting for the Technical Support Team.

Copying and Pasting Text

Copy Selected Text
1. Select text.
2. Click Copy button.
3. Move to desired location.
4. Click Paste button.

Copy

Copying selected text can be useful in documents that contain repetitive portions of text. You can use this function to insert duplicate portions of text in a document instead of retyping the text. After you have selected text, copy the text to a different location with the Copy and Paste buttons in the Clipboard group in the Home tab or using the mouse. You can also use the keyboard shortcut, Ctrl + C, to copy text.

To use the mouse to copy text, select the text and then position the I-beam pointer inside the selected text until it becomes an arrow pointer. Hold down the left mouse button and hold down the Ctrl key. Drag the arrow pointer (displays with a small gray box and a box containing a plus symbol) to the location where you want the copied text inserted (make sure the insertion point, which displays as a grayed vertical bar, is positioned in the desired location) and then release the mouse button and then the Ctrl key.

Project 5a Copying Text

1. Open **WordBlock01.docx**.
2. Save the document with Save As and name it **WordL1_C3_P5**.
3. Copy the text in the document to the end of the document by completing the following steps:
   a. Select all of the text in the document and include one blank line below the text. ***Hint: Click the Show/Hide ¶ button to turn on the display of nonprinting characters. When you select the text, select one of the paragraph markers below the text.***
   b. Click the Copy button in the Clipboard group.
   c. Move the insertion point to the end of the document.
   d. Click the Paste button in the Clipboard group.
4. Copy the text again at the end of the document. To do this, position the insertion point at the end of the document, and then click the Paste button in the Clipboard group. (This inserts a copy of the text from the Clipboard.)
5. Save **WordL1_C3_P5.docx**.

1. With **WordL1_C3_P5.docx** open, select all of the text in the document using the mouse and include one blank line below the text. (Consider turning on the display of nonprinting characters.)
2. Move the I-beam pointer inside the selected text until it becomes an arrow pointer.
3. Hold down the Ctrl key and then the left mouse button. Drag the arrow pointer (displays with a box with a plus symbol inside) to the end of the document, release the mouse button, and then release the Ctrl key.

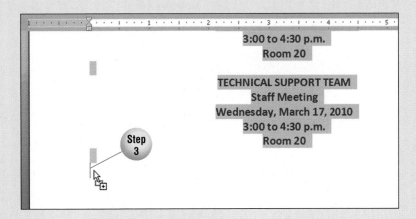

Step 3

3:00 to 4:30 p.m.
Room 20

TECHNICAL SUPPORT TEAM
Staff Meeting
Wednesday, March 17, 2010
3:00 to 4:30 p.m.
Room 20

4. Deselect the text.
5. Make sure all text fits on one page. If not, consider deleting any extra blank lines.
6. Save, print, and then close **WordL1_C3_P5.docx**.

Project **6** Create a Contract Negotiations Document

You will use the Clipboard to copy and paste paragraphs to and from paragraphs in separate documents to create a contract negotiations document. You will also use the Paste Special dialog box to paste text in the contract negotiation document as unformatted text.

Using the Clipboard

Use the Clipboard to collect and paste multiple items. You can collect up to 24 different items and then paste them in various locations. To display the Clipboard task pane, click the Clipboard group dialog box launcher located in the lower right corner of the Clipboard group. The Clipboard task pane displays at the left side of the screen in a manner similar to what you see in Figure 3.16.

QUICK STEPS

Use Clipboard
1. Click Clipboard group dialog box launcher.
2. Select and copy desired text.
3. Move to desired location.
4. Click desired option in Clipboard task pane.

Figure 3.16 Clipboard Task Pane

Click this button to paste all of the Clipboard items into the document.

Click this button to clear all items from the Clipboard.

5 of 24 - Clipboard ▾ ✕

🔲 Paste All   ✖ Clear All

Click an item to paste:

📄 5. If RM, at any time, grants additional sick leave or assistance to any em...

📄 3. An employee shall report to his/her RM supervisor that he/she i...

📄 1. All employees will be credited with eight (8) hours of sick leave for e...

📄 4. Each employee requested by RM to be away from regular base ...

📄 2. Employees transferring to another location at their own request due to bid...

Options ▾

HINT

You can copy items to the Clipboard from various Office applications and then paste them into any Office file.

✖ Clear All

Select text or an object you want to copy and then click the Copy button in the Clipboard group. Continue selecting text or items and clicking the Copy button. To insert an item, position the insertion point in the desired location and then click the option in the Clipboard task pane representing the item. Click the Paste All button to paste all of the items in the Clipboard into the document. If the copied item is text, the first 50 characters display beside the button on the Clipboard task pane. When all desired items are inserted, click the Clear All button to remove any remaining items.

Project 6a Collecting and Pasting Paragraphs of Text

1. Open **WordContItems01.docx**.
2. Turn on the display of the Clipboard task pane by clicking the Clipboard group dialog box launcher. (If the Clipboard task pane list box contains any text, click the Clear All button located toward the top of the task pane.)
3. Select paragraph 1 in the document (the 1. is not selected) and then click the Copy button in the Clipboard group.
4. Select paragraph 3 in the document (the 3. is not selected) and then click the Copy button in the Clipboard group.
5. Close **WordContItems01.docx**.

Step 2

6. Paste the paragraphs by completing the following steps:
   a. Press Ctrl + N to display a new blank document. (If the Clipboard task pane does not display, click the Clipboard group dialog box launcher.)
   b. Type **CONTRACT NEGOTIATION ITEMS** centered and bolded.
   c. Press the Enter key, turn off bold, and return the paragraph alignment back to left.
   d. Click the Paste All button in the Clipboard task pane to paste both paragraphs in the document.
   e. Click the Clear All button in the Clipboard task pane.

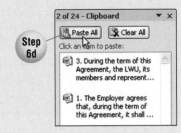

7. Open **WordContract01.docx**.
8. Select and then copy each of the following paragraphs:
   a. Paragraph 2 in the *Transfers and Moving Expenses* section.
   b. Paragraph 4 in the *Transfers and Moving Expenses* section.
   c. Paragraph 1 in the *Sick Leave* section.
   d. Paragraph 3 in the *Sick Leave* section.
   e. Paragraph 5 in the *Sick Leave* section.
9. Close **WordContract01.docx**.
10. Make sure the insertion point is positioned at the end of the document and then paste the paragraphs by completing the following steps:
    a. Click the button in the Clipboard task pane representing paragraph 2. (When the paragraph is inserted in the document, the paragraph number changes to 3.)
    b. Click the button in the Clipboard task pane representing paragraph 4.
    c. Click the button in the Clipboard task pane representing paragraph 3.
    d. Click the button in the Clipboard task pane representing paragraph 5.

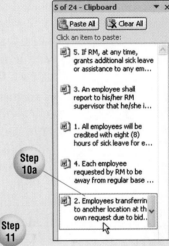

11. Click the Clear All button located toward the top of the Clipboard task pane.
12. Close the Clipboard task pane.
13. Save the document and name it **WordL1_C3_P6**.
14. Print and then close **WordL1_C3_P6.docx**.

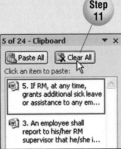

CHAPTER summary

- Number paragraphs with the Numbering button in the Paragraph group in the Home tab and insert bullets before paragraphs with the Bullets button.

- Remove all paragraph formatting from a paragraph by pressing the keyboard shortcut, Ctrl + Q, and remove all character and paragraph formatting by clicking the Clear Formatting button in the Font group.

- The AutoCorrect Options button displays when the AutoFormat feature inserts numbers. Click this button to display options for undoing and/or stopping automatic numbering.

- Bulleted lists with hanging indents are automatically created when a paragraph begins with *, >, or -. The type of bullet inserted depends on the type of character entered.

- You can turn off automatic numbering and bullets at the AutoCorrect dialog box with the AutoFormat As You Type tab selected.

- A paragraph created in Word contains an invisible frame and you can insert a border around this frame. Click the Border button arrow to display a drop-down list of border choices.

- Apply shading to text by clicking the Shading button arrow and then clicking the desired color at the drop-down gallery.

- Use options at the Borders and Shading dialog box with the Borders tab selected to add a customized border to a paragraph or selected paragraphs and use options with Shading tab selected to add shading or a pattern to a paragraph or selected paragraphs.

- With the Sort button in the Paragraph group in the Home tab, you can sort text arranged in paragraphs alphabetically by the first character, which includes numbers, symbols, or letters.

- By default, tabs are set every 0.5 inch. These settings can be changed on the Ruler or at the Tabs dialog box.

- Use the Alignment button at the left side of the Ruler to select a left, right, center, or decimal tab. When you set a tab on the Ruler, any default tabs to the left are automatically deleted.

- After a tab has been set on the Ruler, it can be moved or deleted using the mouse pointer.

- At the Tabs dialog box, you can set any of the four types of tabs as well as a bar tab at a specific measurement. You can also set tabs with preceding leaders and clear one tab or all tabs. Preceding leaders can be periods, hyphens, or underlines.

- Cut, copy, and paste text using buttons in the Clipboard group or with keyboard shortcuts.

- When selected text is pasted, the Paste Options button displays in the lower right corner of the text with options for specifying how you want information pasted in the document.

- With the Office Clipboard, you can collect up to 24 items and then paste them in various locations in a document.

COMMANDS review

FEATURE	RIBBON TAB, GROUP	BUTTON, OPTION	KEYBOARD SHORTCUT
Borders	Home, Paragraph		
Borders and Shading dialog box	Home, Paragraph	, Borders and Shading	
Bullets	Home, Paragraph		
Clear character and paragraph formatting	Home, Font		
Clear paragraph formatting			Ctrl + Q
Clipboard task pane	Home, Clipboard		
Copy text	Home, Clipboard		Ctrl + C
Cut text	Home, Clipboard		Ctrl + X
New Line command			Shift + Enter
Numbering	Home, Paragraph		
Paragraph dialog box	Home, Paragraph		
Paste text	Home, Clipboard		Ctrl + V
Shading	Home, Paragraph		
Sort Text dialog box	Home, Paragraph		
Tabs dialog box	Home, Paragraph	, Tabs	

CONCEPTS check

Test Your Knowledge

Completion: In the space provided at the right, indicate the correct term, symbol, or command.

1. The Numbering button is located in this group in the Home tab. _____

2. Automate the creation of bulleted paragraphs with this button in the Home tab. _____

3. This button displays when the AutoFormat feature inserts numbers. _____

4. You can turn off automatic numbering and bullets at the AutoCorrect dialog box with this tab selected.

     _____

5. Bulleted lists with hanging indents are automatically created when you begin a paragraph with the asterisk symbol (*), the hyphen (-), or this symbol.

     _____

6. The Borders button is located in this group in the Home tab.

     _____

7. Use options at this dialog box with the Borders tab selected to add a customized border to a paragraph or selected paragraphs.

     _____

8. Sort text arranged in paragraphs alphabetically by the first character, which includes numbers, symbols, or this.

     _____

9. By default, each tab is set apart from the other by this measurement.

     _____

10. This is the default tab type.

     _____

11. When setting tabs on the Ruler, choose the tab type with this button.

     _____

12. Tabs can be set on the Ruler or here.

     _____

13. This group in the Home tab contains the Cut, Copy, and Paste buttons.

     _____

14. To copy selected text with the mouse, hold down this key while dragging selected text.

     _____

15. With this task pane, you can collect up to 24 items and then paste the items in various locations in the document.

     _____

SKILLS check
Demonstrate Your Proficiency

Assessment

1   **APPLY PARAGRAPH FORMATTING TO A COMPUTER ETHICS DOCUMENT**

    1. Open **WordDocument07.docx**.
    2. Save the document with Save As and name it **WordL1_C3_A1**.
    3. Move the insertion point to the end of the document and then type the text shown in Figure 3.17.
    4. Change the Quick Styles set to *Formal*.
    5. Apply the Heading 1 style to the three headings in the document.
    6. Apply the Paper theme.

7. Select the paragraphs of text in the *Computer Ethics* section and then apply numbering formatting.
8. Select the paragraphs of text in the *Technology Timeline* section and then apply bullet formatting.
9. Insert the following paragraph of text between paragraphs 2 and 3 in the *Computer Ethics* section: Find sources relating to the latest federal and/or state legislation on privacy protection.
10. Apply Blue-Gray, Accent 6, Lighter 60% paragraph shading to the three headings in the document.
11. Apply Blue-Gray, Accent 6, Lighter 80% paragraph shading to the numbered paragraphs in the *Computer Ethics* section and the bulleted paragraphs in the *Technology Timeline* and *ACLU Fair Electronic Monitoring Policy* sections.
12. Save, print, and then close **WordL1_C3_A1.docx**.

Figure 3.17 Assessment 1

ACLU Fair Electronic Monitoring Policy

➢ Notice to employees of the company's electronic monitoring practices

➢ Use of a signal to let an employee know he or she is being monitored

➢ Employee access to all personal data collected through monitoring

➢ No monitoring of areas designed for the health or comfort of employees

➢ The right to dispute and delete inaccurate data

➢ A ban on the collection of data unrelated to work performance

➢ Restrictions on the disclosure of personal data to others without the employee's consent

Assessment

2 TYPE TABBED TEXT AND APPLY FORMATTING TO A COMPUTER SOFTWARE DOCUMENT

1. Open **WordDocument14.docx**.
2. Save the document with Save As and name it **WordL1_C3_A2**.
3. Move the insertion point to the end of the document and then type the tabbed text as shown in Figure 3.18. Before typing the text in columns, set left tabs at the 0.75-inch, 2.75-inch, and 4.5-inch marks on the Ruler.
4. Apply the Heading 1 style to the three headings in the document (*Productivity Software, Personal-Use Software,* and *Software Training Schedule*).
5. Change the Quick Styles set to *Distinctive*.
6. Apply the Opulent theme.
7. Select the productivity software categories in the *Productivity Software* section (from *Word processing* through *Computer-aided design*) and then sort the text alphabetically.
8. With the text still selected, apply bullet formatting.
9. Select the personal-use software categories in the *Personal-Use Software* section (from *Personal finance software* through *Games and entertainment software*) and then sort the text alphabetically.

10. With the text still selected, apply bullet formatting.
11. Apply a single-line border to the top and a double-line border to the bottom of the three headings in the document and then apply paragraph shading of your choosing to each heading.
12. Select the text in columns and then move the tab symbols on the Ruler as follows:
    a. Move the tab at the 0.75-inch mark to the 1-inch mark.
    b. Move the tab at the 4.5-inch mark to the 4-inch mark.
13. Save, print, and then close **WordL1_C3_A2.docx**.

Figure 3.18 Assessment 2

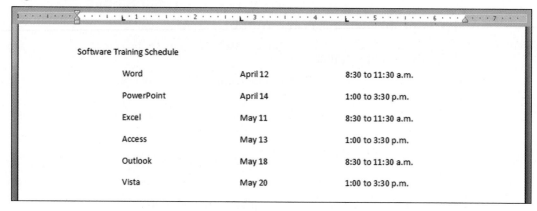

Software Training Schedule		
Word	April 12	8:30 to 11:30 a.m.
PowerPoint	April 14	1:00 to 3:30 p.m.
Excel	May 11	8:30 to 11:30 a.m.
Access	May 13	1:00 to 3:30 p.m.
Outlook	May 18	8:30 to 11:30 a.m.
Vista	May 20	1:00 to 3:30 p.m.

Assessment

3 TYPE AND FORMAT A TABLE OF CONTENTS DOCUMENT

1. At a new blank document, type the document shown in Figure 3.19 with the following specifications:
   a. Change the font to 11-point Cambria.
   b. Bold and center the title as shown.
   c. Before typing the text in columns, display the Tabs dialog box and then set left tabs at the 1-inch mark and the 1.5-inch mark, and a right tab with dot leaders at the 5.5-inch mark.
2. Save the document and name it **WordL1_C3_A3**.
3. Print **WordL1_C3_A3.docx**.
4. Select the text in columns and then move the tab symbols on the Ruler as follows:
   a. Delete the left tab symbol that displays at the 1.5-inch mark.
   b. Set a new left tab at the 0.5-inch mark.
   c. Move the right tab at the 5.5-inch mark to the 6-inch mark.
5. Apply paragraph borders and shading of your choosing to enhance the visual appeal of the document.
6. Save, print, and then close **WordL1_C3_A3.docx**.

Figure 3.19 Assessment 3

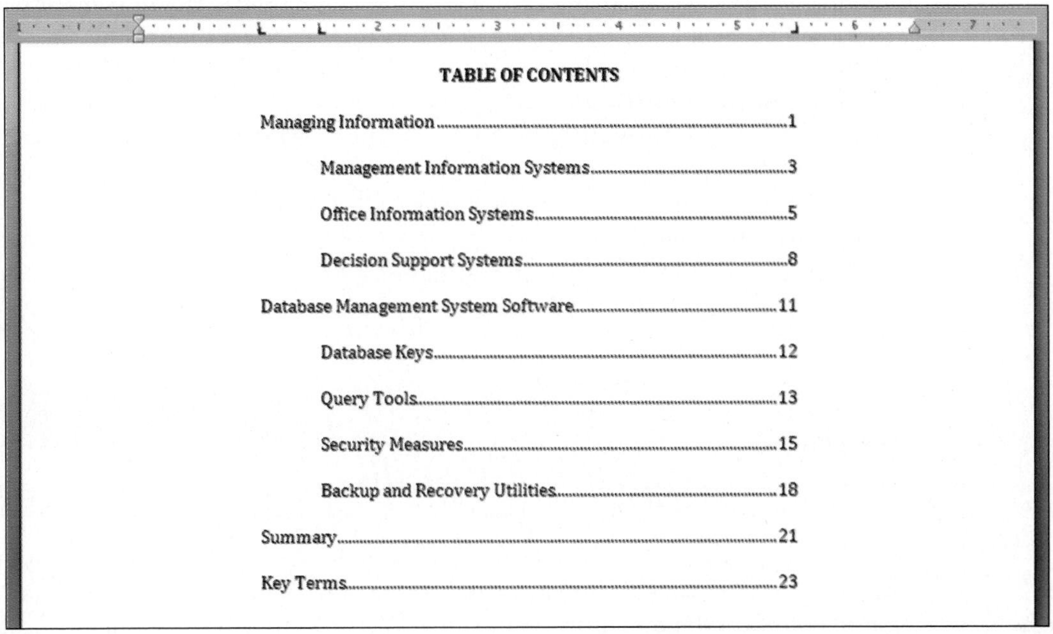
TABLE OF CONTENTS

Managing Information....................1
Management Information Systems....................3
Office Information Systems....................5
Decision Support Systems....................8
Database Management System Software....................11
Database Keys....................12
Query Tools....................13
Security Measures....................15
Backup and Recovery Utilities....................18
Summary....................21
Key Terms....................23

Assessment 4

FORMAT A BUILDING CONSTRUCTION AGREEMENT DOCUMENT

1. Open **WordAgreement02.docx**.
2. Save the document with Save As and name it **WordL1_C3_A4**.
3. Select and then delete the paragraph that begins *Supervision of Work*.
4. Select and then delete the paragraph that begins *Exclusions*.
5. Move the paragraph that begins *Financing Arrangements* above the paragraph that begins *Start of Construction*.
6. Open **WordDocument11.docx**.
7. Turn on the display of the Clipboard.
8. Select and then copy the first paragraph.
9. Select and then copy the second paragraph.
10. Select and then copy the third paragraph.
11. Close **WordDocument11.docx** without saving the changes.
12. With **WordL1_C3_A4.docx** open, paste the *Supervision* paragraph above the *Changes and Alterations* paragraph and match the destination formatting.
13. Paste the *Pay Review* paragraph above the *Possession of Residence* paragraph and match the destination formatting.
14. Clear all items from the Clipboard and then close the Clipboard.
15. Save, print, and then close **WordL1_C3_A4.docx**.

Assessment 5

HYPHENATE WORDS IN A REPORT

1. In some Word documents, especially documents with left and right margins wider than 1 inch, the right margin may appear quite ragged. If the paragraph alignment is changed to justified, the right margin will appear even, but there

will be extra space added throughout the line. In these situations, hyphenating long words that fall at the end of the text line provides the document with a more balanced look. Use Word's Help feature to learn how to automatically hyphenate words in a document.

2. Open **WordReport01.docx**.
3. Save the document with Save As and name it **WordL1_C3_A5**.
4. Automatically hyphenate words in the document, limiting the consecutive hyphens to 2. *Hint: Specify the number of consecutive hyphens at the Hyphenation dialog box.*
5. Save, print, and then close **WordL1_C3_A5.docx**.

CASE study
Apply Your Skills

Part 1

You are the assistant to Gina Coletti, manager of La Dolce Vita, an Italian restaurant. She has been working on updating and formatting the lunch menu. She has asked you to complete the menu by opening the **WordMenu.docx** document (located in the Word2007L1C3 folder), determining how the appetizer section is formatted, and then applying the same formatting to the *Soup and Salad*; *Sandwiches, Calzones and Burgers*; and *Individual Pizzas* sections. Save the document and name it **WordL1_C3_CS_P1**. Print and then close the document.

Part 2

Ms. Coletti has reviewed the completed menu and is pleased with the menu but wants to add a page border around the entire page to increase visual interest. Open **WordL1_C3_CS_P1.docx** and then save the document and name it **WordL1_C3_CS_P2**. Display the Borders and Shading dialog box with the Page Border tab selected and then experiment with the options available. Apply an appropriate page border to the menu (consider applying an art page border). Save, print, and then close **WordL1_C3_CS_P2.docx**.

Part 3

Each week, the restaurant offers daily specials. Ms. Coletti has asked you to open and format the text in the **WordMenuSpecials.docx** document. She has asked you to format the specials menu in a similar manner as the main menu but to make some changes to make it unique from the main menu. Apply the same page border to the specials menu document that you applied to the main menu document. Save the document and name it **WordL1_C3_CS_P3**. Print and then close the document.

Part 4

You have been asked by the head chef to research a new recipe for an Italian dish. Using the Internet, find a recipe that interests you and then prepare a Word document containing the recipe and ingredients. Use bullets before each ingredient and use numbering for each step in the recipe preparation. Save the document and name it **WordL1_C3_CS_P4**. Print and then close the document.

CHAPTER

Formatting Pages

PERFORMANCE OBJECTIVES

Upon successful completion of Chapter 4, you will be able to:

- Change document views
- Navigate in a document with Document Map and Thumbnails
- Change margins, page orientation, and paper size in a document
- Format pages at the Page Setup dialog box
- Insert a page break, blank page, and cover page
- Insert page numbering
- Insert and edit predesigned headers and footers
- Insert a watermark, page color, and page border
- Find and replace text and formatting

word Chapter 4

Tutorial 4.1
Organizing Documents
Tutorial 4.2
Enhancing Documents
Tutorial 4.3
Searching within a Document

A document generally displays in Print Layout view. You can change this default view with buttons in the View area on the Status bar or with options in the View tab. Use the Document Map and Thumbnails features to navigate in a document. A Word document, by default, contains 1-inch top, bottom, left, and right margins. You can change these default margins with the Margins button in the Page Setup group in the Page Layout tab or with options at the Page Setup dialog box. You can insert a variety of features in a Word document including a page break, blank page, and cover page as well as page numbers, headers, footers, a watermark, page color, and page border. Use options at the Find and Replace dialog box to search for specific text or formatting and replace with other text or formatting.

Note: Before beginning computer projects, copy to your storage medium the Word2007L1C4 subfolder from the Word2007L1 folder on the CD that accompanies this textbook and then make Word2007L1C4 the active folder.

You will open a document containing information on computer input and output devices, change document views, navigate in the document using Document Map and Thumbnails, and show and hide white space at the top and bottom of pages.

Changing the View

By default a Word document displays in Print Layout view. This view displays the document on the screen as it will appear when printed. Other views are available such as Draft and Full Screen Reading. Change views with buttons in the View area on the Status bar or with options in the View tab. The buttons in the View area on the Status bar are identified in Figure 4.1. Along with the View buttons, the Status bar also contains a Zoom slider bar as shown in Figure 4.1. Drag the button on the Zoom slider bar to increase or decrease the size of display, or click the Zoom Out button to decrease size and click the Zoom In to increase size.

Figure 4.1 Viewing Buttons and Zoom Slider Bar

Zoom Out

Zoom In

Draft

Displaying a Document in Draft View

Change to Draft view and the document displays in a format for efficient editing and formatting. At this view, margins and other features such as headers and footers do not display on the screen. Change to Draft view by clicking the Draft button in the View section on the Status bar or click the View tab and then click the Draft button in the Document Views group.

Displaying a Document in Full Screen Reading View

Full Screen Reading

The Full Screen Reading view displays a document in a format for easy viewing and reading. Change to Full Screen Reading view by clicking the Full Screen Reading button in the View section on the Status bar or by clicking the View tab and then clicking the Full Screen Reading button in the Document Views group.

Navigate in Full Screen Reading view using the keys on the keyboard as shown in Table 4.1. You can also navigate in Full Screen Reading view with options from the View Options button that displays toward the top right side of the screen or with the Next Screen and Previous Screen buttons located at the top of the window and also located at the bottom of each page.

You can customize the Full Screen Reading view with some of the options from the View Options drop-down list. Display this list by clicking the View Options button located in the upper right corner of the Full Screen Reading window.

Table 4.1 Keyboard Commands in Full Screen Reading View

Press this key	To complete this action
Page Down key or spacebar	Move to the next page or section
Page Up key or Backspace key	Move to the previous page or section
Right Arrow key	Move to next page
Left Arrow key	Move to previous page
Home	Move to first page in document
End	Move to last page in document
Esc	Return to previous view

Project 1a Changing Views

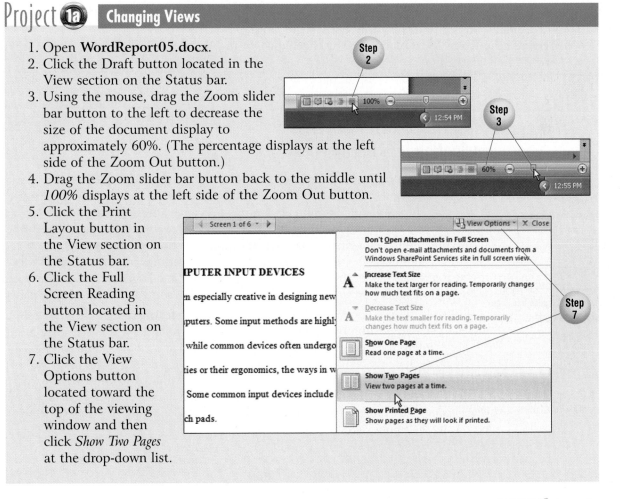

1. Open **WordReport05.docx**.
2. Click the Draft button located in the View section on the Status bar.
3. Using the mouse, drag the Zoom slider bar button to the left to decrease the size of the document display to approximately 60%. (The percentage displays at the left side of the Zoom Out button.)
4. Drag the Zoom slider bar button back to the middle until *100%* displays at the left side of the Zoom Out button.
5. Click the Print Layout button in the View section on the Status bar.
6. Click the Full Screen Reading button located in the View section on the Status bar.
7. Click the View Options button located toward the top of the viewing window and then click *Show Two Pages* at the drop-down list.

8. Click the Next Screen button to display the next two pages in the viewing window.

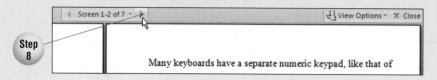

Step 8

Many keyboards have a separate numeric keypad, like that of

9. Click the Previous Screen button to display the previous two pages.
10. Click the View Options button located toward the top of the viewing window and then click *Show One Page* at the drop-down list.
11. Practice navigating using the actions shown in Table 4.1. (Try all of the actions in Table 4.1 except pressing the Esc key since that action will close Full Screen Reading view.)
12. Increase the size of the text by clicking the View Options button and then clicking the *Increase Text Size* option.

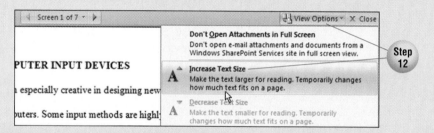

Step 12

13. Press the Home key to display the first viewing page.
14. Decrease the size of the text by clicking the View Options button and then clicking the *Decrease Text Size* option.
15. Click the Close button located in the upper right corner of the screen.

Navigating in a Document

Navigate with Document Map
1. Click View tab.
2. Click *Document Map* check box.
3. Click desired heading in navigation pane.

Navigate with Thumbnails
1. Click View tab.
2. Click *Thumbnails* check box.
3. Click desired thumbnail in navigation pane.

Word includes a number of features you can use to navigate in a document. Along with the navigating features you have already learned, you can also navigate using the Document Map and Thumbnails features. To navigate using the Document Map feature, click the View tab and then click the *Document Map* check box in the Show/Hide group. This displays a navigation pane at the left side of the screen as shown in Figure 4.2. Document Map displays any headings formatted with styles or text that looks like headings, such as short lines set in a larger type size. Navigate to a specific location in the document by clicking the heading in the navigation pane.

To navigate in a document using the Thumbnails feature, click the View tab and then click the Thumbnails check box in the Show/Hide group. This displays a thumbnail of each page in the navigation pane at the left side of the screen. You can switch between Thumbnails and Document Map by clicking the Switch Navigation Window button that displays at the top of the navigation pane and then clicking the desired option at the drop-down list. Close the navigation pane by clicking the *Thumbnails* check box to remove the check mark or by clicking the Close button located in the upper right corner of the pane.

Figure 4.2 Navigation Pane

Switch Navigation Window button

Navigation pane

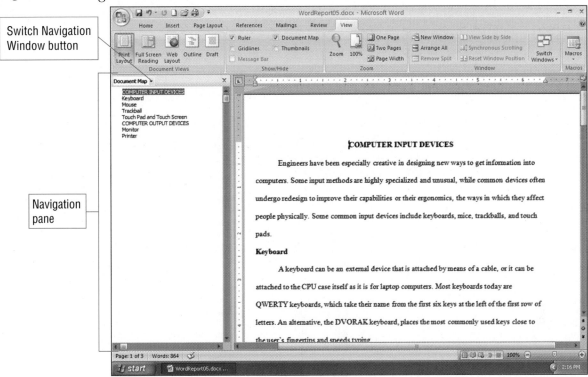

Project 1b Navigating Using Document Map

1. With **WordReport05.docx** open, click the View tab and then click the *Document Map* check box.
2. Click the *COMPUTER OUTPUT DEVICES* title that displays in the navigation pane.

Step 1

Step 2

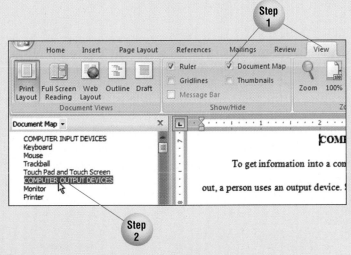

3. Click the *Keyboard* heading that displays in the navigation pane.
4. Click the *Document Map* check box to remove the check mark.

5. Click the *Thumbnails* check box in the Show/Hide group in the View tab.
6. Click the number 3 thumbnail in the navigation pane.
7. Click the number 1 thumbnail in the navigation pane.
8. Close the navigation pane by clicking the Close button located in the upper right corner of the navigation pane.

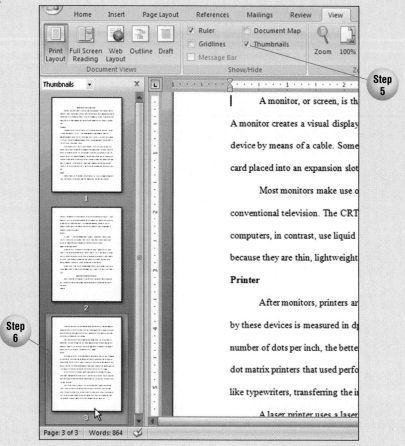

QUICK STEPS

Hiding/Showing White Space in Print Layout View

Hide White Space
1. Position mouse pointer at top of page until pointer displays as *Hide White Space* icon.
2. Double-click left mouse button.

Show White Space
1. Position mouse pointer on thin line separating pages until pointer displays as *Show White Space* icon.
2. Double-click left mouse button.

In Print Layout view, a page displays as it will appear when printed including the white space at the top and bottom of the page representing the default margins. To save space on the screen in Print Layout view, you can remove the white space by positioning the mouse pointer at the top edge or bottom edge of a page or between pages until the pointer displays as the *Hide White Space* icon and then double-clicking the left mouse button. To redisplay the white space, position the mouse pointer on the thin, black line separating pages until the pointer turns into the *Show White Space* icon and then double-click the left mouse button.

1. With **WordReport05.docx** open, make sure the document displays in Print Layout view.
2. Press Ctrl + Home to move the insertion point to the beginning of the document.
3. Hide the white spaces at the top and bottom of pages by positioning the mouse pointer at the top edge of the page until the pointer turns into the *Hide White Space* icon and then double-clicking the left mouse button.
4. Scroll through the document and notice the display of pages.
5. Redisplay the white spaces at the top and bottom of pages by positioning the mouse pointer on any thin, black, horizontal line separating pages until the pointer turns into the *Show White Space* icon and then double-clicking the left mouse button.

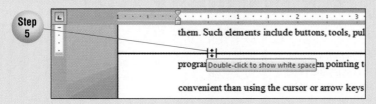

6. Close **WordReport05.docx**.

Project **2** **Format a Document on Online Etiquette Guidelines**

You will open a document containing information on guidelines for online etiquette and then change the margins, page orientation, and page size.

Changing Page Setup

The Page Setup group in the Page Layout tab contains a number of options for affecting pages in a document. With options in the group you can perform such actions as changing margins, orientation, and page size and inserting page breaks. The Pages group in the Insert tab contains three buttons for inserting a page break, blank page, and cover page.

Changing Margins

Change page margins with options at the Margins drop-down list as shown in Figure 4.3. To display this list, click the Page Layout tab and then click the Margins button in the Page Setup group. To change the margins, click one of the preset margins that display in the drop-down list. Be aware that most printers contain a required margin (between one-quarter and three-eighths inch) because printers cannot print to the edge of the page.

QUICK STEPS

Change Margins
1. Click Page Layout tab.
2. Click Margins button.
3. Click desired margin option.

Figure 4.3 Margins Drop-down List

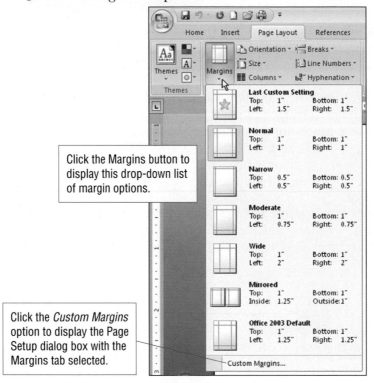

Click the Margins button to display this drop-down list of margin options.

Click the *Custom Margins* option to display the Page Setup dialog box with the Margins tab selected.

Project 2a   Changing Margins

1. Open **WordNetiquette.docx**.
2. Save the document with Save As and name it **WordL1_C4_P2**.
3. Click the Page Layout tab.
4. Click the Margins button in the Page Setup group and then click the *Office 2003 Default* option.
5. Save **WordL1_C4_P2.docx**.

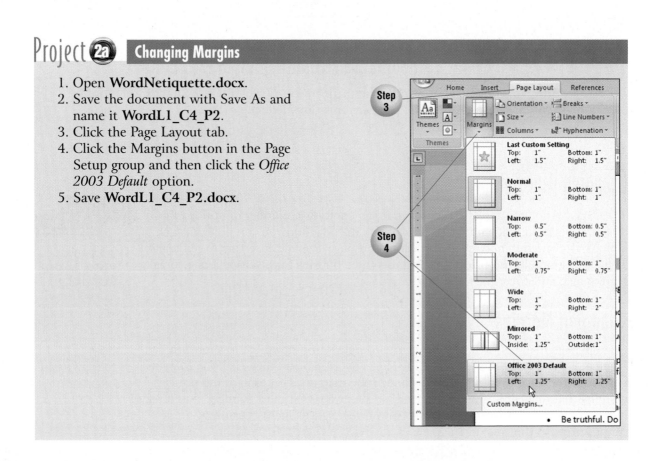

Step 3

Step 4

Changing Page Orientation

Click the Orientation button in the Page Setup group in the Page Layout tab and two options display—*Portrait* and *Landscape*. At the portrait orientation, which is the default, the page is 11 inches tall and 8.5 inches wide. At the landscape orientation, the page is 8.5 inches tall and 11 inches wide. Change the page orientation and the page margins automatically change.

Can you picture some instances in which you might use a landscape orientation? Suppose you are preparing a company's annual report and you need to include a couple of tables that have several columns of text. If you use the default portrait orientation, the columns would need to be quite narrow, possibly so narrow that reading becomes difficult. Changing the orientation to landscape results in three more inches of usable space. Also, you are not committed to using landscape orientation for the entire document. You can use portrait and landscape in the same document. To do this, select the text, display the Page Setup dialog box, click the desired orientation, and change the *Apply to* option box to *Selected text*.

Change Page Orientation
1. Click Page Layout tab.
2. Click Orientation button.
3. Click desired orientation.

Project 2b — Changing Page Orientation

1. With **WordL1_C4_P2.docx** open, make sure the Page Layout tab is selected.
2. Click the Orientation button in the Page Setup group.
3. Click *Landscape* at the drop-down list.
4. Scroll through the document and notice how the text displays on the page in landscape orientation.
5. Save **WordL1_C4_P2.docx**.

Step 2

Step 3

Changing Page Size

By default, Word uses a page size of 8.5 inches wide and 11 inches tall. You can change this default setting with options at the Size drop-down list shown in Figure 4.4. Display this drop-down list by clicking the Size button in the Page Setup group in the Page Layout tab.

Change Page Size
1. Click Page Layout tab.
2. Click Size button.
3. Click desired size option.

Figure 4.4 Size Drop-down List

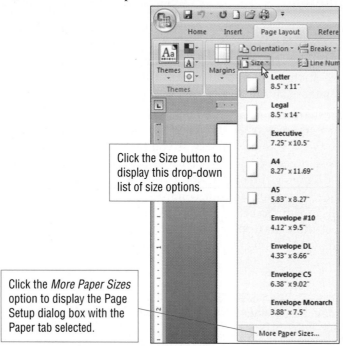

Click the Size button to display this drop-down list of size options.

Click the *More Paper Sizes* option to display the Page Setup dialog box with the Paper tab selected.

Project 2c   Changing Page Size

1. With **WordL1_C4_P2.docx** open, make sure the Page Layout tab is selected.
2. Click the Orientation button in the Page Setup group and then click *Portrait* at the drop-down list. (This changes the orientation back to the default.)
3. Click the Size button in the Page Setup group.
4. Click the A5 option (displays with *5.83″ × 8.27″* below *A5*). If this option is not available, choose an option with a similar size.
5. Scroll through the document and notice how the text displays on the page.
6. Click the Size button and then click *Legal* (displays with *8.5″ × 14″* below *Legal*).
7. Scroll through the document and notice how the text displays on the page.
8. Click the Size button and then click *Letter* (displays with *8.5″ × 11″* below *Letter*). (This returns the size back to the default.)
9. Save **WordL1_C4_P2.docx**.

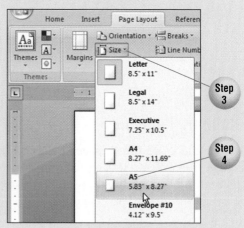

Step 3

Step 4

Changing Margins at the Page Setup Dialog Box

The Margins button in the Page Setup group provides you with a number of preset margins. If these margins do not fit your needs, you can set specific margins at the Page Setup dialog box with the Margins tab selected as shown in Figure 4.5. Display this dialog box by clicking the Page Setup group dialog box launcher or by clicking the Margins button and then clicking *Custom Margins* at the bottom of the drop-down list.

To change margins, select the current measurement in the *Top*, *Bottom*, *Left*, or *Right* text box, and then type the new measurement. You can also increase a measurement by clicking the up-pointing arrow at the right side of the text box. Decrease a measurement by clicking the down-pointing arrow. As you make changes to the margin measurements at the Page Setup dialog box, the sample page in the *Preview* section illustrates the effects of the margin changes.

QUICK STEPS

Change Margins at Page Setup Dialog Box
1. Click Page Layout tab.
2. Click Page Setup group dialog box launcher.
3. Specify desired margins.
4. Click OK.

Change Page Size at Page Setup Dialog Box
1. Click Page Layout tab.
2. Click Size button.
3. Click *More Paper Sizes* at drop-down list.
4. Specify desired size.
5. Click OK.

Figure 4.5 Page Setup Dialog Box with Margins Tab Selected

Notice the default settings for the top, bottom, left, and right margins.

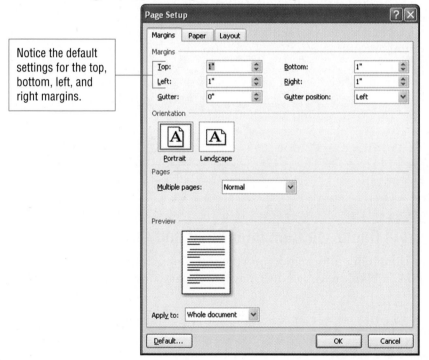

Changing Paper Size at the Page Setup Dialog Box

The Size button drop-down list contains a number of preset page sizes. If these sizes do not fit your needs, you can specify page size at the Page Setup dialog box with the Paper tab selected. Display this dialog box by clicking the Size button in the Page Setup group and then clicking *More Paper Sizes* that displays at the bottom of the drop-down list.

1. With **WordL1_C4_P2.docx** open, make sure the Page Layout tab is selected.
2. Click the Page Setup group dialog box launcher.
3. At the Page Setup dialog box with the Margins tab selected, click the down-pointing arrow at the right side of the *Top* text box until *0.5"* displays.
4. Click the down-pointing arrow at the right side of the *Bottom* text box until *0.5"* displays.
5. Select the current measurement in the *Left* text box and then type **0.75**.
6. Select the current measurement in the *Right* text box and then type **0.75**.
7. Click OK to close the dialog box.
8. Click the Size button in the Page Setup group and then click *More Paper Sizes* at the drop-down list.
9. At the Page Setup dialog box with the Paper tab selected, click the down-pointing arrow at the right side of the *Paper size* option and then click *A4* at the drop-down list.
10. Click OK to close the dialog box.
11. Scroll through the document and notice how the text displays on the page.
12. Click the Size button in the Page Setup group and then click *Letter* at the drop-down list.
13. Save, print, and then close **WordL1_C4_P2.docx**.

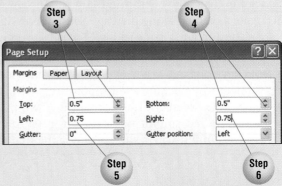

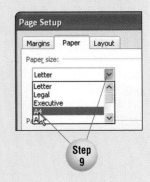

Project ③ **Customize a Report on Computer Input and Output Devices**

You will open a document containing information on computer input and output devices and then insert page breaks, a blank page, a cover page, and page numbering.

Inserting a Page Break

Insert Page Break
1. Click Insert tab.
2. Click Page Break button.
OR
Press Ctrl + Enter.

With the default top and bottom margins of one inch, approximately nine inches of text print on the page. At approximately the ten-inch mark, Word automatically inserts a page break. You can insert your own page break in a document with the keyboard shortcut, Ctrl + Enter, or with the Page Break button in the Pages group in the Insert tab.

A page break inserted by Word is considered a *soft* page break and a page break inserted by you is considered a *hard* page break. Soft page breaks automatically adjust if you add or delete text from a document. A hard page break does not adjust and is therefore less flexible than a soft page break. If you add or delete text from a document with a hard page break, check the break to determine whether it is still in a desirable location. In Draft view, a hard page break displays as a row of dots with the words Page Break in the center. To delete a page break, position the insertion point immediately below the page break and then press the Backspace key or change to Draft view, position the insertion point on the page break, and then press the Delete key.

Project 3a — Inserting Page Breaks

1. Open **WordReport05.docx**.
2. Save the document with Save As and name it **WordL1_C4_P3**.
3. Change the top margin by completing the following steps:
   a. Click the Page Layout tab.
   b. Click the Page Setup group dialog box launcher.
   c. At the Page Setup dialog box, click the Margins tab and then type 1.5 in the *Top* text box.
   d. Click OK to close the dialog box.

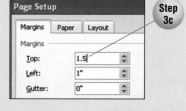

Step 3c

4. Insert a page break at the beginning of the heading *Mouse* by completing the following steps:
   a. Position the insertion point at the beginning of the heading *Mouse* (located toward the bottom of page 1).
   b. Click the Insert tab and then click the Page Break button in the Pages group.

Step 4b

Step 4a

Mouse

5. Move the insertion point to the beginning of the title *COMPUTER OUTPUT DEVICES* (located at the bottom of page 2) and then insert a page break by pressing Ctrl + Enter.
6. Move the insertion point to the beginning of the heading *Printer* and then press Ctrl + Enter to insert a page break.
7. Delete the page break by completing the following steps:
   a. Click the Draft button in the view area on the Status bar.
   b. With the insertion point positioned at the beginning of the heading *Printer*, press the Backspace key. (This displays the page break in the document.)
   c. Press the Backspace key again to delete the page break.
   d. Click the Print Layout button in the view area of the Status bar.
8. Save **WordL1_C4_P3.docx**.

Inserting a Blank Page

Click the Blank Page button in the Pages group in the Insert tab to insert a blank page at the position of the insertion point. This might be useful in a document where you want to insert a blank page for an illustration, graphic, or figure.

Insert Blank Page
1. Click Insert tab.
2. Click Blank Page button.

Inserting a Cover Page

QUICK
STEPS

Insert Cover Page
1. Click Insert tab.
2. Click Cover Page button.
3. Click desired cover page at drop-down list.

If you are preparing a document for distribution to others or you want to simply improve the visual appeal of your document, consider inserting a cover page. With the Cover Page button in the Pages group in the Insert tab, you can insert a predesigned and formatted cover page and then type personalized text in specific locations on the page. Click the Cover Page button and a drop-down list displays similar to the one shown in Figure 4.6. The drop-down list provides a visual representation of the cover page. Scroll through the list and then click the desired cover page.

A predesigned cover page contains location placeholders where you can enter specific information. For example, a cover page might contain the placeholder *[Type the document title]*. Click anywhere in the placeholder text and the placeholder text is selected. With the placeholder text selected, type the desired text. You can delete a placeholder by clicking anywhere in the placeholder text, clicking the placeholder tab, and then pressing the Delete key.

HINT

A cover page provides a polished and professional look to a document.

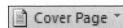

Figure 4.6 Cover Page Drop-down List

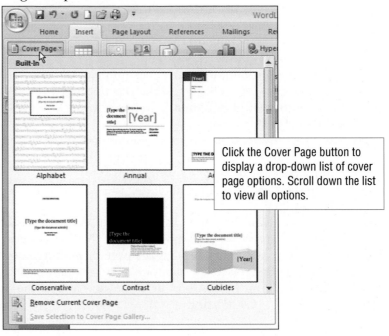

Click the Cover Page button to display a drop-down list of cover page options. Scroll down the list to view all options.

1. With **WordL1_C4_P3.docx** open, create a blank page by completing the following steps:
   a. Move the insertion point to the beginning of the heading *Touch Pad and Touch Screen* located on the second page.
   b. Click the Insert tab.
   c. Click the Blank Page button in the Pages group.
2. Insert a cover page by completing the following steps:
   a. Press Ctrl + Home to move the insertion point to the beginning of the document.
   b. Click the Cover Page button in the Pages group.
   c. At the drop-down list, scroll down and then click the *Motion* cover page.
   d. Click anywhere in the placeholder text *[Type the document title]* and then type **Computer Devices**.

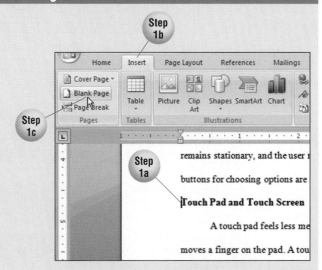

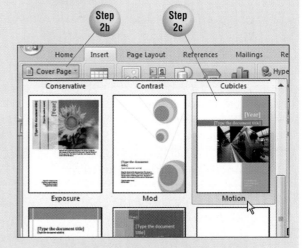

e. Click the placeholder text *[Year]*. Click the down-pointing arrow that displays at the right side of the placeholder and then click the Today button that displays at the bottom of the drop-down calendar.

f. Click anywhere in the placeholder text *[Type the company name]* and then type **Drake Computing**.

Step 2e

Step 2f

g. Click anywhere in the placeholder text *[Type the author name]* and then type your first and last names.

3. Remove the blank page you created in Step 1 by completing the following steps:

a. Move the insertion point to the beginning of page 5 immediately left of the heading *Touch Pad and Touch Screen*.

b. Click the Draft button in the View section on the Status bar.

c. Press the Backspace key until the heading *Touch Pad and Touch Screen* displays a double-space below the previous paragraph of text.

d. Click the Print Layout button in the View section on the Status bar.

4. Save **WordL1_C4_P3.docx**.

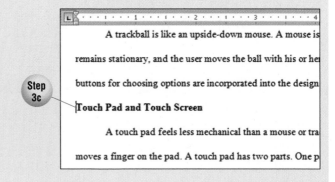

Step 3c

Inserting Predesigned Page Numbering

Word, by default, does not print page numbers on a page. If you want to insert page numbering in a document, use the Page Number button in the Header & Footer group in the Insert tab. When you click the Page Number button, a drop-down list displays with options for specifying the page number location. Point to an option at this list and a drop-down list displays of predesigned page number formats. Scroll through the options in the drop-down list and then click the desired option. If you want to change the format of page numbering in a document, double-click the page number, select the page number text, and then apply the desired formatting. You can remove page numbering from a document by clicking the Page Number button and then clicking *Remove Page Numbers* at the drop-down list.

Project 3C   Inserting Predesigned Page Numbering

1. With **WordL1_C4_P3.docx** open, insert page numbering by completing the following steps:
   a. Move the insertion point so it is positioned on any character in the title *COMPUTER INPUT DEVICES*.
   b. Click the Insert tab.
   c. Click the Page Number button in the Header & Footer group and then point to *Top of Page*.
   d. Scroll through the drop-down list and then click the *Brackets 2* option.

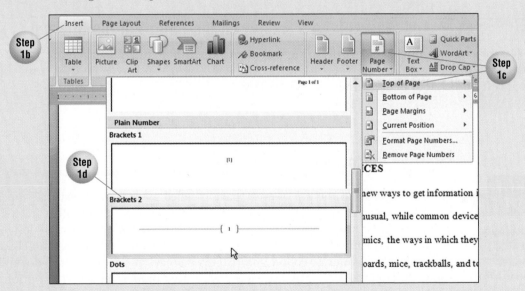

2. Double-click the document to make it active and then scroll through the document and notice the page numbering that displays at the top of each page except the cover page. (The cover page and text are divided by a section break, which you will learn more about in Chapter 5. Word considers the cover page as page 1 but does not include the numbering on the page.)
3. Remove the page numbering by clicking the Insert tab, clicking the Page Number button, and then clicking *Remove Page Numbers* at the drop-down list.

4. Click the Page Number button, point to *Bottom of Page*, scroll down the drop-down list and then click the *Circle* option.

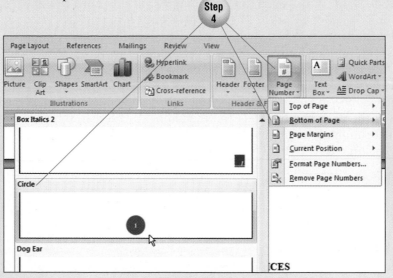

5. Save, print, and then close **WordL1_C4_P3.docx**.

P roject ④ **Add Elements to a Report on the Future of the Internet**

You will open a document containing information on the future of the Internet, insert a predesigned header and footer in the document, remove a header, and format and delete header and footer elements.

Inserting Predesigned Headers and Footers

Insert Predesigned Header
1. Click Insert tab.
2. Click Header button.
3. Click desired option at drop-down list.
4. Type text in specific placeholders in header.

Text that appears at the top of every page is called a ***header*** and text that appears at the bottom of every page is referred to as a ***footer***. Headers and footers are common in manuscripts, textbooks, reports, and other publications. Insert a predesigned header in a document by clicking the Insert tab and then clicking the Header button in the Header & Footer group. This displays the Header drop-down list as shown in Figure 4.7. At this list, click the desired predesigned header option and the header is inserted in the document. The header is visible in Print Layout view but not Draft view.

A predesigned header or footer may contain location placeholders where you can enter specific information. For example, a header might contain the placeholder *[Type the document title]*. Click anywhere in the placeholder text and all of the placeholder text is selected. With the placeholder text selected, type the desired text. You can delete a placeholder by clicking anywhere in the placeholder text, clicking the placeholder tab, and then pressing the Delete key.

Figure 4.7 Header Drop-down List

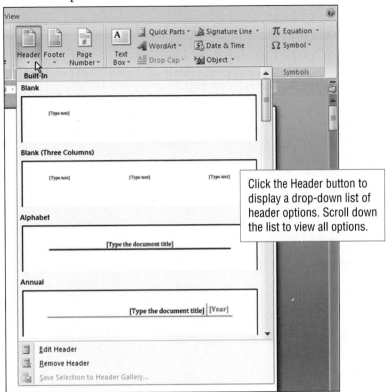

Click the Header button to display a drop-down list of header options. Scroll down the list to view all options.

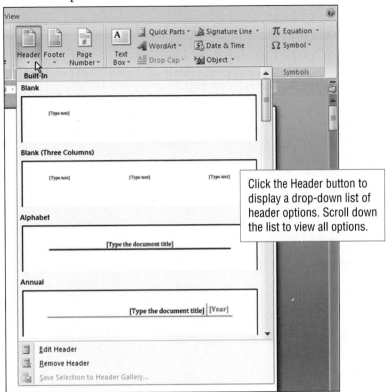

Project **4a**   **Inserting a Predesigned Header in a Document**

1. Open **WordReport02.docx**.
2. Save the document with Save As and name it **WordL1_C4_P4**.
3. Make the following changes to the document:
   a. Select the entire document, change the line spacing to *2*, and then deselect the document.
   b. Change the Quick Styles set to *Formal*. (*Hint: Use the Changes Styles button in the Styles group in the Home tab.*)
   c. Apply the *Heading 1* style to the title *FUTURE OF THE INTERNET*.
   d. Apply the *Heading 2* style to the headings *Satellite Internet Connections*, *Second Internet*, *Internet Services for a Fee*, and *Internet in 2030*.
   e. Move the insertion point to the beginning of the heading *INTERNET IN 2030* (located at the bottom of page 2) and then insert a page break by clicking the Insert tab and then clicking the Page Break button in the Pages group.

4. Press Ctrl + Home to move the insertion point to the beginning of the document and then insert a header by completing the following steps:
   a. If necessary, click the Insert tab.
   b. Click the Header button in the Header & Footer group.
   c. Scroll to the bottom of the drop-down list that displays and then click *Tiles*.

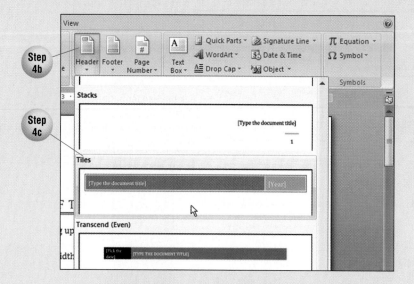

d. Click anywhere in the placeholder text *[Type the document title]* and then type Future of the Internet.
e. Click anywhere in the placeholder text *[Year]* and then type the current year.
f. Double-click in the document text. (This makes the document text active and dims the header.)

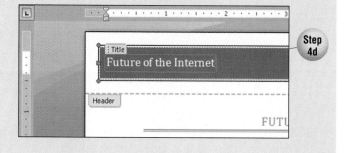

5. Scroll through the document to see how the header will print.
6. Save and then print **WordL1_C4_P4.docx**.

QUICK STEPS

Insert Predesigned Footer
1. Click Insert tab.
2. Click Footer button.
3. Click desired option at drop-down list.
5. Type text in specific placeholders in footer.

Insert a predesigned footer in the same manner as inserting a header. Click the Footer button in the Header & Footer group in the Insert tab and a drop-down list displays similar to the Header drop-down list shown in Figure 4.7. Click the desired footer and the predesigned footer formatting is applied to the document.

Removing a Header or Footer

Remove a header from a document by clicking the Insert tab and then clicking the Header button in the Header & Footer group. At the drop-down list that displays, click the *Remove Header* option. Complete similar steps to remove a footer.

1. With **WordL1_C4_P4.docx** open, press Ctrl + Home to move the insertion point to the beginning of the document.
2. Remove the header by clicking the Insert tab, clicking the Header button in the Header & Footer group, and then clicking the *Remove Header* option at the drop-down menu.

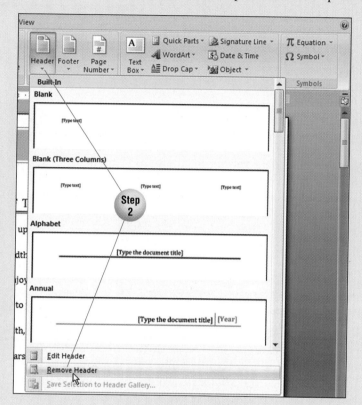

3. Insert a footer in the document by completing the following steps:
   a. Click the Footer button in the Header & Footer group.
   b. Click *Alphabet* at the drop-down list.

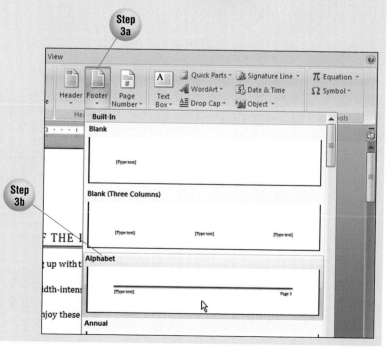

c. Click anywhere in the placeholder text *[Type text]* and then type Future of the Internet.

d. Double-click in the document text. (This makes the document text active and dims the footer.)

4. Scroll through the document to see how the footer will print.

5. Save and then print **WordL1_C4_P4.docx**.

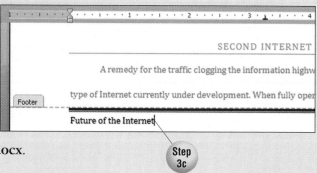

Step
3c

HINT

You can double-click a header or footer in Print Layout view to display the header or footer pane for editing.

Editing a Predesigned Header or Footer

Predesigned headers and footers contain elements such as page numbers and a title. You can change the formatting of the element by clicking the desired element and then applying the desired formatting. You can also select and then delete an item.

Project 4C **Formatting and Deleting Header and Footer Elements**

1. With **WordL1_C4_P4.docx** open, remove the footer by clicking the Insert tab, clicking the Footer button, and then clicking *Remove Footer* at the drop-down list.

2. Insert and then format a header by completing the following steps:

a. Click the Header button in the Header & Footer group in the Insert tab, scroll in the drop-down list, and then click *Motion (Odd Page)*. (This header inserts the document title as well as the page number.)

Step
2a

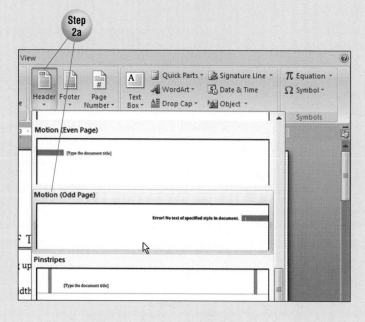

    b. Delete the document title from the header by clicking anywhere in the text *FUTURE OF THE INTERNET*, selecting the text, and then pressing the Delete key.

    c. Double-click in the document text.

3. Insert and then format a footer by completing the following steps:

    a. Click the Insert tab.

    b. Click the Footer button, scroll down the drop-down list, and then click *Motion (Odd Page)*.

    c. Click on any character in the date that displays in the footer, select the date, and then type the current date.

    d. Select the date, turn on bold, and then change the font size to 12.

    e. Double-click in the document text.

4. Scroll through the document to see how the header and footer will print.

5. Save, print, and then close **WordL1_C4_P4.docx**.

Project ⑤ Format a Report on Robots

You will open a document containing information on the difficulties of creating a humanlike robot and then insert a watermark, change page background color, and insert a page border.

Formatting the Page Background

The Page Background group in the Page Layout tab contains three buttons for customizing a page background. Click the Watermark button and choose a predesigned watermark from a drop-down list. If a document is going to be viewed on-screen or on the Web, consider adding a page color. In Chapter 3, you learned how to apply borders and shading to text at the Borders and Shading dialog box. This dialog box also contains options for inserting a page border.

Inserting a Watermark

A watermark is a lightened image that displays behind text in a document. Using watermarks is an excellent way to add visual appeal to a document. Word provides a number of predesigned watermarks you can insert in a document. Display these watermarks by clicking the Watermark button in the Page Background group in the Page Layout tab. Scroll through the list of watermarks and then click the desired option.

Changing Page Color

Use the Page Color button in the Page Background group to apply background color to a document. This background color is intended for viewing a document on-screen or on the Web. The color is visible on the screen but does not print. Insert a page color by clicking the Page Color button and then clicking the desired color at the color palette.

QUICK STEPS

Insert Watermark
1. Click Page Layout tab.
2. Click Watermark button.
3. Click desired option at drop-down list.

Change Page Color
1. Click Page Layout tab.
2. Click Page Color button.
3. Click desired option at color palette.

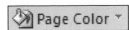

1. Open **WordReport07.docx** and then save the document and name it **WordL1_C4_P5**.
2. Apply the Heading 1 style to the title *ROBOTS AS ANDROIDS* and the Heading 2 style to the five headings in the document.
3. Change the Quick Styles set to *Formal*.
4. Insert a page break at the beginning of the heading *Tactile Perception*.
5. Insert a watermark by completing the following steps:
   a. Move the insertion point to the beginning of the document.
   b. Click the Page Layout tab.
   c. Click the Watermark button in the Page Background group.
   d. At the drop-down list, click the *CONFIDENTIAL 1* option.

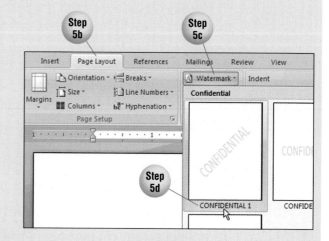

6. Scroll through the document and notice how the watermark displays behind the text.
7. Remove the watermark and insert a different one by completing the following steps:
   a. Click the Watermark button in the Page Background group and then click *Remove Watermark* at the drop-down list.
   b. Click the Watermark button and then click *DO NOT COPY 1* at the drop-down list.

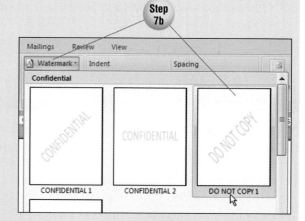

8. Scroll through the document and notice how the watermark displays.
9. Move the insertion point to the beginning of the document.
10. Click the Page Color button in the Page Background group and then click *Aqua, Accent 5, Lighter 80%* at the color palette.
11. Save **WordL1_C4_P5.docx**.

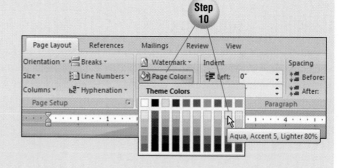

Inserting a Page Border

To improve the visual appeal of a document, consider inserting a page border. When you insert a page border in a multiple-page document, the border prints on each page. To insert a page border, click the Page Borders button in the Page Background group in the Page Layout tab. This displays the Borders and Shading dialog box with the Page Border tab selected as shown in Figure 4.8. At this dialog box, you can specify the border style, color, and width.

The dialog box contains an option for inserting a page border containing an image. To display the images available, click the down-pointing arrow at the right side of the *Art* list box. Scroll down the drop-down list and then click the desired image. (This feature may need to be installed the first time you use it.)

Insert Page Border
1. Click Page Layout tab.
2. Click Page Borders button.
3. Specify desired options at dialog box.

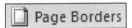

Figure 4.8 Borders and Shading Dialog Box with Page Border Tab Selected

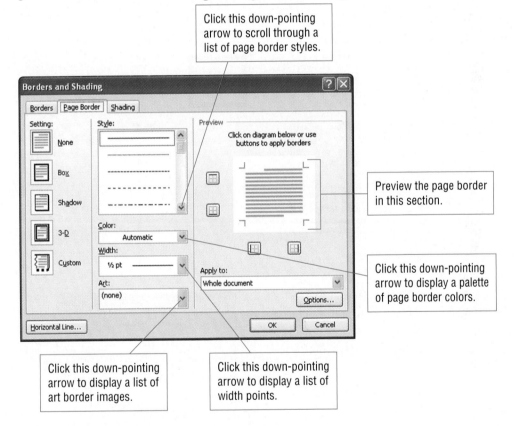

Click this down-pointing arrow to scroll through a list of page border styles.

Preview the page border in this section.

Click this down-pointing arrow to display a palette of page border colors.

Click this down-pointing arrow to display a list of art border images.

Click this down-pointing arrow to display a list of width points.

1. With **WordL1_C4_P5.docx** open, remove the page color by clicking the Page Color button in the Page Background group and then clicking *No Color* at the color palette.
2. Insert a page border by completing the following steps:
   a. Click the Page Borders button in the Page Background group in the Page Layout tab.
   b. Click the *Box* option in the *Setting* section.
   c. Scroll down the list of line styles in the *Style* list box until the end of the list displays and then click the third line from the end.
   d. Click the down-pointing arrow at the right of the *Color* list box and then click *Red, Accent 2, Darker 25%* at the color palette.
   e. Click OK to close the dialog box.

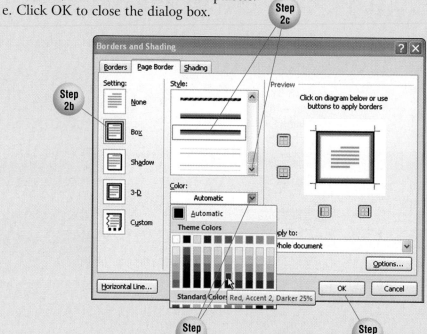

3. Save and then print **WordL1_C4_P5**.
4. Insert an image page border by completing the following steps:
   a. Click the Page Borders button in the Page Background group.
   b. Click the down-pointing arrow at the right side of the *Art* list box and then click the border image shown at the right.
   c. Click OK to close the dialog box.
5. Save, print, and then close **WordL1_C4_P5.docx**.

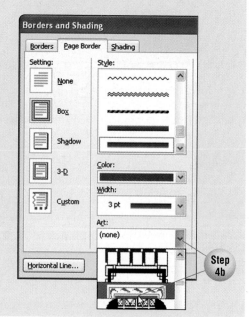

Project **6** **Format a Lease Agreement Document**

You will open a lease agreement document, search for specific text and replace it with other text, and then search for specific formatting and replace it with other formatting.

Finding and Replacing Text and Formatting

With Word's Find feature you can search for specific characters or formatting. With the Find and Replace feature, you can search for specific characters or formatting and replace them with other characters or formatting. The Find button and the Replace button are located in the Editing group in the Home tab.

Finding Text

With the Find feature, you can search a document for specific text. To use the Find feature, click the Find button in the Editing group in the Home tab or use the keyboard shortcut, Ctrl + F. This displays the Find and Replace dialog box with the Find tab selected as shown in Figure 4.9. Type the text you want to find in the *Find what* text box. Click the Find Next button and Word searches for and selects the first occurrence of the text in the document. Make corrections to the text if needed and then search for the next occurrence by clicking the Find Next button again. Click the Cancel button to close the Find and Replace dialog box.

QUICK STEPS

Find Text
1. Click Find button in Home tab.
2. Type search text.
3. Click Find Next button.

Figure 4.9 Find and Replace Dialog Box with Find Tab Selected

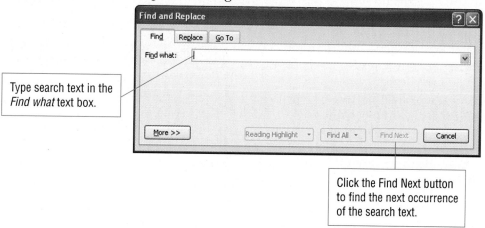

Type search text in the *Find what* text box.

Click the Find Next button to find the next occurrence of the search text.

Highlighting Find Text

You can use the Find feature to highlight specific text in a document. This can help you easily scan a document for every occurrence of the specific text. To find and highlight text, click the Find button, type the text you want highlighted in the *Find what* text box, click the Reading Highlight button, and then click *Highlight All* at the drop-down list. All occurrences of the text in the document are highlighted. To remove highlighting, click the Reading Highlight button and then click *Clear Highlighting* at the drop-down list.

Project 6a Finding Text and Finding and Highlighting Text

1. Open **WordAgreement01.docx** and then save the document and name it **WordL1_C4_P6**.
2. Find all occurrences of *lease* by completing the following steps:
   a. Click the Find button in the Editing group in the Home tab.
   b. At the Find and Replace dialog box with the Find tab selected, type **lease** in the *Find what* text box.
   c. Click the Find Next button.

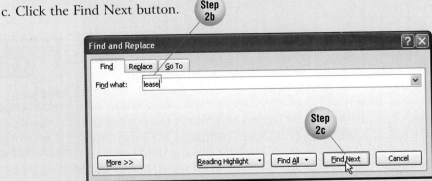

   d. Continue clicking the Find Next button until a message displays telling you that Word has finished searching the document. At this message, click OK.
3. Highlight all occurrences of *Premises* in the document by completing the following steps:
   a. At the Find and Replace dialog box with the Find tab selected, select the text in the *Find what* text box and then type **Premises**.
   b. Click the Reading Highlight button and then click *Highlight All* at the drop-down list.
   c. Click in the document to make it active and then scroll through the document and notice the occurrences of highlighted text.
   d. Click in the dialog box to make it active.
   e. Click the Reading Highlight button and then click *Clear Highlighting* at the drop-down list.

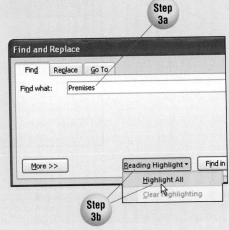

4. Click the Close button to close the Find and Replace dialog box.

Finding and Replacing Text

To find and replace text, click the Replace button in the Editing group in the Home tab or use the keyboard shortcut, Ctrl + H. This displays the Find and Replace dialog box with the Replace tab selected as shown in Figure 4.10. Type the text you want to find in the *Find what* text box, press the Tab key, and then type the replacement text.

Figure 4.10 Find and Replace Dialog Box with the Replace Tab Selected

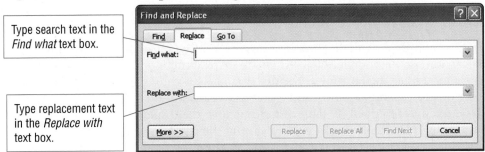

Type search text in the *Find what* text box.

Type replacement text in the *Replace with* text box.

QUICK STEPS

Find and Replace Text
1. Click Replace button in Home tab.
2. Type search text.
3. Press Tab key.
4. Type replace text.
5. Click Replace or Replace All button.

The Find and Replace dialog box contains several command buttons. Click the Find Next button to tell Word to find the next occurrence of the characters. Click the Replace button to replace the characters and find the next occurrence. If you know that you want all occurrences of the characters in the *Find what* text box replaced with the characters in the *Replace with* text box, click the Replace All button. This replaces every occurrence from the location of the insertion point to the beginning or end of the document (depending on the search direction). Click the Cancel button to close the Find and Replace dialog box.

HINT

If the Find and Replace dialog box is in the way of specific text, drag the dialog box to a different location.

Project 6b   **Finding and Replacing Text**

1. With **WordL1_C4_P6.docx** open, make sure the insertion point is positioned at the beginning of the document.
2. Find all occurrences of *Lessor* and replace with *Tracy Hartford* by completing the following steps:
   a. Click the Replace button in the Editing group in the Home tab.
   b. At the Find and Replace dialog box with the Replace tab selected, type Lessor in the *Find what* text box.
   c. Press the Tab key to move the insertion point to the *Replace with* text box.
   d. Type Tracy Hartford.
   e. Click the Replace All button.

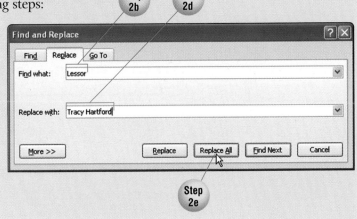

Step 2b

Step 2d

Step 2e

f. At the message *Word has completed its search of the document and has made 11 replacements*, click OK. (Do not close the Find and Replace dialog box.)

3. With the Find and Replace dialog box still open, complete steps similar to those in Step 2 to find all occurrences of *Lessee* and replace with *Michael Iwami*.

4. Close the Find and Replace dialog box.

5. Save **WordL1_C4_P6.docx**.

Choosing Check Box Options

The Find and Replace dialog box contains a variety of check boxes with options you can choose for completing a search. To display these options, click the More button located at the bottom of the dialog box. This causes the Find and Replace dialog box to expand as shown in Figure 4.11. Each option and what will occur if it is selected is described in Table 4.2. To remove the display of options, click the Less button. (The Less button was previously the More button.) Note that if you make a mistake when replacing text, you can close the Find and Replace dialog box and then click the Undo button on the Quick Access toolbar.

Figure 4.11 Expanded Find and Replace Dialog Box

Specify search options with options in this section.

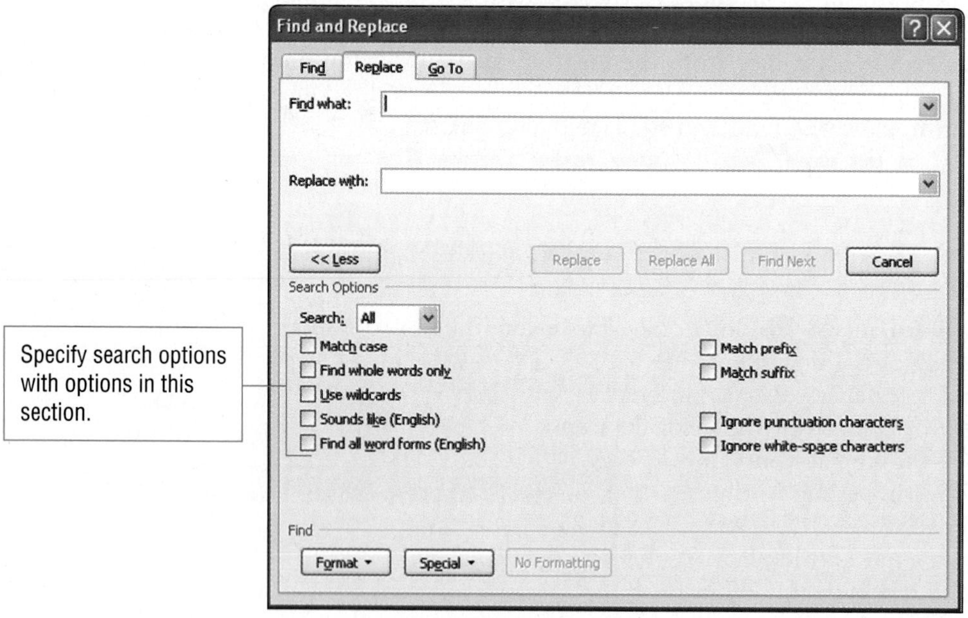

Table 4.2 Options at the Expanded Find and Replace Dialog Box

Choose this option	*To*
Match case	Exactly match the case of the search text. For example, if you search for *Book* and select the *Match case* option, Word will stop at *Book* but not *book* or *BOOK*.
Find whole words only	Find a whole word, not a part of a word. For example, if you search for *her* and did not select *Find whole words only*, Word would stop at *there*, *here*, *hers*, etc.
Use wildcards	Search for wildcards, special characters, or special search operators.
Sounds like	Match words that sound alike but are spelled differently such as *know* and *no*.
Find all word forms	Find all forms of the word entered in the *Find what* text box. For example, if you enter *hold*, Word will stop at *held* and *holding*.
Match prefix	Find only those words that begin with the letters in the *Find what* text box. For example, if you enter *per*, Word will stop at words such as *perform* and *perfect* but skip words such as *super* and *hyperlink*.
Match suffix	Find only those words that end with the letters in the *Find what* text box. For example, if you enter *ly*, Word will stop at words such as *accurately* and *quietly* but skip over words such as *catalyst* and *lyre*.
Ignore punctuation characters	Ignore punctuation within characters. For example, if you enter *US* in the *Find what* text box, Word will stop at *U.S.*
Ignore white space characters	Ignore spaces between letters. For example, if you enter *F B I* in the *Find what* text box, Word will stop at *FBI*.

1. With **WordL1_C4_P6.docx** open, make sure the insertion point is positioned at the beginning of the document.
2. Find all word forms of the word *lease* and replace with *rent* by completing the following steps:

   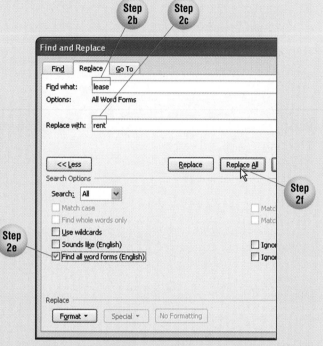

   a. Click the Replace button in the Editing group in the Home tab.
   b. At the Find and Replace dialog box with the Replace tab selected, type lease in the *Find what* text box.
   c. Press the Tab key and then type rent in the *Replace with* text box.
   d. Click the More button.
   e. Click the *Find all word forms* option. (This inserts a check mark in the check box.)
   f. Click the Replace All button.
   g. At the message telling you that Replace All is not recommended with Find All Word Forms, click OK.
   h. At the message *Word has completed its search of the document and has made 6 replacements*, click OK.
   i. Click the *Find all word forms* option to remove the check mark.
3. Find the word *less* and replace with the word *minus* and specify that you want Word to find only those words that end in *less* by completing the following steps:

   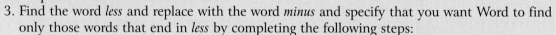

   a. At the expanded Find and Replace dialog box, select the text in the *Find what* text box and then type less.
   b. Select the text in the *Replace with* text box and then type minus.
   c. Click the *Match suffix* check box to insert a check mark and tell Word to find only words that end in *less*.
   d. Click the Replace All button.
   e. At the message telling you that 2 replacements were made, click OK.
   f. Click the *Match suffix* check box to remove the check mark.
   g. Click the Less button.
   h. Close the Find and Replace dialog box.
4. Save **WordL1_C4_P6.docx**.

Finding and Replacing Formatting

With options at the Find and Replace dialog box with the Replace tab selected, you can search for characters containing specific formatting and replace them with other characters or formatting. To specify formatting in the Find and Replace dialog box, click the More button and then click the Format button that displays toward the bottom of the dialog box. At the pop-up list that displays, identify the type of formatting you want to find.

Project 6d   Finding and Replacing Fonts

1. With **WordL1_C4_P6.docx** open, move the insertion point to the beginning of the document.
2. Find text set in 12-point Candara bold dark red and replace it with text set in 14-point Calibri bold dark blue by completing the following steps:
   a. Click the Replace button in the Editing group.
   b. At the Find and Replace dialog box, press the Delete key. (This deletes any text that displays in the *Find what* text box.)
   c. Click the More button. (If a check mark displays in any of the check boxes, click the option to remove the check mark.)
   d. With the insertion point positioned in the *Find what* text box, click the Format button located toward the bottom of the dialog box and then click *Font* at the pop-up list.
   e. At the Find Font dialog box, change the Font to *Candara*, the Font style to *Bold*, the Size to *12*, and the Font color to *Dark Red* (first color option from the left in the *Standard Colors* section).
   f. Click OK to close the Find Font dialog box.
   g. At the Find and Replace dialog box, click inside the *Replace with* text box and then delete any text that displays.
   h. Click the Format button located toward the bottom of the dialog box and then click *Font* at the pop-up list.

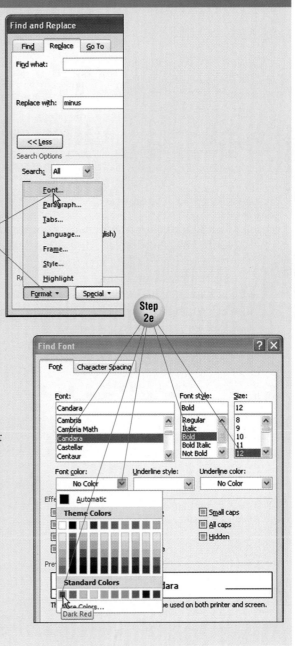

i. At the Replace Font dialog box, change the Font to *Calibri*, the Font style to *Bold*, the Size to *14*, and the Font color to *Dark Blue* (second color option from the right in the *Standard Colors* section).

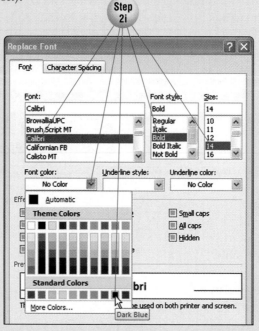

j. Click OK to close the Replace Font dialog box.
k. At the Find and Replace dialog box, click the Replace All button.
l. At the message telling you that the search of the document is complete and eight replacements were made, click OK.
m. Click in the *Find what* text box and then click the No Formatting button.
n. Click in the *Replace with* text box and then click the No Formatting button.
o. Click the Less button.
p. Close the Find and Replace dialog box.
3. Save, print, and then close **WordL1_C4_P6.docx**.

CHAPTER summary

- You can change the document view with buttons in the View section on the Status bar or with options in the View tab.
- Print Layout is the default view, which can be changed to other views such as Draft view or Full Screen Reading view.
- The Draft view displays the document in a format for efficient editing and formatting.
- Use the Zoom slider bar to change the percentage of the display.
- Full Screen Reading view displays a document in a format for easy viewing and reading.
- Navigate in Full Screen Reading view using keys on the keyboard or with the Next and Previous buttons.
- Navigate in a document using the Document Map or Thumbnails features. Click the *Document Map* check box in the View tab or the *Thumbnails* check box and a navigation pane displays at the left side of the screen.
- In Print Layout view, you can remove the white space at the top and bottom of pages.
- By default, a Word document contains 1-inch top, bottom, left, and right margins. Change margins with preset margin settings at the Margins drop-down list or with options at the Page Setup dialog box with the Margins tab selected.
- The default page orientation is portrait, which can be changed to landscape with the Orientation button in the Page Setup group in the Page Layout tab.
- The default page size is 8.5 by 11 inches, which can be changed with options at the Size drop-down list or options at the Page Setup dialog box with the Paper tab selected.
- The page break that Word inserts automatically is a soft page break. A page break that you insert is a hard page break. Insert a page break with the Page Break button in the Pages group in the Insert tab or by pressing Ctrl + Enter.
- Insert a blank page in a document by clicking the Blank Page button in the Pages group in the Insert tab.
- Insert a predesigned and formatted cover page by clicking the Cover Page button in the Pages group in the Insert tab and then clicking the desired option at the drop-down list.
- Insert predesigned and formatted page numbering by clicking the Page Number button in the Header & Footer group in the Insert tab, specifying the desired location of page numbers, and then clicking the desired page numbering option.
- Text that appears at the top of every page is called a header and text that appears at the bottom of every page is called a footer.
- You can insert predesigned headers and footers in a document with the Header button and the Footer button in the Header & Footer group in the Insert tab.
- A header or footer displays in Print Layout view but will not display in Draft view.
- You can remove and/or edit predesigned headers and footers.

- A watermark is a lightened image that displays behind text in a document. Use the Watermark button in the Page Background group in the Page Layout tab to insert a watermark.

- Insert page color in a document with the Page Color button in the Page Background group. Page color is designed for viewing a document on-screen and does not print.

- Click the Page Borders button in the Page Background group and the Borders and Shading dialog box with the Page Border tab selected displays. Use options at this dialog box to insert a page border or an image page border in a document.

- Use the Find feature to search for specific characters or formatting. Use the Find and Replace feature to search for specific characters or formatting and replace with other characters or formatting.

- At the Find and Replace dialog box, click the Find Next button to find the next occurrence of the characters and/or formatting. Click the Replace button to replace the characters or formatting and find the next occurrence, or click the Replace All button to replace all occurrences of the characters or formatting.

- Click the More button at the Find and Replace dialog box to display additional options for completing a search.

COMMANDS review

FEATURE	RIBBON TAB, GROUP	BUTTON	KEYBOARD SHORTCUT
Blank page	Insert, Pages	Blank Page	
Borders and Shading dialog box with Page Border tab selected	Page Layout, Page Background	Page Borders	
Cover page	Insert, Pages	Cover Page	
Document Map	View, Show/Hide	Document Map	
Draft view	View, Document Views		
Find and Replace dialog box with Find tab selected	Home, Editing	Find	Ctrl + F
Find and Replace dialog box with Replace tab selected	Home, Editing	Replace	Ctrl + H
Footer	Insert, Header & Footer		
Full Screen Reading view	View, Document Views		
Header	Insert, Header & Footer		
Margins	Page Layout, Page Setup		
Orientation	Page Layout, Page Setup	Orientation	
Page break	Insert, Pages	Page Break	Ctrl + Enter
Page color	Page Layout, Page Background	Page Color	
Page numbering	Insert, Header & Footer		
Page Setup dialog box with Margins tab selected	Page Layout, Page Setup	, *Custom Margins;* or Page Setup group dialog box launcher	
Page Setup dialog box with Paper tab selected	Page Layout, Page Setup	Size , *More Paper Sizes*	
Page size	Page Layout, Page Setup	Size	
Print Layout view	View, Document Views		
Thumbnails	View, Show/Hide	Thumbnails	
Watermark	Page Layout, Page Background	Watermark	

CONCEPTS check

Test Your Knowledge

Completion: In the space provided at the right, indicate the correct term, symbol, or command.

1. This is the default measurement for the top, bottom, left, and right margins.

_____

2. This view displays a document in a format for efficient editing and formatting.

_____

3. This view displays a document in a format for easy viewing and reading.

_____

4. The Document Map check box is located in this group in the View tab.

_____

5. Insert a check mark in the *Document Map* or *Thumbnails* check box and this displays at the left side of the screen.

_____

6. To remove white space, double-click this icon.

_____

7. This is the default page orientation.

_____

8. Set specific margins at this dialog box with the Margins tab selected.

_____

9. Press these keys on the keyboard to insert a page break.

_____

10. The Cover Page button is located in the Pages group in this tab.

_____

11. Text that appears at the top of every page is called this.

_____

12. A footer displays in Print Layout view, but not this view.

_____

13. A lightened image that displays behind text in a document is called this.

_____

14. The Page Borders button displays in this group in the Page Layout tab.

_____

15. If you want to replace every occurrence of what you are searching for in a document, click this button at the Find and Replace dialog box.

_____

16. Click this option at the Find and Replace dialog box if you are searching for a word and all of its forms.

_____

SKILLS check
Demonstrate Your Proficiency

Assessment

1 FORMAT A SOFTWARE LIFE CYCLE DOCUMENT AND CREATE A COVER PAGE

1. Open **WordDocument05.docx** and then save the document and name it **WordL1_C4_A1**.
2. Select the entire document, change the line spacing to 2, and then deselect the document.
3. Apply the Heading 1 style to the title of the document and apply the Heading 2 style to the headings in the document.
4. Change the Quick Styles set to *Fancy*.
5. Change the theme colors to *Flow*.
6. Insert a page break at the beginning of the heading *Testing*.
7. Move the insertion point to the beginning of the document and then insert the *Austere* cover page.
8. Insert the following text in the specified fields:
   a. Insert the current year in the *[Year]* placeholder.
   b. Insert your school's name in the *[Type the company name]* placeholder.
   c. If a name displays below your school's name, select the name and then type your first and last names.
   d. Insert *software life cycle* in the *[TYPE THE DOCUMENT TITLE]* placeholder (the placeholder will convert the text you type to all uppercase letters).
   e. Click the text below the document title, click the Abstract tab, and then press the Delete key twice.
9. Move the insertion point to any character in the title *COMMERCIAL LIFE CYCLE* and then insert the Box Italics 2 page numbering at the bottom of the pages (the page numbering will not appear on the cover page).
10. Save, print, and then close **WordL1_C4_A1.docx**.

Assessment

2 FORMAT AN INTELLECTUAL PROPERTY REPORT AND INSERT HEADERS AND FOOTERS

1. Open **WordReport03.docx** and then save the document and name it **WordL1_C4_A2**.
2. Select the entire document and then change the line spacing to 2 and the font to 12-point Constantia.
3. Select text from the beginning of the first paragraph of text to just above the *REFERENCES* title located toward the end of the document and then indent the first line to 0.25 inch.
4. Apply the Heading 1 style to the titles *PROPERTY PROTECTION ISSUES* and *REFERENCES* (located toward the end of the document).
5. Apply the Heading 2 style to the headings in the document.
6. Change the Quick Styles set to *Distinctive*.
7. Center the *PROPERTY PROTECTION ISSUES* and *REFERENCES* titles.
8. Select and then hang indent the paragraphs below the *REFERENCES* title.

9. Insert a page break at the beginning of the *REFERENCES* title.
10. Move the insertion point to the beginning of the document and then insert the Exposure header. Type Property Protection Issues in the *[Type the document title]* placeholder and, if necessary, insert the current date in the *[Pick the date]* placeholder.
11. Insert the Pinstripes footer and type your first and last names in the *[Type text]* placeholder.
12. Save and then print **WordL1_C4_A2.docx**.
13. Remove the header and footer.
14. Insert the *Austere (Odd Page)* footer and then make the following changes:
    a. Delete the *[Type the company name]* placeholder.
    b. Select the text and page number in the footer and then change the font to 10-point Constantia bold.
15. Insert the DRAFT 1 watermark in the document.
16. Insert a page border of your choosing to the document.
17. Save, print, and then close **WordL1_C4_A2.docx**.

Assessment

3 FORMAT A REAL ESTATE AGREEMENT

1. Open **WordContract02.docx** and then save the document and name it **WordL1_C4_A3**.
2. Find all occurrences of *BUYER* (matching the case) and replace with *James Berman*.
3. Find all occurrences of *SELLER* (matching the case) and replace with *Mona Trammell*.
4. Find all word forms of the word *buy* and replace with *purchase*.
5. Search for 14-point Tahoma bold formatting in dark red and replace with 12-point Times New Roman bold formatting in black.
6. Insert page numbers at the bottom of each page.
7. Save, print, and then close **WordL1_C4_A3.docx**.

CASE study

Apply Your Skills

You work for Citizens for Consumer Safety, a non-profit organization providing information on household safety. Your supervisor, Melinda Johansson, has asked you to attractively format a document on smoke detectors. She will be using the document as an informational handout during a presentation on smoke detectors. Open the document named **WordSmokeDetectors.docx** and then save the document and name it **WordL1_C4_CS_P1**. Apply a theme to the document and apply appropriate styles to the title and headings. Ms. Johansson has asked you to change the page orientation and then change the left and right margins to 1.5 inches. She wants the extra space at the left and right margins so audience members can write notes in the margins. Use the Help feature or experiment with the options in the Header & Footer Tools Design tab and figure out how to number pages on every page but the first page. Insert page numbering in the document that prints at the top right side of every page except the first page. Save, print, and then close **WordL1_C4_CS_P1.docx**.

After reviewing the formatted document on smoke detectors, Ms. Johansson has decided that she wants the document to print in the default orientation and she is not happy with the theme and style choices. She also noticed that the term "smoke alarm" should be replaced with "smoke detector." She has asked you to open and then format the original document. Open **WordSmokeDetectors.docx** and then save the document and name it **WordL1_C4_CS_P2**. Apply a theme to the document (other than the one you chose for Part 1) and apply styles to the title and headings. Search for all occurrences of *smoke alarm* and replace with *smoke detector*. Insert a cover page of your choosing and insert the appropriate information in the page. Use the Help feature or experiment with the options in the Header & Footer Tools Design tab and figure out how to insert an odd-page and even-page footer in a document. Insert an odd-page footer that prints the page number at the right margin and insert an even-page footer that prints the page number at the left margin. You do not want the footer to print on the cover page so make sure you position the insertion point below the cover page before inserting the footers. After inserting the footers in the document, you decide that they need to be moved down the page to create more space between the last line of text on a page and the footer. Use the Help feature or experiment with the options in the Header & Footer Tools Design tab to figure out how to move the footers down and then edit each footer so they display 0.3″ from the bottom of the page. Save, print, and then close **WordL1_C4_CS_P2.docx**.

Ms. Johansson has asked you to prepare a document on infant car seats and car seat safety. She wants this informational car seat safety document available for distribution at a local community center. Use the Internet to find Web sites that provide information on child and infant car seats and car seat safety. Write a report on the information you find that includes at least the following information:

- Description of the types of car seats (such as rear-facing, convertible, forward-facing, built-in, and booster)
- Safety rules and guidelines
- Installation information
- Specific child and infant seat models
- Sites on the Internet that sell car seats
- Price ranges
- Internet sites providing safety information

Format the report using a theme and styles and include a cover page and headers and/or footers. Save the completed document and name it **WordL1_C4_CS_P3**. Print and then close the document.

Editing and Formatting Documents

ASSESSING proficiency

In this unit, you have learned to create, edit, save, and print Word documents. You also learned to format characters, paragraphs, and pages.

word Unit 1

Note: Before beginning unit assessments, copy to your storage medium the Word2007L1U1 subfolder from the Word2007L1 folder on the CD that accompanies this textbook and then make Word2007L1U1 the active folder.

Assessment 1 Format *Designing an Effective Web Site* Document

1. Open **WordDocument08.docx** and then save the document and name it **WordL1_U1_A1**.
2. Complete a spelling and grammar check.
3. Select from the paragraph that begins *Make your home page work for you.* through the end of the document and then apply bullet formatting.
4. Select and then bold the first sentence of each bulleted paragraph.
5. Apply paragraph border and shading to the document title.
6. Save and then print **WordL1_U1_A1.docx**.
7. Change the top, left, and right margins to 1.5 inches.
8. Select the bulleted paragraphs, change the paragraph alignment to justified, and then insert numbering.
9. Select the entire document and then change the font to 12-point Constantia.
10. Insert the text shown in Figure U1.1 after paragraph number 2. (The number 3. should be inserted preceding the text you type.)
11. Save, print, and then close **WordL1_U1_A1.docx**.

Figure U1.1 Assessment 1

Avoid a cluttered look. In design, less is more. Strive for a clean look to your pages, using ample margins and white space.

Assessment 2 Format *Accumulated Returns* Document

1. Open **WordDocument09.docx** and then save the document and name it **WordL1_U1_A2**.
2. Select the entire document and then make the following changes:
   a. Click the No Spacing style.
   b. Change the line spacing to 1.5.
   c. Change the font to 12-point Cambria.
   d. Apply 6 points of spacing after paragraphs.

3. Select the title *TOTAL RETURN CHARTS*, change the font to 14-point Corbel bold, change the alignment to center, and apply paragraph shading of your choosing.
4. Bold the following text that appears at the beginning of the second through the fifth paragraphs:
   Average annual total return:
   Annual total return:
   Accumulation units:
   Accumulative rates:
5. Select the paragraphs of text in the body of the document (all paragraphs except the title) and then change the paragraph alignment to justified.
6. Select the paragraphs that begin with the bolded words, sort the paragraphs, and then indent the text 0.5 inch from the left margin.
7. Insert a watermark that prints *DRAFT* diagonally across the page.
8. Save, print, and then close **WordL1_U1_A2.docx**.

Assessment 3 Format Computer Ethics Report

1. Open **WordReport04.docx** and then save the document and name it **WordL1_U1_A3**.
2. Apply the *Foundry* theme to the document.
3. Apply the Heading 1 style to the titles *FUTURE OF COMPUTER ETHICS* and *REFERENCES*.
4. Apply the Heading 2 style to the headings in the document.
5. Change the Quick Styles set to *Modern*.
6. Change the theme colors to *Opulent*.
7. Center the two titles (*FUTURE OF COMPUTER ETHICS* and *REFERENCES*).
8. Hang indent the paragraphs of text below the *REFERENCES* title.
9. Insert page numbering that prints at the bottom of each page.
10. Save, print, and then close **WordL1_U1_A3.docx**.

Assessment 4 Set Tabs and Type Division Income Text in Columns

1. At a new blank document, type the text shown in Figure U1.2 with the following specifications:
   a. Bold and center the title as shown.
   b. You determine the tab settings for the text in columns.
   c. Select the entire document and then change the font to 12-point Arial.
2. Save the document and name it **WordL1_U1_A4**.
3. Print and then close **WordL1_U1_A4.docx**.

Figure U1.2 Assessment 4

INCOME BY DIVISION

	2007	2008	2009
Public Relations	$14,375	$16,340	$16,200
Database Services	9,205	15,055	13,725
Graphic Design	18,400	21,790	19,600
Technical Support	5,780	7,325	9,600

Assessment 5 Set Tabs and Type Table of Contents Text

1. At a new blank document, type the text shown in Figure U1.3 with the following specifications:
   a. Bold and center the title as shown.
   b. You determine the tab settings for the text in columns.
   c. Select the entire document, change the font to 12-point Bookman Old Style (or a similar serif typeface), and then change the line spacing to 1.5.
2. Save the document and name it **WordL1_U1_A5**.
3. Print and then close **WordL1_U1_A5.docx**.

Figure U1.3 Assessment 5

TABLE OF CONTENTS

Online Shopping... 2

Online Services... 4

Peer-to-Peer Online Transactions.............................. 5

Transaction Payment Methods.................................... 8

Transaction Security and Encryption........................ 11

Establishing a Web Site..14

Assessment 6 Format Union Agreement Contract

1. Open **WordContract01.docx** and then save the document and name it **WordL1_U1_A6**.
2. Find all occurrences of *REINBERG MANUFACTURING* and replace with *MILLWOOD ENTERPRISES*.
3. Find all occurrences of *RM* and replace with *ME*.
4. Find all occurrences of *LABOR WORKER'S UNION* and replace with *SERVICE EMPLOYEE'S UNION*.
5. Find all occurrences of *LWU* and replace with *SEU*.
6. Select the entire document and then change the font to 12-point Cambria and the line spacing to double.
7. Select the numbered paragraphs in the *Transfers and Moving Expenses* section and change to bullets.
8. Select the numbered paragraphs in the *Sick Leave* section and change to bullets.
9. Change the page orientation to landscape and the top margin to 1.5″.
10. Save and then print **WordL1_U1_A6.docx**.
11. Change the page orientation to portrait and the left margin (previously the top margin) back to 1″.
12. Insert a footer that prints *Union Agreement* at the left margin and the page number at the right margin.

13. Insert a cover page of your choosing and insert *UNION AGREEMENT* as the document name and *Millwood Enterprises* as the company name. Include any additional information required by the cover page.
14. Save, print, and then close **WordL1_U1_A6.docx**.

Assessment 7 Copy and Paste Text in Health Plan Document

1. Open **WordKeyLifePlan.docx** and then save the document and name it **WordL1_U1_A7**.
2. Open **WordDocument15.docx** and then turn on the display of the Clipboard task pane. Make sure the Clipboard is empty.
3. Copy to the Clipboard the heading *Plan Highlights* and the six paragraphs of text below the heading.
4. Copy to the Clipboard the heading *Plan Options* and the two paragraphs of text below the heading.
5. Copy to the Clipboard the heading *Quality Assessment* and the six paragraphs of text below the heading.
6. Close **WordDocument15.docx**.
7. With **WordL1_U1_A7.docx** open, display the Clipboard task pane.
8. Move the insertion point to the beginning of the *Provider Network* heading, paste the *Plan Options* item from the Clipboard, and match the destination formatting.
9. With the insertion point positioned at the beginning of the *Provider Network* heading, paste the *Plan Highlights* item from the Clipboard, and match the destination formatting.
10. Move the insertion point to the end of the document, paste the *Quality Assessment* item from the Clipboard, and match the destination formatting.
11. Clear the Clipboard and then close it.
12. Apply the Heading 1 style to the title, *KEY LIFE HEALTH PLAN*.
13. Apply the Heading 2 style to the headings in the document.
14. Change to a Quick Styles set of your choosing (other than the default).
15. Change to a theme of your choosing (other than the default).
16. Insert a page border of your choosing in the document.
17. Insert a header or footer of your choosing in the document.
18. Add a cover page of your choosing to the document.
19. Save, print, and then close **WordL1_U1_A7.docx**.

WRITING activities

The following activities give you the opportunity to practice your writing skills along with demonstrating an understanding of some of the important Word features you have mastered in this unit. Use correct grammar, appropriate word choices, and clear sentence constructions. Follow the steps explained below to improve your writing skills.

The Writing Process

Plan: Gather ideas, select which information to include, and choose the order in which to present the information.

Checkpoints

What is the purpose?

What information do the readers need in order to reach your intended conclusion?

Write: Following the information plan and keeping the reader in mind, draft the document using clear, direct sentences that say what you mean.

Checkpoints

What are the subpoints for each main thought?

How can you connect paragraphs so the reader moves smoothly from one idea to the next?

Revise: Improve what is written by changing, deleting, rearranging, or adding words, sentences, and paragraphs.

Checkpoints

Is the meaning clear?

Do the ideas follow a logical order?

Have you included any unnecessary information?

Have you built your sentences around strong nouns and verbs?

Edit: Check spelling, sentence construction, word use, punctuation, and capitalization.

Checkpoints

Can you spot any redundancies or clichés?

Can you reduce any phrases to an effective word (for example, change *the fact that* to *because*)?

Have you used commas only where there is a strong reason for doing so?

Did you proofread the document for errors that your spell checker cannot identify?

Publish: Prepare a final copy that could be reproduced and shared with others.

Checkpoints

Which design elements, for example, bolding and different fonts, would help highlight important ideas or sections?

Would charts or other graphics help clarify meaning?

Activity 1 Write Hyphenation Steps and Hyphenate Computer Text in Health Plan Document

Use Word's Help feature to learn about hyphenating text in a document. Learn how to hyphenate text automatically as well as manually. Create a document that contains the following:

1. Include an appropriate title that is bolded and centered.
2. Write the steps required to automatically hyphenate text in a document.
3. Write the steps required to manually hyphenate text in a document.

Save the document and name it **WordL1_U1_Hyphen**. Print and then close **WordL1_U1_Hyphen.docx**. Open **WordL1_U1_A3.docx** and then save the document and name it **WordL1_U1_Act01**. Manually hyphenate text in the document. Save, print, and then close **WordL1_U1_Act01.docx**.

Activity 2 Write Information on Customizing Spelling and Grammar

Use Word's Help feature to learn about grammar and style options. Learn about grammar options and what they detect and style options and what they detect. Also, learn how to set rules for grammar and style. Once you have determined this information, create a document describing at least two grammar options and at least two style options. Also include in this document the steps required to change the writing style from grammar only to grammar and style. Save the completed document and name it **WordL1_U1_Act02**. Print and then close **WordL1_U1_Act02.docx**.

INTERNET research

Research Business Desktop Computer Systems

You hold a part-time job at a local newspaper, *The Daily Chronicle*, where you conduct Internet research for the staff writers. Mr. Woods, the editor, has decided to purchase nine new desktop computers for the staff. He has asked you to identify at least three Macintosh PCs that can be purchased directly over the Internet, and he requests that you put your research and recommendations in writing. Mr. Woods is looking for solid, reliable, economical, and powerful desktop computers with good warranties and service plans. He has given you a budget of $1,300 per unit.

Search the Internet for three desktop Macintosh computer systems from three different manufacturers. Consider price, specifications (processor speed, amount of RAM, hard drive space, and monitor type and size), performance, warranties, and service plans when making your choice of systems. Print your research findings and include them with your report. (For helpful information on choosing a PC, read the article "Factors to Consider When Buying a PC," which is available in the Computer Concepts Resource Center at EMC/Paradigm's Web site. Go to www.emcp.com; click College Division and then click Resource Center for either *Computer Technology* or *Computers: Exploring Concepts*. Choose Student and then select the article under "Practical Tips for Computer Users.")

Using Word, write a brief report in which you summarize the capabilities and qualities of each of the three computer systems you recommend. Include a final paragraph detailing which system you suggest for purchase and why. If possible, incorporate user opinions and/or reviews about this system to support your decision. At the end of your report, include a table comparing the computer system. Format your report using the concepts and techniques you learned in Unit 1. Save the report and name it **WordL1_U1_InternetResearch**. Print and then close the file.

Level 1

Microsoft®

word

Unit 2: Enhancing and Customizing Documents

- ➤ Applying Formatting and Inserting Objects
- ➤ Maintaining Documents
- ➤ Creating Tables and SmartArt
- ➤ Merging Documents

Benchmark Microsoft® Word 2007 Level 1

Microsoft Certified Application Specialist Skills—Unit 2

Reference No.	Skill	Pages
1	**Creating and Customizing Documents**	
1.1	Create and format documents	
1.1.1	Use document templates	216-217
1.2	Lay out documents	
1.2.3	Create and design the appearance of columns	155-159
2	**Formatting Content**	
2.3	Control pagination	
2.3.2	Create and revise sections	154-155, 155-159
3	**Working with Visual Content**	
3.1	Insert illustrations	
3.1.1	Create SmartArt graphics	251-259
3.1.2	Add pictures from files and clip art	169-174
3.1.3	Add shapes to a document	177-184
3.2	Format illustrations	
3.2.1	Change text wrapping style	170-174
3.2.2	Size, crop, scale, and rotate images	170-174
3.2.4	Apply contrast, brightness, and coloration	169-172
3.2.5	Include text in SmartArt graphics and shapes	257-259
3.2.6	Reduce picture file size	169-172
3.3	Format text graphically	
3.3.1	Add and edit WordArt	184-185
3.3.2	Create Pull Quotes	175-177
3.3.3	Create and revise drop caps	162
3.4	Insert and modify text boxes	
3.4.1	Create text boxes	180-181
3.4.2	Design the appearance of text boxes	180-181
3.4.3	Connect text boxes with a link	182-183
4	**Organizing Content**	
4.2	Use tables and lists to organize content	225-229
4.2.1	Convert text to tables and lists and convert tables to text	247
4.2.2	Sort text	248
4.3	Modify tables	
4.3.1	Format tables with Quick Styles	229-230
4.3.2	Change table properties and options	234-236
4.3.3	Combine and split table cells	236-238
4.3.4	Calculate numbers in tables	249-251
4.3.5	Modify cell contents direction and position	243-244
4.5	Merge documents and data sources	
4.5.1	Create a data source and a main document	272-274, 275-276
4.5.2	Complete a merge with form letters	277, 283-285, 285-288
4.5.3	Merge envelopes and labels	278-280, 280-281
5	**Reviewing Documents**	
5.1	Navigate documents	
5.1.2	Change window views	201-205
6	**Sharing and Securing Content**	
6.1	Prepare documents for sharing	
6.1.1	Save a document in different formats	199-201

Note: The Level 1 and Level 2 texts each address approximately half of the Microsoft Certified Application Specialist skills. Complete coverage of the skills is offered in the combined Level 1 and Level 2 text titled *Benchmark Series Microsoft® Word 2007: Levels 1 and 2,* which has been approved as certified courseware and which displays the Microsoft Certified Application Specialist logo on the cover.

CHAPTER 5

Applying Formatting and Inserting Objects

PERFORMANCE OBJECTIVES

Upon successful completion of Chapter 5, you will be able to:

- Insert section breaks
- Create and format text in columns
- Hyphenate words automatically and manually
- Create a drop cap
- Insert symbols, special characters, and the date and time
- Use the Click and Type feature
- Vertically align text
- Insert, format, and customize pictures, clip art images, text boxes, shapes, and WordArt

Tutorial 5.1
Creating Presentable Documents
Tutorial 5.2
Using Additional Features

To apply page or document formatting to only a portion of the document, insert a section break. You can insert a continuous section break or a section break that begins a new page. A section break is useful when formatting text in columns. The hyphenation feature hyphenates words at the end of lines, creating a less ragged margin. Use buttons in the Text and Symbols groups in the Insert tab to insert symbols, special characters, and the date and time. With the Click and Type feature, you can position the insertion point at various locations in the document and change the paragraph alignment. Use the *Vertical alignment* option at the Page Setup dialog box with the Layout tab selected to align text vertically on the page. Along with these features, you will also learn how to increase the visual appeal of a document by inserting and customizing images such as pictures, clip art, text boxes, shapes, and WordArt.

Note: Before beginning computer projects, copy to your storage medium the Word2007L1C5 subfolder from the Word2007L1 folder on the CD that accompanies this textbook and then make Word2007L1C5 the active folder.

Project **1** Format a Document on Computer Input Devices

You will format into columns text in a document on computer input devices, improve the readability of the document by hyphenating long words, and improve the visual appeal by inserting a drop cap.

Inserting a Section Break

Insert a Section Break
1. Click Page Layout tab.
2. Click Breaks button.
3. Click section break type in drop-down list.

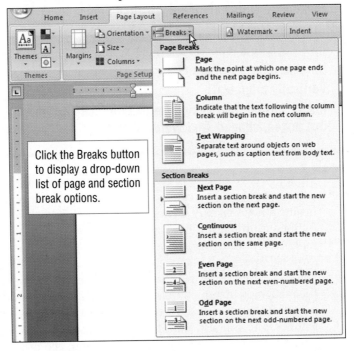

You can change the layout and formatting of specific portions of a document by inserting section breaks. For example, you can insert section breaks and then change margins for the text between the section breaks. If you want to format specific text in a document into columns, insert a section break.

Insert a section break in a document by clicking the Page Layout tab, clicking the Breaks button in the Page Setup group, and then clicking the desired option in the *Section Breaks* section of the drop-down list shown in Figure 5.1. You can insert a section break that begins a new page or a continuous section break that does not begin a new page. A continuous section break separates the document into sections but does not insert a page break. Click one of the other three options in the *Section Breaks* section of the Breaks drop-down list if you want to insert a section break that begins a new page.

Figure 5.1 Breaks Button Drop-down List

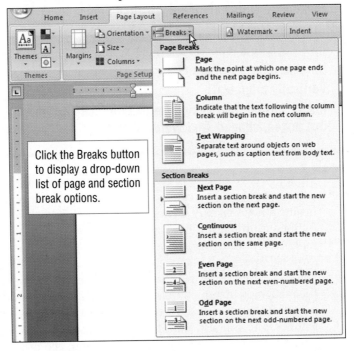

Click the Breaks button to display a drop-down list of page and section break options.

HINT
If you delete a section break, the text that follows the section break takes on the formatting of the text preceding the break.

A section break inserted in a document is not visible in Print Layout view. Click the Draft button and a section break displays in the document as a double row of dots with the words *Section Break* in the middle. Depending on the type of section break you insert, text follows *Section Break*. For example, if you insert a continuous section break, the words *Section Break (Continuous)* display in the middle of the row of dots. To delete a section break, change to Draft view, position the insertion point on the section break, and then press the Delete key.

1. Open **WordDocument16.docx** and then save it and name it **WordL1_C5_P1**.
2. Insert a continuous section break by completing the following steps:
   a. Move the insertion point to the beginning of the *Keyboard* heading.
   b. Click the Page Layout tab.
   c. Click the Breaks button in the Page Setup group and then click *Continuous* in the *Section Breaks* section of the drop-down list.
3. Click the Draft button in the view area on the Status bar and then notice the section break that displays across the screen.
4. Click the Print Layout button in the view area on the Status bar.
5. With the insertion point positioned at the beginning of the *Keyboard* heading, change the left and right margins to 1.5 inches. (The margin changes affect only the text after the continuous section break.)
6. Save and then print **WordL1_C5_P1.docx**.

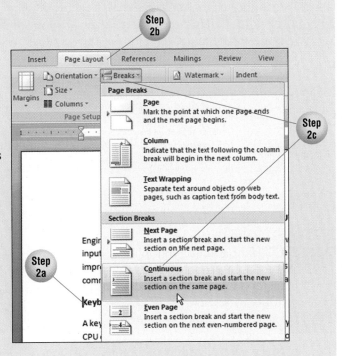

Creating Columns

When preparing a document containing text, an important point to consider is the readability of the document. Readability refers to the ease with which a person can read and understand groups of words. The line length of text in a document can enhance or detract from the readability of text. If the line length is too long, the reader may lose his or her place on the line and have a difficult time moving to the next line below. To improve the readability of some documents such as newsletters or reports, you may want to set the text in columns. One common type of column is newspaper, which is typically used for text in newspapers, newsletters, and magazines. Newspaper columns contain text that flows up and down in the document.

Create newspaper columns with the Columns button in the Page Setup group in the Page Layout tab or with options from the Columns dialog box. The Columns button creates columns of equal width. Use the Columns dialog box to create columns with varying widths. A document can include as many columns as room available on the page. Word determines how many columns can be included on the page based on the page width, the margin widths, and the size and spacing of the columns. Columns must be at least one-half inch in width. Changes in columns affect the entire document or the section of the document in which the insertion point is positioned.

QUICK STEPS

Create Columns
1. Click Page Layout tab.
2. Click Columns button.
3. Click on desired number of columns.

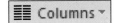

1. With **WordL1_C5_P1.docx** open, make sure the insertion point is positioned below the section break and then return the left and right margins to 1 inch.
2. Delete the section break by completing the following steps:
   a. Click the Draft button in the view area on the Status bar.
   b. Position the insertion point on the section break.

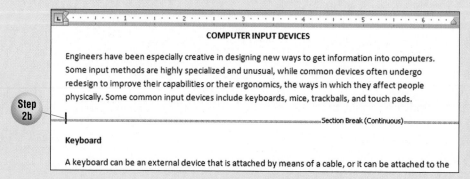

COMPUTER INPUT DEVICES

Engineers have been especially creative in designing new ways to get information into computers. Some input methods are highly specialized and unusual, while common devices often undergo redesign to improve their capabilities or their ergonomics, the ways in which they affect people physically. Some common input devices include keyboards, mice, trackballs, and touch pads.

Step 2b

Section Break (Continuous)

Keyboard

A keyboard can be an external device that is attached by means of a cable, or it can be attached to the

   c. Press the Delete key.
   d. Click the Print Layout button in the view area on the Status bar.
3. Move the insertion point to the beginning of the first paragraph of text in the document and then insert a continuous section break.
4. Format the text into columns by completing the following steps:
   a. Make sure the insertion point is positioned below the section break.
   b. Click the Page Layout tab.
   c. Click the Columns button in the Page Setup group.
   d. Click *Two* at the drop-down list.
5. Save **WordL1_C5_P1.docx**.

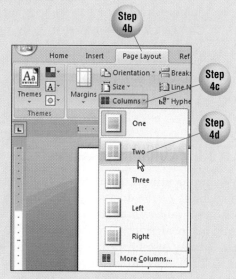

Step 4b

Step 4c

Step 4d

Creating Columns with the Columns Dialog Box

You can use the Columns dialog box to create newspaper columns that are equal or unequal in width. To display the Columns dialog box shown in Figure 5.2, click the Columns button in the Page Setup group of the Page Layout tab and then click *More Columns* at the drop-down list.

Figure 5.2 Columns Dialog Box

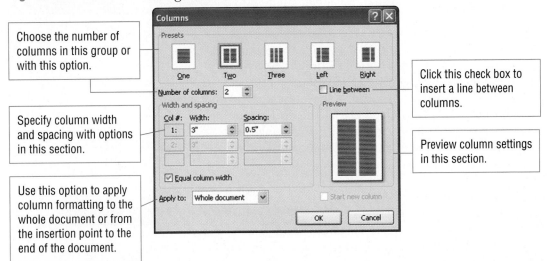

Choose the number of columns in this group or with this option.

Specify column width and spacing with options in this section.

Use this option to apply column formatting to the whole document or from the insertion point to the end of the document.

Click this check box to insert a line between columns.

Preview column settings in this section.

With options at the Columns dialog box you can specify the style and number of columns, enter your own column measurements, and create unequal columns. You can also insert a line between columns. By default, column formatting is applied to the whole document. With the *Apply to* option at the bottom of the Columns dialog box, you can change this from *Whole document* to *This point forward*. At the *This point forward* option, a section break is inserted and the column formatting is applied to text from the location of the insertion point to the end of the document or until other column formatting is encountered. The *Preview* section of the dialog box displays an example of how the columns will appear in your document.

Removing Column Formatting

To remove column formatting using the Columns button, position the insertion point in the section containing columns, click the Page Layout tab, click the Columns button, and then click *One* at the drop-down list. You can also remove column formatting at the Columns dialog box by selecting the *One* option in the *Presets* section.

Inserting a Column Break

When formatting text into columns, Word automatically breaks the columns to fit the page. At times, column breaks may appear in an undesirable location. You can insert a column break by positioning the insertion point where you want the column to end, clicking the Page Layout tab, clicking the Breaks button, and then clicking *Column* at the drop-down list.

HINT
You can also insert a column break with the keyboard shortcut, Ctrl + Shift + Enter.

1. With **WordL1_C5_P1.docx** open, delete the section break by completing the following steps:
   a. Click the Draft button in the view area on the Status bar.
   b. Position the insertion point on the section break and then press the Delete key.
   c. Click the Print Layout button in the view area on the Status bar.
2. Remove column formatting by clicking the Columns button in the Page Setup group in the Page Layout tab and then clicking *One* at the drop-down list.
3. Format text in columns by completing the following steps:
   a. Position the insertion point at the beginning of the first paragraph of text in the document.
   b. Click the Columns button in the Page Setup group and then click *More Columns* at the drop-down list.
   c. At the Columns dialog box, click *Two* in the *Presets* section.
   d. Click the down-pointing arrow at the right of the *Spacing* option box until *0.3″* displays.
   e. Click the *Line between* check box to insert a check mark.
   f. Click the down-pointing arrow at the right side of the *Apply to* option box and then click *This point forward* at the drop-down list.
   g. Click OK to close the dialog box.
4. Insert a column break by completing the following steps:
   a. Position the insertion point at the beginning of the *Mouse* heading.
   b. Click the Breaks button in the Page Setup group and then click *Column* at the drop-down list.

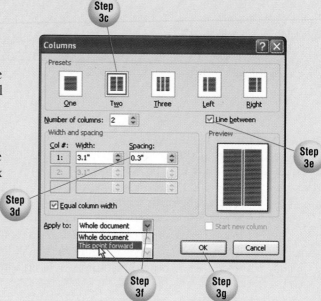

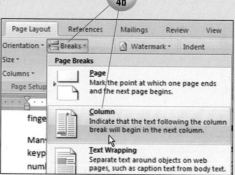

5. Save and then print **WordL1_C5_P1.docx**.

Balancing Columns on a Page

In a document containing text formatted into columns, Word automatically lines up (balances) the last line of text at the bottom of each column, except the last page. Text in the first column of the last page may flow to the end of the page, while the text in the second column may end far short of the end of the page. You can balance columns by inserting a continuous section break at the end of the text.

Project 1d Formatting and Balancing Columns of Text

1. With **WordL1_C5_P1.docx** open, delete the column break by completing the following steps:
   a. Position the insertion point at the beginning of the *Mouse* heading.
   b. Click the Draft button in the view area on the Status bar.
   c. Position the insertion point on the column break.

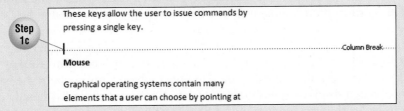

These keys allow the user to issue commands by pressing a single key.

Step 1c

··Column Break····

Mouse

Graphical operating systems contain many elements that a user can choose by pointing at

   d. Press the Delete key.
   e. Click the Print Layout button in the view area on the Status bar.
2. Select the entire document and then change the font to 12-point Constantia.
3. Move the insertion point to the end of the document and then balance the columns by clicking the Page Layout tab, clicking the Breaks button, and then clicking *Continuous* at the drop-down list.
4. Apply the Aqua, Accent 5, Lighter 60% paragraph shading to the title *COMPUTER INPUT DEVICES*.
5. Apply the Aqua, Accent 5, Lighter 80% paragraph shading to each of the headings in the document.
6. Insert page numbering that prints at the bottom of each page.
7. Save **WordL1_C5_P1.docx**.

Hyphenating Words

In some Word documents, especially documents with left and right margins wider than 1 inch, or text set in columns, the right margin may appear quite ragged. To improve the display of text lines by making line lengths more uniform, consider hyphenating long words that fall at the end of a text line. When using the hyphenation feature, you can tell Word to hyphenate words automatically in a document or you can manually insert hyphens.

Automatically Hyphenating Words

QUICK STEPS

Automatic Hyphenation
1. Click Page Layout tab.
2. Click Hyphenation button.
3. Click *Automatic* at drop-down list.

Manual Hyphenation
1. Click Page Layout tab.
2. Click Hyphenation button.
3. Click *Manual* at drop-down list.
4. Click Yes or No to hyphenate indicated words.
5. When complete, click OK.

To automatically hyphenate words in a document, click the Page Layout tab, click the Hyphenation button in the Page Setup group, and then click *Automatic* at the drop-down list. Scroll through the document and check to see if hyphens display in appropriate locations within the words. If, after hyphenating words in a document, you want to remove all hyphens, immediately click the Undo button on the Quick Access toolbar. This must be done immediately after hyphenating since the Undo feature undoes only the last function.

Manually Hyphenating Words

If you want to control where a hyphen appears in a word during hyphenation, choose manual hyphenation. To do this, click the Page Layout tab, click the Hyphenation button in the Page Setup group, and then click *Manual* at the drop-down list. This displays the Manual Hyphenation dialog box as shown in Figure 5.3. (The word in the *Hyphenate at* text box will vary.) At this dialog box, click Yes to hyphenate the word as indicated in the *Hyphenate at* text box; click No if you do not want the word hyphenated; or click Cancel to cancel hyphenation. You can also reposition the hyphen in the *Hyphenate at* text box. Word displays the word with syllable breaks indicated by a hyphen. The position where the word will be hyphenated displays as a blinking black bar. If you want to hyphenate at a different location in the word, position the blinking black bar where you want the hyphen and then click Yes. Continue clicking Yes or No at the Manual Hyphenation dialog box. Be careful with words ending in *-ed*. Several two-syllable words can be divided before that final syllable, for example, *noted*. However, one-syllable words ending in *-ed* should not be divided. An example is *served*. Watch for this type of occurrence and click No to cancel the hyphenation. At the hyphenation complete message, click OK.

HINT

Avoid dividing words at the ends of more than two consecutive lines.

b꜀ꜞ Hyphenation ▾

Figure 5.3 Manual Hyphenation Dialog Box

Click Yes to hyphenate the word at this location or move to a different syllable break and then click Yes.

Manual Hyphenation: English (U.S.)

Hyphenate at: er-go▮nom-ics

[Yes]   [No]   [Cancel]

1. With **WordL1_C5_P1.docx** open, hyphenate words automatically by completing the following steps:
   a. Press Ctrl + Home and then click the Page Layout tab.
   b. Click the Hyphenation button in the Page Setup group and then click *Automatic* at the drop-down list.

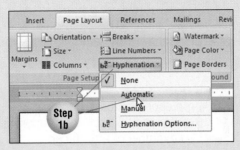

2. Scroll through the document and notice the automatic hyphenations.
3. Click the Undo button to remove the hyphens.
4. Manually hyphenate words by completing the following steps:
   a. Click the Hyphenation button in the Page Setup group and then click *Manual* at the drop-down list.

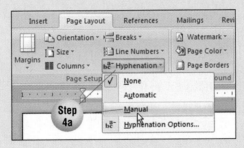

   b. At the Manual Hyphenation dialog box, make one of the following choices:
      • Click Yes to hyphenate the word as indicated in the *Hyphenate at* text box.
      • Move the hyphen in the word to a more desirable location, and then click Yes.
      • Click No if you do not want the word hyphenated.
   c. Continue clicking Yes or No at the Manual Hyphenation dialog box.
   d. At the hyphenation complete message, click OK.
5. Save **WordL1_C5_P1.docx**.

If you want to remove all hyphens in a document, immediately click the Undo button on the Quick Access toolbar. To delete a few, but not all, of the optional hyphens inserted during hyphenation, use the Find and Replace dialog box. To do this, you would display the Find and Replace dialog box with the Replace tab selected, insert an optional hyphen symbol in the *Find what* text box (to do this, click the More button, click the Special button and then click *Optional Hyphen* at the pop-up list), and make sure the *Replace with* text box is empty. Complete the find and replace, clicking the Replace button to replace the hyphen with nothing or clicking the Find Next button to leave the hyphen in the document.

Creating a Drop Cap

QUICK STEPS

Create Drop Cap
1. Click Insert tab.
2. Click Drop Cap button.
3. Click desired type in drop-down list.

A≣ Drop Cap ▾

Use a drop cap to enhance the appearance of text. A drop cap is the first letter of the first word of a paragraph that is set into a paragraph, as shown below. Drop caps identify the beginning of major sections or parts of a document. Create a drop cap with the Drop Cap button in the Text group in the Insert tab. You can choose to set the drop cap in the paragraph or in the margin. At the Drop Cap dialog box, you can specify a font, the numbers of lines you want the letter to drop, and the distance you want the letter positioned from the text of the paragraph. You can drop cap the first word by selecting the word first and then clicking the Drop Cap button.

D rop caps look best when set in a paragraph containing text set in a proportional font. Here is an example of a drop cap.

Project 1f Inserting Drop Caps

1. With **WordL1_C5_P1.docx** open, create a drop cap by completing the following steps:
   a. Position the insertion point on the first word of the first paragraph of text (*Engineers*).
   b. Click the Insert tab.
   c. Click the Drop Cap button in the Text group.
   d. Click *In margin* at the drop-down gallery.
2. Looking at the drop cap, you decide that you do not like it in the margin and want it to be a little smaller. To change the drop cap, complete the following steps:
   a. With the E in the word *Engineers* selected, click the Drop Cap button in the Text group and then click *None* at the drop-down gallery.
   b. Click the Drop Cap button and then click *Drop Cap Options* at the drop-down gallery.
   c. At the Drop Cap dialog box, click *Dropped* in the *Position* section.
   d. Change the font to Times New Roman.
   e. Change the *Lines to drop* option to *2*.
   f. Click OK to close the dialog box.
   g. Click outside the drop cap to deselect it.
3. Save **WordL1_C5_P1.docx**.

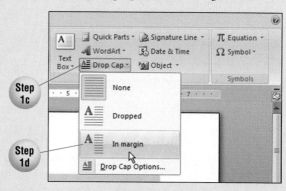

Step 1c

Step 1d

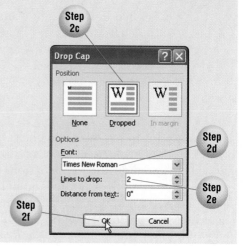

Step 2c

Step 2d

Step 2e

Step 2f

Inserting Symbols and Special Characters

You can use the Symbol button in the Insert tab to insert special symbols in a document. Click the Symbol button in the Symbols group in the Insert tab and a drop-down list displays with the most recently inserted symbols along with a *More Symbols* option. Click one of the symbols that displays in the list to insert it in the document or click the *More Symbols* option to display the Symbol dialog box as shown in Figure 5.4. At the Symbol dialog box, double-click the desired symbol, and then click Close; or click the desired symbol, click the Insert button, and then click Close.

QUICK STEPS

Insert a Symbol
1. Click Insert tab.
2. Click Symbol button.
3. Click desired symbol in drop-down list.
OR
1. Click Insert tab.
2. Click Symbol button.
3. Click *More Symbols*.
4. Double-click desired symbol.
5. Click Close.

Figure 5.4 Symbol Dialog Box with Symbols Tab Selected

Use the *Font* option to select the desired set of characters.

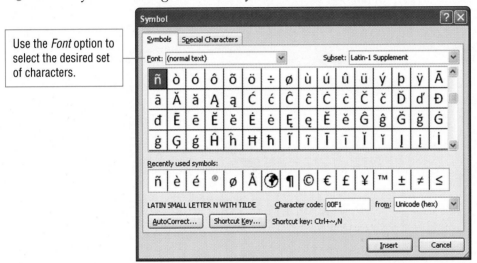

At the Symbol dialog box with the Symbols tab selected, you can change the font with the *Font* option. When you change the font, different symbols display in the dialog box. Click the Special Characters tab at the Symbol dialog box and a list of special characters displays along with keyboard shortcuts to create the special character.

Project 1g Inserting Symbols and Special Characters

1. With **WordL1_C5_P1.docx** open, press Ctrl + End to move the insertion point to the end of the document.
2. Press the Enter key once, type Prepared by:, and then press the spacebar once.
3. Type the first name Matthew.
4. Insert the last name *Viña* by completing the following steps:
   a. Type Vi.
   b. Click the Symbol button in the Symbols group in the Insert tab.
   c. Click *More Symbols* at the drop-down list.

d. At the Symbol dialog box, make sure the *Font* option displays as *(normal text)* and then double-click the ñ symbol (first symbol from the left in the twelfth row).

e. Click the Close button.

f. Type a.

5. Press Shift + Enter.

6. Insert the keyboard symbol (⌨) by completing the following steps:

a. Click the Symbol button and then click *More Symbols*.

b. At the Symbol dialog box, click the down-pointing arrow at the right side of the *Font* option and then click *Wingdings* at the drop-down list. (You will need to scroll down the list to display this option.)

c. Double-click ⌨ (eighth symbol from the left in the second row).

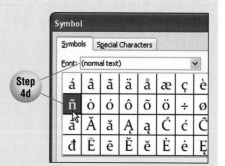

Step 4d

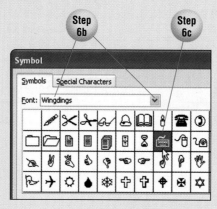

Step 6b   Step 6c

d. Click the Close button.

7. Type SoftCell Technologies.

8. Insert the registered trademark symbol (®) by completing the following steps:

a. Click the Symbol button and then click *More Symbols*.

b. At the Symbol dialog box, click the Special Characters tab.

c. Double-click the ® symbol (tenth option from the top).

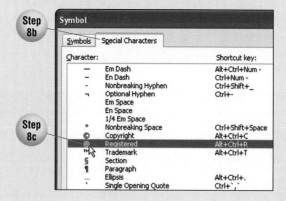

Step 8b

Step 8c

d. Click the Close button.

e. Press Shift + Enter.

9. Select the keyboard symbol (⌨) and then change the font size to 18.

10. Save **WordL1_C5_P1.docx**.

Inserting the Date and Time

Use the Date & Time button in the Text group in the Insert tab to insert the current date and time in a document. Click this button and the Date and Time dialog box displays as shown in Figure 5.5 (your date will vary from what you see in the figure). At the Date and Time dialog box, click the desired date and/or time format in the *Available formats* list box.

QUICK STEPS

Insert Date and Time
1. Click Insert tab.
2. Click Date and Time button.
3. Click option in list box.
4. Click OK.

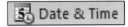

Figure 5.5 Date and Time Dialog Box

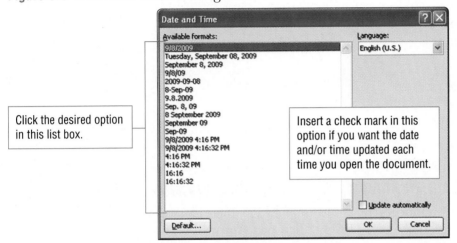

If the *Update automatically* check box does not contain a check mark, the date and/or time are inserted in the document as normal text that you can edit in the normal manner. You can also insert the date and/or time as a field. The advantage to inserting the date or time as a field is that the field can be updated with the Update Field keyboard shortcut, F9. Insert a check mark in the *Update automatically* check box to insert the data and/or time as a field. You can also insert the date as a field using the keyboard shortcut Alt + Shift + D, and insert the time as a field with the keyboard shortcut Alt + Shift + T.

Project 1b Inserting the Date and Time

1. With **WordL1_C5_P1.docx** open, press Ctrl + End and make sure the insertion point is positioned below the company name.
2. Insert the current date by completing the following steps:
   a. Click the Date & Time button in the Text group in the Insert tab.

b. At the Date and Time dialog box, click the third option from the top in the *Available formats* group.

c. Click in the *Update automatically* check box to insert a check mark.

d. Click OK to close the dialog box.

3. Press Shift + Enter.

4. Insert the current time by pressing Alt + Shift + T.

5. Save **WordL1_C5_P1.docx**.

6. Update the time by clicking the time and then pressing F9.

7. Save, print, and then close **WordL1_C5_P1.docx**.

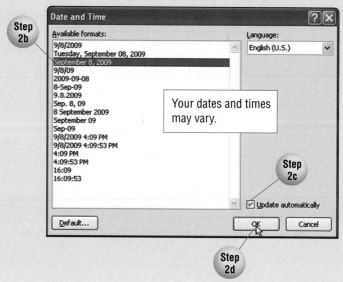

Step 2b

Your dates and times may vary.

Step 2c

Step 2d

P roject ② **Create an Announcement about Supervisory Training**

You will create an announcement about upcoming supervisory training and use the click and type feature to center and right align text. You will vertically center the text on the page and insert and format a picture to add visual appeal to the announcement.

Using the Click and Type Feature

QUICK STEPS

Use Click and Type
1. Hover mouse at left margin, between left and right margin, or at right margin.
2. Double-click left mouse button.

Word contains a click and type feature you can use to position the insertion point at a specific location and alignment in the document. This feature allows you to position one or more lines of text as you write (type), rather than typing the text and then selecting and reformatting the text, which requires multiple steps.

To use click and type, make sure the document displays in Print Layout view and then hover the mouse pointer at the location where you want the insertion point positioned. As you move the mouse pointer, you will notice that the pointer displays with varying horizontal lines representing the alignment. Double-click the mouse button and the insertion point is positioned at the location of the mouse pointer. Turn off the click and type feature by clicking the Office button and then clicking Word Options. Click the Advanced option in the left panel, click the *Enable click and type* check box to remove the check mark, and then click OK.

If the horizontal lines do not display next to the mouse pointer when you double-click the mouse button, a left tab is set at the position of the insertion point. If you want to change the alignment and not set a tab, make sure the horizontal lines display near the mouse pointer before double-clicking the mouse.

Project 2a Using Click and Type

1. At a blank document, create the centered text shown in Figure 5.6 by completing the following steps:
   a. Position the I-beam pointer between the left and right margins at about the 3.25-inch mark on the horizontal ruler and the top of the vertical ruler.
   b. When the center alignment lines display below the I-beam pointer, double-click the left mouse button.

   c. Type the centered text shown in Figure 5.6. Press Shift + Enter to end each text line.
2. Change to right alignment by completing the following steps:
   a. Position the I-beam pointer near the right margin at approximately the 1.5-inch mark on the vertical ruler until the right alignment lines display at the left side of the I-beam pointer.
   b. Double-click the left mouse button.
   c. Type the right-aligned text shown in Figure 5.6. Press Shift + Enter to end the text line.
3. Select the centered text and then change the font to 14-point Candara bold and the line spacing to double.
4. Select the right-aligned text, change the font to 10-point Candara bold, and then deselect the text.
5. Save the document and name it **WordL1_C5_P2**.

Figure 5.6 Project 2a

SUPERVISORY TRAINING

Maximizing Employee Potential

Wednesday, February 10, 2010

Training Center

9:00 a.m. to 3:30 p.m.

Sponsored by

Cell Systems

Vertically Aligning Text

Text in a Word document is aligned at the top of the page by default. You can change this alignment with the *Vertical alignment* option at the Page Setup dialog box with the Layout tab selected as shown in Figure 5.7. Display this dialog box by clicking the Page Layout tab, clicking the Page Setup group dialog box launcher, and then clicking the Layout tab at the Page Setup dialog box.

Figure 5.7 Page Setup Dialog Box with Layout Tab Selected

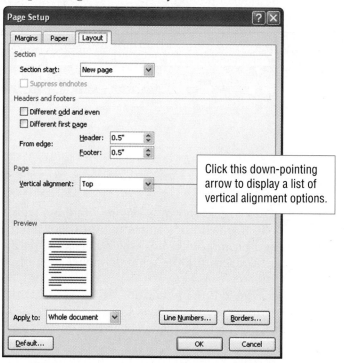

Click this down-pointing arrow to display a list of vertical alignment options.

Vertically Align Text
1. Click Page Layout tab.
2. Click Page Setup dialog box launcher.
3. Click Layout tab.
4. Click desired alignment.
5. Click OK.

The *Vertical alignment* option from the Page Setup dialog box contains four choices—*Top*, *Center*, *Justified*, and *Bottom*. The default setting is *Top*, which aligns text at the top of the page. Choose *Center* if you want text centered vertically on the page. The *Justified* option will align text between the top and the bottom margins. The *Center* option positions text in the middle of the page vertically, while the *Justified* option adds space between paragraphs of text (not within) to fill the page from the top to bottom margins. If you center or justify text, the text does not display centered or justified on the screen in the Draft view, but it does display centered or justified in the Print Layout view. Choose the *Bottom* option to align text in the document vertically along the bottom of the page.

1. With **WordL1_C5_P2.docx** open, click the Page Layout tab and then click the Page Setup group dialog box launcher.
2. At the Page Setup dialog box, click the Layout tab.
3. Click the down-pointing arrow at the right side of the *Vertical alignment* option box and then click *Center* at the drop-down list.
4. Click OK to close the dialog box.
5. Save and then print **WordL1_C5_P2.docx**.

Page Setup

| Margins | Paper | Layout |

Section

Section start: New page

☐ Suppress endnotes

Headers and footers

☐ Different odd and even
☐ Different first page

Header: 0.5"
From edge:
Footer: 0.5"

Step 2

Page

Vertical alignment: Top

Top
Center
Justified
Bottom

Step 3

Preview

Inserting an Image

You can insert an image such as a picture or clip art in a Word document with buttons in the Illustrations group in the Insert tab. Click the Picture button to display the Insert Picture dialog box where you can specify the desired picture file or click the Clip Art button and then choose from a variety of images available at the Clip Art task pane. When you insert a picture or a clip art image in a document, the Picture Tools Format Tab displays as shown in Figure 5.8.

Figure 5.8 Picture Tools Format Tab

Customizing and Formatting an Image

With options in the Adjust group in the Picture Tools Format tab you can recolor the picture or clip art image and change the brightness and contrast of the image. You can also reset the picture or clip art back to its original color or change to a different image. Use the Compress Pictures button to compress the size of the image file. Word provides predesigned styles you can apply to your image. These styles are available in the Picture Styles group along with buttons for changing the image border and applying effects to the image. Use options in the Arrange group to position the image on the page, specify text wrapping in relation to the image, align the image with other objects in the document, and rotate the image. Use the Crop button in the Size group to remove any unnecessary parts of the image and specify the image size with the *Shape Height* and *Shape Width* measurement boxes.

Sizing an Image

You can change the size of an image with the *Shape Height* and *Shape Width* measurement boxes in the Size group in the Picture Tools Format tab or with the sizing handles that display around the selected image. To change size with a sizing handle, position the mouse pointer on a sizing handle until the pointer turns into a double-headed arrow and then hold down the left mouse button. Drag the sizing handle in or out to decrease or increase the size of the image and then release the mouse button. Use the middle sizing handles at the left or right side of the image to make the image wider or thinner. Use the middle sizing handles at the top or bottom of the image to make the image taller or shorter. Use the sizing handles at the corners of the image to change both the width and height at the same time.

Moving an Image

Move an image to a specific location on the page with options from the Position button drop-down gallery. The Position button is located in the Arrange group in the Picture Tools Format tab. When you choose an option at the Position button drop-down gallery, the image is moved to the specified location on the page and square text wrapping is applied to the image.

You can also move the image by dragging it to the desired location. Before dragging an image, you must first choose a text wrapping style by clicking the Text Wrapping button in the Arrange group and then clicking the desired wrapping style at the drop-down list. After choosing a wrapping style, move the image by positioning the mouse pointer on the image border until the arrow pointer turns into a four-headed arrow. Hold down the left mouse button, drag the image to the desired position, and then release the mouse button. To help precisely position an image, consider turning on gridlines. Do this by clicking the Align button in the Arrange group in the Picture Tools Format tab and then clicking *Show Gridlines*.

Rotate the image by positioning the mouse pointer on the green, round rotation handle until the pointer displays as a circular arrow. Hold down the left mouse button, drag in the desired direction, and then release the mouse button.

Inserting a Picture

To insert a picture in a document, click the Insert tab and then click the Picture button in the Illustrations group. At the Insert Picture dialog box, navigate to the folder containing the desired picture and then double-click the picture. Use buttons in the Picture Tools Format tab to format and customize the picture. You can insert a picture from a Web page by opening the Web page, opening a Word document, and then dragging the picture from the Web page to the document. If the picture is linked, the link (rather than the image) will display in your document.

1. With **WordL1_C5_P2.docx** open, return the vertical alignment back to *Top* by completing the following steps:
   a. Click the Page Layout tab.
   b. Click the Page Setup group dialog box launcher.
   c. At the Page Setup dialog box, click the Layout tab.
   d. Click the down-pointing arrow at the right side of the *Vertical alignment* option box and then click *Top* at the drop-down list.
   e. Click OK to close the dialog box.
2. Select and then delete the text *Sponsored by* and the text *Cell Systems*.
3. Select the remaining text and change the line spacing to single.
4. Move the insertion point to the beginning of the document and then press the Enter key until the first line of text displays at approximately the 3-inch mark on the vertical ruler.
5. Insert a picture by completing the following steps:
   a. Click the Insert tab.
   b. Click the Picture button in the Illustrations group.
   c. At the Insert Picture dialog box, navigate to your Word2007L1C5 folder.
   d. Double-click **Mountain.jpg** in the list box.
6. Crop the picture by completing the following steps:
   a. Click the Crop button in the Size group.
   b. Position the mouse pointer on the bottom, middle crop handle (displays as a short black line) until the pointer turns into the crop tool (displays as a small, black T).
   c. Hold down the left mouse button, drag up to just below the mountain as shown at the right, and then release the mouse button.
   d. Click the Crop button in the Size group to turn off the feature.

Step 6c

Maximizing Employee

7. Increase the size of the picture by clicking in the *Shape Width* measurement box, typing 5, and then pressing Enter.
8. Move the picture behind the text by clicking the Text Wrapping button in the Arrange group and then clicking *Behind Text* at the drop-down list.

Step 8

9. Rotate the image by clicking the Rotate button in the Arrange group and then clicking *Flip Horizontal* at the drop-down list.

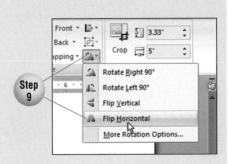

Step 9

10. Change the picture color by clicking the Recolor button in the Adjust group and then clicking the second option from the left in the Light Variations section (*Accent color 1 Light*).

11. After looking at the coloring you decide to return to the original color by clicking the Recolor button in the Adjust group and then clicking the option in the *No Recolor* section.

12. Click the Brightness button in the Adjust group and then click *+10%* at the drop-down gallery.

13. Click the Contrast button in the Adjust group and then click *-10%* at the drop-down gallery.

14. Apply a picture style by clicking the More button at the right side of the picture styles and then clicking *Soft Edge Rectangle* (first image from the left in the second row).

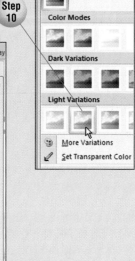

Step 10

Step 12

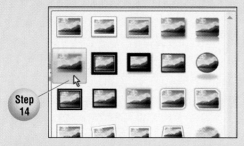

Step 14

15. Compress the picture by completing the following steps:
    a. Click the Compress Pictures button in the Adjust group.
    b. At the Compress Pictures dialog box, click the *Apply to selected pictures only* check box to insert a check mark.
    c. Click OK.

16. Position the mouse pointer on the border of the selected picture until the pointer turns into a four-headed arrow and then drag the picture so it is positioned behind the text.

17. Click outside the picture to deselect it.

18. Save, print, and then close **WordL1_C5_P2.docx**.

Step 15b

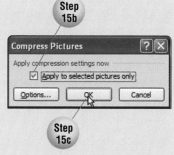

Step 15c

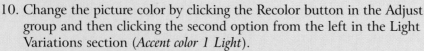

Project ③ **Customize a Report on Robots**

You will open a report on robots and then add visual appeal to the report by inserting and formatting a clip art image and a built-in text box.

Inserting a Clip Art Image

Microsoft Office includes a gallery of media images you can insert in a document such as clip art, photographs, and movie images, as well as sound clips. To insert an image in a Word document, click the Insert tab and then click the Clip Art button in the Illustrations group. This displays the Clip Art task pane at the right side of the screen as shown in Figure 5.9.

Figure 5.9 Clip Art Task Pane

Type the search word or topic in this text box.

Use this option to specify where to search.

Use this option to specify the type of files for which you are searching.

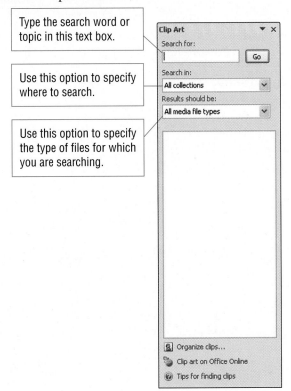

To view all picture, sound, and motion files, make sure the *Search for* text box in the Clip Art task pane does not contain any text and then click the Go button. When the desired image is visible, click the image to insert it in the document. Use buttons in the Picture Tools Format tab shown in Figure 5.8 to format and customize the clip art image.

By default (unless it has been customized), the Clip Art task pane looks for all media images and sound clips found in all locations. You can narrow the search to specific locations and to specific images. The *Search in* option at the Clip Art task pane has a default setting of *All collections*. This can be changed to *My Collections*, *Office Collections*, and *Web Collections*. The *Results should be* option has a default setting of *All media file types*. Click the down-pointing arrow at the right side of this option to display media types. To search for a specific media type, remove the check mark before all options at the drop-down list but the desired type. For example, if you are searching only for photograph images, remove the check mark before Clip Art, Movies, and Sounds.

If you are searching for specific images, click in the *Search for* text box, type the desired topic, and then click the Go button. For example, if you want to find images related to business, click in the *Search for* text box, type business, and then click the Go button. Clip art images related to *business* display in the viewing area of the task pane. If you are connected to the Internet, Word will search for images at the Office Online Web site matching the topic.

QUICK STEPS

Insert Clip Art Image
1. Click Insert tab.
2. Click Clip Art button.
3. Type search word or topic.
4. Press Enter.
5. Click desired image.

HINT
You can drag a clip art image from the Clip Art task pane to your document.

1. Open **WordReport07.docx** and then save the document and name it **WordL1_C5_P3**.
2. Apply the Heading 1 style to the title *ROBOTS AS ANDROIDS* and apply the Heading 2 style to the headings in the document.
3. Change the Quick Styles set to *Modern*. **Hint: Do this with the Change Styles button in the Styles group in the Home tab.**
4. Insert a clip art image by completing the following steps:

   a. Move the insertion point so it is positioned at the beginning of the first paragraph of text (the sentence that begins *Robotic factories are increasingly . . .*).
   b. Click the Insert tab.
   c. Click the Clip Art button in the Illustrations group.
   d. At the Clip Art task pane, select any text that displays in the *Search for* text box, type computer, and then press Enter.
   e. Click the computer image in the list box as shown at the right.
   f. Close the Clip Art task pane by clicking the Close button (contains an X) located in the upper right corner of the task pane.
5. Crop the clip art image by completing the following steps:

   a. Click the Crop button in the Size group.
   b. Position the mouse pointer on the top middle crop handle (displays as a short black line) until the pointer turns into the crop tool.
   c. Hold down the left mouse button, drag down to just above the top of the computer as shown at the right, and then release the mouse button.
   d. Click the Crop button in the Size group to turn off the feature.
6. Decrease the size of the picture by clicking in the *Shape Height* measurement box, typing 1.3, and then pressing Enter.
7. Change the text wrapping by clicking the Text Wrapping button in the Arrange group and then clicking *Square* at the drop-down list.
8. Rotate the image by clicking the Rotate button in the Arrange group and then clicking *Flip Horizontal* at the drop-down list.
9. Change the picture color by clicking the Recolor button in the Adjust group and then clicking the second option from the left in the Light Variations section (*Accent color 1 Light*).
10. Click the Picture Effects button in the Picture Styles group, point to *Shadow*, and then click the *Offset Diagonal Bottom Left* option (last option in the top row of the *Outer* section).

    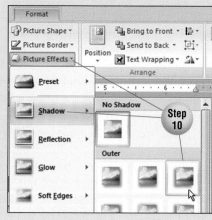

11. Position the mouse pointer on the border of the selected picture until the pointer turns into a four-headed arrow and then drag the picture so it is positioned as shown at the right.

    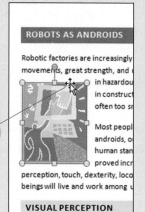

12. Click outside the clip art image to deselect it.
13. Save **WordL1_C5_P3.docx**.

Inserting and Customizing a Pull Quote

Use a pull quote in a document such as an article to attract attention. A pull quote is a quote from an article that is "pulled out" and enlarged and positioned in an attractive location on the page. Some advantages of pull quotes are that they reinforce important concepts, summarize your message, and break up text blocks to make them easier to read. If you use multiple pull quotes in a document, keep them in order to ensure clear comprehension for readers.

You can insert a pull quote in a document with a predesigned built-in text box. Display the available pull quote built-in text boxes by clicking the Insert tab and then clicking the Text Box button in the Text group. Click the desired pull quote from the drop-down list that displays and the built-in text box is inserted in the document. Type the quote inside the text box and then format the text and/or customize the text box. Use buttons in the Text Box Tools Format tab shown in Figure 5.10 to format and customize the built-in text box.

Inserting Pull Quote
1. Click Insert tab.
2. Click Text Box button.
3. Click desired pull quote.

Figure 5.10 Text Box Tools Format Tab

With options in the Text group in the Text Box Tools Format tab, you can draw a text box, change text direction in a text box, and link text boxes. Apply predesigned styles to a text box with options in the Text Box Styles group. You can also change the shape, shape fill, and shape outline. Add and customize shadows and 3-D effects with options in the Shadow Effects and 3-D Effects groups. Use options in the Arrange group to position the text box on the page, specify text wrapping in relation to the text box, align the text box with other objects in the document, and rotate the text box. Specify the image size with the *Shape Height* and *Shape Width* measurement boxes in the Size group.

1. With **WordL1_C5_P3.docx** open, click the Insert tab.
2. Click the Text Box button in the Text group.
3. Scroll down the drop-down list and then click the *Contrast Quote* option.

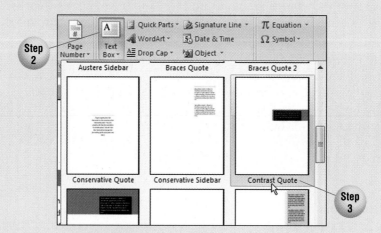

4. Type the following text in the text box: "The task of creating a humanlike body has proved incredibly difficult."
5. Click the More button at the right side of the Text Box Styles group.

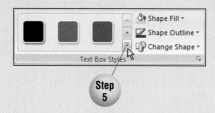

6. Click the blue *Diagonal Gradient - Accent 1* option at the drop-down gallery (second option from the left in the sixth row).
7. Click the Shadow Effects button in the Shadow Effects group and then click the *Shadow Style 5* option in the *Drop Shadow* section (first option from the left in the second row).

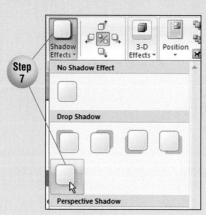

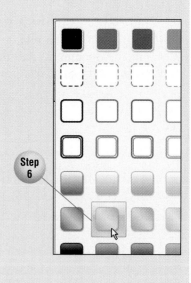

8. Position the mouse pointer on the border of the selected text box until the pointer turns into a four-headed arrow and then drag the text box so it is positioned as shown below.

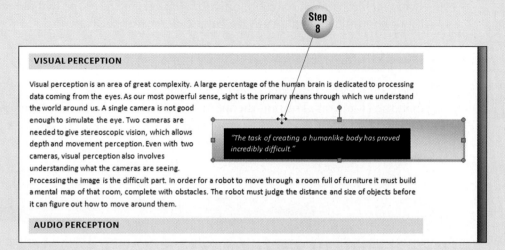

9. Save, print, and then close **WordL1_C5_P3.docx**.

Project ④ Prepare a Company Flyer

You will prepare a company flyer by inserting and customizing shapes, text boxes, and WordArt.

Drawing Shapes

QUICK STEPS

Draw a Shape
1. Click Insert tab.
2. Click Shapes button.
3. Click desired shape at drop-down list.
4. Drag in document screen to create shape.

Use the Shapes button in the Insert tab to draw shapes in a document including lines, basic shapes, block arrows, flow chart shapes, callouts, stars, and banners. Click a shape and the mouse pointer displays as crosshairs (plus sign). Position the crosshairs where you want the shape to begin, hold down the left mouse button, drag to create the shape, and then release the mouse button. This inserts the shape in the document and also displays the Drawing Tools Format tab shown in Figure 5.11. Use buttons in this tab to change the shape, apply a style to the shape, arrange the shape, and change the size of the shape. This tab contains many of the same options and buttons as the Picture Tools Format tab and the Text Box Tools Format tab.

Figure 5.11 Drawing Tools Format Tab

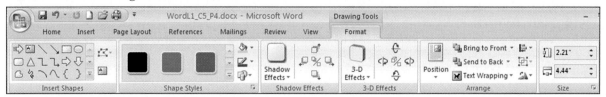

If you choose a shape in the *Lines* section of the drop-down list, the shape you draw is considered a *line drawing*. If you choose an option in the other sections of the drop-down list, the shape you draw is considered an ***enclosed object***. When drawing an enclosed object, you can maintain the proportions of the shape by holding down the Shift key while dragging with the mouse to create the shape.

Copying Shapes

To copy a shape, select the shape and then click the Copy button in the Clipboard group in the Home tab. Position the insertion point at the location where you want the copied image and then click the Paste button. You can also copy a selected shape by holding down the Ctrl key while dragging the shape to the desired location.

Project 4a   Drawing Arrow Shapes

1. At a blank document, press the Enter key twice and then draw an arrow shape by completing the following steps:
   a. Click the Insert tab.
   b. Click the Shapes button in the Illustrations group and then click the *Striped Right Arrow* shape in the *Block Arrows* section.

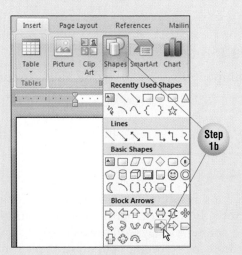

   c. Position the mouse pointer (displays as crosshairs) in the document at approximately the 1-inch mark on the horizontal ruler and the 0.5-inch mark on the vertical ruler.
   d. Hold down the Shift key and the left mouse button, drag to the right until the tip of the arrow is positioned at approximately the 5.5-inch mark on the horizontal ruler, and then release the mouse button and the Shift key.
2. Format the arrow by completing the following steps:
   a. Click in the *Shape Height* measurement box in the Size group, type 2.4, and then press Enter.
   b. Click in the *Shape Width* measurement box in the Size group, type 4.5, and then press Enter.

c. Click the More button at the right side of the Shape Styles group and then click the green *Linear Up Gradient - Accent 3* option at the drop-down gallery (fourth option from the left in the fifth row).

d. Click the 3-D Effects button in the 3-D Effects group and then click *3-D Style 6* in the *Perspective* section.

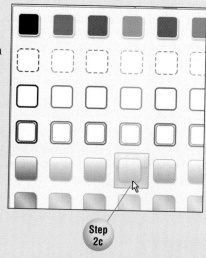

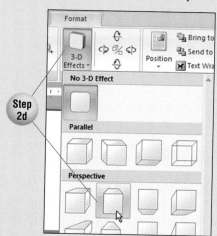

e. Click the 3-D Effects button, point to *3-D Color*, and then click the *Olive Green, Accent 3, Darker 50%* color.

3. Copy the arrow by completing the following steps:
   a. With the insertion point positioned in the arrow (mouse pointer displays with four-headed arrow attached), hold down the Ctrl key.
   b. Drag down until the outline of the copied arrow displays just below the top arrow, release the mouse button, and then release the Ctrl key.
   c. Copy the arrow again by holding down the Ctrl key and then dragging the outline of the copied arrow just below the second arrow.

4. Flip the middle arrow by completing the following steps:
   a. Click the middle arrow to select it.
   b. Click the Rotate button in the Arrange group and then click *Flip Horizontal* at the drop-down gallery.

5. Insert text in the top arrow by completing the following steps:
   a. Click the top arrow.
   b. Click the Edit Text button in the Insert Shapes group in the Drawing Tools Format tab.
   c. Click the Home tab.
   d. Change the font size to 16, turn on bold, and then change the font color to Olive Green, Accent 3, Darker 50%.

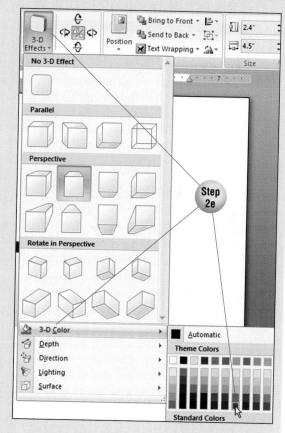

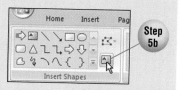

e. Click the Center button in the Paragraph group.
f. Type Financial.
g. Click the Text Box Tools Format tab.
h. Click the Text Direction button in the Text group.

6. Complete steps similar to those in Step 5 to insert the word *Direction* in the middle arrow. (Click twice on the Text Direction button to insert *Direction* in the tip of the arrow.)

7. Complete steps similar to those in Step 5 to insert the word *Retirement* in the bottom arrow.

8. Save the document and name it **WordL1_C5_P4**.

9. Print the document.

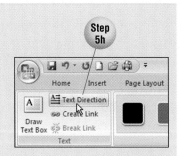
Step 5h

QUICK STEPS

Drawing and Formatting a Text Box

Draw a Text Box
1. Click Insert tab.
2. Click Text Box button in Text group.
3. Click *Draw Text Box*.
4. Drag in document screen to create box.

You can use the built-in text boxes provided by Word or you can draw your own text box. To draw a text box, click the Insert tab, click the Text Box button in the Text group, and then click *Draw Text Box* at the drop-down list. The mouse pointer displays as crosshairs. Position the crosshairs in the document and then drag to create the text box. When a text box is selected, the Text Box Tools Format tab displays as shown in Figure 5.11. Use buttons in this tab to format text boxes in the same manner as formatting built-in text boxes.

Project 4b   Inserting a Text Box in a Shape

1. With **WordL1_C5_P4.docx** open, delete the bottom arrow by completing the following steps:
   a. Click the bottom arrow. (This displays a border around the arrow.)
   b. Position the mouse pointer on the border (displays with four-headed arrow attached) and then click the left mouse button.
   c. Press the Delete key.

2. Insert a shape below the two arrows by completing the following steps:
   a. Click the Insert tab.
   b. Click the Shapes button in the Illustrations group and then click the *Bevel* shape in the *Basic Shapes* section.
   c. Scroll down the document to display the blank space below the bottom arrow.
   d. Position the mouse pointer (displays as crosshairs) in the document at approximately the 1-inch mark on the horizontal ruler and the 6.5-inch mark on the vertical ruler and then click the left mouse button. (This inserts a bevel shape in the document.)

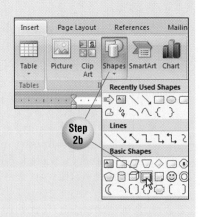
Step 2b

3. Format the shape by completing the following steps:
   a. Click in the *Shape Height* measurement box in the Size group, type 1.7, and then press Enter.
   b. Click in the *Shape Width* measurement box in the Size group, type 4.5, and then press Enter.
   c. Click the More button at the right side of the Shape Styles group and then click the *Linear Up Gradient - Accent 3* option at the drop-down gallery (fourth option from the left in the fifth row).
   d. Click the Shape Outline button arrow in the Shape Styles group and then click the *Olive Green, Accent 3, Darker 50%* color at the drop-down gallery.

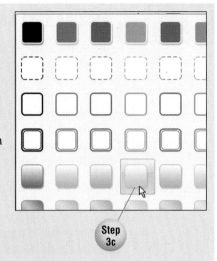

Step 3c

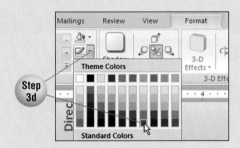

Step 3d

4. Insert a text box inside the shape by completing the following steps:
   a. Click the Insert tab.
   b. Click the Text Box button in the Text group and then click *Draw Text Box* at the drop-down list.
   c. Click inside the bevel shape.

Step 4c

5. Format the text box by completing the following steps:
   a. Click in the *Shape Width* measurement box in the Size group, type 3.5, and then press Enter.
   b. Drag the text box so it is centered inside the bevel shape.
   c. Click the Shape Fill button arrow in the Text Box Styles group and then click *No Fill* at the drop-down gallery.
   d. Click the Shape Outline button arrow in the Text Box Styles group and then click *No Outline* at the drop-down gallery.
6. Insert text inside the text box by completing the following steps:
   a. With the text box selected, click the Home tab.
   b. Change the font size to 24 points, turn on bold, and change the font color to Olive Green, Accent 3, Darker 50%.
   c. Click the Center button in the Paragraph group.
   d. Change the line spacing to 1.
   e. Type Retirement Financial Consulting. (Your shape and text box should appear as shown at the right.)
7. Save and then print **WordL1_C5_P4.docx**.

Step 6e

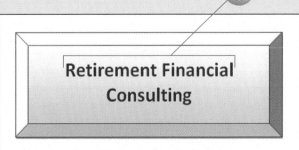

Link Text Boxes
1. Select first text box.
2. Click Create Link button.
3. Click empty text box.

⊖⊙ Create Link

Linking Text Boxes

You can create several text boxes and then have text flow from one text box to another by linking the text boxes. To do this, draw the desired text boxes and then select the first text box you want in the link. Click the Create Link button in the Text group in the Text Box Tools Format tab and the mouse pointer displays with a link image attached. Click an empty text box to link it with the selected text box. To break a link between two boxes, select the first text box in the link, click the Break Link button in the Text group, and then click the linked text box. When you break a link, all of the text is placed in the selected text box.

Project **4C**   **Linking Text Boxes**

1. With **WordL1_C5_P4.docx** open, delete the text in the arrow shapes by completing the following steps:
   a. Click *Financial* located in the top arrow.
   b. Drag through *Financial* to select it. (You will need to drag down to select the word since the word displays vertically rather than horizontally.)
   c. Press the Delete key.
   d. Click *Direction* in the bottom arrow.
   e. Select *Direction* and then press the Delete key.
2. Draw a text box inside the top arrow by completing the following steps:
   a. Click the Insert tab.
   b. Click the Text Box button in the Text group and then click *Draw Text Box* at the drop-down list.
   c. Draw a text box inside the top arrow.

Step
1b

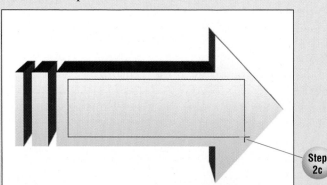

Step
2c

3. Format the text box by completing the following steps:
   a. Change the height measurement to *1"* and the width measurement to *3"*.
   b. Click the Shape Fill button arrow and then click *No Fill*.
   c. Click the Shape Outline button arrow and then click *No Outline*.
   d. Make sure the text box is centered in the arrow.
4. Copy the text box to the bottom arrow.
5. Click the text box in the top arrow to select it.

6. Link the top text box with the text box in the second arrow by clicking the Create Link button in the Text group and then clicking the text box in the second arrow.
7. With the top text box selected, make the following changes:
   a. Click the Home tab.
   b. Change the font size to 16 points, the font color to Olive Green, Accent 3, Darker 50%, and turn on bold.
   c. Change the line spacing to single.
   d. Click the Center button in the Paragraph group.
   e. Type Miller-Callahan Financial Services can help you plan for retirement and provide you with information to determine your financial direction. (The text will flow to the text box in the bottom arrow.)
8. Save **WordL1_C5_P4.docx**.

Selecting Objects

When a document contains a number of objects you may need to select multiple objects and then perform tasks such as formatting, moving, or aligning the objects. To select multiple objects, click the Select button in the Editing group in the Home tab and then click *Select Objects* at the drop-down list. Using the mouse, draw a border around the objects you want to select. When you click *Select Objects* at the drop-down list, the option in the drop-down list becomes active and the mouse arrow at the left side of the option displays with an orange background. To turn off object selecting, click the Select button and then click *Select Objects*. (This removes the orange background from the mouse arrow at the left side of the option.)

Select Objects
1. Click Select button.
2. Click *Select Objects*.
3. Draw border around objects to select.

Project 🔟 **Selecting, Moving, and Aligning Objects**

1. With **WordL1_C5_P4.docx** open, select the beveled shape and text box inside the shape by completing the following steps:
   a. Click the Zoom Out button located at the left side of the Zoom slider bar until *60%* displays at the left side of the button.
   b. Click the Home tab.
   c. Click the Select button in the Editing group and then click *Select Objects* at the drop-down list.
   d. Using the mouse, draw a border around the bevel shape. (When you release the mouse button, the shape is selected as well as the text box inside the shape.)

Step 1a

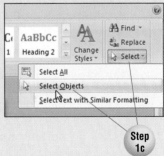

Step 1c

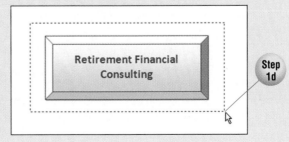

Retirement Financial Consulting

Step 1d

e. Position the mouse pointer on the border of the selected shape until the pointer displays as a four-headed arrow and then drag the shape down so the bottom of the shape is positioned at approximately the 8.5-inch mark on the vertical ruler.

f. Click outside the selected objects.

2. Select and move the arrows by completing the following steps:

a. Using the mouse, draw a border around the two arrows. (When you release the mouse button the arrows are selected as well as the text boxes in the arrows.)

b. Drag the arrows down so they are positioned just above the bevel shape.

c. Click outside the selected objects.

3. Select and then align all of the objects by completing the following steps:

a. Using the mouse, draw a border around the two arrows and the bevel shape.

b. Click the Drawing Tools Format tab.

c. Click the Align button in the Arrange group and then click *Align Center* at the drop-down list.

d. Click outside the selected objects.

e. Turn off object selecting by clicking the Select button in the Editing group and then clicking *Select Objects* at the drop-down list.

4. Save **WordL1_C5_P4.docx**.

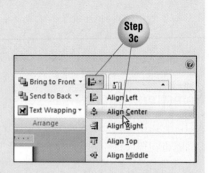

Creating and Modifying WordArt Text

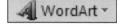

Create WordArt Text
1. Click Insert tab.
2. Click WordArt button.
3. Click desired WordArt style.
4. Type WordArt text.
5. Click OK.

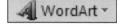
WordArt ▾

Use the WordArt feature to distort or modify text to conform to a variety of shapes. Consider using WordArt to create a company logo, letterhead, flier title, or heading. Insert WordArt in a document by clicking the Insert tab, clicking the WordArt button in the Text group, and then clicking the desired WordArt style at the drop-down list. Type the WordArt text at the Edit WordArt text dialog box and then click OK. You can also change the WordArt font and font size at the Edit WordArt Text dialog box.

You can customize WordArt with options and buttons in the WordArt Tools Format tab as shown in Figure 5.12. This tab displays when WordArt is selected in a document. With options and buttons at the WordArt Tools Format tab you can edit WordArt and change spacing, apply a WordArt style, change the shape fill and outline, apply shadow and 3-D effects, and arrange and size the WordArt.

Figure 5.12 WordArt Tools Format Tab

1. With **WordL1_C5_P4.docx** open, press Ctrl + Home to move the insertion point to the beginning of the document.
2. Insert WordArt by completing the following steps:
   a. Click the Insert tab.
   b. Click the WordArt button in the Text group and then click *WordArt style 15* at the drop-down list.

   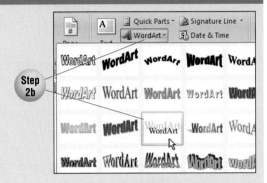
   Step 2b

   c. Type Miller-Callahan Financial Services in the Edit WordArt Text box and then click OK.
3. Format the WordArt text by completing the following steps:
   a. Click in the *Shape Height* measurement box, type 1, and then press Enter.
   b. Click in the *Shape Width* measurement box, type 6.5, and then press Enter.

   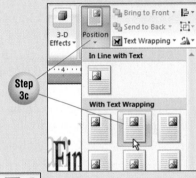
   Step 3c

   c. Click the Position button in the Arrange group and then click the middle option in the top row of the *With Text Wrapping* section (the option named *Position Top Center with Square Text Wrapping*).
   d. Click the Shadow Effects button in the Shadow Effects group and then click *Shadow Style 2* at the drop-down gallery (second option from the left in the top row of the *Drop Shadow* section).

   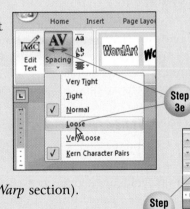
   Step 3d

   e. Click the Spacing button in the Text group and then click *Loose* at the drop-down list.
   f. Click the Shape Outline button arrow in the WordArt Styles group and then click the *Olive Green, Accent 3, Darker 50%* option.
   g. Click the Change WordArt Shape button in the WordArt Styles group and then click *Can Up* (third shape from the left in the top row of the *Warp* section).

   Step 3e

   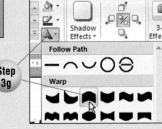
   Step 3g

4. Return the display to 100%.
5. Click outside the WordArt to deselect it.
6. Make sure that all of the objects fit on one page. Consider deleting blank lines between shapes to make sure all of the objects fit on the page.
7. Save, print, and then close **WordL1_C5_P4.docx**.

CHAPTER summary

- Insert a section break in a document to apply formatting to a portion of a document. You can insert a continuous section break or a section break that begins a new page. View a section break in Draft view since section breaks are not visible in Print Layout view.

- Set text in columns to improve readability of documents such as newsletters or reports. Format text in columns using the Columns button in the Page Setup group in the Page Layout tab or with options at the Columns dialog box.

- Remove column formatting with the Columns button in the Page Layout tab or at the Columns dialog box. Balance column text on the last page of a document by inserting a continuous section break at the end of the text.

- Improve the display of text lines by hyphenating long words that fall at the end of the line. You can automatically or manually hyphenate words in a document.

- To enhance the appearance of text, use drop caps to identify the beginning of major sections or parts of a paragraph. Create drop caps with the Drop Cap button in the Text group in the Insert tab.

- Insert symbols with options at the Symbol dialog box with the Symbols tab selected and insert special characters with options at the Symbol dialog box with the Special Characters tab selected.

- Click the Date & Time button in the Text group in the Insert tab to display the Date and Time dialog box. Insert the date or time with options at this dialog box or with keyboard shortcuts. If the date or time is inserted as a field, update the field with the Update Field key, F9.

- Use the click and type feature to center, right-align, and left-align text.

- Vertically align text in a document with the *Vertical alignment* option at the Page Setup dialog box with the Layout tab selected.

- Insert an image such as a picture or clip art with buttons in the Illustrations group in the Insert tab.

- Customize and format an image with options and buttons in the Picture Tools Format tab. Size an image with the *Shape Height* and *Shape Width* measurement boxes in the Picture Tools Format tab or with the sizing handles that display around the selected image.

- Move an image with options from the Position button drop-down gallery located in the Picture Tools Format tab or by choosing a text wrapping style and then moving the image by dragging it with the mouse.

- To insert a picture, click the Insert tab, click the Picture button, navigate to the desired folder at the Insert Picture dialog box, and then double-click the picture.

- To insert a clip art image, click the Insert tab, click the Clip Art button, and then click the desired image in the Clip Art task pane.

- Insert a pull quote in a document with a built-in text box by clicking the Insert tab, clicking the Text Box button, and then clicking the desired built-in text box at the drop-down list.

- Draw shapes in a document by clicking the Shapes button in the Illustrations group in the Insert tab, clicking the desired shape at the drop-down list, and then dragging in the document to draw the shape. Customize a shape with options at the Drawing Tools Format tab. Copy a shape by holding down the Ctrl key while dragging the selected shape.

- Draw a text box by clicking the Text Box button in the Text group in the Insert tab, clicking *Draw Text Box* at the drop-down list, and then clicking in the document or dragging in the document. Customize a text box with buttons at the Text Box Tools Format tab.

- Link drawn text boxes with the Create Link button in the Text group in the Text Box Tools Format tab. Break a link with the Break Link button in the Text group.

- Use WordArt to distort or modify text to conform to a variety of shapes. Customize WordArt with options at the WordArt Tools Format tab.

COMMANDS review

FEATURE	RIBBON TAB, GROUP	BUTTON	OPTION	KEYBOARD SHORTCUT
Continuous section break	Page Layout, Page Setup	Breaks ▾	Continuous	
Columns dialog box	Page Layout, Page Setup	Columns ▾	More Columns	
Columns	Page Layout, Page Setup	Columns ▾		
Hyphenate words automatically	Page Layout, Page Setup	Hyphenation ▾	Automatic	
Manual Hyphenation dialog box	Page Layout, Page Setup	Hyphenation ▾	Manual	
Drop cap	Insert, Text	Drop Cap ▾		
Symbol dialog box	Insert, Symbols	Ω Symbol ▾		
Date and Time dialog box	Insert, Text	Date & Time		
Insert date				Alt + Shift + D
Insert time				Alt + Shift + T
Update field				F9
Page Setup dialog box	Page Layout, Page Setup	▣		
Insert Picture dialog box	Insert, Illustrations	▣		
Clip Art task pane	Insert, Illustrations	▣		
Pull quote (Built-in text box)	Insert, Text	A		
Shapes	Insert, Illustrations	▣		
Text box	Insert, Text	A	Draw Text Box	
Link text box	Text Box Tools Format, Text	Create Link		
Select objects	Home, Editing	Select ▾	Select Objects	
WordArt	Insert, Text	WordArt ▾		

CONCEPTS check

Completion: In the space provided at the right, indicate the correct term, symbol, or command.

1. View a section break in this view. _____

2. Format text into columns with the Columns button located in this group in the Page Layout tab. _____

3. Balance column text on the last page of a document by inserting this type of break at the end of the text. _____

4. The first letter of the first word of a paragraph that is set into a paragraph is called this. _____

5. The Symbol button is located in this tab. _____

6. This is the keyboard shortcut to insert the current date. _____

7. Use this feature to position the insertion point at a specific location and alignment in a document. _____

8. Vertically align text with the *Vertical alignment* option at the Page Setup dialog box with this tab selected. _____

9. Insert an image in a document with buttons in this group in the Insert tab. _____

10. Customize and format an image with options and buttons in this tab. _____

11. Size an image with the sizing handles that display around the selected image or with these boxes in the Picture Tools Format tab. _____

12. Click the Picture button in the Insert tab and this dialog box displays. _____

13. Click the Clip Art button in the Insert tab and this displays at the right side of the screen. _____

14. This is the term for a quote that is enlarged and positioned in an attractive location on the page. _____

15. Format text boxes with options and buttons in this tab. _____

16. The Shapes button is located in this tab. _____

17. To copy a selected shape, hold down this key while dragging the shape.

_____

18. Link text boxes using this button in the Text group.

_____

19. To select multiple objects in a document, click the Select button in the Editing group in the Home tab and then click this option.

_____

20. Use this feature to distort or modify text to conform to a variety of shapes.

_____

SKILLS check
Demonstrate Your Proficiency

Assessment

1 ADD VISUAL APPEAL TO A REPORT ON THE FUTURE OF THE INTERNET

1. Open **WordReport02.docx** and then save the document and name it **WordL1_C5_A1**.
2. Remove the first line indent by selecting text from the beginning of the first paragraph of text to the end of the document and then dragging the First Line Indent marker on the horizontal ruler to the 0" mark.
3. Apply the Heading 1 style to the title of the report and apply the Heading 2 style to the headings in the report.
4. Change the Quick Styles set to *Formal*.
5. Format the text from the first paragraph to the end of the document into two columns with 0.4 inches between columns.
6. Select the title *FUTURE OF THE INTERNET* and then change the font size to 16 points, increase the spacing after the title to 12 points and, if necessary center-align the title.
7. Balance the text on the second page.
8. Insert a clip art image related to *satellite*. (Choose the clip art image that is available with Word and does not require downloading. This clip art image is blue and black and contains a satellite and a person holding a telephone and a briefcase.)
9. Make the following customizations to the clip art image:
   a. Change the height to 1.3".
   b. Apply tight text wrapping.
   c. Recolor the clip art image to Accent color 6 Dark.
   d. Change the brightness to +10%.
   e. Drag the image so it is positioned at the left margin in the *Satellite Internet Connections* section.
10. Insert the *Alphabet Quote* built-in text box and then make the following customizations:
   a. Type the following text in the text box: "A remedy for the traffic clogging the information highway is Internet2."

b. Select the text and then change the font size to 12 and change the line spacing to 1.15.

c. Apply the Linear Up Gradient - Accent 6 style to the text box (last option in the fifth row of the Text Box Styles drop-down gallery).

d. Apply a shadow effect of your choosing to the text box.

e. Drag the box so it is positioned above the SATELLITE INTERNET CONNECTIONS heading in the first column, below the SECOND INTERNET heading in the second column, and centered between the left and right margins.

11. Press Ctrl + End to move the insertion point to the end of the document. (The insertion point will be positioned below the continuous section break you inserted on the second page to balance the columns of text.)

12. Change back to one column.

13. Press the Enter key twice and then create a shape of your choosing and make the following customizations:

a. Recolor the shape to match the color formatting in the document or the built-in text box.

b. Position the shape centered between the left and right margins.

c. Make any other changes to enhance the visual appeal of the shape.

d. Draw a text box inside the shape.

e. Remove the shape fill and the shape outline.

f. Type the following text inside the text box: ☙Felicité Compagnie❧. Insert the ☙ and ❧ symbols at the Symbol dialog box with the Wingdings font selected. Insert the é symbol at the Symbol dialog box with the *(normal text)* font selected.

g. Insert the current date below ☙*Felicité Compagnie*❧ and insert the current time below the date.

h. Select and then center the text in the text box.

14. Manually hyphenate the document (do not hyphenate headings or proper names).

15. Create a drop cap with the first letter of the word *The* that begins the first paragraph of text.

16. Save, print, and then close **WordL1_C5_A1.docx**.

Assessment

2 CREATE A SALES MEETING ANNOUNCEMENT

1. Create an announcement about an upcoming sales meeting with the following specifications:

a. Insert the company name *Inlet Development Company* as WordArt text.

b. Insert the following text in the document:

> National Sales Meeting
> Northwest Division
> Ocean View Resort
> August 23 through 25, 2010

c. Insert the picture named ***Ocean.jpg*** and size and position the picture behind the text.

d. Make any formatting changes to the WordArt, text, and picture to enhance the visual appeal of the document.

2. Save the announcement document and name it **WordL1_C5_A2**.

3. Print and then close **WordL1_C5_A2.docx**.

CASE study

Apply Your Skills

Part 1

You work for Honoré Financial Services and have been asked by the office manager, Jason Monroe, to prepare an information newsletter. Mr. Monroe has asked you open the document named **WordBudget.docx** and then format it into columns. You determine the number of columns and any additional enhancements to the columns. He also wants you to proofread the document and correct any spelling and grammatical errors. Save the completed newsletter and name it **WordL1_C5_CS_P1** and then print the newsletter. When Mr. Monroe reviews the newsletter, he decides that it needs additional visual appeal. He wants you to insert visual elements in the newsletter such as WordArt, clip art, a built-in text box, and/or a drop cap. Save **WordL1_C5_CS_P1.docx** and then print and close the document.

Part 2

Honoré Financial Services will be offering a free workshop on Planning for Financial Success. Mr. Monroe has asked you to prepare an announcement containing information on the workshop. You determine what to include in the announcement such as the date, time, location, and so forth. Enhance the announcement by inserting a picture or clip art and by applying formatting such as font, paragraph alignment, and borders. Save the completed document and name it **WordL1_C5_CS_P2**. Print and then close the document.

Part 3

Honoré Financial Services has adopted a new slogan and Mr. Monroe has asked you to create a shape with the new slogan inside. Experiment with the shadow and 3-D effects available at the Text Box Tools Format tab and then create a shape and enhance the shape with shadow and/or 3-D effects. Insert the new Honoré Financial Services slogan "Retirement Planning Made Easy" in the shape. Include any additional enhancements to improve the visual appeal of the shape and slogan. Save the completed document and name it **WordL1_C5_CS_P3**. Print and then close the document.

Part 4

Mr. Monroe has asked you to prepare a document containing information on teaching children how to budget. Use the Internet to find Web sites and articles that provide information on how to teach children to budget their money. Write a synopsis of the information you find and include at least four suggestions on how to teach children to manage their money. Format the text in the document into newspaper columns. Add additional enhancements to improve the appearance of the document. Save the completed newsletter and name it **WordL1_C5_CS_P4**. Print and then close the document.

CHAPTER

Maintaining Documents

PERFORMANCE OBJECTIVES

Upon successful completion of Chapter 6, you will be able to:

- Create and rename a folder
- Select, delete, copy, move, rename, and print documents
- Save documents in different file formats
- Open, close, arrange, split, maximize, minimize, and restore documents
- Insert a file into an open document
- Print specific pages and sections in a document
- Print multiple copies of a document
- Print envelopes and labels
- Create a document using a Word template

Tutorial 6.1
Managing Folders and Multiple Documents
Tutorial 6.2
Printing Documents

Almost every company that conducts business maintains a filing system. The system may consist of documents, folders, and cabinets; or it may be a computerized filing system where information is stored on the computer's hard drive or other storage medium. Whatever type of filing system a business uses, daily maintenance of files is important to a company's operation. In this chapter, you will learn to maintain files (documents) in Word, including such activities as creating additional folders and copying, moving, and renaming documents. You will also learn how to create and print documents, envelopes, and labels and create a document using a Word template.

Note: Before beginning computer projects, copy to your storage medium the Word2007L1C6 subfolder from the Word2007L1 folder on the CD that accompanies this textbook and then make Word2007L1C6 the active folder.

 **Project ① Manage Documents**

You will perform a variety of file management tasks including creating and renaming a folder; selecting and then deleting, copying, cutting, pasting, and renaming documents; deleting a folder; and opening, printing, and closing a document.

Maintaining Documents

Many file (document) management tasks can be completed at the Open dialog box (and some at the Save As dialog box). These tasks can include copying, moving, printing, and renaming documents; opening multiple documents; and creating a new folder and renaming a folder.

Creating a Folder

Create a Folder
1. Display Open dialog box.
2. Click Create New Folder button.
3. Type folder name.
4. Press Enter.

Create New Folder

Up One Level

Back

In Word, documents are grouped logically and placed in *folders*. The main folder on a storage medium is called the *root folder* and you can create additional folders within the root folder. At the Open or Save As dialog box, documents display in the list box preceded by a document icon and folders are preceded by a folder icon. Create a new folder by clicking the Create New Folder button located on the dialog box toolbar. At the New Folder dialog box, type a name for the folder, and then press Enter. The new folder becomes the active folder. A folder name can contain a maximum of 255 characters. Numbers, spaces, and symbols can be used in the folder name, except those symbols explained in Chapter 1 in the "Naming a Document" section.

If you want to make the previous folder the active folder, click the Up One Level button on the dialog box toolbar. Clicking this button changes to the folder that is up one level from the current folder. After clicking the Up One Level button, the Back button becomes active. Click this button and the previously active folder becomes active again. You can also use the keyboard shortcut, Alt + 2, to move up one level and make the previous folder active.

Project 1a Creating a Folder

1. Create a folder named *Correspondence* on your storage medium by completing the following steps:
   a. Display the Open dialog box and open the Word2007L1C6 folder on your storage medium.
   b. Click the Create New Folder button located on the dialog box toolbar.
   c. At the New Folder dialog box, type Correspondence.
   d. Click OK or press Enter. (The Correspondence folder is now the active folder.)

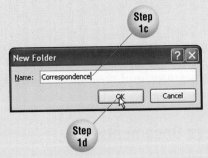

Step 1c

Step 1d

2. Change back to the Word2007L1C6 folder by clicking the Up One Level button on the dialog box toolbar.

Renaming a Folder

As you organize your files and folders, you may decide to rename a folder. Rename a folder using the Tools button in the Open or Save As dialog box or using a shortcut menu. To rename a folder using the Tools button, display the Open or Save As dialog box, click the folder you want to rename, click the Tools button located in the lower left corner of the dialog box, and then click *Rename* at the drop-down list. This selects the folder name and inserts a border around the name. Type the new name for the folder and then press Enter. To rename a folder using a shortcut menu, display the Open dialog box, right-click the folder name in the list box, and then click *Rename* at the shortcut menu. Type a new name for the folder and then press Enter.

QUICK STEPS

Rename a Folder
1. Display Open dialog box.
2. Right-click folder.
3. Click *Rename*.
4. Type new name.
5. Press Enter.

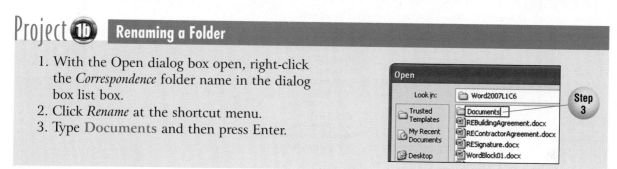

Project 1b   Renaming a Folder

1. With the Open dialog box open, right-click the *Correspondence* folder name in the dialog box list box.
2. Click *Rename* at the shortcut menu.
3. Type **Documents** and then press Enter.

Selecting Documents

You can complete document management tasks on one document or selected documents. To select one document, display the Open dialog box, and then click the desired document. To select several adjacent documents (documents that display next to each other), click the first document, hold down the Shift key, and then click the last document. To select documents that are not adjacent, click the first document, hold down the Ctrl key, click any other desired documents, and then release the Ctrl key.

Deleting Documents

At some point, you may want to delete certain documents from your storage medium or any other drive or folder in which you may be working. To delete a document, display the Open or Save As dialog box, select the document, and then click the Delete button on the dialog box toolbar. At the dialog box asking you to confirm the deletion, click Yes. To delete a document using a shortcut menu, right-click the document name in the list box, click *Delete* at the shortcut menu, and then click Yes at the confirmation dialog box.

QUICK STEPS

Delete Folder/ Document
1. Display Open dialog box.
2. Click folder or document name.
3. Click Delete button.
4. Click Yes.

Delete

Deleting to the Recycle Bin

Documents deleted from the hard drive are automatically sent to the Windows Recycle Bin. If you accidentally delete a document to the Recycle Bin, it can be easily restored. To free space on the drive, empty the Recycle Bin on a periodic basis. Restoring a document from or emptying the contents of the Recycle Bin is completed at the Windows desktop (not in Word). To display the Recycle Bin, minimize the Word window, and then double-click the *Recycle Bin* icon located on the Windows desktop. At the Recycle Bin, you can restore file(s) and empty the Recycle Bin.

HINT
Remember to empty the Recycle Bin on a regular basis.

1. Open **WordDocument04.docx** and then save the document and name it **WordL1_C6_P1**.
2. Close **WordL1_C6_P1.docx**.
3. Delete **WordL1_C6_P1.docx** by completing the following steps:
   a. Display the Open dialog box.
   b. Click *WordL1_C6_P1.docx* to select it.
   c. Click the Delete button on the dialog box toolbar.

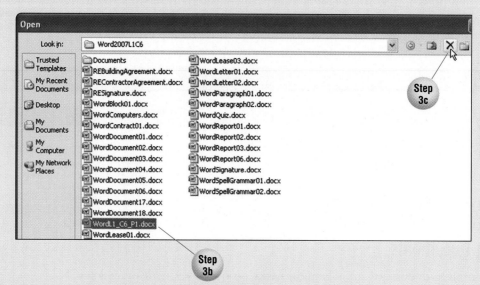

   d. At the question asking if you want to delete **WordL1_C6_P1.docx**, click Yes.
4. Delete selected documents by completing the following steps:
   a. At the Open dialog box, click *WordReport01.docx*.
   b. Hold down the Shift key and then click *WordReport03.docx*.
   c. Position the mouse pointer on a selected document and then click the *right* mouse button.
   d. At the shortcut menu that displays, click *Delete*.
   e. At the question asking if you want to delete the items, click Yes.
5. Open **WordDocument01.docx** and then save the document and name it **Keyboards**.
6. Save a copy of the **Keyboards.docx** document in the Documents folder by completing the following steps. (If your system does not contain this folder, check with your instructor to determine if another folder is available for you to use.)
   a. With **Keyboards.docx** open, click the Office button and then click *Save As*.
   b. At the Save As dialog box, double-click the *Documents* folder located at the beginning of the list box (folders are listed before documents).
   c. Click the Save button located in the lower right corner of the dialog box.
7. Close **Keyboards.docx**.
8. Display the Open dialog box and then click the Up One Level button to return to the Word2007L1C6 folder.

Copying and Moving Documents

You can copy a document to another folder without opening the document first. To do this, use the Copy and Paste options from a shortcut menu at the Open or Save As dialog box. You can copy a document or selected documents into the same folder. When you do this, Word names the document(s) "Copy of xxx" (where *xxx* is the current document name). You can copy one document or selected documents into the same folder.

Remove a document from one folder and insert it in another folder using the Cut and Paste options from the shortcut menu at the Open dialog box. To do this, display the Open dialog box, position the arrow pointer on the document to be removed (cut), click the *right* mouse button, and then click *Cut* at the shortcut menu. Change to the desired folder, position the arrow pointer in a white area in the list box, click the *right* mouse button, and then click *Paste* at the shortcut menu.

Copy Documents
1. Display Open dialog box.
2. Right-click document name.
3. Click *Copy*.
4. Navigate to desired folder.
5. Right-click blank area.
6. Click *Paste*.

Project 1d Copying Documents

1. At the Open dialog box with Word2007L1C6 the active folder, copy a document to another folder by completing the following steps:
   a. Position the arrow pointer on **WordDocument02.docx**, click the *right* mouse button, and then click *Copy* at the shortcut menu.
   b. Change to the Documents folder by double-clicking *Documents* at the beginning of the list box.
   c. Position the arrow pointer in any white area (not on a document name) in the list box, click the *right* mouse button, and then click *Paste* at the shortcut menu.
2. Change back to the Word2007L1C6 folder by clicking the Up One Level button located on the dialog box toolbar.
3. Copy several documents to the Documents folder by completing the following steps:
   a. Click once on **WordDocument01.docx**. (This selects the document.)
   b. Hold down the Ctrl key, click **WordDocument04.docx**, click **WordDocument05.docx**, and then release the Ctrl key.
   c. Position the arrow pointer on one of the selected documents, click the *right* mouse button, and then click *Copy* at the shortcut menu.
   d. Double-click the *Documents* folder.
   e. Position the arrow pointer in any white area in the list box, click the *right* mouse button, and then click *Paste* at the shortcut menu.
4. Click the Up One Level button to return to the Word2007L1C6 folder.
5. Move **WordQuiz.docx** to the Documents folder by completing the following steps:
   a. Position the arrow pointer on **WordQuiz.docx**, click the *right* mouse button, and then click *Cut* at the shortcut menu.
   b. Double-click *Documents* to make it the active folder.
   c. Position the arrow pointer in the white area in the list box, click the *right* mouse button, and then click *Paste* at the shortcut menu.
6. Click the Up One Level button to return to the Word2007L1C6 folder.

Renaming Documents

At the Open dialog box, use the *Rename* option from the Tools drop-down list to give a document a different name. The *Rename* option changes the name of the document and keeps it in the same folder. To use Rename, display the Open dialog box, click once on the document to be renamed, click the Tools button, and then click *Rename* at the drop-down list. This causes a black border to surround the document name and the name to be selected. Type the desired name and then press Enter. You can also rename a document by right-clicking the document name at the Open dialog box and then clicking *Rename* at the shortcut menu. Type the desired name for the document and then press the Enter key.

Project 1e   Renaming Documents

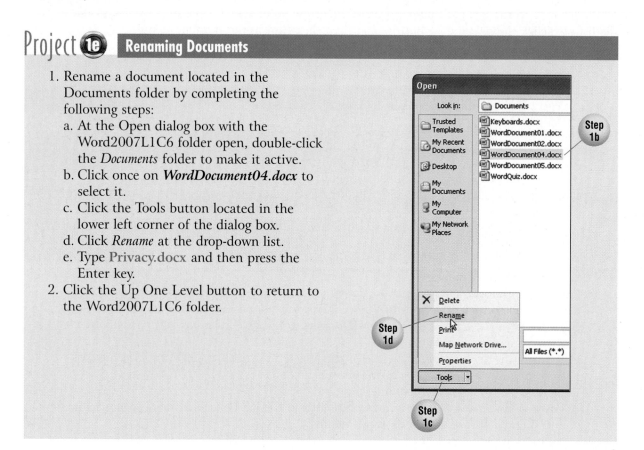

1. Rename a document located in the Documents folder by completing the following steps:
   a. At the Open dialog box with the Word2007L1C6 folder open, double-click the *Documents* folder to make it active.
   b. Click once on ***WordDocument04.docx*** to select it.
   c. Click the Tools button located in the lower left corner of the dialog box.
   d. Click *Rename* at the drop-down list.
   e. Type **Privacy.docx** and then press the Enter key.
2. Click the Up One Level button to return to the Word2007L1C6 folder.

Deleting a Folder

As you learned earlier in this chapter, you can delete a document or selected documents. Delete a folder and all its contents in the same manner as deleting a document.

Project ⑪ **Deleting a Folder**

1. At the Open dialog box, click the *Documents* folder to select it.
2. Click the Delete button on the dialog box toolbar.

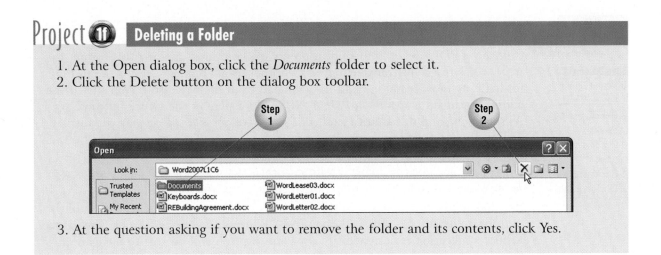

3. At the question asking if you want to remove the folder and its contents, click Yes.

Opening and Printing Multiple Documents

To open more than one document, select the documents in the Open dialog box, and then click the Open button. You can also open multiple documents by positioning the arrow pointer on one of the selected documents, clicking the *right* mouse button, and then clicking *Open* at the shortcut menu. Up to this point, you have opened a document and then printed it. With the *Print* option from the Tools drop-down list or the *Print* option from the shortcut menu at the Open dialog box, you can print a document or several documents without opening them.

HINT
Open a recently opened document by clicking the Office button and then clicking the document in the drop-down list.

Project ⑲ **Opening and Printing Multiple Documents**

1. Select *WordDocument01.docx*, *WordDocument02.docx*, *WordDocument03.docx*, and *WordDocument04.docx*.
2. Click the Open button located toward the lower right corner of the dialog box.
3. Close the open documents.
4. Display the Open dialog box and then select *WordDocument03.docx* and *WordDocument04.docx*.
5. Click the Tools button located in the lower left corner of the dialog box.
6. Click *Print* at the drop-down list.

Saving a Document in a Different Format

When you save a document, the document is automatically saved as a Word document. If you need to share a document with someone who is using a different Word processing program or a different version of Word, you can save the document in another format. You can also save a Word document as a Web page, in rich text format, as plain text, or in PDF format. To save a document with a different format, display the Save As dialog box, click the down-pointing arrow at the right side of the *Save as type* option, and then click the desired format at the drop-down list.

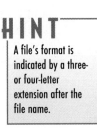

HINT
A file's format is indicated by a three- or four-letter extension after the file name.

You can also save a document in a different format with the *Save As* option at the Office button drop-down list. Click the Office button, point to *Save As*, and a side menu displays with options for saving a document in the default format, saving the document as a template, in Office 97 to 2003 format as well as PDF format.

QUICK STEPS

Save Document in Different Format
1. Open document.
2. Click Office button, *Save As.*
3. Click *Save as type* option.
4. Click desired type.
5. Click Save button.

The portable document format (PDF) was developed by Adobe Systems and is a format that captures all of the elements of a file as an electronic image. You can view a PDF file on any application on any computer, making this format the most widely used for transferring files to other users. Before saving a file in PDF format, you must install an add-in download from the Microsoft Web site. If the add-in download is installed, *PDF or XPS* will display in the Office button Save As side menu and if it is not installed, *Find add-ins for other file formats* will display. To download the add-in, click the *Find add-ins for other file formats* option and then follow the steps in the Word Help window.

When you click the *PDF or XPS* option at the Save As side menu, the Save As dialog box displays with *PDF (*.pdf)* specified as the *Save as type* option. At this dialog box, type a name in the *File name* text box and then click the Publish button. By default, the file will open in PDF format in Adobe Reader. The Adobe Reader application is designed to view your file. You will be able to navigate in the file but you will not be able to make any changes to the file. You can open a PDF file in your browser window by clicking the File option on the browser menu bar and then clicking *Open*. At the Open dialog box, browse to the appropriate folder and then double-click the desired file. You may need to change the *Files of type* option to *All Files.*

The Open dialog box generally displays only Word documents, which are documents containing the *.docx* extension. If you want to display all files, display the Open dialog box, click the down-pointing arrow at the right side of the *Files of type* option, and then click *All Files (*.*)* at the drop-down list.

Project 1h   Saving a Document in Different Formats

1. Open **WordDocument18.docx**.
2. Click the Office button, point to *Save As,* and then click *Word 97-2003 Document* at the side menu.
3. At the Save As dialog box, check to make sure that the *Save as type* option displays as *Word 97-2003 Document (*.doc)* and then type WordDocument18in2003format.
4. Click the Save button.
5. Save the document in PDF file format by completing the following steps:
   a. Click the Office button, point to *Save As,* and then click *PDF or XPS* in the side menu. (If this option does not display, the PDF add-in has not been installed.)
   b. At the Save As dialog box with the *Save as type* option set at *PDF (*.pdf),* click the Publish button.
6. Scroll through the document in Adobe Reader.
7. Close Adobe Reader by clicking the Close button located in the upper right corner of the window.
8. Save the document as plain text by completing the following steps:
   a. Click the Office button and then click *Save As.*
   b. At the Save As dialog box, type WordDocument18PlainText in the *File name* text box.

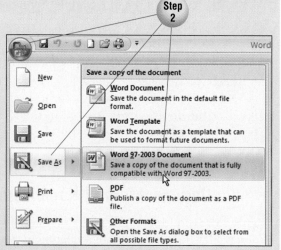

c. Click the down-pointing arrow at the right side of the *Save as type* option, scroll down the drop-down list, and then click *Plain Text (*.txt)*.

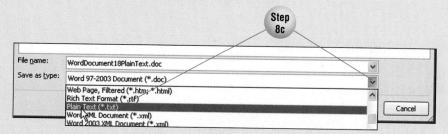

Step
8c

| File name: | WordDocument18PlainText.doc | ⌄ |
| Save as type: | Word 97-2003 Document (*.doc) | ⌄ |

Web Page, Filtered (*.htm; *.html)
Rich Text Format (*.rtf)
Plain Text (*.txt)
Word XML Document (*.xml)
Word 2003 XML Document (*.xml)

Cancel

    d. Click the Save button.
    e. At the File Conversion dialog box, click OK.
  9. Close the document.
10. Display the Open dialog box and, if necessary, display all files. To do this, click the down-pointing arrow at the right side of the *Files of type* option, and then click *All Files (*.*)* at the drop-down list. (This displays all files containing any extension.)
11. Double-click ***WordDocument18PlainText.txt*** in the list box. (If a File Conversion dialog box displays, click OK. Notice that the character and margin formatting has been removed from the document.)
12. Close the document.
13. Display the Open dialog box, change the *Files of type* option to *Word Documents (*.docx),* and then close the dialog box.

Project ② Manage Multiple Documents

You will work with windows by arranging, maximizing, restoring, and minimizing windows; move selected text between split windows; compare formatting of documents side by side; print specific text, pages, and multiple copies; and create and modify document properties.

Working with Windows

You can open multiple documents and move the insertion point between the documents. You can also move and copy information between documents or compare the contents of documents. The maximum number of documents that you can have open at one time depends on the memory of your computer system and the amount of data in each document. When you open a new window, it is placed on top of the original window. Once multiple windows are open, you can resize the windows to see all or a portion of them on the screen.

    When a document is open, a button displays on the Taskbar. This button represents the open document and contains a document icon, and the document name. (Depending on the length of the document name and the size of the button, not all of the name may be visible.) Another method for determining what documents are open is to click the View tab and then click the Switch Windows button in the Window group. The document name that displays in the list with

HINT
Press Ctrl + F6 to switch between open documents.

HINT
Press Ctrl + W or Ctrl + F4 to close the active document window.

the check mark in front of it is the ***active*** document. The active document is the document containing the insertion point. To make one of the other documents active, click the document name. If you are using the keyboard, type the number shown in front of the desired document.

Arranging Windows

Arrange Windows
1. Open documents.
2. Click View tab.
3. Click Arrange All.

If you have more than one document open, you can arrange them so a portion of each document displays. The portions that display are the titles (if present) and opening paragraphs of each document. Seeing this information is helpful if you are preparing a report that needs to incorporate key ideas from several documents.

To arrange a group of open documents, click the View tab and then click the Arrange All button in the Window group. Figure 6.1 shows a document screen with four documents open that have been arranged.

Figure 6.1 Arranged Documents

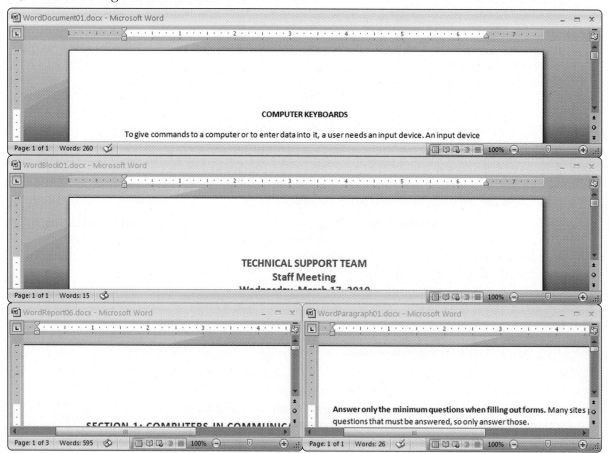

Maximizing, Restoring, and Minimizing Documents

Minimize Maximize

Use the Maximize and Minimize buttons in the active document window to change the size of the window. The Maximize button is the button in the upper right corner of the active document immediately to the left of the Close button. (The Close button is the button containing the *X*.) The Minimize button is located immediately to the left of the Maximize button.

If you arrange all open documents and then click the Maximize button in the active document, the active document expands to fill the document screen. In addition, the Maximize button changes to the Restore button. To return the active document back to its size before it was maximized, click the Restore button. If you click the Minimize button in the active document, the document is reduced and a button displays on the Taskbar representing the document. To maximize a document that has been minimized, click the button on the Taskbar representing the document.

Restore

Arranging, Maximizing, Restoring, and Minimizing Windows

Note: If you are using Word on a network system that contains a virus checker, you may not be able to open multiple documents at once. Continue by opening each document individually.

1. Open the following documents: **WordBlock01.docx**, **WordDocument01.docx**, **WordParagraph01.docx**, and **WordReport06.docx**.
2. Arrange the windows by clicking the View tab and then clicking the Arrange All button in the Window group.
3. Make **WordDocument01.docx** the active document by positioning the arrow pointer on the title bar for **WordDocument01.docx** and then clicking the left mouse button.
4. Close **WordDocument01.docx**.
5. Make **WordParagraph01.docx** active and then close it.
6. Make **WordReport06.docx** active and minimize it by clicking the Minimize button in the upper right corner of the active window.
7. Maximize **WordBlock01.docx** by clicking the Maximize button at the right side of the Title bar. (The Maximize button is the button at the right side of the Title bar, immediately left of the Close button.)
8. Close **WordBlock01.docx**.
9. Restore **WordReport06.docx** by clicking the button on the Taskbar representing the document.
10. Maximize **WordReport06.docx**.

Step 7

Step 9

Splitting a Window

You can divide a window into two *panes*, which is helpful if you want to view different parts of the same document at one time. You may want to display an outline for a report in one pane, for example, and the portion of the report that you are editing in the other. The original window is split into two panes that extend horizontally across the screen.

Split a window by clicking the View tab and then clicking the Split button in the Window group. This causes a wide gray line to display in the middle of the screen and the mouse pointer to display as a double-headed arrow pointing up and down with a small double line between. Move this double-headed arrow pointer up or down, if desired, by dragging the mouse or by pressing the up- and/or down-pointing arrow keys on the keyboard. When the double-headed arrow is positioned at the desired location in the document, click the left mouse button or press the Enter key.

You can also split the window with the split bar. The split bar is the small gray horizontal bar above the up scroll arrow on the vertical scroll bar. To split the window with the split bar, position the arrow pointer on the split bar until it turns

QUICK STEPS

Split Window
1. Open document.
2. Click View tab.
3. Click Split button.
OR
Drag split bar.

Split

into a short double line with an up- and down-pointing arrow. Hold down the left mouse button, drag the double-headed arrow into the document screen to the location where you want the window split, and then release the mouse button. With the window split, you may decide you want to move certain objects or sections of text. Do this by selecting the desired object or text and then dragging and dropping it across the split bar.

When a window is split, the insertion point is positioned in the bottom pane. To move the insertion point to the other pane with the mouse, position the I-beam pointer in the other pane, and then click the left mouse button. To remove the split line from the document, click the View tab and then click the Remove Split button in the Window group. You can also double-click the split bar or drag the split bar to the top or bottom of the screen.

Project 2b — Moving Selected Text between Split Windows

1. With **WordReport06.docx** open, save the document with Save As and name it **WordL1_C6_P2**.
2. Click the View tab and then click the Split button in the Window group.
3. With the split line displayed in the middle of the document screen, click the left mouse button.

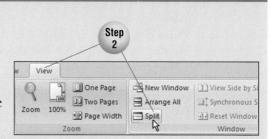
Step 2

4. Move the first section below the second section by completing the following steps:
   a. Click the Home tab.
   b. Select the *SECTION 1: COMPUTERS IN COMMUNICATION* section from the title to right above *SECTION 2: COMPUTERS IN ENTERTAINMENT*.
   c. Click the Cut button in the Clipboard group in the Home tab.
   d. Position the arrow pointer at the end of the document in the bottom window pane and then click the left mouse button.
   e. Click the Paste button in the Clipboard group in the Home tab.
   f. Change the number in the two titles to *SECTION 1: COMPUTERS IN ENTERTAINMENT* and *SECTION 2: COMPUTERS IN COMMUNICATION*.
5. Remove the split from the window by clicking the View tab and then clicking the Remove Split button in the Window group.
6. If the Section 2 title displays at the bottom of the first page, move the insertion point to the beginning of the title and then press Ctrl + Enter to insert a page break.
7. Save **WordL1_C6_P2.docx**.

Viewing Documents Side by Side

If you want to compare the contents of two documents, open both documents, click the View tab, and then click the View Side by Side button in the Window group. Both documents are arranged in the screen side by side as shown in Figure 6.2. By default synchronous scrolling is active. With this feature active, scrolling in one document causes the same scrolling to occur in the other document. This feature is useful in situations where you want to compare text, formatting, or other features between documents. If you want to scroll in one document and not the other, click the Synchronous Scrolling button in the Window group in the View tab to turn it off.

Figure 6.2 Viewing Documents Side by Side

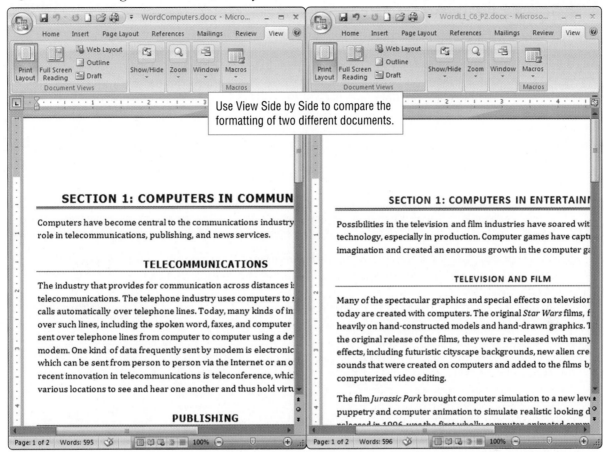

Use View Side by Side to compare the formatting of two different documents.

Project 2G Viewing Documents Side by Side

1. With **WordL1_C6_P2.docx** open, open **WordComputers.docx**.
2. Click the View tab and then click the View Side by Side button in the Window group.

Step 2

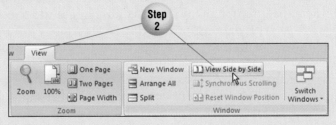

3. Scroll through both documents simultaneously. Notice the difference between the two documents. (The title and headings are set in a different font and color.) Select and then format the title and headings in **WordL1_C6_P2.docx** so they match the formatting in **WordComputers.docx**.
4. Save **WordL1_C6_P2.docx**.
5. Make **WordComputers.docx** the active document and then close it.

Inserting a File

If you want to insert the contents of one document into another, use the Object button in the Text group in the Insert tab. Click the Object button arrow and then click *Text from File* and the Insert File dialog box displays. This dialog box contains similar features as the Open dialog box. Navigate to the desired folder and then double-click the document you want to insert in the open document.

Project 2d Inserting a File

1. With **WordL1_C6_P2.docx** open, move the insertion point to the end of the document.
2. Insert a file into the open document by completing the following steps:
   a. Click the Insert tab.
   b. Click the Object button arrow in the Text group.
   c. Click *Text from File* at the drop-down list.
   d. At the Insert File dialog box, navigate to the Word2007L1C6 folder and then double-click ***WordDocument17.docx***.
3. Check the formatting of the inserted text and format it to match the formatting of the original text.
4. Save **WordL1_C6_P2.docx**.

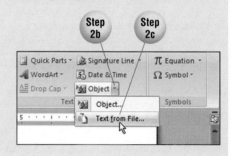

Previewing a Document

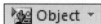

Before printing a document, you may want to view the document as it will appear when printed. To do this, display the document in Print Preview by clicking the Office button, pointing to the *Print* option, and then clicking *Print Preview*. The page where the insertion point is located displays in the screen in a manner similar to Figure 6.3. With options in the Print Preview tab, you can send the document to the printer, change the page setup, change the zoom display, and customize the preview window. Viewing a document in Print Preview is especially useful for making sure that a letter is positioned attractively on the page. For example, use Print Preview to help you center letters vertically, which means allowing equal space above and below the beginning and end of the letter.

Figure 6.3 Document in Print Preview

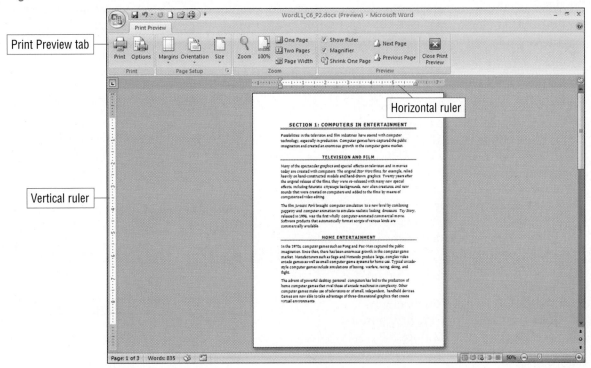

Print Preview tab

Horizontal ruler

Vertical ruler

Project 2e   **Previewing the Document**

1. With **WordL1_C6_P2.docx** open, press Ctrl + Home to move the insertion point to the beginning of the document.
2. Preview the document by clicking the Office button, pointing to the *Print* option, and then clicking *Print Preview*.
3. Click the Two Pages button in the Zoom group in the Print Preview tab. (This displays the first two pages in the document.)

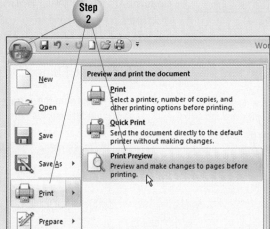

Step 2

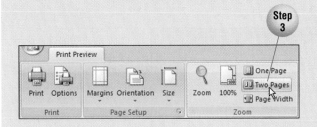

Step 3

4. Click the Next Page button in the Preview group. (This displays the third page.)
5. Click the Previous Page button in the Preview group. (This redisplays the first two pages.)
6. Click the One Page button in the Zoom group.
7. Change the page orientation by clicking the Orientation button in the Page Setup group and then clicking *Landscape* at the drop-down list.

8. After looking at the page in landscape orientation, you decide to return to portrait orientation. To do this, click the Orientation button in the Page Setup group and then click *Portrait* at the drop-down list.
9. Change margins by completing the following steps:
   a. Click the Margins button in the Page Setup group and then click *Custom Margins* at the drop-down list.
   b. At the Page Setup dialog box with the Margins tab selected, change the top margin to 1.25".
   c. Click OK to close the dialog box.
10. Change the Zoom by completing the following steps:
    a. Click the Zoom button in the Zoom group.
    b. At the Zoom dialog box, click the *75%* option.
    c. Click OK to close the dialog box.
    d. After viewing the document in 75% view, click the Zoom button.
    e. At the Zoom dialog box, click the *Whole page* option.
    f. Click OK to close the dialog box.
11. Click the Close Print Preview button.
12. Save **WordL1_C6_P2.docx**.

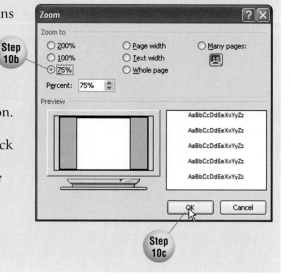

Step 10b

Step 10c

Printing Documents

In Chapter 1, you learned to print at the Print dialog box the document displayed in the document screen. By default, one copy of all pages of the currently open document prints. With options at the Print dialog box, you can specify the number of copies to print and also specific pages for printing. To display the Print dialog box shown in Figure 6.4, click the Office button and then click *Print* or press Ctrl + P.

Figure 6.4 Print Dialog Box

Make sure the correct printer displays here.

Click the down-pointing arrow to display a list of installed printers.

Click this button to set options for the selected printer such as paper size, layout, orientation, paper source, and paper quality.

Specify the amount of text to print with options in this section of the dialog box.

Print multiple copies of a document by increasing this number.

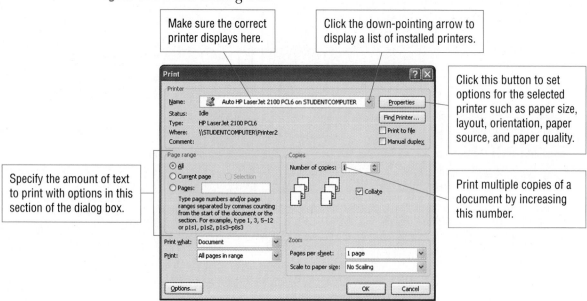

Printing Specific Text or Pages

The *Page range* section of the Print dialog box contains settings you can use to specify the amount of text you want printed. At the default setting of *All*, all pages of the current document are printed. Choose the *Current page* option to print the page where the insertion point is located. If you want to select and then print a portion of the document, choose the *Selection* option at the Print dialog box. This prints only the text that has been selected in the current document. (This option is dimmed unless text is selected in the document.)

With the *Pages* option, you can identify a specific page, multiple pages, and/or a range of pages. If you want specific multiple pages printed, use a comma (,) to indicate *and* and use a hyphen (-) to indicate *through*. For example, to print pages 2 and 5, you would type *2,5* in the *Pages* text box. To print pages 6 through 10, you would type *6-10*.

Project ㉑   Printing Specific Text and Pages

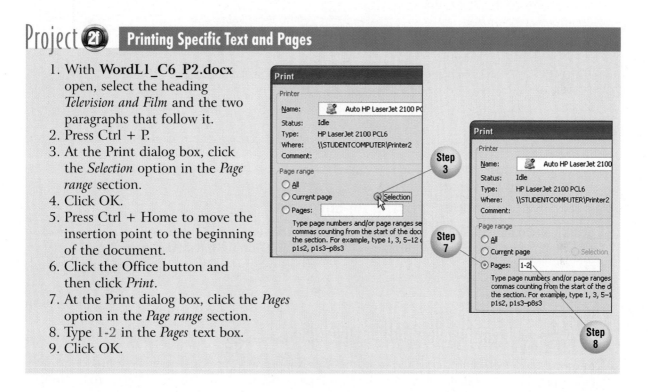

1. With **WordL1_C6_P2.docx** open, select the heading *Television and Film* and the two paragraphs that follow it.
2. Press Ctrl + P.
3. At the Print dialog box, click the *Selection* option in the *Page range* section.
4. Click OK.
5. Press Ctrl + Home to move the insertion point to the beginning of the document.
6. Click the Office button and then click *Print*.
7. At the Print dialog box, click the *Pages* option in the *Page range* section.
8. Type *1-2* in the *Pages* text box.
9. Click OK.

Printing Multiple Copies

If you want to print more than one copy of a document, use the *Number of copies* option from the Print dialog box. If you print several copies of a document containing multiple pages, Word prints the pages in the document collated. For example, if you print two copies of a three-page document, pages 1, 2, and 3 are printed, and then the pages are printed a second time. Printing pages collated is helpful but takes more printing time. To speed up the printing time, you can tell Word *not* to print the pages collated. To do this, remove the check mark from the *Collate* option at the Print dialog box. With the check mark removed, Word will print all copies of the first page, and then all copies of the second page, and so on.

1. With **WordL1_C6_P2.docx** open, press Ctrl + P.
2. Type 2 in the *Number of copies* text box.
3. Click the *Pages* option in the *Page range* section.
4. Type 1,3.
5. Click the *Collate* check box in the *Copies* section to remove the check mark.
6. Click OK.
7. Close **WordL1_C6_P2.docx**.

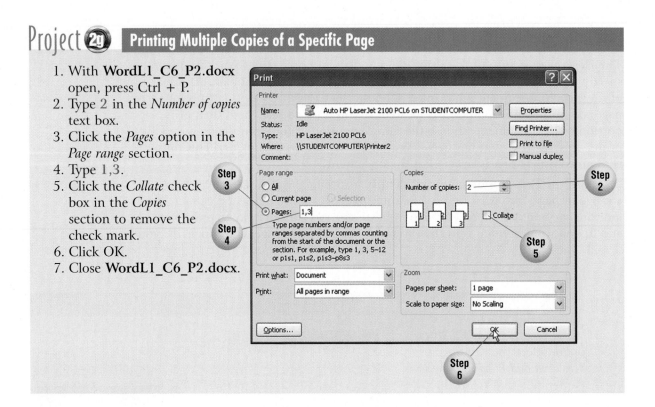

Step 3

Step 4

Step 2

Step 5

Step 6

Project 3   Create and Print an Envelope

You will create an envelope document and type the return address and delivery address using envelope addressing guidelines issued by the United States Postal Service.

Create Envelope
1. Click Mailings tab.
2. Click Envelopes button.
3. Type delivery address.
4. Click in *Return address* text box.
5. Type return address.
6. Click Add to Document button or Print button.

Creating and Printing Envelopes

Word automates the creation of envelopes with options at the Envelopes and Labels dialog box with the Envelopes tab selected as shown in Figure 6.5. Display this dialog box by clicking the Mailings tab and then clicking the Envelopes button in the Create group. At the dialog box, type the delivery address in the *Delivery address* text box and the return address in the *Return address* text box. You can send the envelope directly to the printer by clicking the Print button or insert the envelope in the current document by clicking the Add to Document button.

Figure 6.5 Envelopes and Labels Dialog Box with Envelopes Tab Selected

Type the delivery name and address in this text box.

Type the return name and address in this text box.

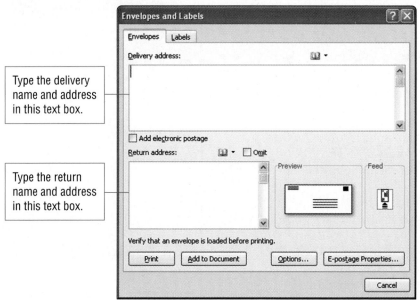

If you enter a return address before printing the envelope, Word will display the question *Do you want to save the new return address as the default return address?* At this question, click Yes if you want the current return address available for future envelopes. Click No if you do not want the current return address used as the default. If a default return address displays in the *Return address* section of the dialog box, you can tell Word to omit the return address when printing the envelope. To do this, click the *Omit* check box to insert a check mark.

The Envelopes and Labels dialog box contains a *Preview* sample box and a *Feed* sample box. The *Preview* sample box shows how the envelope will appear when printed and the *Feed* sample box shows how the envelope should be inserted into the printer.

When addressing envelopes, consider following general guidelines issued by the United States Postal Service (USPS). The USPS guidelines suggest using all capital letters with no commas or periods for return and delivery addresses. Figure 6.6 shows envelope addresses following the USPS guidelines. Use abbreviations for street suffixes (such as *ST* for *STREET* and *AVE* for *Avenue*). For a complete list of address abbreviations, visit the www.emcp.net/usps site and then search for *Official USPS Abbreviations*.

Project ③ Printing an Envelope

1. At a blank document, create an envelope that prints the delivery address and return address shown in Figure 6.6. Begin by clicking the Mailings tab.
2. Click the Envelopes button in the Create group.

3. At the Envelopes and Labels dialog box with the Envelopes tab selected, type the delivery address shown in Figure 6.6 (the one containing the name *GREGORY LINCOLN*). (Press the Enter key to end each line in the name and address.)
4. Click in the *Return address* text box. (If any text displays in the *Return address* text box, select and then delete it.)
5. Type the return address shown in Figure 6.6 (the one containing the name *WENDY STEINBERG*). (Press the Enter key to end each line in the name and address.)
6. Click the Add to Document button.
7. At the message *Do you want to save the new return address as the default return address?*, click No.
8. Save the document and name it **WordL1_C6_P3**.
9. Print and then close **WordL1_C6_P3.docx**. *Note: Manual feed of the envelope may be required. Please check with your instructor.*

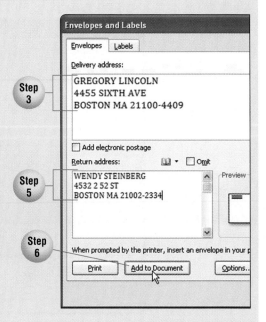

Figure 6.6 Project 3

WENDY STEINBERG
4532 S 52 ST
BOSTON MA 21002-2334

GREGORY LINCOLN
4455 SIXTH AVE
BOSTON MA 21100-4409

roject ④ **Create and Print an Envelope and Mailing Labels**
You will open a letter document and then create an envelope using the inside address of the letter and then create mailing labels containing the inside address.

If you open the Envelopes and Labels dialog box in a document containing a name and address (the name and address lines must end with a press of the Enter key and not Shift + Enter), the name and address are automatically inserted in the *Delivery address* section of the dialog box. To do this, open a document containing a name and address and then display the Envelopes and Labels dialog box. The name and address are inserted in the *Delivery address* section as they appear in the letter and may not conform to the USPS guidelines. The USPS guidelines for addressing envelopes are only suggestions, not requirements.

1. Open **WordLetter01.docx**.
2. Click the Mailings tab.
3. Click the Envelopes button in the Create group.
4. At the Envelopes and Labels dialog box (with the Envelopes tab selected), make sure the delivery address displays properly in the *Delivery address* section.
5. If any text displays in the *Return address* section, insert a check mark in the *Omit* check box (located to the right of the *Return address* option). (This tells Word not to print the return address on the envelope.)
6. Click the Print button.

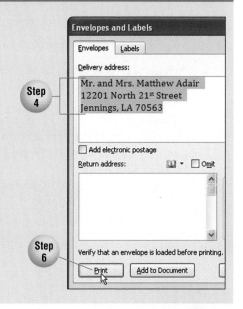

Step 4

Step 6

Creating and Printing Labels

Use Word's labels feature to print text on mailing labels, file labels, disk labels, or other types of labels. Word includes a variety of predefined formats for labels that can be purchased at an office supply store. To create a sheet of mailing labels with the same name and address using the default options, click the Labels button in the Create group in the Mailings tab. At the Envelopes and Labels dialog box with the Labels tab selected as shown in Figure 6.7, type the desired address in the *Address* text box. Click the New Document button to insert the mailing label in a new document or click the Print button to send the mailing label directly to the printer.

Figure 6.7 Envelopes and Labels Dialog Box with Labels Tab Selected

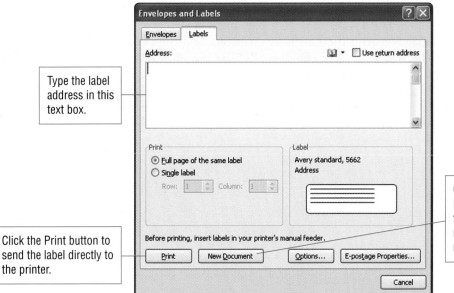

Type the label address in this text box.

Click the Print button to send the label directly to the printer.

Click the New Document button to insert the mailing label in a new document.

1. With **WordLetter01.docx** open, create mailing labels with the delivery address. Begin by clicking the Mailings tab.
2. Click the Labels button in the Create group.
3. At the Envelopes and Labels dialog box with the Labels tab selected, make sure the delivery address displays properly in the *Address* section.
4. Click the New Document button.
5. Save the mailing label document and name it **WordL1_C6_P4.docx**.
6. Print and then close **WordL1_C6_P4.docx**.
7. Close **WordLetter01.docx**.

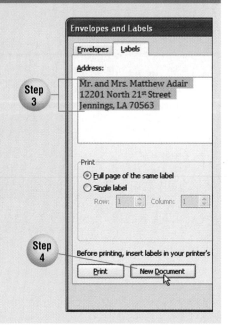

Step 3

Step 4

roject **5** **Create Mailing Labels**

You will create mailing labels containing varying names and addresses.

If you open the Envelopes and Labels dialog box with the Labels tab selected in a document containing a name and address, the name and address are automatically inserted in the *Address* section of the dialog box. To enter different names in each of the mailing labels, start at a clear document screen, display the Envelopes and Labels dialog box with the Labels tab selected, and then click the New Document button. The Envelopes and Labels dialog box is removed from the screen and the document screen displays with label forms. The insertion point is positioned in the first label form. Type the name and address in this label and then press the Tab key to move the insertion point to the next label. Pressing Shift + Tab will move the insertion point to the preceding label.

Changing Label Options

Click the Options button at the Envelopes and Labels dialog box with the Labels tab selected and the Label Options dialog box displays as shown in Figure 6.8. At the Label Options dialog box, choose the type of printer, the desired label product, and the product number. This dialog box also displays information about the selected label such as type, height, width, and paper size. When you select a label, Word automatically determines label margins. If, however, you want to customize these default settings, click the Details button at the Label Options dialog box.

Figure 6.8 Label Options Dialog Box

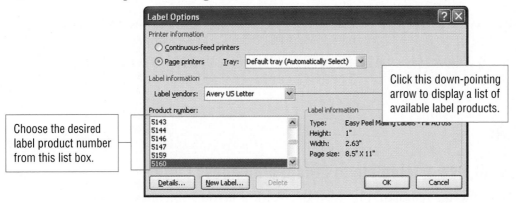

Click this down-pointing arrow to display a list of available label products.

Choose the desired label product number from this list box.

Project 5 | Creating Customized Mailing Labels

1. At a blank document, click the Mailings tab.
2. Click the Labels button in the Create group.
3. At the Envelopes and Labels dialog box with the Labels tab selected, click the Options button.
4. At the Label Options dialog box, click the down-pointing arrow at the right side of the *Label vendors* option and then click *Avery US Letter* at the drop-down list.
5. Scroll down the *Product number* list box and then click *5160*.
6. Click OK or press Enter.
7. At the Envelopes and Labels dialog box, click the New Document button.
8. At the document screen, type the first name and address shown in Figure 6.9 in the first label.
9. Press the Tab key twice to move the insertion point to the next label and then type the second name and address shown in Figure 6.9.

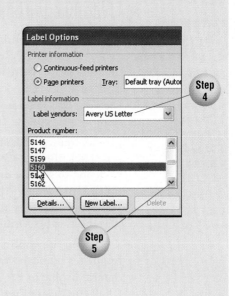

Step 4

Step 5

word Level 1

Maintaining Documents   **215**

10. Continue in this manner until all names and addresses in Figure 6.9 have been typed.
11. Save the document and name it **WordL1_C6_P5**.
12. Print and then close **WordL1_C6_P5.docx**.
13. At the blank document, close the document without saving changes.

Figure 6.9 Project 5

DAVID LOWRY	MARCELLA SANTOS	KEVIN DORSEY
12033 S 152 ST	394 APPLE BLOSSOM	26302 PRAIRIE DR
HOUSTON TX 77340	FRIENDSWOOD TX 77533	HOUSTON TX 77316
AL AND DONNA SASAKI	JACKIE RHYNER	MARK AND TINA ELLIS
1392 PIONEER DR	29039 107 AVE E	607 FORD AVE
BAYTOWN TX 77903	HOUSTON TX 77302	HOUSTON TX 77307

Project ⑥ Use a Template to Create a Business Letter

You will use a letter template provided by Word to create a business letter.

Creating a Document Using a Template

QUICK STEPS

Create Document using a Template
1. Click Office button, New.
2. Click *Installed Templates.*
3. Double-click desired template.

Word includes a number of template documents formatted for specific uses. Each Word document is based on a template document with the Normal template the default. With Word templates, you can easily create a variety of documents such as letters, faxes, and awards, with specialized formatting. Templates are available in the *Templates* section of the New Document dialog box. You can choose an installed template or choose from a variety of templates available online.

To create a document based on a template, display the New Document dialog box, click the *Installed Templates* option in the *Templates* section, and then double-click the desired template in the *Installed Templates* list box. This causes a template document to open that contains formatting as well as specific locations where you enter text. Locations for personalized text display in placeholders. Click the placeholder text and then type the personalized text.

If you are connected to the Internet, Microsoft offers a number of predesigned templates you can download. Templates are grouped into categories and the category names display in the *Microsoft Office Online* section of the New Document dialog box. Click the desired template category in the list box and available templates display at the right. Click the desired template and then click the Download button.

Project ⑥ Creating a Letter Using a Template

1. Click the Office button and then click *New* at the drop-down list.
2. At the New Document dialog box, display available templates by clicking *Installed Templates* in the *Templates* section.
3. Scroll through the list of installed templates and then double-click the ***Equity Letter*** template.

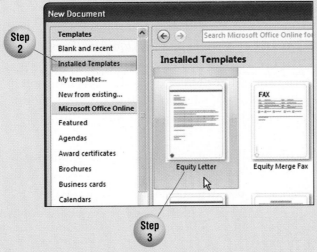

4. At the letter document, click the placeholder text *[Pick the date]*, click the down-pointing arrow at the right side of the placeholder, and then click the Today button located at the bottom of the calendar.
5. Click in the name that displays below the date, select the name, and then type your first and last names.
6. Click the placeholder text *[Type the sender company name]* and then type Sorenson Funds.
7. Click the placeholder text *[Type the sender company address]*, type 4400 Jackson Avenue, press the Enter key, and then type Seattle, WA 98021.
8. Click the placeholder text *[Type the recipient name]* and then type Ms. Jennifer Gonzalez.
9. Click the placeholder text *[Type the recipient address]*, type 12990 California Avenue, press the Enter key, and then type Seattle, WA 98022.
10. Click the placeholder text *[Type the salutation]* and then type Dear Ms. Gonzalez:.
11. Insert a file in the document by completing the following steps:
    a. Click anywhere in the three paragraphs of text in the body of the letter and then click the Delete key.
    b. Click the Insert tab.
    c. Click the Object button arrow in the Text group and then click *Text from File* at the drop-down list.
    d. At the Insert File dialog box, navigate to the Word2007L1C6 folder on your storage medium and then double-click ***WordLetter02.docx***.
12. Click the placeholder text *[Type the closing]* and then type Sincerely,.
13. Delete one blank line above Sincerely.
14. Click the placeholder text *[Type the sender title]* and then type Financial Consultant.
15. Save the document and name it **WordL1_C6_P6**.
16. Print and then close **WordL1_C6_P6.docx**.

CHAPTER summary

- Group Word documents logically into folders. Create a new folder at the Open or Save As dialog box.
- You can select one or several documents at the Open dialog box. Copy, move, rename, delete, print, or open a document or selected documents.
- Use the *Cut*, *Copy*, and *Paste* options from the Open dialog box shortcut menu to move or copy a document from one folder to another.
- Delete documents and/or folders with the Delete button on the Open or Save As dialog box toolbar or the *Delete* option from the shortcut menu.
- You can open multiple documents and print multiple documents at the Open dialog box.
- Save a document in a different format with the *Save As* side menu at the Office button drop-down list or with the *Save as type* option at the Save As dialog box.
- Move among the open documents by clicking the button on the Taskbar representing the desired document, or by clicking the View tab, clicking the Switch Windows button in the Window group, and then clicking the desired document name.
- View a portion of all open documents by clicking the View tab and then clicking the Arrange All button in the Window group.
- Use the Minimize, Maximize, and Restore buttons located in the upper right corner of the window to reduce or increase the size of the active window.
- Divide a window into two panes by clicking the View tab and then clicking the Split button in the Window group. This enables you to view different parts of the same document at one time.
- View the contents of two open documents side by side by clicking the View tab, and then clicking the View Side by Side button in the Window group.
- Insert a document into the open document by clicking the Insert tab, clicking the Object button arrow, and then clicking *Text from File* at the drop-down list. At the Insert File dialog box, double-click the desired document.
- Preview a document to display how the document will appear when printed. Use options and buttons in the Print Preview tab to customize the view and to format text in the document.
- Customize a print job with options at the Print dialog box. Use the *Page range* section to specify the amount of text you want printed; use the *Pages* option to identify a specific page, multiple pages, and/or a range of pages for printing; and use the *Number of copies* option to print more than one copy of a document.
- With Word's envelope feature you can create and print an envelope at the Envelopes and Labels dialog box with the Envelopes tab selected.
- If you open the Envelopes and Labels dialog box in a document containing a name and address (with each line ending with a press of the Enter key), that information is automatically inserted in the *Delivery address* text box in the dialog box.
- Use Word's labels feature to print text on mailing labels, file labels, disk labels, or other types of labels.
- Word includes a number of template documents you can use to create a variety of documents. Display the list of template documents by clicking the Office button and then clicking *New* at the drop-down list.

COMMANDS review

FEATURE	RIBBON TAB, GROUP	BUTTON	OPTION	KEYBOARD SHORTCUT
Open dialog box				Ctrl + O
Save As dialog box			Save As	
Print dialog box			Print	Ctrl + P
Arrange all documents	View, Window	Arrange All		
Minimize document				
Maximize document				
Restore				
Split window	View, Window	Split		
View documents side by side	View, Window	View Side by Side		
Insert file	Insert, Text	Object ▾	Text from File	
Preview document			Print, Print Preview	
Envelopes and Labels dialog box with Envelopes tab selected	Mailings, Create			
Envelopes and Labels dialog box with Labels tab selected	Mailings, Create			
New Document dialog box			New	

CONCEPTS check

Test Your Knowledge

Completion: In the space provided at the right, indicate the correct term, command, or number.

1. Create a new folder with this button at the Open or Save As dialog box. _____

2. Click this button at the Open dialog box to make the previous folder active. _____

3. Using the mouse, select nonadjacent documents at the Open dialog box by holding down this key while clicking the desired documents.

       _____

4. Documents deleted from the hard drive are automatically sent to this bin.

       _____

5. Copy a document to another folder without opening the document with the *Copy* option and this option from the Open dialog box shortcut menu.

       _____

6. Save a document in a different file format with this option at the Save As dialog box.

       _____

7. Click this button in the Window group in the View tab to arrange all open documents so a portion of each document displays.

       _____

8. Click this button and the active document fills the editing window.

       _____

9. Click this button to reduce the active document to a button on the Taskbar.

       _____

10. To display documents side by side, click this button in the Window group in the View tab.

       _____

11. Display the Insert File dialog box by clicking the Object button arrow in the Insert tab and then clicking this option.

       _____

12. Display a document in this view to determine how a document will appear when printed.

       _____

13. Type this in the *Pages* text box in the *Page range* section of the Print dialog box to print pages 3 through 6 of the open document.

       _____

14. Type this in the *Pages* text box in the *Page range* section of the Print dialog box to print page 4 and 9 of the open document.

       _____

15. The Envelopes button is located in the Create group in this tab.

       _____

16. Click the *Installed Templates* option at this dialog box to display a list of templates.

       _____

SKILLS check
Demonstrate Your Proficiency

Assessment

1 MANAGE DOCUMENTS

1. Display the Open dialog box with Word2007L1C6 the active folder and then create a new folder named *CheckingTools*.
2. Copy (be sure to copy and not cut) all documents that begin with *WordSpellGrammar* into the CheckingTools folder.
3. With the CheckingTools folder as the active folder, rename **WordSpellGrammar01.docx** to **Technology.docx**.
4. Rename **WordSpellGrammar02.docx** to **Software.docx**.
5. Make Word2007L1C6 the active folder.
6. Delete the CheckingTools folder and all documents contained within it.
7. Open **WordBlock01.docx**, **WordLease03.docx**, and **WordDocument04.docx**.
8. Make **WordLease03.docx** the active document.
9. Make **WordBlock01.docx** the active document.
10. Arrange all of the windows.
11. Make **WordDocument04.docx** the active document and then minimize it.
12. Minimize the remaining documents.
13. Restore **WordBlock01.docx**.
14. Restore **WordLease03.docx**.
15. Restore **WordDocument04.docx**.
16. Maximize and then close **WordBlock01.docx** and then maximize and close **WordDocument04.docx**.
17. Maximize **WordLease03.docx** and then save the document and name it **WordL1_C6_A1**.
18. Open **WordDocument18.docx**.
19. View the **WordL1_C6_A1.docx** document and **WordDocument18.docx** document side by side.
20. Scroll through both documents simultaneously and notice the formatting differences between the title and headings in the two documents. Change the font size and apply shading to the title and headings in **WordL1_C6_A1.docx** to match the font size and shading of the title and headings in **WordDocument18.docx**.
21. Make **WordDocument18.docx** active and then close it.
22. Save **WordL1_C6_A1.docx**.
23. Move the insertion point to the end of the document and then insert the document named **WordSignature.docx**.
24. Save, print, and then close **WordL1_C6_A1.docx**.

Assessment

2 CREATE AN ENVELOPE

1. At a blank document, create an envelope with the text shown in Figure 6.10.
2. Save the envelope document and name it **WordL1_C6_A2**.
3. Print and then close **WordL1_C6_A2.docx**.

Figure 6.10 Assessment 2

DR ROSEANNE HOLT
21330 CEDAR DR
LOGAN UT 84598

GENE MIETZNER
4559 CORRIN AVE
SMITHFIELD UT 84521

Assessment

3 CREATE MAILING LABELS

1. Create mailing labels with the names and addresses shown in Figure 6.11. Use a label option of your choosing. (You may need to check with your instructor before choosing an option.)
2. Save the document and name it **WordL1_C6_A3**.
3. Print and then close **WordL1_C6_A3.docx**.
4. At the clear document screen, close the document screen without saving changes.

Figure 6.11 Assessment 3

SUSAN LUTOVSKY	JIM AND PAT KIEL	IRENE HAGEN
1402 MELLINGER DR	413 JACKSON ST	12930 147TH AVE E
FAIRHOPE OH 43209	AVONDALE OH 43887	CANTON OH 43296
VINCE KILEY	LEONARD KRUEGER	HELGA GUNDSTROM
14005 288TH S	13290 N 120TH	PO BOX 3112
CANTON OH 43287	CANTON OH 43291	AVONDALE OH 43887

Assessment

4 PREPARE A FAX

1. Open the Equity fax template from the New Document dialog box and then insert the following information in the specified fields.

> To: Frank Gallagher
> From: (your first and last names)
> Fax: (206) 555-9010
> Pages: 3
> Phone: (206) 555-9005
> Date: (insert current date)
> Re: Consultation Agreement
> CC: Jolene Yin
> Insert an X in the *For Review* check box
> Comments: Please review the Consultation Agreement and advise me of any legal issues.

2. Save the fax document and name it **WordL1_C6_A4**.
3. Print and then close the document.

Assessment

5 SAVE A DOCUMENT AS A WEB PAGE

1. Experiment with the *Save as type* option at the Save As dialog box and figure out how to save a document as a single file Web page.
2. Open **WordComputers.docx**, display the Save As dialog box, and then change the save as type to a single file Web page. Click the Change Title button that displays in the Save As dialog box. At the Set Page Title dialog box, type Computers in Communication and Entertainment and then close the dialog box. Click the Save button in the Save As dialog box and at the message telling you that some features are not supported by Web browsers, click the Continue button.
3. Close the WordComputers.mht file.
4. Open your Web browser and then open the WordComputers.mht file.
5. Close WordComputers.mht and then close your Web browser.

CASE study
Apply Your Skills

Part 1

You are the office manager for the real estate company, Macadam Realty, and have been asked by the senior sales associate, Lucy Hendricks, to organize contract forms into a specific folder. Create a new folder named *RealEstate* and then copy into the folder documents that begin with the letters "RE." Ms. Hendricks has also asked you to prepare mailing labels for Macadam Realty. Include the name,

Macadam Realty, and the address 100 Third Street, Suite 210, Denver, CO 80803, on the labels. Use a decorative font for the label and make the *M* in *Macadam* and the *R* in *Realty* larger and more pronounced than surrounding text. ***Hint: Format text in the label by selecting text, right-clicking in the selected text, and then choosing the desired option at the shortcut menu.*** Save the completed document and name it **WordL1_C6_CS_P1**. Print and then close the document.

Part 2

One of your responsibilities is to format contract forms. Open the document named **REContractorAgreement.docx** and then save it and name it **WordL1_C6_CS_P2**. The sales associate has asked you to insert signature information at the end of the document and so you decide to insert at the end of the document the file named **RESignature.docx**. With **WordL1_C6_CS_P2.docx** still open, open **REBuildingAgreement.docx**. Format the **WordL1_C6_CS_P2.docx** document so it is formatted in a manner similar to the **REBuildingAreement.docx** document. Consider the following when specifying formatting: margins, fonts, and paragraph shading. Save, print, and then close **WordL1_C6_CS_P2.docx**. Close **REBuildingAgreement.docx**.

Part 3

As part of the organization of contracts, Ms. Hendricks has asked you to insert document properties for the **REBuildingAgreement.docx** and **WordL1_C6_CS_P2.docx** documents. Use the Help feature to learn how to insert document properties. With the information you learn from the Help feature, open each of the two documents separately and then insert document properties in the following fields (you determine the information to type): *Author* (type your first and last names), *Title*, *Subject*, *Keywords*, and *Category*. Print the document properties for each document (change the *Print what* option at the Print dialog box to *Document properties*). Save each document with the original name and close the documents.

Part 4

A client of the real estate company, Anna Hurley, is considering purchasing several rental properties and has asked for information on how to locate real estate rental forms. Using the Internet, locate at least three Web sites that offer real estate rental forms. Write a letter to Anna Hurley at 2300 South 22nd Street, Denver, CO 80205. In the letter, list the Web sites you found and include information on which site you thought offered the most resources. Also include in the letter that Macadam Realty is very interested in helping her locate and purchase rental properties. Save the document and name it **WordL1_C6_CS_P4**. Create an envelope for the letter and add it to the letter document. Save, print, and then close **WordL1_C6_CS_P4.docx**. (You may need to manually feed the envelope in the printer.)

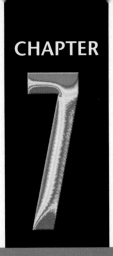

CHAPTER 7

Creating Tables and SmartArt

PERFORMANCE OBJECTIVES

Upon successful completion of Chapter 7, you will be able to:

- Create, edit, and format a table
- Change the table design and layout
- Sort text in a table
- Perform calculations on data in a table
- Create and format a SmartArt diagram
- Create and format a SmartArt organizational chart

word Chapter 7

Tutorial 7.1
Using Tables
Tutorial 7.2
Working with Charts

Some Word data can be organized in a table, which is a combination of columns and rows. With the Tables feature, you can insert data in columns and rows. This data can consist of text, values, and formulas. In this chapter you will learn how to create and format a table and insert and format data in the table. Word includes a SmartArt feature that provides a number of predesigned diagrams and organizational charts. Use this feature to create and then customize a diagram or organizational chart.

Note: Before beginning computer projects, copy to your storage medium the Word2007L1C7 subfolder from the Word2007L1 folder on the CD that accompanies this textbook and then make Word2007L1C7 the active folder.

Project ① Create and Format Tables with Company Information

You will create a table containing contact information and another containing information on plans offered by the company. You will then change the design and layout of both tables.

Creating a Table

Use the Tables feature to create boxes of information called *cells*. A cell is the intersection between a row and a column. A cell can contain text, characters, numbers, data, graphics, or formulas. Create a table by clicking the Insert tab,

Create a Table
1. Click Insert tab.
2. Click Table button.
3. Drag to create desired number of columns and rows.
4. Click mouse button.
OR
1. Click Insert tab.
2. Click Table button.
3. Click *Insert Table*.
4. Specify number of columns and rows.
5. Click OK.

clicking the Table button, dragging down and to the right until the correct number of rows and columns displays, and then clicking the mouse button. You can also create a table with options at the Insert Table dialog box. Display this dialog box by clicking the Table button in the Tables group in the Insert tab and then clicking *Insert Table* at the drop-down list.

Figure 7.1 shows an example of a table with four columns and three rows. Various parts of the table are identified in Figure 7.1 such as the gridlines, move table column marker, end-of-cell marker, end-of-row marker, and the resize handle. In a table, nonprinting characters identify the end of a cell and the end of a row. To view these characters, click the Show/Hide ¶ button in the Paragraph group in the Home tab. The end-of-cell marker displays inside each cell and the end-of-row marker displays at the end of a row of cells. These markers are identified in Figure 7.1.

When you create a table, the insertion point is located in the cell in the upper left corner of the table. Cells in a table contain a cell designation. Columns in a table are lettered from left to right, beginning with *A*. Rows in a table are numbered from top to bottom beginning with *1*. The cell in the upper left corner of the table is cell A1. The cell to the right of A1 is B1, the cell to the right of B1 is C1, and so on.

Figure 7.1 Table

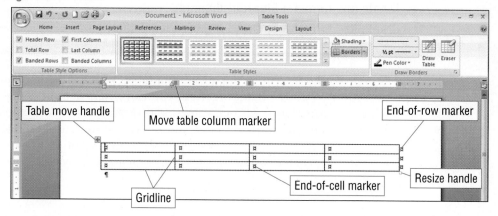

When the insertion point is positioned in a cell in the table, move table column markers display on the horizontal ruler. These markers represent the end of a column and are useful in changing the width of columns. Figure 7.1 identifies a move table column marker.

Entering Text in Cells

With the insertion point positioned in a cell, type or edit text. Move the insertion point to other cells with the mouse by clicking in the desired cell. If you are using the keyboard, press the Tab key to move the insertion point to the next cell or press Shift + Tab to move the insertion point to the previous cell.

If the text you type does not fit on one line, it wraps to the next line within the same cell. Or, if you press Enter within a cell, the insertion point is moved to the next line within the same cell. The cell vertically lengthens to accommodate the text, and all cells in that row also lengthen. Pressing the Tab key in a table causes the insertion point to move to the next cell in the table. If you want to move the

HINT
You can create a table within a table, creating a *nested* table.

HINT
Pressing the Tab key in a table moves the insertion point to the next cell. Pressing Ctrl + Tab moves the insertion point to the next tab within a cell.

insertion point to a tab stop within a cell, press Ctrl + Tab. If the insertion point is located in the last cell of the table and you press the Tab key, Word adds another row to the table. Insert a page break within a table by pressing Ctrl + Enter. The page break is inserted between rows, not within.

Moving the Insertion Point within a Table

To move the insertion point to a different cell within the table using the mouse, click in the desired cell. To move the insertion point to different cells within the table using the keyboard, refer to the information shown in Table 7.1.

Table 7.1 Insertion Point Movement within a Table Using the Keyboard

To move the insertion point	Press these keys
To next cell	Tab
To preceding cell	Shift + Tab
Forward one character	Right Arrow key
Backward one character	Left Arrow key
To previous row	Up Arrow key
To next row	Down Arrow key
To first cell in the row	Alt + Home
To last cell in the row	Alt + End
To top cell in the column	Alt + Page Up
To bottom cell in the column	Alt + Page Down

Project 1a Creating a Table

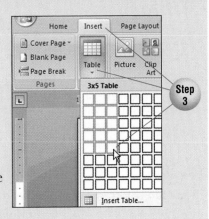

1. At a blank document, turn on bold, and then type the title CONTACT INFORMATION shown in Figure 7.2.
2. Turn off bold and then press the Enter key.
3. Create the table shown in Figure 7.2. To do this, click the Insert tab, click the Table button in the Tables group, drag down and to the right until the number above the grid displays as *3x5*, and then click the mouse button.
4. Type the text in the cells as indicated in Figure 7.2. Press the Tab key to move to the next cell or press Shift + Tab to move to the preceding cell. (If you accidentally press the Enter key within a cell, immediately press the Backspace key. Do not press Tab after typing the text in the last cell. If you do, another row is inserted in the table. If this happens, immediately click the Undo button on the Quick Access toolbar.)
5. Save the table and name it **WordL1_C7_P1**.

Figure 7.2 Project 1a

CONTACT INFORMATION

Maggie Rivera	First Trust Bank	(203) 555-3440
Regina Stahl	United Fidelity	(301) 555-1221
Justin White	Key One Savings	(360) 555-8966
Les Cromwell	Madison Trust	(602) 555-4900
Cecilia Nordyke	American Financial	(509) 555-3995

You can also create a table with options at the Insert Table dialog box shown in Figure 7.3. To display this dialog box, click the Insert tab, click the Table button in the Tables group, and then click *Insert Table.* At the Insert Table dialog box, enter the desired number of columns and rows and then click OK.

Figure 7.3 Insert Table Dialog Box

Use these options to specify the numbers of columns and rows.

Project 1b   Creating a Table with the Insert Table Dialog Box

1. With **WordL1_C7_P1.docx** open, press Ctrl + End to move the insertion point below the table.
2. Press the Enter key twice.
3. Turn on bold and then type the title OPTIONAL PLAN PREMIUM RATES shown in Figure 7.4.
4. Turn off bold and then press the Enter key.
5. Click the Insert tab, click the Table button in the Tables group, and then click *Insert Table* at the drop-down list.
6. At the Insert Table dialog box, type 3 in the *Number of columns* text box. (The insertion point is automatically positioned in this text box.)
7. Press the Tab key (this moves the insertion point to the *Number of rows* option) and then type 5.
8. Click OK.
9. Type the text in the cells as indicated in Figure 7.4. Press the Tab key to move to the next cell or press Shift + Tab to move to the preceding cell. To indent the text in cells B2 through B5 and cells C2 through C5, press Ctrl + Tab to move the insertion to a tab within cells and then type the text.
10. Save **WordL1_C7_P1.docx**.

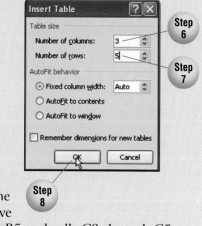

Step 6

Step 7

Step 8

Figure 7.4 Project 1b

OPTIONAL PLAN PREMIUM RATES

Waiting Period	Plan 2010 Employees	Basic Plan Employees
60 days	0.79%	0.67%
90 days	0.59%	0.49%
120 days	0.35%	0.30%
180 days	0.26%	0.23%

Changing the Table Design

When you create a table, the Table Tools Design tab is selected and the tab contains a number of options for enhancing the appearance of the table as shown in Figure 7.5. With options in the Table Styles group, apply a predesigned style that applies color and border lines to a table. Maintain further control over the predesigned style formatting applied to columns and rows with options in the Table Style Options group. For example, if your table contains a total column, you would insert a check mark in the *Total Row* option. Apply additional design formatting to cells in a table with the Shading and Borders buttons in the Table Styles group. Draw a table or draw additional rows and/or columns in a table by clicking the Draw Table button in the Draw Borders group. Click this button and the mouse pointer turns into a pencil. Drag in the table to create the desired columns and rows. Click the Eraser button and the mouse pointer turns into an eraser. Drag through the column and/or row lines you want to erase in the table.

HINT
Draw a freeform table by clicking the Insert tab, clicking the Table button, and then clicking the *Draw Table* option. Drag in the document to create the table.

 Draw Table Eraser

Figure 7.5 Table Tools Design Tab

1. With **WordL1_C7_P1.docx** open, click in any cell in the top table.
2. Apply a table style by completing the following steps:
   a. Click the Table Tools Design tab.
   b. Click the More button at the right side of the table styles in the Table Styles group.
   c. Click the *Medium Grid 3 - Accent 5* style (second table style from the *right* in the tenth row in the *Built-in* section).

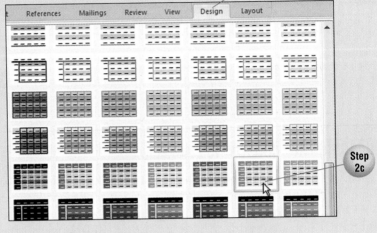

Step 2a

Step 2c

3. After looking at the table, you realize that the first row is not a header row and the first column should not be formatted differently than the other columns. To format the first row and first column in the same manner as the other rows and columns, click the *Header Row* check box and the *First Column* check box in the Table Style Options to remove the check marks.

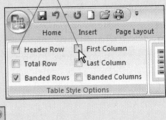

Step 3

4. Click in any cell in the bottom table, apply the Dark List - Accent 5 table style (second option from the *right* in the eleventh row in the Built-in section), and then remove the check mark from the *First Column* check box.
5. Add color borders to the top table by completing the following steps:
   a. Click in any cell in the top table.
   b. Click the Pen Color button arrow in the Draw Borders group and then click the *Orange, Accent 6, Darker 50%* color.
   c. Click the Line Weight button in the Draw Borders group and then click *1 ½ pt* at the drop-down list. (When you choose a line weight, the Draw Table button is automatically activated.)

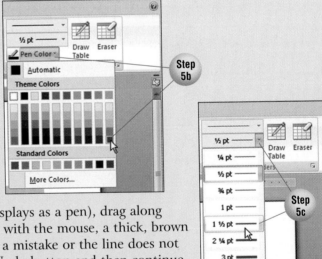

Step 5b

Step 5c

   d. Using the mouse (mouse pointer displays as a pen), drag along each side of the table. (As you drag with the mouse, a thick, brown border line is inserted. If you make a mistake or the line does not display as you intended, click the Undo button and then continue drawing along each side of the table.)
6. Drag along each side of the bottom table.
7. Click the Line Weight button in the Draw Borders group and then click *1 pt* at the drop-down list.
8. Drag along the row boundary separating the first row from the second row in the bottom table.
9. Click the Draw Table button to turn off the feature.
10. Save **WordL1_C7_P1.docx**.

Selecting Cells

You can apply formatting to an entire table or to specific cells, rows, or columns in a table. To identify cells for formatting, select the specific cells using the mouse or the keyboard.

Selecting in a Table with the Mouse

Use the mouse pointer to select a cell, row, column, or an entire table. Table 7.2 describes methods for selecting a table with the mouse. The left edge of each cell, between the left column border and the end-of-cell marker or first character in the cell, is called the *cell selection bar*. When you position the mouse pointer in the cell selection bar, it turns into a small, black arrow pointing up and to the right. Each row in a table contains a *row selection bar*, which is the space just to the left of the left edge of the table. When you position the mouse pointer in the row selection bar, the mouse pointer turns into an arrow pointing up and to the right.

Table 7.2 Selecting in a Table with the Mouse

To select this	Do this
A cell	Position the mouse pointer in the cell selection bar at the left edge of the cell until it turns into a small, black arrow pointing up and to the right and then click the left mouse button.
A row	Position the mouse pointer in the row selection bar at the left edge of the table until it turns into an arrow pointing up and to the right and then click the left mouse button.
A column	Position the mouse pointer on the uppermost horizontal gridline of the table in the appropriate column until it turns into a short, black down-pointing arrow and then click the left mouse button.
Adjacent cells	Position the mouse pointer in the first cell to be selected, hold down the left mouse button, drag the mouse pointer to the last cell to be selected, and then release the mouse button.
All cells in a table	Click the table move handle; or position the mouse pointer in any cell in the table, hold down the Alt key, and then double-click the left mouse button. You can also position the mouse pointer in the row selection bar for the first row at the left edge of the table until it turns into an arrow pointing up and to the right, hold down the left mouse button, drag down to select all rows in the table, and then release the left mouse button.
Text within a cell	Position the mouse pointer at the beginning of the text and then hold down the left mouse button as you drag the mouse across the text. (When a cell is selected, the cell background color changes to blue. When text within cells is selected, only those lines containing text are selected.)

Selecting in a Table with the Keyboard

In addition to the mouse, you can also use the keyboard to select specific cells within a table. Table 7.3 displays the commands for selecting specific amounts of a table.

Table 7.3 Selecting in a Table with the Keyboard

To select	Press
The next cell's contents	Tab
The preceding cell's contents	Shift + Tab
The entire table	Alt + 5 (on numeric keypad with Num Lock off)
Adjacent cells	Hold down Shift key, then press an arrow key repeatedly.
A column	Position insertion point in top cell of column, hold down Shift key, then press down-pointing arrow key until column is selected.

If you want to select only text within cells, rather than the entire cell, press F8 to turn on the Extend mode and then move the insertion point with an arrow key. When a cell is selected, the cell background color changes to blue. When text within a cell is selected, only those lines containing text are selected.

Project 1d   Selecting and Formatting Cells in a Table

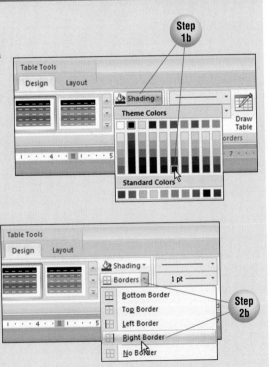

1. With **WordL1_C7_P1.docx** open, apply shading to a row by completing the following steps:
   a. Position the mouse pointer in the row selection bar at the left edge of the first row in the bottom table until the pointer turns into an arrow pointing up and to the right and then click the left mouse button. (This selects the entire first row of the bottom table.)
   b. Click the Shading button arrow in the Table Styles group and then click the *Red, Accent 2, Darker 50%* color.
2. Apply a border line to a column by completing the following steps:
   a. Position the mouse pointer on the uppermost horizontal gridline of the first column in the bottom table until the pointer turns into a short, down-pointing arrow and then click the left mouse button.
   b. Click the Borders button arrow and then click *Right Border* at the drop-down list. (This inserts a 1 point dark orange border line at the right side of the column.)

Step 1b

Step 2b

3. Complete steps similar to those in Step 2 to insert a border line at the right side of the second column.
4. Apply italic formatting to a column by completing the following steps:
   a. Position the insertion point in the first cell of the first row in the top table.
   b. Hold down the Shift key and then press the Down Arrow key four times. (This should select all cells in the first column.)
   c. Press Ctrl + I.
5. Save **WordL1_C7_P1.docx**.

Changing Table Layout

To further customize a table, consider changing the table layout by inserting or deleting columns and rows and specifying cell alignments. Change table layout with options at the Table Tools Layout tab shown in Figure 7.6. Use options and buttons in the tab to select specific cells, delete and insert rows and columns, merge and split cells, specify cell height and width, sort data in cells, and insert a formula.

HINT
Some table layout options are available at a shortcut menu that can be viewed by right-clicking a table.

Figure 7.6 Table Tools Layout Tab

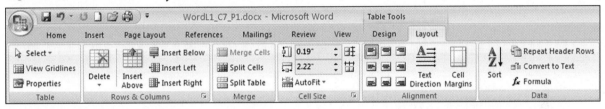

Selecting with the Select Button

Along with selecting cells with the keyboard and mouse, you can also select specific cells with the Select button in the Table group in the Table Tools Layout tab. To select with this button, position the insertion point in the desired cell, column, or row and then click the Select button. At the drop-down list that displays, specify what you want to select—the entire table or a column, row, or cell.

Inserting and Deleting Rows and Columns

With buttons in the Rows & Columns group in the Table Tools Layout tab, you can insert a row or column and delete a row or column. Click the button in the group that inserts the row or column in the desired location such as above, below, to the left, or to the right. Add a row to the bottom of a table by positioning the insertion point in the last cell and then pressing the Tab key. To delete a table, row, or column, click the Delete button and then click the option identifying what you want to delete. If you make a mistake while formatting a table, immediately click the Undo button on the Quick Access toolbar.

Project 1e Selecting, Inserting, and Deleting Columns and Rows

1. With **WordL1_C7_P1.docx** open, select a column and apply formatting by completing the following steps:
   a. Click in any cell in the first column in the top table.
   b. Click the Table Tools Layout tab.
   c. Click the Select button in the Table group and then click *Select Column* at the drop-down list.

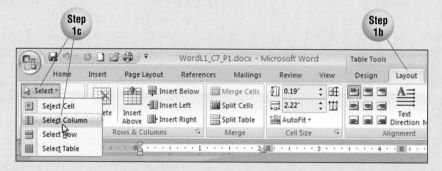

Step 1c

Step 1b

   d. With the first column selected, press Ctrl + I to remove italics and then press Ctrl + B to apply bold formatting.
2. Select a row and apply formatting by completing the following steps:
   a. Click in any cell in the first row in the bottom table.
   b. Click the Select button in the Table group and then click *Select Row* at the drop-down list.
   c. With the first row selected in the bottom table, press Ctrl + I to apply italic formatting.
3. Insert a new row in the bottom table and type text in the new cells by completing the following steps:
   a. Click in the cell containing the text *60 days*.

b. Click the Insert Above button in the Rows & Columns group.

c. Type 30 days in the first cell of the new row, type 0.85% in the middle cell of the new row (make sure you press Ctrl + Tab before typing the text), and type 0.81% in the third cell of the new row (make sure you press Ctrl + Tab before typing the text).

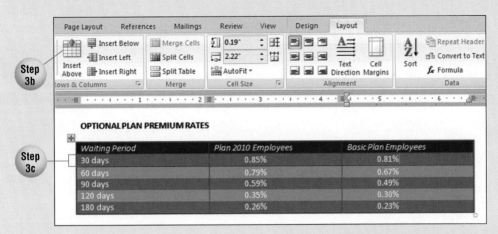

4. Insert three new rows in the top table and type text in the new cells by completing the following steps:

a. Select the three rows of cells that begin with the names *Regina Stahl*, *Justin White*, and *Les Cromwell*.

b. Click the Insert Below button in the Rows & Columns group.

c. Type the following text in the new cells:

Teresa Getty	Meridian Bank	(503) 555-9800
Michael Vazquez	New Horizon Bank	(702) 555-2435
Samantha Roth	Cascade Mutual	(206) 555-6788

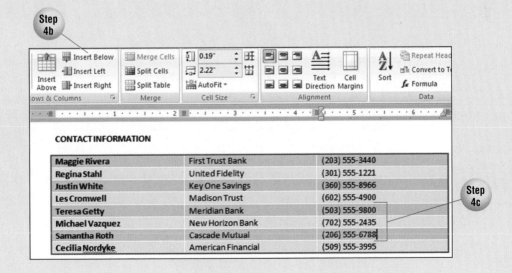

5. Delete a row by completing the following steps:
   a. Click in the cell containing the name *Les Cromwell*.
   b. Click the Delete button in the Rows & Columns group and then click *Delete Rows* at the drop-down list.
6. Insert a new column and type text in the new cells by completing the following steps:
   a. Click in the cell containing the text *First Trust Bank*.
   b. Click the Insert Left button in the Rows & Columns group.
   c. Type the following text in the news cells:

B1	=	Vice President
B2	=	Loan Officer
B3	=	Account Manager
B4	=	Branch Manager
B5	=	President
B6	=	Vice President
B7	=	Regional Manager

7. Save **WordL1_C7_P1.docx**.

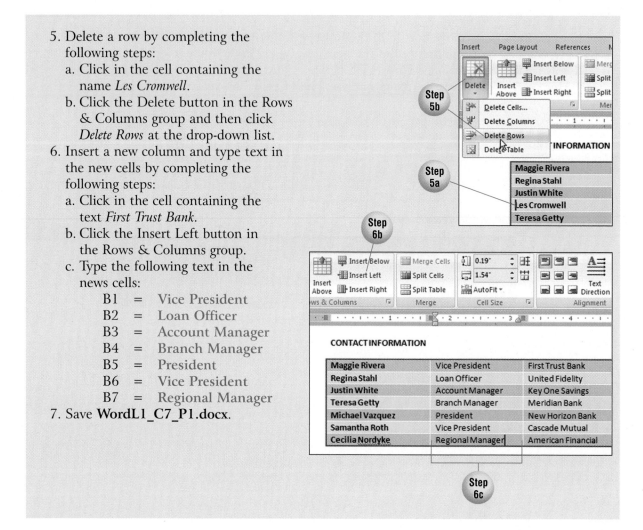

Merging and Splitting Cells and Tables

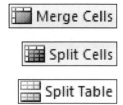

Click the Merge Cells button in the Merge group in the Table Tools Layout tab to merge selected cells and click the Split Cells button to split the currently active cell. When you click the Split Cells button, the Split Cells dialog box displays where you specify the number of columns or rows into which you want to split the active cell. If you want to split one table into two tables, position the insertion point in a cell in the row that you want to be the first row in the new table and then click the Split Table button.

1. With **WordL1_C7_P1.docx** open, insert a new row and merge cells in the row by completing the following steps:

   a. Click in the cell containing the text *Waiting Period* (located in the bottom table).

   b. Click the Insert Above button in the Rows & Columns group.

   c. With all of the cells in the new row selected, click the Merge Cells button in the Merge group.

   d. Type OPTIONAL PLAN PREMIUM RATES and then press Ctrl + E to center-align the text in the cell. (The text you type will be italicized.)

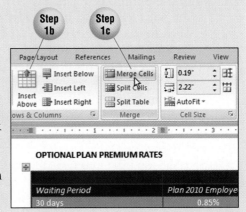

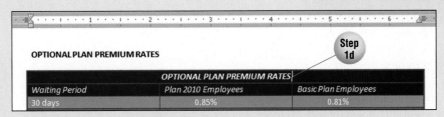

2. Select and then delete the text *OPTIONAL PLAN PREMIUM RATES* that displays above the bottom table.

3. Insert rows and text in the top table and merge cells by completing the following steps:

   a. Click in the cell containing the text *Maggie Rivera*.

   b. Click the Table Tools Layout tab.

   c. Click the Insert Above button twice. (This inserts two rows at the top of the table.)

   d. With the cells in the top row selected, click the Merge Cells button in the Merge group.

   e. Type CONTACT INFORMATION, NORTH and then press Ctrl + E to change the paragraph alignment to center.

   f. Type the following text in the four cells in the new second row.

       Name   Title   Company   Telephone

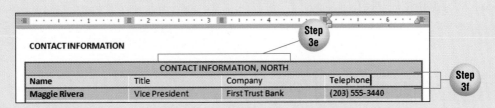

4. Apply heading formatting to the new top row by completing the following steps:

   a. Click the Table Tools Design tab.

   b. Click the *Header Row* check box in the Table Style Options dialog box.

5. Select and then delete the text *CONTACT INFORMATION* that displays above the top table.

6. Split a cell by completing the following steps:

   a. Click in the cell containing the telephone number *(360) 555-8966*.

   b. Click the Table Tools Layout tab.

c. Click the Split Cells button in the Merge group.

d. At the Split Cells dialog box, click OK. (The telephone number will wrap to a new line. You will change this in the next project.)

e. Click in the new cell.

f. Type x453 in the new cell. If AutoCorrect automatically capitalizes the *x*, hover the mouse pointer over the *X* until the AutoCorrect Options button displays. Click the AutoCorrect Options button and then click *Undo Automatic Capitalization* or click *Stop Auto-capitalizing First Letter of Table Cells.*

Telephone	
(203) 555-3440	
(301) 555-1221	
(360) 555-	x453
8966	
(503) 555-9800	

Step 6f

7. Split the cell containing the telephone number *(206) 555-6788* and then type x2310 in the new cell. (If necessary, make the *x* lowercase.)

8. Split the top table into two tables by completing the following steps:

   a. Click in the cell containing the name *Teresa Getty.*

   b. Click the Split Table button in the Merge group.

   c. Click in the cell containing the name *Teresa Getty* (in the first row of the new table).

   d. Click the Insert Above button.

   e. With the new row selected, click the Merge Cells button.

   f. Type CONTACT INFORMATION, SOUTH in the new row and then press Ctrl + E to center-align the text.

9. Draw a dark orange border at the bottom of the top table and the top of the middle table by completing the following steps:

   a. Click the Table Tools Design tab.

   b. Click the Line Weight button in the Draw Borders group and then click *1 ½ pt* at the drop-down list. (This activates the Draw Table button.)

   c. Using the mouse (pointer displays as a pen), drag along the bottom border of the top table.

   d. Drag along the top border of the middle table.

   e. Click the Draw Table button to turn it off.

10. Save and then print **WordL1_C7_P1.docx**.

11. Delete the middle table by completing the following steps:

    a. Click in any cell in the middle table.

    b. Click the Table Tools Layout tab.

    c. Click the Delete button in the Rows & Columns group and then click *Delete Table* at the drop-down list.

12. Save **WordL1_C7_P1.docx**.

Customizing Cell Size

Distribute Rows

Distribute Columns

When you create a table, column width and row height are equal. You can customize the width of columns or height of rows with buttons in the Cell Size group in the Table Tools Layout tab. Use the *Table Row Height* measurement box to increase or decrease the height of rows and use the *Table Column Width* measurement box to increase or decrease the width of columns. The Distribute Rows button will distribute equally the height of selected rows and the Distribute Columns button will distribute equally the width of selected columns.

You can also change column width using the move table column markers on the horizontal ruler or by using the table gridlines. To change column width using the horizontal ruler, position the mouse pointer on a move table column marker until it turns into a left and right arrow, and then drag the marker to the desired position. Hold down the Shift key while dragging a table column marker and the horizontal ruler remains stationary while the table column marker moves. Hold down the Alt key while dragging a table column marker and measurements display on the horizontal ruler. To change column width using gridlines, position the arrow pointer on the gridline separating columns until the insertion point turns into a left and right arrow with a vertical line between and then drag the gridline to the desired position. If you want to see the column measurements on the horizontal ruler as you drag a gridline, hold down the Alt key.

Adjust row height in a manner similar to adjusting column width. You can drag the adjust table row marker on the vertical ruler or drag the gridline separating rows. Hold down the Alt key while dragging the adjust table row marker or the row gridline and measurements display on the vertical ruler.

Use the AutoFit button in the Cell Size group to make the column widths in a table automatically fit the contents. To do this, position the insertion point in any cell in the table, click the AutoFit button in the Cell Size group, and then click *AutoFit Contents* at the drop-down list.

Project 1g — Changing Column Width and Row Height

1. With **WordL1_C7_P1.docx** open, change the width of the first column in the top table by completing the following steps:
   a. Click in the cell containing the name *Maggie Rivera*.
   b. Position the mouse pointer on the move table column marker that displays just right of the 1.5-inch marker on the horizontal ruler until the pointer turns into an arrow pointing left and right.

   Step 1d

Name		Title
Maggie Rivera		Vice P
Regina Stahl		Loan C

   c. Hold down the Shift key and then the left mouse button.
   d. Drag the marker to the 1.25-inch mark, release the mouse button and then release the Shift key.
2. Complete steps similar to those in Step 1 to drag the move table column marker that displays just right of the 3-inch mark on the horizontal ruler to the 2.5-inch mark. (Make sure the text *Account Manager* in the second column does not wrap to the next line. If it does, slightly increase the width of the column.)
3. Change the width of the third column in the top table by completing the following steps:
   a. Position the mouse pointer on the gridline separating the third and fourth columns until the pointer turns into a left- and right-pointing arrow with a vertical double line between.

   Step 3b

	1.4"		2.38"	
CONTACT INFORMATION, NORTH				
Company			Telephone	
First Trust Bank			(203) 555-3440	
United Fidelity			(301) 555-1221	
Key One Savings			(360) 555-8966	x453

   b. Hold down the Alt key and then the left mouse button, drag the gridline to the left until the measurement for the third column on the horizontal ruler displays as *1.4"*, and then release the Alt key and then the mouse button.

4. Position the mouse pointer on the gridline that separates the telephone number *(360) 555-8966* from the extension *x453* and then drag the gridline to the 5.25-inch mark on the horizontal ruler.

5. Drag the right border of the top table to the 5.75-inch marker on the horizontal ruler.

6. Autofit the columns in the bottom table by completing the following steps:
   a. Click in any cell in the bottom table.
   b. Click the AutoFit button in the Cell Size group and then click *AutoFit Contents* at the drop-down list.

7. Increase the height of the first row in the bottom table by completing the following steps:
   a. Make sure the insertion point is located in one of the cells in the bottom table.
   b. Position the mouse pointer on the top adjust table row marker on the vertical ruler.
   c. Hold down the left mouse button and hold down the Alt key.
   d. Drag the adjust table row marker down until the first row measurement on the vertical ruler displays as *0.36"*, release the mouse button and then the Alt key.

8. Increase the height of the first row in the top table by completing the following steps:
   a. Click in any cell in the top table.
   b. Position the arrow pointer on the gridline that displays at the bottom of the top row until the arrow pointer turns into an up- and down-pointing arrow with a vertical double line between.
   c. Hold down the left mouse button and then hold down the Alt key.
   d. Drag the gridline down until the first row measurement on the vertical ruler displays as *0.36"* and release the mouse button and then the Alt key.

9. Save **WordL1_C7_P1.docx**.

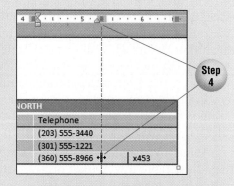

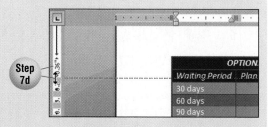

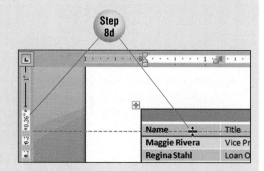

Changing Cell Alignment

The Alignment group in the Table Tools Layout tab contains a number of buttons for specifying the horizontal and vertical alignment of text in cells. The buttons contain a visual representation of the alignment and you can also hover the mouse pointer over a button to determine the alignment.

1. With **WordL1_C7_P1.docx** open, click in the top cell in the top table (the cell containing the title *CONTACT INFORMATION, NORTH*).
2. Click the Align Center button in the Alignment group in the Table Tools Layout tab.
3. Format and align text in the second row in the table by completing the following steps:
   a. Select the second row.
   b. Press Ctrl + B (this turns off bold for the entry in the first cell) and then press Ctrl + B again (this turns on bold for all entries in the second row).
   c. Click the Align Top Center button in the Alignment group.
4. Click in the top cell in the bottom table and then click the Align Center button in the Alignment group.
5. Save, print, and then close **WordL1_C7_P1.docx**.

Project **2** Create and Format Tables with Employee Information

You will create and format a table containing information on the names and departments of employees of Tri-State Products and also insert a table containing additional information on employees and then format the table.

Changing Cell Margin Measurements

By default, cells in a table contain specific margin settings. Top and bottom margins in a cell have a default measurement of *0"* and left and right margins have a default setting of *0.08"*. Change these default settings with options at the Table Options dialog box shown in Figure 7.7. Display this dialog box by clicking the Cell Margins button in the Alignment group in the Table Tools Layout tab. Use the options in the *Default cell margins* section to change the top, bottom, left, and/or right cell margin measurements.

Figure 7.7 Table Options Dialog Box

Use options in this section to increase and/or decrease margin measurements in cells.

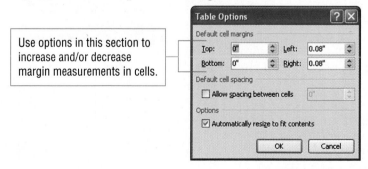

Changes to cell margins will affect all cells in a table. If you want to change the cell margin measurements for one cell or for selected cells, position the insertion point in the cell or select the desired cells, and then click the Properties button in the Table group in the Table Tools Layout tab. (You can also click the Cell Size group dialog box launcher.) At the Table Properties dialog box that displays, click the Cell tab and then the Options button that displays in the lower right corner of the dialog box. This displays the Cell Options dialog box shown in Figure 7.8.

Figure 7.8 Cell Options Dialog Box

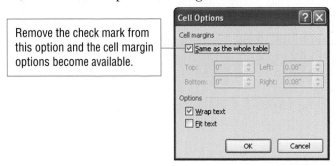

Remove the check mark from this option and the cell margin options become available.

Before setting the new cell margin measurements, remove the check mark from the *Same as the whole table* option. With the check mark removed from this option, the cell margin options become available. Specify the new cell margin measurements and then click OK to close the dialog box.

Project 2a Changing Cell Margin Measurements

1. Open **WordTable01.docx** and then save the document and name it **WordL1_C7_P2**.
2. Change the top and bottom margins for all cells in the table by completing the following steps:
   a. Position the insertion point in any cell in the table and then click the Table Tools Layout tab.
   b. Click the Cell Margins button in the Alignment group.
   c. At the Table Options dialog box, change the *Top* and *Bottom* measurements to *0.05"*.
   d. Click OK to close the Table Options dialog box.
3. Change the top and bottom cell margin measurements for the first row of cells by completing the following steps:
   a. Select the first row of cells (the cells containing *Name* and *Department*).
   b. Click the Properties button in the Table group.
   c. At the Table Properties dialog box, click the Cell tab.
   d. Click the Options button.
   e. At the Cell Options dialog box, remove the check mark from the *Same as the whole table* option.
   f. Change the *Top* and *Bottom* measurements to *0.1"*.
   g. Click OK to close the Cell Options dialog box.
   h. Click OK to close the Table Properties dialog box.

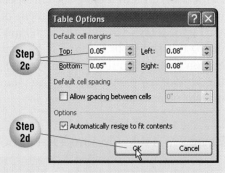

Step 2c

Step 2d

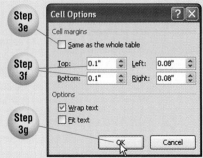

Step 3e

Step 3f

Step 3g

4. Change the left cell margin measurement for specific cells by completing the following steps:
   a. Select all rows in the table *except* the top row.
   b. Click the Cell Size group dialog box launcher.
   c. At the Table Properties dialog box, click the Cell tab.
   d. Click the Options button.
   e. At the Cell Options dialog box, remove the check mark from the *Same as the whole table* option.
   f. Change the *Left* measurement to *0.3"*.
   g. Click OK to close the Cell Options dialog box.
   h. Click OK to close the Table Properties dialog box.
5. Save **WordL1_C7_P2.docx**.

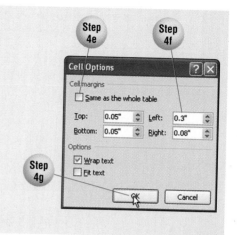

Changing Cell Direction

Change the direction of text in a cell using the Text Direction button in the Alignment group in the Table Tools Layout tab. Each time you click the Text Direction button, the text rotates in the cell 90 degrees.

Text Direction

Changing Table Alignment

By default, a table aligns at the left margin. Change this alignment with options at the Table Properties dialog box with the Table tab selected as shown in Figure 7.9. To change the alignment, click the desired alignment option in the Alignment section of the dialog box.

Figure 7.9 Table Properties Dialog Box with Table Tab Selected

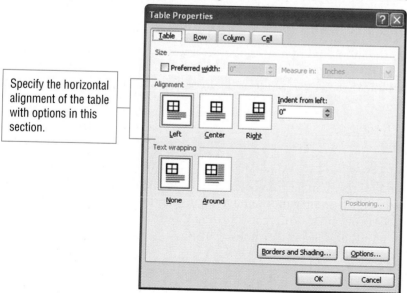

Specify the horizontal alignment of the table with options in this section.

1. With **WordL1_C7_P2.docx** open, insert a new column and change text direction by completing the following steps:
   a. Click in any cell in the first column.
   b. Click the Insert Left button in the Rows & Columns group.
   c. With the cells in the new column selected, click the Merge Cells button in the Merge group.
   d. Type Tri-State Products.
   e. Click the Align Center button in the Alignment group.
   f. Click twice on the Text Direction button in the Alignment group.
   g. With *Tri-State Products* selected, click the Home tab, and then increase the font size to *16*.
2. Autofit the contents by completing the following steps:
   a. Click in any cell in the table.
   b. Click the Table Tools Layout tab.
   c. Click the AutoFit button in the Cell Size group and then click the *AutoFit Contents* at the drop-down list.
3. Change the table alignment by completing the following steps:
   a. Click the Properties button in the Table group in the Table Tools Layout tab.
   b. At the Table Properties dialog box, click the Table tab.
   c. Click the *Center* option in the *Alignment* section.
   d. Click OK.
4. Select the two cells containing the text *Name* and *Department* and then click the Align Center button in the Alignment group.
5. Save **WordL1_C7_P2.docx**.

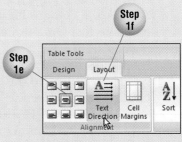

Step 1e
Step 1f

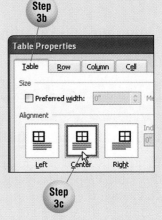

Step 3b
Step 3c

Changing Table Size with the Resize Handle

When you hover the mouse pointer over a table, a resize handle displays in the lower right corner of the table. The resize handle displays as a small, white square. Drag this resize handle to increase and/or decrease the size and proportion of the table.

Moving a Table

Position the mouse pointer in a table and a table move handle displays in the upper left corner. Use this handle to move the table in the document. To move a table, position the mouse pointer on the table move handle until the pointer turns into a four-headed arrow, hold down the left mouse button, drag the table to the desired position, and then release the mouse button.

1. With **WordL1_C7_P2.docx** open, insert a table into the current document by completing the following steps:
   a. Press Ctrl + End to move the insertion point to the end of the document and then press the Enter key.
   b. Click the Insert tab.
   c. Click the Object button arrow in the Text group and then click *Text from File* at the drop-down list.
   d. At the Insert File dialog box, navigate to the Word2007L1C7 folder and then double-click **WordTable02.docx**.
2. Autofit the bottom table by completing the following steps:
   a. Click in any cell in the bottom table.
   b. Click the Table Tools Layout tab.
   c. Click the AutoFit button in the Cell Size group and then click *AutoFit Contents* at the drop-down list.
3. Format the bottom table by completing the following steps:
   a. Click the Table Tools Design tab.
   b. Click the More button that displays at the right side of the Table Styles group and then click the *Medium Shading 1 - Accent 2* style (third style from the left in the fourth row of the *Built-In* section).

Step
3b

   c. Click the First Column check box to remove the check mark.
   d. Select the first and second rows, click the Table Tools Layout tab, and then click the Align Center button in the Alignment group.
   e. Select the second row and then press Ctrl + B to turn on bold.

4. Resize the bottom table by completing the following steps:
   a. Position the mouse pointer on the resize handle located in the lower right corner of the top table.
   b. Hold down the left mouse button, drag down and to the right until the width and height of the table increases approximately one inch, and then release the mouse button.

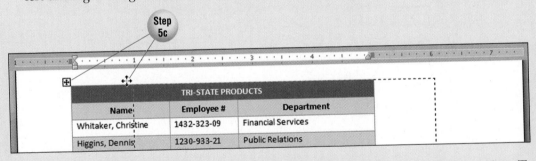

5. Move the bottom table by completing the following steps:
   a. Hover the mouse pointer over the bottom table.
   b. Position the mouse pointer on the table move handle until the pointer displays with a four-headed arrow attached.
   c. Hold down the left mouse button, drag the table so it is positioned equally between the left and right margins, and then release the mouse button.

6. Select the cells in the column below the heading *Employee #* and then click the Align Top Center button in the Alignment group.
7. Save **WordL1_C7_P2.docx**.

Converting Text to a Table

You can create a table and then enter data in the cells or you can create the data and then convert it to a table. To convert text to a table, type the text and separate it with a separator character such as a comma or tab. The separator character identifies where you want text divided into columns. To convert text, select the text, click the Insert tab, click the Table button in the Tables group, and then click *Convert Text to Table* at the drop-down list.

Converting a Table to Text

You can convert a table to text by positioning the insertion point in any cell of the table, clicking the Table Tools Layout tab, and then clicking the Convert to Text button in the Data group. At the Convert Table to Text dialog box, specify the desired separator and then click OK.

Project 2d — Converting Text to a Table

1. With **WordL1_C7_P2.docx** open, press Ctrl + End to move the insertion point to the end of the document and then press the Enter key until the insertion point is positioned approximately a double space below the bottom table.
2. Insert the document named **WordList01.docx** into the current document.
3. Convert the text to a table by completing the following steps:
   a. Select the text you just inserted.
   b. Click the Insert tab.
   c. Click the Table button in the Tables group and then click *Convert Text to Table* at the drop-down list.
   d. At the Convert Text to Table dialog box, type 2 in the *Number of columns* text box.
   e. Click the *AutoFit to contents* option in the *AutoFit behavior* section.
   f. Click the *Commas* option in the *Separate text at* section.
   g. Click OK.
4. Select and merge the cells in the top row (the row containing the title *TRI-STATE PRODUCTS* and then change the alignment to Center.
5. Apply the Medium Shading 1 - Accent 2 style (third style from the left in the fourth row of the *Built-In* section) and remove the check mark from the *First Column* check box in the Table Style Options group in the Table Tools Design tab.
6. Drag the table so it is centered and positioned below the table above.
7. Apply the Medium Shading 1 - Accent 2 style to the top table. Increase the width of the columns so the text *TRI-STATE PRODUCTS* is visible and the text in the second and third columns displays on one line.
8. If necessary, drag the table so it is centered and positioned above the middle table. Make sure the three tables fit on one page.
9. Save, print, and then close **WordL1_C7_P2.docx**.

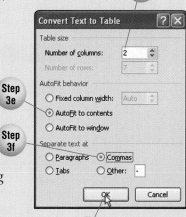

Step 3d

Step 3e

Step 3f

Step 3g

roject **3** **Sort and Calculate Sales Data**

You will sort data in tables on Tri-State Products sales and then insert formulas to calculate total sales, average sales, and top sales.

Sorting Text in a Table

With the Sort button in the Data group in the Table Tools Layout tab, you can sort text in selected cells in a table in ascending alphabetic or numeric order. To sort text, select the desired rows in the table and then click the Sort button in the Data group. At the Sort dialog box, specify the column containing the text on which you want to sort, and then click OK.

Project **3a**   Sorting Text in a Table

1. Open **WordTable03.docx** and then save the document and name it **WordL1_C7_P3**.
2. Sort text in the top table by completing the following steps:
   a. Select all of the rows containing names (from *Novak, Diana* through *Sogura, Jeffrey*).
   b. Click Table Tools Layout tab.
   c. Click the Sort button in the Data group.
   d. At the Sort dialog box, click OK. (This sorts the last names in the first column in alphabetical order.)

3. After looking at the table, you decide to sort by 2009 Sales. To do this, complete the following steps:
   a. With the rows still selected, click the Sort button in the Data group.
   b. At the Sort dialog box, click the down-pointing arrow at the right side of the *Sort by* option box and then click *Column 2* at the drop-down list.
   c. Click OK.
   d. Deselect the rows.
4. Save **WordL1_C7_P3.docx**.

Performing Calculations in a Table

You can use the Formula button in the Data group in the Table Tools Layout tab to insert formulas that calculate data in a table. Numbers in cells in a table can be added, subtracted, multiplied, and divided. In addition, you can calculate averages, percentages, and minimum and maximum values. You can calculate data in a Word table, but for complex calculations use an Excel worksheet.

To perform a calculation on data in a table, position the insertion point in the cell where you want the result of the calculation inserted and then click the Formula button in the Data group in the Table Tools Layout tab. This displays the Formula dialog box shown in Figure 7.10. At this dialog box, accept the default formula that displays in the *Formula* text box or type the desired calculation, and then click OK.

Figure 7.10 Formula Dialog Box

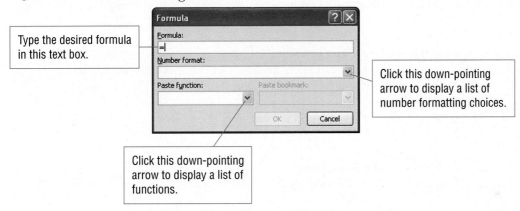

Type the desired formula in this text box.

Click this down-pointing arrow to display a list of number formatting choices.

Click this down-pointing arrow to display a list of functions.

You can use four basic operators when writing a formula including the plus sign (+) for addition, the minus sign (hyphen) for subtraction, the asterisk (*) for multiplication, and the forward slash (/) for division. If a calculation contains two or more operators, Word calculates from left to right. If you want to change the order of calculation, use parentheses around the part of the calculation to be performed first.

In the default formula, the **SUM** part of the formula is called a *function*. Word provides other functions you can use to write a formula. These functions are available with the *Paste function* option in the Formula dialog box. For example, you can use the AVERAGE function to average numbers in cells.

Specify the numbering format with the *Number format* option at the Formula dialog box. For example, if you are calculating money amounts, you can specify that the calculated numbers display with no numbers or two numbers following the decimal point.

1. With **WordL1_C7_P3.docx** open, insert a formula by completing the following steps:
   a. Click in cell B9 (the empty cell located immediately below the cell containing the amount *$623,214*).
   b. Click the Table Tools Layout tab.
   c. Click the Formula button in the Data group.
   d. At the Formula dialog box, make sure *=SUM(ABOVE)* displays in the *Formula* option box.
   e. Click the down-pointing arrow at the right side of the *Number format* option box and then click *#,##0* at the drop-down list (top option in the list).
   f. Click OK to close the Formula dialog box.
   g. At the table, type a dollar sign ($) before the number just inserted in cell B9.

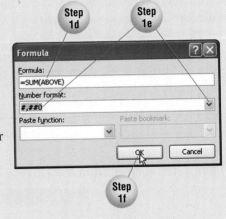

Step 1d   Step 1e

Step 1f

2. Complete steps similar to those in Steps 1c through 1g to insert a formula in cell C9 (the empty cell located immediately below the cell containing the amount *$635,099*).
3. Complete steps similar to those in Steps 1c through 1g to insert in the bottom table formulas that calculate totals. Insert formulas in the cells in the *Total* row and *Total* column. When inserting formulas in cells F3 through F6, you will need to change the formula to *=SUM(LEFT)*.
4. Insert a formula that calculates the average of amounts by completing the following steps:
   a. Click in cell B10 in the top table. (Cell B10 is the empty cell immediately right of the cell containing the word *Average*.)
   b. Click the Formula button in the Data group.
   c. At the Formula dialog box, delete the formula in the *Formula* text box *except* the equals sign.
   d. With the insertion point positioned immediately right of the equals sign, click the down-pointing arrow at the right side of the *Paste function* option box and then click *AVERAGE* at the drop-down list.
   e. With the insertion point positioned between the left and right parentheses, type B2:B8. (When typing cell designations in a formula, you can type either uppercase or lowercase letters.)

Step 4e

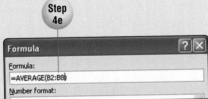

   f. Click the down-pointing arrow at the right side of the *Number format* option box and then click *#,##0* at the drop-down list (top option in the list).
   g. Click OK to close the Formula dialog box.
   h. Type a dollar sign ($) before the number just inserted in cell B10.
5. Complete steps similar to those in Steps 4b through 4h to insert a formula in cell C10 in the top table that calculates the average of cells C2 through C8.

6. Complete steps similar to those in Steps 4b through 4h to insert a formula in cell B7 in the bottom table that calculates the average of cells B2 through B5. Complete similar steps to insert in cell C7 the average of cells C2 through C5; insert in cell D7 the average of cells D2 through D5; insert in cell E7 the average of cells E2 through E5; and insert in cell F7 the average of cells F2 through F5.

7. Insert a formula that calculates the maximum number by completing the following steps:
   a. Click in cell B11 in the top table (the empty cell immediately right of the cell containing the word *Top Sales*).
   b. Click the Formula button in the Data group.
   c. At the Formula dialog box, delete the formula in the *Formula* text box *except* the equals sign.
   d. With the insertion point positioned immediately right of the equals sign, click the down-pointing arrow at the right side of the *Paste function* option box and then click *MAX* at the drop-down list. (You will need to scroll down the list to display the *MAX* option.)
   e. With the insertion point positioned between the left and right parentheses, type B2:B8.
   f. Click the down-pointing arrow at the right side of the *Number format* option box and then click *#,##0* at the drop-down list (top option in the list).
   g. Click OK to close the Formula dialog box.
   h. Type a dollar sign ($) before the number just inserted in cell B11.

Step 7d

8. Complete steps similar to those in Steps 7b through 7h to insert the maximum number in cell C11.

9. Apply formatting to each table to enhance the visual appeal of the tables.

10. Save, print, and then close **WordL1_C7_P3.docx**.

Project 4 **Prepare and Format a Diagram**

You will prepare a process diagram identifying steps in the production process and then apply formatting to enhance the diagram.

Creating SmartArt

With Word's SmartArt feature you can insert diagrams and organizational charts in a document. SmartArt offers a variety of predesigned diagrams and organizational charts that are available at the Choose a SmartArt Graphic dialog box shown in Figure 7.11. At this dialog box, *All* is selected in the left panel and all available predesigned diagrams display in the middle panel.

HINT

Use SmartArt to communicate your message and ideas in a visual manner.

SmartArt

Figure 7.11 Choose a SmartArt Graphic Dialog Box

Double-click the desired SmartArt graphic in this panel.

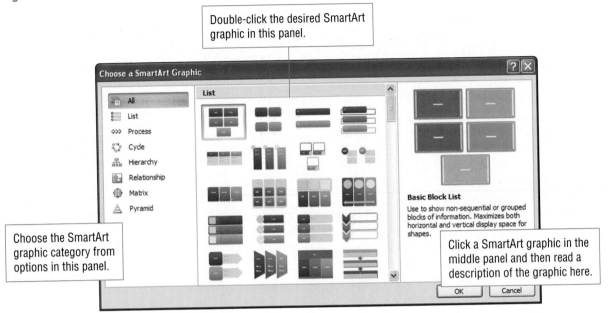

Choose the SmartArt graphic category from options in this panel.

Click a SmartArt graphic in the middle panel and then read a description of the graphic here.

Inserting and Formatting a SmartArt Diagram

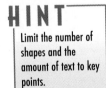

Insert a SmartArt Diagram
1. Click Insert tab.
2. Click SmartArt button.
3. Double-click desired diagram.

Predesigned diagrams display in the middle panel of the Choose a SmartArt Graphic dialog box. Use the scroll bar at the right side of the middle panel to scroll down the list of diagram choices. Click a diagram in the middle panel and the name of the diagram displays in the right panel along with a description of the diagram type. SmartArt includes diagrams for presenting a list of data; showing data processes, cycles, and relationships; and presenting data in a matrix or pyramid. Double-click a diagram in the middle panel of the dialog box and the diagram is inserted in the document.

When you double-click a diagram at the dialog box, the diagram is inserted in the document and a text pane displays at the left side of the diagram. You can type text in the diagram in the text pane or directly in the diagram. Apply design formatting to a diagram with options at the SmartArt Tools Design tab shown in Figure 7.12. This tab is active when the diagram is inserted in the document. With options and buttons in this tab you add objects, change the diagram layout, apply a style to the diagram, and reset the diagram back to the original formatting.

HINT
Limit the number of shapes and the amount of text to key points.

Figure 7.12 SmartArt Tools Design Tab

Project 4a   Inserting and Formatting a Diagram

1. At a blank document, insert the diagram shown in Figure 7.13 by completing the
   following steps:
   a. Click the Insert tab.
   b. Click the SmartArt button in the Illustrations group.
   c. At the Choose a SmartArt Graphic
      dialog box, click *Process* in the left
      panel and then double-click the
      Alternating Flow diagram (last option
      in the top row).

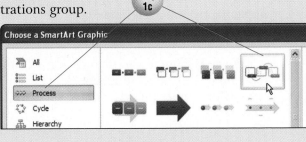

Step
1c

   d. If a *Type your text here* text pane does
      not display at the left side of the
      diagram, click the Text Pane button
      in the Create Graphic group to display the pane.
   e. With the insertion point positioned after the top bullet
      in the *Type your text here* text pane, type Design.
   f. Click *[Text]* that displays below *Design* and then type
      Mock-up.
   g. Continue clicking occurrences of *[Text]* and typing text
      so the text pane displays as shown at the right.
   h. Close the text pane by clicking the Close button
      (contains an X) that displays in the upper right corner
      of the pane. (You can also click the Text Pane button in
      the Create Graphic group.)
2. Change the diagram colors by clicking the Change Colors
   button in the SmartArt Styles group and then clicking the
   first option in the *Colorful* section (*Colorful – Accent Colors*).

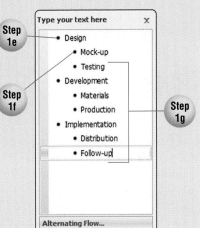

Step
1e

Step
1f

Step
1g

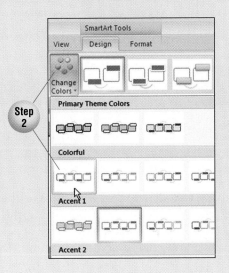

Step
2

3. Apply a style by clicking the More button that displays at the right side of the SmartArt Styles group and then clicking the second option from the left in the top row of the *3-D* section (*Inset*).

4. Copy the diagram and then change the layout by completing the following steps:
   a. Click inside the diagram border but outside of any shapes.
   b. Click the Home tab and then click the Copy button in the Clipboard group.
   c. Press Ctrl + End, press the Enter key once, and then press Ctrl + Enter to insert a page break.
   d. Click the Paste button in the Clipboard group.
   e. Click the bottom diagram.
   f. Click the SmartArt Tools Design tab.
   g. Click the middle layout (*Continuous Block Process*) in the Layouts group.
   h. Click outside the diagram to deselect it.

5. Save the document and name it **WordL1_C7_P4**.

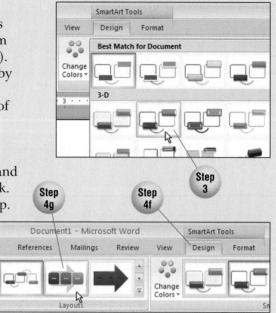

Figure 7.13 Project 4a

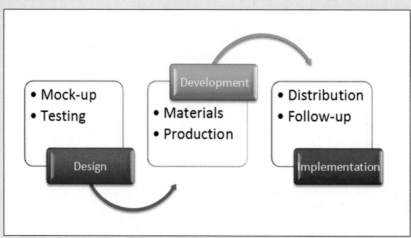

Apply formatting to a diagram with options at the SmartArt Tools Format tab shown in Figure 7.14. With options and buttons in this tab you can change the size and shape of objects in the diagram; apply shape styles and WordArt styles; change the shape fill, outline, and effects; and arrange and size the diagram.

Figure 7.14 SmartArt Tools Format Tab

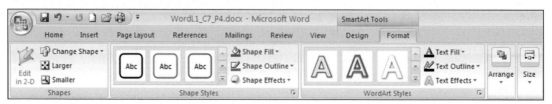

Arranging and Moving a SmartArt Diagram

Before moving a SmartArt diagram, you must select a text wrapping style. Select a text wrapping style with the Arrange button in the SmartArt Tools Format tab. Click the Arrange button, click the Position button, and then click the desired position at the drop-down gallery. You can also choose a text wrapping by clicking the Arrange button, clicking Text Wrapping, and then clicking the desired wrapping style at the drop-down list. Move the diagram by positioning the arrow pointer on the diagram border until the pointer turns into a four-headed arrow, holding down the left mouse button, and then dragging the diagram to the desired location. Nudge selected shape(s) with the up, down, left, or right arrow keys on the keyboard.

Project ④ℓ Formatting Diagrams

1. With **WordL1_C7_P4.docx** open, format shapes by completing the following steps:
    a. Click the diagram on the first page to select it (light turquoise border surrounds the diagram).
    b. Click the SmartArt Tools Format tab.
    c. In the diagram, click the rectangle shape containing the word *Design*.
    d. Hold down the Shift key and then click the shape containing the word *Development*.
    e. With the Shift key still down, click the shape containing the word *Implementation*. (All three shapes should now be selected.)
    f. Click the Change Shape button in the Shapes group.
    g. Click the seventh shape from the left in the second row of the *Block Arrows* section (the Pentagon shape).
    h. With the shapes still selected, click the Larger button in the Shapes group.
    i. With the shapes still selected, click the Shape Outline button arrow in the Shape Styles group and then click the red color *Red, Accent 2*.

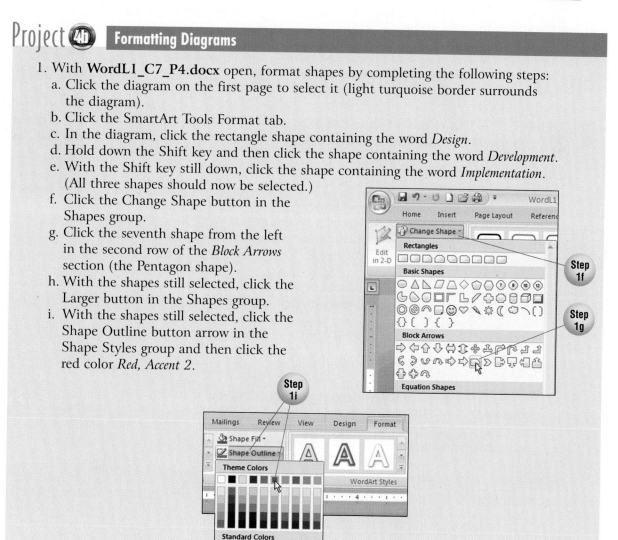

j. Click inside the diagram border but outside any shape. (This deselects the shapes but keeps the diagram selected.)

2. Change the size of the diagram by completing the following steps:
   a. Click the Size button located at the right side of the tab.
   b. Click in the *Height* measurement box, type 4, and then press Enter.

3. Position the diagram by completing the following steps:
   a. Click the Arrange button located toward the right side of the tab.
   b. Click the Position button.
   c. Click the middle option in the second row of the *With Text Wrapping* section (the *Position in Middle Center with Square Text Wrapping* option).

4. Format the bottom diagram by completing the following steps:
   a. Press Ctrl + End to move to the end of the document and then click in the bottom diagram to select it.
   b. Hold down the Shift key and then click each of the three shapes.
   c. Click the More button at the right side of the styles in the WordArt Styles group.
   d. Click the last WordArt style in the lower right corner of the drop-down gallery (*Fill - Accent 1, Metal Bevel, Reflection*).

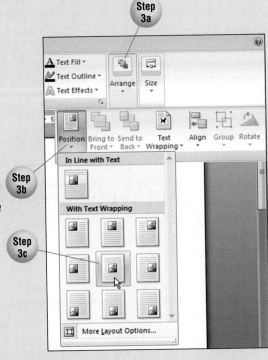

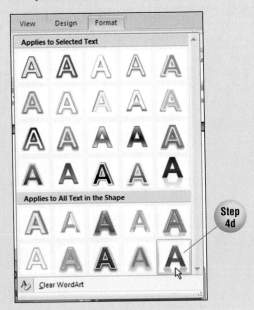

e. Click the Text Outline button arrow in the WordArt Styles group and then click the light blue color in the *Standard Colors* section (the seventh color from the left).

f. Click the Text Effects button in the WordArt Styles group, point to *Glow* at the drop-down list, and then click the last option in the top row.

g. Click inside the diagram border but outside any shape.

5. Arrange the diagram by clicking the Arrange button, clicking the Position button, and then clicking the middle option in the second row of the *With Text Wrapping* section (the *Position in Middle Center with Square Text Wrapping* option).

6. Save, print, and then close **WordL1_C7_P4.docx**.

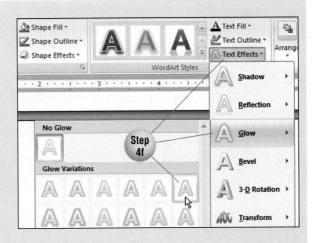

Project ⑤ Prepare and Format a Company Organizational Chart

You will prepare an organizational chart for a company and then apply formatting to enhance the visual appeal of the organizational chart.

Creating an Organizational Chart with SmartArt

If you need to visually illustrate hierarchical data, consider creating an organizational chart with a SmartArt option. To display organizational chart SmartArt options, click the Insert tab and then click the SmartArt button in the Illustrations group. At the Choose a SmartArt Graphic dialog box, click *Hierarchy* in the left panel. Organizational chart options display in the middle panel of the dialog box. Double-click the desired organizational chart and the chart is inserted in the document. Type text in a diagram by selecting the shape and then typing text in the shape or you can type text in the *Type your text here* window that displays at the left side of the diagram. Format a SmartArt organizational chart with options and buttons in the SmartArt Tools Design tab similar to the one shown in Figure 7.12 and the SmartArt Tools Format tab similar to the one shown in Figure 7.14.

Insert an Organizational Chart
1. Click Insert tab.
2. Click SmartArt button.
3. Click *Hierarchy.*
4. Double-click desired organizational chart.

1. At a blank document, create the organizational chart shown in Figure 7.15. To begin, click the Insert tab.
2. Click the SmartArt button in the Illustrations group.
3. At the Choose a SmartArt Graphic dialog box, click *Hierarchy* in the left panel of the dialog box and then double-click the first option in the middle panel, *Organization Chart*.

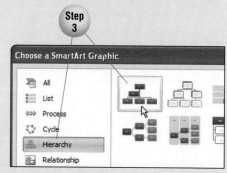

4. If a *Type your text here* window displays at the left side of the organizational chart, close the pane by clicking the Text Pane button in the Create Graphic group.
5. Delete one of the boxes in the organizational chart by clicking the border of the box in the lower right corner to select it and then pressing the Delete key. (Make sure that the selection border that surrounds the box is a solid line and not a dashed line. If a dashed line displays, click the box border again. This should change it to a solid line.)
6. With the bottom right box selected, click the Add Shape button arrow and then click the *Add Shape Below* option.

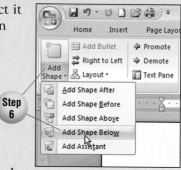

7. Click *[Text]* in the top box, type Blaine Willis, press the Enter key, and then type President. Click in each of the remaining boxes and type the text as shown in Figure 7.15.
8. Click the More button located at the right side of the styles in the SmartArt Styles group and then click the *Inset* style in the *3-D* section (second option from the left in the top row of the *3-D* section).
9. Click the Change Colors button in the SmartArt Styles group and then click the *Colorful Range - Accent Colors 4 to 5* in the *Colorful* section (fourth option from the left in the *Colorful* row).
10. Click the SmartArt Tools Format tab.
11. Click the tab (displays with a right- and left-pointing triangle) that displays at the left side of the diagram border. (This displays the *Type your text here* window.)

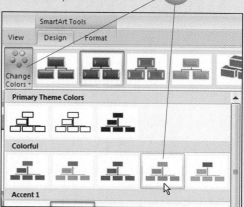

12. Using the mouse, select the text that displays in the *Type your text here* window.
13. Click the Change Shape button in the Shapes group and then click the *Round Same Side Corner Rectangle* option (second option from the *right* in the top row).
14. Click the Shape Outline button arrow in the Shape Styles group and then click the dark blue color (second color from the *right* in the *Standard Colors* section).

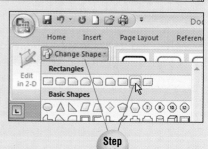

15. Click the Size button located at the right side of the tab and then change the height to 4″ and the width to 6.5″.
16. Click outside the chart to deselect it.
17. Save the document and name it **WordL1_C7_P5**.
18. Print and then close the document.

Figure 7.15 **Project 5**

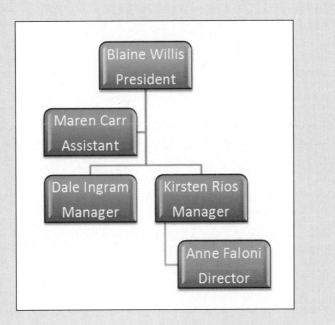

CHAPTER summary

- Use the Tables feature to create columns and rows of information. Create a table with the Table button in the Tables group in the Insert tab or with options at the Insert Table dialog box.

- A cell is the intersection between a row and a column. The lines that form the cells of the table are called gridlines. Columns in a table are lettered from left to right beginning with *A*. Rows are numbered from top to bottom beginning with *1*.

- Move the insertion point to cells in a document using the mouse by clicking in the desired cell or use the keyboard commands shown in Table 7.1.

- Change the table design with options and buttons in the Table Tools Design tab.

- Refer to Table 7.2 for a list of mouse commands for selecting specific cells in a table.

- Refer to Table 7.3 for a list of keyboard commands for selecting specific cells in a table.

- Change the layout of a table with options and buttons in the Table Tools Layout tab.

- You can select a table, column, row, or cell using the Select button in the Table group in the Table Tools Layout tab.

- Insert and delete columns and rows with buttons in the Rows & Columns group in the Table Tools Layout tab.

- Merge selected cells with the Merge Cells button and split cells with the Split Cells button, both located in the Merge group in the Table Tools Layout tab.

- Change column width and row height using the height and width measurement boxes in the Cell Size group in the Table Tools Layout tab; by dragging move table column markers on the horizontal ruler, adjust table row markers on the vertical ruler, gridlines in the table; or with the AutoFit button in the Cell Size group.

- Change alignment of text in cells with buttons in the Alignment group in the Table Tools Layout tab.

- Change cell margins with options in the Table Options dialog box.

- Change text direction in a cell with the Text Direction button in the Alignment group.

- Change the table alignment at the Table Properties dialog box with the Table tab selected.

- You can use the resize handle to change the size of the table and use the table move handle to move the table.

- Convert text to a table with the *Convert Text to Table* option at the Table button drop-down list. Convert a table to text with the Convert to Text button in the Data group in the Table Tools Layout tab.

- Sort selected rows in a table with the Sort button in the Data group.

- Perform calculations on data in a table by clicking the Formula button in the Data group in the Table Tools Layout tab and then specifying the formula and number format at the Formula dialog box.

- Use the SmartArt feature to insert predesigned diagrams and organizational charts in a document. Click the SmartArt button in the Insert tab to display the Choose a SmartArt Graphic dialog box.
- Format a SmartArt diagram or organizational chart with options and buttons in the SmartArt Tools Design tab and the SmartArt Tools Format tab.
- To move a SmartArt diagram, first choose a position or a text wrapping style with the Arrange button in the SmartArt Tools Format tab.

COMMANDS review

FEATURE	RIBBON TAB, GROUP	BUTTON	OPTION
Table	Insert, Tables		
Insert Table dialog box	Insert, Tables		Insert Table
Draw table	Table Tools Design, Draw Borders		
Insert column left	Table Tools Layout, Rows & Columns	Insert Left	
Insert column right	Table Tools Layout, Rows & Columns	Insert Right	
Insert row above	Table Tools Layout, Rows & Columns		
Insert row below	Table Tools Layout, Rows & Columns	Insert Below	
Delete table	Table Tools Layout, Rows & Columns		Delete Table
Delete row	Table Tools Layout, Rows & Columns		Delete Rows
Delete column	Table Tools Layout, Rows & Columns		Delete Columns
Merge cells	Table Tools Layout, Merge	Merge Cells	
Split cells dialog box	Table Tools Layout, Merge	Split Cells	
AutoFit table contents	Table Tools Layout, Cell Size	AutoFit ▼	
Cell alignment	Table Tools Layout, Alignment		
Table Options dialog box	Table Tools Layout, Alignment		
Cell direction	Table Tools Layout, Alignment		
Convert text to table	Insert, Tables		Convert Text to Table
Convert table to text	Table Tools Layout, Data	Convert to Text	

continued

FEATURE	RIBBON TAB, GROUP	BUTTON	OPTION
Sort text in table	Table Tools Layout, Data	A↓Z	
Formula dialog box	Table Tools Layout, Data	ƒx Formula	
Choose a SmartArt Graphic dialog box	Insert, Illustrations		

CONCEPTS check

Test Your Knowledge

Completion: In the space provided at the right, indicate the correct term, command, or number.

1. The Table button is located in this tab. _____

2. This is another name for the lines that form the cells of the table. _____

3. Use this keyboard shortcut to move the insertion point to the previous cell. _____

4. Use this keyboard shortcut to move the insertion point to a tab within a cell. _____

5. This tab contains table styles you can apply to a table. _____

6. Click this button in the Table Tools Layout tab to insert a column at the left side of the column containing the insertion point. _____

7. Insert and delete columns and rows with buttons in this group in the Table Tools Layout tab. _____

8. One method for changing column width is dragging this on the horizontal ruler. _____

9. Use this button in the Cell Size group to make the column widths in a table automatically fit the contents. _____

10. Change the table alignment at this dialog box with the Table tab selected. _____

11. Hover the mouse pointer over a table and this displays in the lower right corner of the table. _____

12. Position the mouse pointer in a table and this displays in the upper left corner. _____

13. Display the Formula dialog box by clicking the Formula button in this group in the Table Tools Layout tab.

_____

14. The SmartArt button is located in this tab.

_____

15. Click the SmartArt button and this dialog box displays.

_____

16. If you need to visually illustrate hierarchical data, consider creating this with the SmartArt feature.

_____

SKILLS check
Demonstrate Your Proficiency

Assessment

1 CREATE AND FORMAT A PROPERTY REPLACEMENT COSTS TABLE

1. At a blank document, create the table shown in Figure 7.16 with the following specifications:
   a. Create a table with two columns and eight rows.
   b. Merge the cells in the top row and then change the alignment to Align Center.
   c. Type the text in the cells as shown in Figure 7.16.
   d. Right-align the cells containing the money amounts as well as the blank line below the last amount (cells B2 through B8).
   e. Autofit the contents of the cells.
   f. Apply the Light List – Accent 4 table style.
   g. Remove the check mark from the *First Column* check box.
   h. Draw a green (Olive Green, Accent 3, Darker 25%) 1½ pt border around the table.
   i. Change the font size to 14 for the text in cell A1.
   j. Use the resize handle located in the lower right corner of the table and increase the width and height of the table by approximately one inch.
2. Click in the *Accounts receivable* cell and insert a row below. Type Equipment in the new cell at the left and type $83,560 in the new cell at the right.
3. Insert a formula in cell B9 that sums the amounts in cell B2 through B8. (Insert a dollar sign before the amount in cell B9.)
4. Save the document and name it **WordL1_C7_A1**.
5. Print and then close **WordL1_C7_A1.docx**.

Figure 7.16 **Assessment 1**

PROPERTY Replacement Costs	
Business personal property	$1,367,340
Earnings and expenses	$945,235
Domestic and foreign transit	$123,400
Accounts receivable	$95,460
Legal liability	$75,415
Computer coverage	$53,098
Total	

Assessment

2 FORMAT A TABLE CONTAINING TRANSPORTATION SERVICE INFORMATION

1. Open **WordTable04.docx** and then save the document and name it **WordL1_C7_A2**.
2. Format the table so it appears as shown in Figure 7.17.
3. Position the table in the middle of the page.
4. Save, print, and then close **WordL1_C7_A2.docx**.

Figure 7.17 **Assessment 2**

Metro Area Transportation Services	*Service*	*Telephone*
	Langley City Transit	
	Subway and bus information	(507) 555-3049
	Service status hotline	(507) 555-4123
	Travel information	(507) 555-4993
	Valley Rail Road	
	Railway information	(202) 555-2300
	Status hotline	(202) 555-2343
	Travel information	(202) 555-2132
	Mainline Bus	
	Bus routes	(507) 555-6530
	Emergency hotline	(507) 555-6798
	Travel information	(507) 555-7542
	Village Travel Card	
	Village office	(507) 555-1232
	Card inquiries	(507) 555-1930

Assessment

3 CREATE AND FORMAT A COMPANY DIAGRAM

1. At a blank document, create the SmartArt diagram shown in Figure 7.18 with the following specifications:
   a. Use the Titled Matrix diagram.
   b. Apply the Colorful - Accent Colors SmartArt style.
   c. Type all of the text shown in Figure 7.18.
   d. Select all of the text and then apply the Gradient Fill - Accent 4, Reflection WordArt style.
2. Save the document and name it **WordL1_C7_A3**.
3. Print and then close **WordL1_C7_A3.docx**.

Figure 7.18 Assessment 3

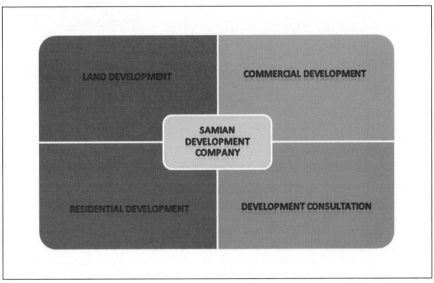

Assessment

4 CREATE AND FORMAT A COMPANY ORGANIZATIONAL CHART

1. At a blank document, create the organizational chart shown in Figure 7.19 with the following specifications:
   a. Use the Hierarchy organizational chart.
   b. Select the top text box and insert a shape above.
   c. Select the top right text box and then add a shape below.
   d. Type the text shown in the organizational chart in Figure 7.19.
   e. Apply the Colorful Range - Accent Colors 2 to 3 option.
   f. Increase the height to 4.5″ and the width to 6.5″.
   g. Position the organizational chart in the middle of the page.
2. Save the document and name it **WordL1_C7_A4**.
3. Print and then close **WordL1_C7_A4.docx**.

Figure 7.19 Assessment 4

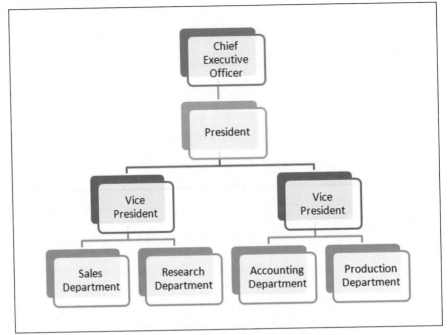

Assessment

5 INSERT FORMULAS IN A TABLE

1. In this chapter, you learned how to insert formulas in a table. Experiment with writing formulas (consider using the Help feature or other reference) and then open **WordTable05.docx**. Save the document and name it **WordL1_C7_A5**.
2. Format the table so it appears as shown in Figure 7.20.
3. Insert a formula in cell B13 that sums the amounts in cells B6 through B12. Complete similar steps to insert a formula in cell C13, D13, and E13.
4. Insert a formula in cell B14 that subtracts the amount in B4 from the amount in B13. *(Hint: The formula should look like this: =(B4-B13).)* Complete similar steps to insert a formula in cells C14, D14, and E14.
5. Save, print, and then close **WordL1_C7_A5.docx**.

Figure 7.20 Assessment 5

TRI-STATE PRODUCTS			
Financial Analysis			
	2007	**2008**	**2009**	**2010**
Revenue	$1,450,348	$1,538,239	$1,634,235	$1,523,455
Expenses				
Facilities	$250,220	$323,780	$312,485	$322,655
Materials	$93,235	$102,390	$87,340	$115,320
Payroll	$354,390	$374,280	$380,120	$365,120
Benefits	$32,340	$35,039	$37,345	$36,545
Marketing	$29,575	$28,350	$30,310	$31,800
Transportation	$4,492	$5,489	$5,129	$6,349
Miscellaneous	$4,075	$3,976	$4,788	$5,120
Total				
Net Revenue				

CASE study
Apply Your Skills

Part 1

You have recently been hired as an accounting clerk for a landscaping business, Landmark Landscaping, which has two small offices in your city. The accounting clerk prior to you kept track of monthly sales using Word, and the manager would prefer that you continue using that application. Open the file named **WordMonthlySales.docx** and then save the document and name it **WordL1_C7_CS_P1**. After reviewing the information, you decide that a table would be a better way of maintaining and displaying the data. Convert the data to a table and modify its appearance so that it is easy to read and understand. Insert a total row at the bottom of the table and then insert formulas to sum the totals in the columns containing amounts. Apply formatting to the table to enhance the visual appeal. Determine a color theme for the table and then continue that same color theme when preparing other documents for Landmark Landscaping. Save, print, and then close the document.

Part 2

The president of Landmark Landscaping has asked you to prepare an organizational chart for the company that will become part of the company profile. Use a SmartArt organizational chart and create a chart with the following company titles (in the order shown below):

President			
Westside Manager		**Eastside Manager**	
Landscape Architect	Landscape Director	Landscape Architect	Landscape Director
	Assistant		Assistant

Format the organizational chart to enhance the visual appeal and apply colors that match the color scheme you chose for the company in Part 1. Save the document and name it **WordL1_C7_CS_P2**. Print and then close the document.

Part 3

As part of the company profile, the president of the company would like to include a diagram that represents the services offered by the company and use the diagram as a company marketing tool. Use SmartArt to create a diagram that contains the following services: Maintenance Contracts, Planting Services, Landscape Design, and Landscape Consultation. Format the diagram to enhance the visual appeal and apply colors that match the color scheme you chose for the company in Part 1. Save the document and name it **WordL1_C7_CS_P3**. Print and then close the document.

Part 4

Since the SmartArt feature is new and others in the company will need training on the feature, the office manager has started a training document with information on using SmartArt. He has asked you to add information on keyboard shortcuts for working with shapes. Use the Help feature to learn about the keyboard shortcuts available for working with shapes and then create a table and insert the information in the table. Format the table to enhance the visual appeal and apply colors that match the color scheme you chose for the company in Part 1. Save the document and name it **WordL1_C7_CS_P4**. Print and then close the document.

Part

5

One of the landscape architects has asked you to prepare a table containing information on trees that need to be ordered next month. She would also like to have you include the Latin name for the trees since this is important when ordering. Create a table that contains the common name of the tree, the Latin name, the number required, and the price per tree as shown in Figure 7.21. Use the Internet (or any other resource available to you) to find the Latin name of each tree listed in Figure 7.21. Create a column in the table that multiplies the number of trees required by the price and include this formula for each tree. Format and enhance the table so it is attractive and easy to read. Save the document and name it **WordL1_C7_CS_P5**. Print and then close the document.

Figure 7.21 Case Study, Part 5

Douglas Fir, 15 required, $1.99 per tree
White Elm, 10 required, $2.49 per tree
Western Hemlock, 10 required, $1.89 per tree
Red Maple, 8 required, $6.99 per tree
Ponderosa Pine, 5 required, $2.69 per tree

CHAPTER

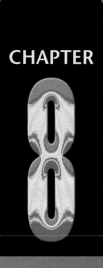

Merging Documents

PERFORMANCE OBJECTIVES

Upon successful completion of Chapter 8, you will be able to:

word Chapter 8

- Create and merge letters, envelopes, labels, and a directory
- Create custom fields for a merge
- Edit main documents and data source files
- Input text during a merge

Tutorial 8.1
Using Mail Merge

Word includes a Mail Merge feature you can use to create customized letters, envelopes, labels, directories, e-mail messages, and faxes. The Mail Merge feature is useful for situations where you need to send the same letter to a number of people and create an envelope for each letter. Use Mail Merge to create a main document that contains a letter, envelope, or other data and then merge the main document with a data source. In this chapter, you will use Mail Merge to create letters, envelopes, labels, and directories.

Note: Before beginning computer projects, copy to your storage medium the Word2007L1C8 subfolder from the Word2007L1 folder in the CD that accompanies this textbook and then make Word2007L1C8 the active folder.

roject Merge Letters to Customers

You will create a data source file and a letter main document, and then merge the main document with the records in the data source file.

Completing a Merge

Use buttons and options in the Mailings tab shown in Figure 8.1 to complete a merge. A merge generally takes two files—the *data source* file and the *main document*. The main document contains the standard text along with fields identifying where variable information is inserted during the merge. The data source file contains the variable information that will be inserted in the main document.

Figure 8.1 Mailings Tab

Use the Start Mail Merge button in the Mailings tab to identify the type of main document you want to create and use the Select Recipients button to create a data source file or to specify an existing data source file. You can also use the Mail Merge Wizard to guide you through the merge process. Start the wizard by clicking the Mailings tab, clicking the Start Mail Merge button, and then clicking *Step by Step Mail Merge Wizard*.

Create Data Source File
1. Click Mailings tab.
2. Click Select Recipients button.
3. Click *Type New List* in drop-down list.
4. Type data in predesigned or custom fields.
5. Click OK.

Creating a Data Source File

Before creating a data source file, determine what type of correspondence you will be creating and the type of information you will need to insert in the correspondence. Word provides predetermined field names you can use when creating the data source file. Use these field names if they represent the data you are creating. Variable information in a data source file is saved as a ***record***. A record contains all of the information for one unit (for example, a person, family, customer, client, or business). A series of fields makes one record, and a series of records makes a data source file.

Create a data source file by clicking the Select Recipients button in the Start Mail Merge group in the Mailings tab and then clicking *Type New List* at the drop-down list. At the New Address List dialog box shown in Figure 8.2, use the predesigned fields offered by Word and type the required data or edit the fields by deleting and/or inserting custom fields and then typing the data. Note that fields in the main document correspond to the column headings in the data source file. When all records have been entered, click OK. At the Save Address List dialog box, navigate to the desired folder, type a name for the data source file, and then click OK. Word saves a data source file as an Access database. You do not need Access on your computer to complete a merge with a data source file.

Figure 8.2 New Address List Dialog Box

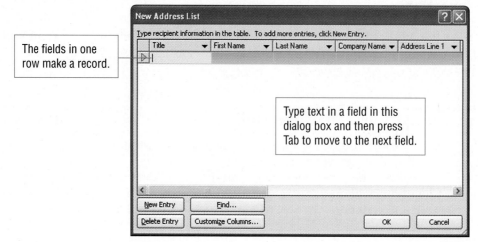

The fields in one row make a record.

Type text in a field in this dialog box and then press Tab to move to the next field.

1. At a blank document, click the Mailings tab.
2. Click the Start Mail Merge button in the Start Mail Merge group and then click *Letters* at the drop-down list.
3. Click the Select Recipients button in the Start Mail Merge group and then click *Type New List* at the drop-down list.

Step 3   **Step 1**

4. At the New Address List dialog box, Word provides you with a number of predesigned fields. Delete the fields you do not need by completing the following steps:
   a. Click the Customize Columns button.
   b. At the Customize Address List dialog box, click *Company Name* to select it and then click the Delete button.

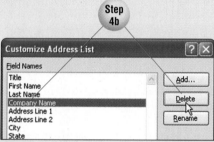

Step 4b

   c. At the message asking if you are sure you want to delete the field, click the Yes button.
   d. Complete steps similar to those in 4b and 4c to delete the following fields:
      Country or Region
      Home Phone
      Work Phone
      E-mail Address
5. Insert a custom field by completing the following steps:
   a. At the Customize Address List box, click the Add button.
   b. At the Add Field dialog box, type *Fund* and then click OK.
   c. Click the OK button to close the Customize Address List dialog box.

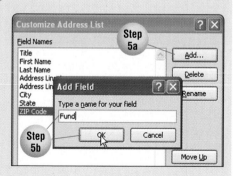

Step 5a

Step 5b

6. At the New Address List dialog box, enter the information for the first client shown in Figure 8.3 by completing the following steps:
   a. Click in the *Title* text box.
   b. Type Mr. and then press the Tab key. (This moves the insertion point to the *First Name* field. You can also press Shift + Tab to move to the previous field.)
   c. Type Kenneth and then press the Tab key.
   d. Type Porter and then press the Tab key.
   e. Type 7645 Tenth Street and then press the Tab key.
   f. Type Apt. 314 and then press the Tab key.
   g. Type New York and then press the Tab key.
   h. Type NY and then press the Tab key.
   i. Type 10192 and then press the Tab key.
   j. Type Mutual Investment Fund and then press the Tab key. (This makes the New Entry button active.)

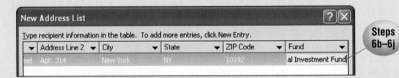

Steps
6b–6j

   k. With the insertion point positioned in the *Title* field, complete steps similar to those in 6b through 6j to enter the information for the three other clients shown in Figure 8.3.
7. After entering all of the information for the last client in Figure 8.3 (Mrs. Wanda Houston), click the OK button located in the bottom right corner of the New Address List dialog box.
8. At the Save Address List dialog box, navigate to the Word2007L1C8 folder on your storage medium, type WordL1_C8_P1_DS in the *File name* text box, and then click the Save button.

Figure 8.3 Project 1a

Title	=	Mr.	Title	=	Ms.
First Name	=	Kenneth	First Name	=	Carolyn
Last Name	=	Porter	Last Name	=	Renquist
Address Line 1	=	7645 Tenth Street	Address Line 1	=	13255 Meridian Street
Address Line 2	=	Apt. 314	Address Line 2	=	(leave this blank)
City	=	New York	City	=	New York
State	=	NY	State	=	NY
Zip Code	=	10192	Zip Code	=	10435
Fund	=	Mutual Investment Fund	Fund	=	Quality Care Fund
Title	=	Dr.	Title	=	Mrs.
First Name	=	Amil	First Name	=	Wanda
Last Name	=	Ranna	Last Name	=	Houston
Address Line 1	=	433 South 17th	Address Line 1	=	566 North 22nd Avenue
Address Line 2	=	Apt. 17-D	Address Line 2	=	(leave this blank)
City	=	New York	City	=	New York
State	=	NY	State	=	NY
Zip Code	=	10322	Zip Code	=	10634
Fund	=	Priority One Fund	Fund	=	Quality Care Fund

Creating a Main Document

QUICK STEPS

Create Main Document
1. Click Mailings tab.
2. Click Start Mail Merge button.
3. Click desired document type at drop-down list.
4. Type main document text and insert fields as needed.

When you begin a mail merge, you specify the type of main document you are creating. After creating and typing the records in the data source file, type the main document. Insert in the main document fields identifying where you want the variable information inserted when the document is merged with the data source file. Use buttons in the Write & Insert Fields group to insert fields and field blocks in the main document.

Insert all of the fields required for the inside address of a letter with the Address Block button in the Write & Insert Fields group. Click this button and the Insert Address Block dialog box displays with a preview of how the fields will be inserted in the document to create the inside address; the dialog box also contains buttons and options for customizing the fields. Click OK and the «AddressBlock» field is inserted in the document. The «AddressBlock» field is an example of a composite field that groups a number of fields together.

Click the Greeting Line button and the Insert Greeting Line dialog box displays with options for customizing how the fields are inserted in the document to create the greeting line. When you click OK at the dialog box the «GreetingLine» composite field is inserted in the document.

If you want to insert an individual field from the data source file, click the Insert Merge Field button. This displays the Insert Merge Field dialog box with a list of fields from the data source file. Click the Insert Merge Field button arrow and a drop-down list displays containing the fields in the data source file. If you want merged data formatted, you can format the merge fields at the main document.

HINT

A field name is inserted in the main document surrounded by chevrons (« and »), which distinguish fields in the main document and do not display in the merged document.

Address Block   Greeting Line

Insert Merge Field ▾

Project 1b Creating a Main Document

1. At the blank document, create the letter shown in Figure 8.4. Begin by clicking the No Spacing style in the Styles group in the Home tab.
2. Press the Enter key six times and then type February 23, 2010.
3. Press the Enter key five times and then insert the address fields by completing the following steps:
   a. Click the Mailings tab and then click the Address Block button in the Write & Insert Fields group.
   b. At the Insert Address Block dialog box, click the OK button.
   c. Press the Enter key twice.
4. Insert the greeting line fields by completing the following steps:
   a. Click the Greeting Line button in the Write & Insert Fields group.
   b. At the Insert Greeting Line dialog box, click the down-pointing arrow at the right of the option box containing the comma (the box to the right of the box containing *Mr. Randall*).
   c. At the drop-down list that displays, click the colon.

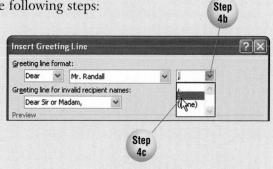

Step 4b

Step 4c

d. Click OK to close the Insert Greeting Line dialog box.

e. Press the Enter key twice.

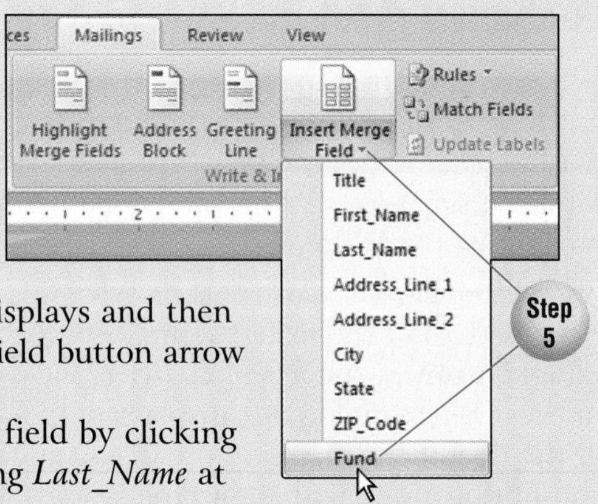

5. Type the letter to the point where «Fund» displays and then insert the «Fund» field by clicking the Insert Merge Field button arrow and then clicking *Fund* at the drop-down list.

6. Type the letter to the point where the «Title» field displays and then insert the «Title» field by clicking the Insert Merge Field button arrow and then clicking *Title* at the drop-down list.

7. Press the spacebar and then insert the «Last_Name» field by clicking the Insert Merge Field button arrow and then clicking *Last_Name* at the drop-down list.

8. Type the remainder of the letter shown in Figure 8.4. (Insert your initials instead of the *XX* at the end of the letter.)

9. Save the document and name it **WordL1_C8_P1_MD**.

Figure 8.4 **Project 1b**

February 23, 2010

«AddressBlock»

«GreetingLine»

McCormack Funds is lowering its expense charges beginning May 1, 2010. The reductions in expense charges mean that more of your account investment performance in the «Fund» is returned to you, «Title» «Last_Name». The reductions are worth your attention because most of our competitors' fees have gone up.

Lowering expense charges is noteworthy because before the reduction, McCormack expense deductions were already among the lowest, far below most mutual funds and variable annuity accounts with similar objectives. At the same time, services for you, our client, will continue to expand. If you would like to discuss this change, please call us at (212) 555-2277. Your financial future is our main concern at McCormack.

Sincerely,

Jodie Langstrom
Director, Financial Services

XX:WordL1_C8_P1_MD.docx

Previewing a Merge

To view how the main document will appear when merged with the first record in the data source file, click the Preview Results button in the Mailings tab. You can view the main document merged with other records by using the navigation buttons in the Preview Results group. This group contains the buttons First Record, Previous Record, Go to Record, Next Record, and Last Record. Click the button that will display the main document merged with the desired record. Viewing the merged document before printing is helpful to ensure that the merged data is correct. To use the Go to Record button, click the button, type the number of the desired record, and then press Enter. Turn off the preview feature by clicking the Preview Results button.

Preview
Results

First   Last
Record   Record

Previous   Next
Record   Record

Merging Documents

To complete the merge, click the Finish & Merge button in the Finish group in the Mailings tab. At the drop-down list that displays, you can choose to merge the records and create a new document, send the merged documents directly to the printer, or send the merged documents by e-mail.

To merge the documents and create a new document with the merged records, click the Finish & Merge button and then click *Edit Individual Documents* at the drop-down list. At the Merge to New Document dialog box, make sure *All* is selected in the *Merge records* section and then click OK. This merges the records in the data source file with the main document and inserts the merged documents in a new document. You can also display the Merge to New Document dialog box by pressing Alt + Shift + N. Press Alt + Shift + M to display the Merge to Printer dialog box.

QUICK STEPS

Merge Documents
1. Click Finish & Merge button.
2. Click *Edit Individual Documents* at drop-down list.
3. Make sure *All* is selected in Merge to New Document dialog box.
4. Click OK.

Finish &
Merge ▾

Project 1G · **Merging the Main Document with the Data Source File**

1. With **WordL1_C8_P1_MD.docx** open, preview the main document merged with the first record in the data source file by clicking the Preview Results button in the Mailings tab.
2. Click the Next Record button to view the main document merged with the second record in the data source file.
3. Click the Preview Results button to turn it off.
4. Click the Finish & Merge button in the Finish group and then click *Edit Individual Documents* at the drop-down list.
5. At the Merge to New Document dialog box, make sure *All* is selected, and then click OK.
6. Save the merged letters and name the document **WordL1_C8_P1_Ltrs**.
7. Print **WordL1_C8_P1_Ltrs.docx**. (This document will print four letters.)
8. Close **WordL1_C8_P1_Ltrs.docx**.
9. Save and then close **WordL1_C8_P1_MD.docx**.

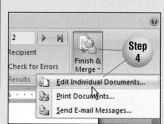

Step 1

Step 2

Step 4

You will use Mail Merge to prepare envelopes with customer names and addresses.

Merging Envelopes

If you create a letter as a main document and then merge it with a data source file, more than likely you will need properly addressed envelopes in which to send the letters. To prepare an envelope main document that is merged with a data source file, click the Mailings tab, click the Start Mail Merge button, and then click *Envelopes* at the drop-down list. This displays the Envelope Options dialog box as shown in Figure 8.5. At this dialog box, specify the desired envelope size, make any other changes, and then click OK.

Figure 8.5 Envelope Options Dialog Box

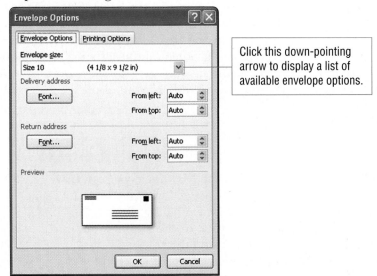

Click this down-pointing arrow to display a list of available envelope options.

The next step in the envelope merge process is to create the data source file or identify an existing data source file. To identify an existing data source file, click the Select Recipients button in the Start Mail Merge group and then click *Use Existing List* at the drop-down list. At the Select Data Source dialog box, navigate to the folder containing the desired data source file and then double-click the file.

With the data source file attached to the envelope main document, the next step is to insert the appropriate fields. Click in the envelope in the approximate location where the recipient's address will appear and a box with a dashed blue border displays. Click the Address Block button in the Write & Insert Fields group and then click OK at the Insert Address Block dialog box.

1. At a blank document, click the Mailings tab.
2. Click the Start Mail Merge button in the Start Mail Merge group and then click *Envelopes* at the drop-down list.
3. At the Envelope Options dialog box, make sure the envelope size is 10 and then click OK.
4. Click the Select Recipients button in the Start Mail Merge group and then click *Use Existing List* at the drop-down list.
5. At the Select Data Source dialog box, navigate to the Word2007L1C8 folder on your storage medium and then double-click the data source file named **WordL1_C8_P1_DS.mdb**.
6. Click in the approximate location in the envelope document where the recipient's address will appear. (This causes a box with a dashed blue border to display. If you do not see this box, try clicking in a different location on the envelope.)

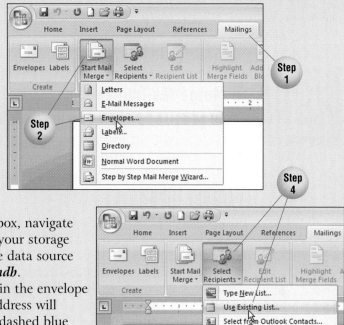

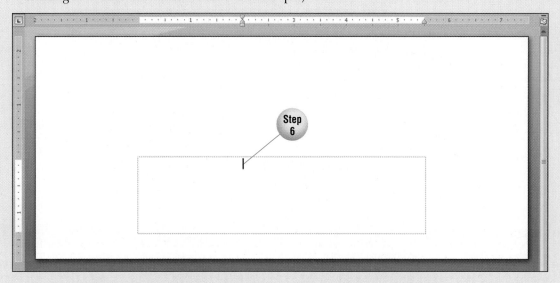

7. Click the Address Block button in the Write & Insert Fields group.
8. At the Insert Address Block dialog box, click the OK button.
9. Click the Preview Results button to see how the envelope appears merged with the first record in the data source file.
10. Click the Preview Results button to turn it off.
11. Click the Finish & Merge button in the Finish group and then click *Edit Individual Documents* at the drop-down list.
12. At the Merge to New Document dialog box, make sure *All* is selected and then click OK.
13. Save the merged envelopes and name the document **WordL1_C8_P2_Envs**.
14. Print **WordL1_C8_P2_Envs.docx**. (This document will print four envelopes.)

15. Close **WordL1_C8_P2_Envs.docx**.
16. Save the envelope main document and name it **WordL1_C8_P2_MD**.
17. Close **WordL1_C8_P2_MD.docx**.

Project ③ Merge Mailing Labels

You will use Mail Merge to prepare mailing labels with customer names and addresses.

Merging Labels

Create mailing labels for records in a data source file in much the same way that you create envelopes. Click the Start Mail Merge button and then click *Labels* at the drop-down list. This displays the Label Options dialog box as shown in Figure 8.6. Make sure the desired label is selected and then click OK to close the dialog box. The next step is to create the data source file or identify an existing data source file. With the data source file attached to the label main document, insert the appropriate fields and then complete the merge.

Figure 8.6 Label Options Dialog Box

Project ③ Merging Mailing Labels

1. At a blank document, click the Mailings tab.
2. Click the Start Mail Merge button in the Start Mail Merge group and then click *Labels* at the drop-down list.

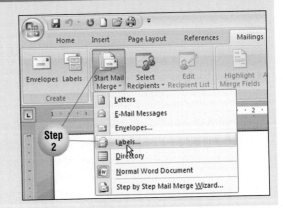

3. At the Label Options dialog box, complete the following steps:
   a. If necessary, click the down-pointing arrow at the right side of the *Label vendors* option and then click *Avery US Letter* at the drop-down list. (If this product vendor is not available, choose a vendor name that offers labels that print on a full page.)
   b. Scroll in the *Product number* list box and then click *5160*. (If this option is not available, choose a label number that prints labels in two or three columns down a full page.)
   c. Click OK to close the dialog box.

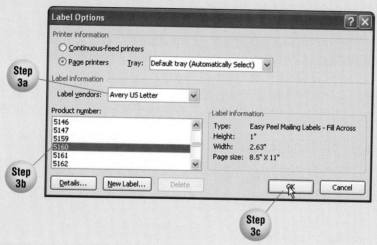

4. Click the Select Recipients button in the Start Mail Merge group and then click *Use Existing List* at the drop-down list.
5. At the Select Data Source dialog box, navigate to the Word2007L1C8 folder on your storage medium and then double-click the data source file named ***WordL1_C8_P1_DS.mdb***.
6. At the labels document, click the Address Block button in the Write & Insert Fields group.
7. At the Insert Address Block dialog box, click the OK button. (This inserts «AddressBlock» in the first label. The other labels contain the «Next Record» field.)
8. Click the Update Labels button in the Write & Insert Fields group. (This adds the «AddressBlock» field after each «Next Record» field in the second and subsequent labels.)
9. Click the Preview Results button to see how the labels appear merged with the records in the data source file.
10. Click the Preview Results button to turn it off.
11. Click the Finish & Merge button in the Finish group and then click *Edit Individual Documents* at the drop-down list.
12. At the Merge to New Document dialog box, make sure *All* is selected, and then click OK.
13. Format the labels by completing the following steps:
    a. Click the Table Tools Layout tab.
    b. Click the Select button in the Table group and then click *Select Table*.
    c. Click the Align Center Left button in the Alignment group.
    d. Click the Home tab and then click the Paragraph group dialog box launcher.
    e. At the Paragraph dialog box, click the up-pointing arrow at the right of *Before* and also at the right of *After* to change the measurement to 0″. Click the up-pointing arrow at the right of the *Inside* option to change the measurement to 0.3″ and then click OK.
14. Save the merged labels and name the document **WordL1_C8_P3_Labels**.
15. Print and then close **WordL1_C8_P3_Labels.docx**.
16. Save the label main document and name it **WordL1_C8_P3_MD**.
17. Close **WordL1_C8_P3_MD.docx**.

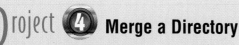

Project 4 — Merge a Directory

You will use Mail Merge to prepare a directory list containing customer names and type of funds.

Merging a Directory

When merging letters, envelopes, or mailing labels, a new form is created for each record. For example, if the data source file merged with the letter contains eight records, eight letters are created. If the data source file merged with a mailing label contains twenty records, twenty labels are created. In some situations, you may want merged information to remain on the same page. This is useful, for example, when creating a list such as a directory or address list.

Begin creating a merged directory by clicking the Start Mail Merge button and then clicking *Directory*. Create or identify an existing data source file and then insert the desired fields in the directory document. You may want to set tabs to insert text in columns.

Project 4 — Merging a Directory

1. At a blank document, click the Mailings tab.
2. Click the Start Mail Merge button in the Start Mail Merge group and then click *Directory* at the drop-down list.
3. Click the Select Recipients button in the Start Mail Merge group and then click *Use Existing List* at the drop-down list.
4. At the Select Data Source dialog box, navigate to the Word2007L1C8 folder on your storage medium and then double-click the data source file named *WordL1_C8_P1_DS.mdb*.

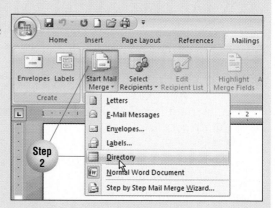

Step 2

5. At the document screen, set left tabs at the 1-inch mark, the 2.5-inch mark, and the 4-inch mark on the Ruler and then press the Tab key. (This moves the insertion point to the tab set at the 1-inch mark.)
6. Click the Insert Merge Field button arrow and then click *Last_Name* at the drop-down list.
7. Press the Tab key to move the insertion point to the 2.5-inch mark.
8. Click the Insert Merge Field button arrow and then click *First_Name* at the drop-down list.
9. Press the Tab key to move the insertion point to the 4-inch mark.
10. Click the Insert Merge Field button arrow and then click *Fund* at the drop-down list.
11. Press the Enter key once.
12. Click the Finish & Merge button in the Finish group and then click *Edit Individual Documents* at the drop-down list.
13. At the Merge to New Document dialog box, make sure *All* is selected, and then click OK. (This merges the fields in the document.)
14. Press Ctrl + Home, press the Enter key once, and then press the Up Arrow key once.

15. Press the Tab key, turn on bold, and then type Last Name.
16. Press the Tab key and then type First Name.
17. Press the Tab key and then type Fund.

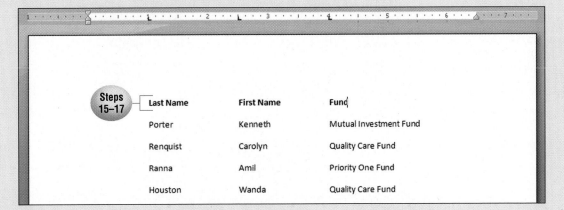

18. Save the directory document and name it **WordL1_C8_P4_Directory**.
19. Print and then close the document.
20. Close the directory main document without saving it.

Editing a Data Source File

Edit a main document in the normal manner. Open the document, make the required changes, and then save the document. Since a data source is actually an Access database file, you cannot open it in the normal manner. Open a data source file for editing using the Edit Recipient List button in the Start Mail Merge group in the Mailings tab. When you click the Edit Recipient List button, the Mail Merge Recipients dialog box displays as shown in Figure 8.7. Select or edit records at this dialog box.

QUICK STEPS

Edit Data Source File
1. Open main document.
2. Click Mailings tab.
3. Click Edit Recipient List button.
4. Make desired changes at Mail Merge Recipients dialog box.
5. Click OK.

roject ⑤ **Select Records and Merge Mailing Labels**

You will use Mail Merge to prepare mailing labels with names and addresses of customers living in Baltimore.

Selecting Specific Records

All of the records in the Mail Merge Recipients dialog box contain a check mark before the first field. If you want to select specific records, remove the check mark from those records you do not want included in a merge. In this way you can select and then merge specific records in the data source file with the main document.

Figure 8.7 Mail Merge Recipients Dialog Box

Select specific records by removing the check marks from those records you do not want included in the merge.

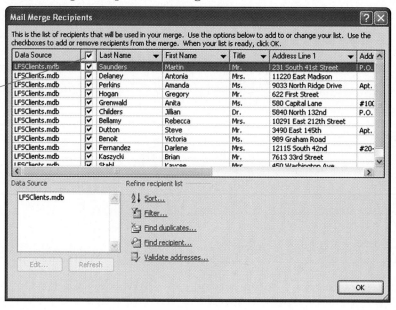

Project 5 Selecting Records and Merging Mailing Labels

1. At a blank document, create mailing labels for customers living in Baltimore. Begin by clicking the Mailings tab.
2. Click the Start Mail Merge button in the Start Mail Merge group and then click *Labels* at the drop-down list.
3. At the Label Options dialog box, make sure *Avery US Letter* displays in the *Label products* option box, and *5160* displays in the *Product number* list box, and then click OK.
4. Click the Select Recipients button in the Start Mail Merge group and then click *Use Existing List* at the drop-down list.
5. At the Select Data Source dialog box, navigate to the Word2007L1C8 folder on your storage medium and then double-click the data source file named **LFSClients.mdb**.
6. Click the Edit Recipient List button in the Start Mail Merge group.
7. At the Mail Merge Recipients dialog box, complete the following steps:
    a. Click the check box located immediately left of the *Last Name* field column heading to remove the check mark. (This removes all of the check marks from the check boxes.)
    b. Click the check box immediately left of each of the following last names: *Saunders, Perkins, Grenwald, Dutton, Fernandez,* and *Stahl.* (These are the customers that live in Baltimore.)
    c. Click OK to close the dialog box.

Step 7a

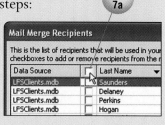

8. At the labels document, click the Address Block button in the Write & Insert Fields group.
9. At the Insert Address Block dialog box, click the OK button.
10. Click the Update Labels button in Write & Insert Fields group.
11. Click the Preview Results button and then click the Next Record button to display each of the labels and make sure only those customers living in Baltimore display.
12. Click the Preview Results button to turn it off.
13. Click the Finish & Merge button in the Finish group and then click *Edit Individual Documents* at the drop-down list.

14. At the Merge to New Document dialog box, make sure *All* is selected, and then click OK.
15. Format the labels by completing the following steps:
    a. Click the Table Tools Layout tab.
    b. Click the Select button in the Table group and then click *Select Table*.
    c. Click the Align Center Left button in the Alignment group.
    d. Click the Home tab and then click the Paragraph group dialog box launcher.
    e. At the Paragraph dialog box, click the up-pointing arrow at the right of *Before* and also at the right of *After* to change the measurement to 0″. Click the up-pointing arrow at the right of the *Inside* option to change the measurement to 0.3″ and then click OK.
16. Save the merged labels and name the document **WordL1_C8_P5_Labels**.
17. Print and then close **WordL1_C8_P5_Labels.docx**.
18. Close the main labels document without saving it.

P roject **6** **Edit Records in a Data Source File**

You will edit records in a data source file and then use Mail Merge to prepare a directory with the edited records that contains customer names, telephone numbers, and cell phone numbers.

Editing Records

A data source file may need editing on a periodic basis to add or delete customer names, update fields, insert new fields, or delete existing fields. To edit a data source file, click the Edit Recipient List button in the Start Mail Merge group. At the Mail Merge Recipients dialog box, click the data source file name in the *Data Source* list box and then click the Edit button that displays below the list box. This displays the Edit Data Source dialog box shown in Figure 8.8. At this dialog box you can add a new entry, delete an entry, find a particular entry, and customize columns.

Figure 8.8 Edit Data Source Dialog Box

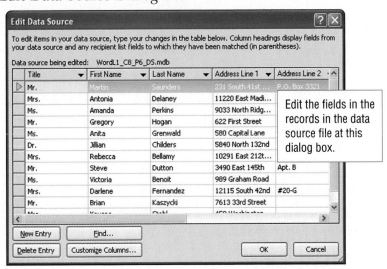

1. Make a copy of the **LFSClients.mdb** file by completing the following steps:
    a. Display the Open dialog box and make Word2007L1C8 the active folder.
    b. If necessary, change the *Files of type* option to *All Files (*.*)*.
    c. Right-click on the **LFSClients.mdb** file and then click *Copy* at the shortcut menu.
    d. Position the mouse pointer in a white portion of the Open dialog box list box (outside of any file name), click the right mouse button, and then click *Paste* at the shortcut menu. (This inserts a copy of the file in the dialog box list box and names the file **Copy of LFSClients.mdb**.)
    e. Right-click on the file name **Copy of LFSClients.mdb** and then click *Rename* at the shortcut menu.
    f. Type WordL1_C8_P6_DS.mdb and then press Enter.
    g. Close the Open dialog box.
2. At a blank document, click the Mailings tab.
3. Click the Select Recipients button and then click *Use Existing List* from the drop-down list.
4. At the Select Data Source dialog box, navigate to the Word2007L1C8 folder on your storage medium and then double-click the data source file named *WordL1_C8_P6_DS.mdb*.
5. Click the Edit Recipient List button in the Start Mail Merge group.
6. At the Mail Merge Recipients dialog box, click *WordL1_C8_P6_DS.mdb* that displays in the *Data Source* list box and then click the Edit button.
7. Delete the record for Steve Dutton by completing the following steps:
    a. Click the square that displays at the beginning of the row for *Mr. Steve Dutton*.
    b. Click the Delete Entry button.

Step 6

    c. At the message asking if you want to delete the entry, click the Yes button.
8. Insert a new record by completing the following steps:
    a. Click the New Entry button in the dialog box.

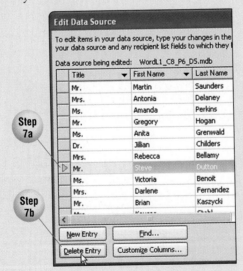

Step 7a

Step 7b

b. Type the following text in the new record in the specified fields:

Title = **Ms.**
First Name = **Jennae**
Last Name = **Davis**
Address Line 1 = **3120 South 21st**
Address Line 2 = (none)
City = **Rosedale**
State = **MD**
ZIP Code = **20389**
Home Phone = **410-555-5774**

9. Insert a new field and type text in the field by completing the following steps:

a. At the Edit Data Source dialog box, click the Customize Columns button.

b. At the message asking if you want to save the changes made to the data source file, click Yes.

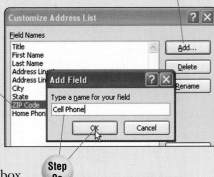

Step 9d

c. At the Customize Address List dialog box, click *ZIP Code* in the *Field Names* list box. (A new field is inserted below the selected field.)

d. Click the Add button.

e. At the Add Field dialog box, type **Cell Phone** and then click OK.

Step 9c

f. You decide that you want the *Cell Phone* field to display after the *Home Phone* field. To move the *Cell Phone* field, make sure it is selected and then click the Move Down button.

g. Click OK to close the Customize Address List dialog box.

Step 9e

h. At the Edit Data Source dialog box, scroll to the right to display the *Cell Phone* field (last field in the file) and then type the following cell phone numbers (after typing each cell phone number, except the last number, press the Down Arrow key to make the next cell below active):

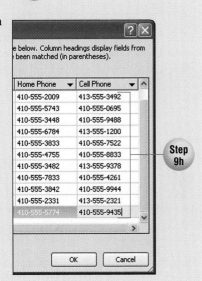

Step 9h

Record 1 = **410-555-1249**
Record 2 = **413-555-3492**
Record 3 = **410-555-0695**
Record 4 = **410-555-9488**
Record 5 = **413-555-1200**
Record 6 = **410-555-7522**
Record 7 = **410-555-8833**
Record 8 = **413-555-9378**
Record 9 = **410-555-4261**
Record 10 = **410-555-9944**
Record 11 = **413-555-2321**
Record 12 = **410-555-9435**

i. Click OK to close the Edit Data Source dialog box.

j. At the message asking if you want to update the recipient list and save changes, click Yes.

k. At the Mail Merge Recipients dialog box, click OK.

10. Create a directory by completing the following steps:

a. Click the Start Mail Merge button and then click *Directory* at the drop-down list.

b. At a blank document, set left tabs on the horizontal ruler at the 1-inch mark, the 3-inch mark, and the 4.5-inch mark.

c. Press the Tab key (this moves the insertion point to the first tab set at the 1-inch mark).

d. Click the Insert Merge Field button arrow and then click *Last_Name* at the drop-down list.

e. Type a comma and then press the spacebar.

f. Click the Insert Merge Field button arrow and then click *First_Name* at the drop-down list.

g. Press the Tab key, click the Insert Merge Field button arrow, and then click *Home_Phone* at the drop-down list.

h. Press the Tab key, click the Insert Merge Field button arrow, and then click *Cell_Phone* at the drop-down list.

i. Press the Enter key once.

j. Click the Finish & Merge button in the Finish group and then click *Edit Individual Documents* at the drop-down list.

k. At the Merge to New Document dialog box, make sure *All* is selected and then click OK. (This merges the fields in the document.)

11. Press Ctrl + Home, press the Enter key once, and then press the Up Arrow key once.

12. Press the Tab key, turn on bold, and then type Name.

13. Press the Tab key and then type Home Phone.

14. Press the Tab key and then type Cell Phone.

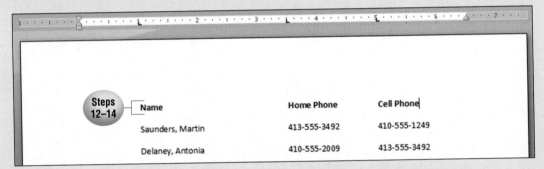

15. Save the directory document and name it **WordL1_C8_P6_Directory**.

16. Print and then close the document.

17. Close the directory main document without saving it.

roject ⑦ **Add Fill-in Fields to a Main Document**

You will edit a form letter and insert sales representative contact information during a merge.

Inputting Text during a Merge

Word's Merge feature contains a large number of Word fields you can insert in a main document. In this chapter, you will learn about the *Fill-in* field that is used for information input at the keyboard during a merge. For more information on the other Word fields, please refer to the on-screen help.

Situations may arise in which you do not need to keep all variable information in a data source file. For example, variable information that changes on a regular basis might include a customer's monthly balance, a product price, and so on. Word lets you input variable information into a document during the merge using the keyboard. A Fill-in field is inserted in a main document by clicking the Rules button in the Write & Insert Fields group in the Mailings tab and then clicking *Fill-in* at the drop-down list. This displays the Insert Word Field: Fill-in dialog box shown in Figure 8.9. At this dialog box, type a short message indicating what should be entered at the keyboard and then click OK. At the Microsoft Word dialog box with the message you entered displayed in the upper left corner, type text you want to display in the document and then click OK. When the Fill-in field or fields are added, save the main document in the normal manner. A document can contain any number of Fill-in fields.

QUICK STEPS

Insert Fill-in Field in Main Document
1. Click Mailings tab.
2. Click Rules button.
3. Click *Fill-in* at drop-down list.
4. Type prompt text.
5. Click OK.
6. Type text to be inserted in document.
7. Click OK.

Figure 8.9 Insert Word Field: Fill-in Dialog Box

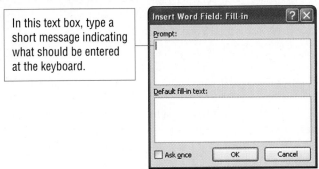

In this text box, type a short message indicating what should be entered at the keyboard.

When you merge the main document with the data source file, the first record is merged with the main document and the Microsoft Word dialog box displays with the message you entered displayed in the upper left corner. Type the required information for the first record in the data source file and then click the OK button. Word displays the dialog box again. Type the required information for the second record in the data source file and then click OK. Continue in this manner until the required information has been entered for each record in the data source file. Word then completes the merge.

Project 7 | **Adding Fill-in Fields to a Main Document**

1. Open the document named **WordL1_C8_P1_MD.docx** (at the message asking if you want to continue, click Yes) and then save the document and name it **WordL1_C8_P7_MD**.
2. Change the second paragraph in the body of the letter to the paragraph shown in Figure 8.10. Insert the first Fill-in field (representative's name) by completing the following steps:
   a. Click the Mailings tab.
   b. Click the Rules button in the Write & Insert Fields group and then click *Fill-in* at the drop-down list.

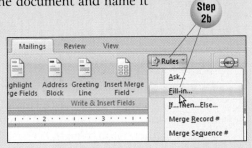

c. At the Insert Word Field: Fill-in dialog box, type Insert rep name in the *Prompt* text box and then click OK.

d. At the Microsoft Office Word dialog box with *Insert rep name* displayed in the upper left corner, type (representative's name) and then click OK.

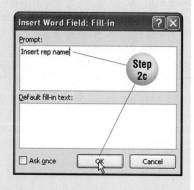

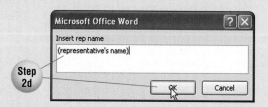

3. Complete steps similar to those in Step 2 to insert the second Fill-in field (phone number), except type Insert phone number in the *Prompt* text box at the Insert Word Field: Fill-in dialog box and type (phone number) at the Microsoft Word dialog box.

4. Save **WordL1_C8_P7_MD.docx**.

5. Merge the main document with the data source file by completing the following steps:
   a. Click the Finish & Merge button and then click *Edit Individual Documents* at the drop-down list.
   b. At the Merge to New Document dialog box, make sure *All* is selected, and then click OK.
   c. When Word merges the main document with the first record, a dialog box displays with the message *Insert rep name* and the text *(representative's name)* selected. At this dialog box, type Marilyn Smythe and then click OK.

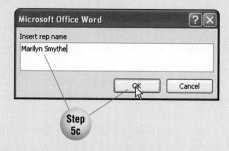

   d. At the dialog box with the message *Insert phone number* and *(phone number)* selected, type (646) 555-8944 and then click OK.
   e. At the dialog box with the message *Insert rep name*, type Anthony Mason (over *Marilyn Smythe*) and then click OK.
   f. At the dialog box with the message *Insert phone number*, type (646) 555-8901 (over the previous number) and then click OK.
   g. At the dialog box with the message *Insert rep name*, type Faith Ostrom (over *Anthony Mason*) and then click OK.
   h. At the dialog box with the message *Insert phone number*, type (646) 555-8967 (over the previous number) and then click OK.
   i. At the dialog box with the message *Insert rep name*, type Thomas Rivers (over *Faith Ostrom*) and then click OK.
   j. At the dialog box with the message *Insert phone number*, type (646) 555-0793 (over the previous number) and then click OK.

6. Save the merged document and name it **WordL1_C8_P7_Ltrs**.

7. Print and then close **WordL1_C8_P7_Ltrs.docx**.

8. Save and then close **WordL1_C8_P7_MD.docx**.

Figure 8.10 Project 7

Lowering expense charges is noteworthy because before the reduction, McCormack expense deductions were already among the lowest, far below most mutual funds and variable annuity accounts with similar objectives. At the same time, services for you, our client, will continue to expand. If you would like to discuss this change, please call our service representative, **(representative's name)**, at **(phone number)**.

CHAPTER summary

- Use the Mail Merge feature to create letters, envelopes, labels, directories, e-mail messages, and faxes, all with personalized information.
- Generally, a merge takes two documents—the data source file containing the variable information and the main document containing standard text along with fields identifying where variable information is inserted during the merge process.
- Variable information in a data source file is saved as a record. A record contains all of the information for one unit. A series of fields makes one record, and a series of records makes a data source file.
- A data source file is saved as an Access database but you do not need Access on your computer to complete a merge with a data source.
- You can use predesigned fields when creating a data source file or you can create your own custom field at the Customize Address List dialog box.
- Use the Address Block button in the Write & Insert Fields group in the Mailings tab to insert all of the fields required for the inside address of a letter. This inserts the «AddressBlock» field, which is considered a composite field because it groups a number of fields together.
- Click the Greeting Line button in the Write & Insert Fields group in the Mailings tab to insert the «GreetingLine» composite field in the document.
- Click the Insert Merge Field button arrow in the Write & Insert Fields group in the Mailings tab to display a drop-down list of fields contained in the data source file.
- Click the Preview Results button in the Mailings tab to view the main document merged with the first record in the data source. Use the navigation buttons in the Preview Results group in the Mailings tab to display the main document merged with the desired record.
- Click the Finish & Merge button in the Mailings tab to complete the merge.
- Select specific records for merging by inserting or removing check marks from the desired records in the Mail Merge Recipients dialog box. Display this dialog box by clicking the Edit Recipient List button in the Mailings tab.
- Edit specific records in a data source file at the Edit Data Source dialog box. Display this dialog box by clicking the Edit Recipient List button in the Mailings tab, clicking the desired data source file name in the *Data Source* list box, and then clicking the Edit button.
- Use the Fill-in field in a main document to insert variable information at the keyboard during a merge.

COMMANDS review

FEATURE	RIBBON TAB, GROUP	BUTTON, OPTION
New Address List dialog box	Mailings, Start Mail Merge	, Type New List
Letter main document	Mailings, Start Mail Merge	, Letters
Envelopes main document	Mailings, Start Mail Merge	, Envelopes
Labels main document	Mailings, Start Mail Merge	, Labels
Directory main document	Mailings, Start Mail Merge	, Directory
Preview merge results	Mailings, Preview Results	
Mail Merge Recipients dialog box	Mailings, Start Mail Merge	
Address Block field	Mailings, Write & Insert Fields	
Greeting Line field	Mailings, Write & Insert Fields	
Insert merge fields	Mailings, Write & Insert Fields	
Fill-in merge field	Mailings, Write & Insert Fields	Rules ▼, Fill-in

CONCEPTS check

Test Your Knowledge

Completion: In the space provided at the right, indicate the correct term, command, or number.

1. A merge generally takes two files—a data source file and this. _____

2. This term refers to all of the information for one unit in a data source file. _____

3. Create a data source file by clicking this button in the Mailings tab and then clicking *Type New List* at the drop-down list.   _____

4. A data source file is saved as this type of file.   _____

5. Create your own custom fields in a data source file with options at this dialog box.   _____

6. Use this button in the Mailings tab to insert all of the required fields for the inside address in a letter.   _____

7. The «GreetingLine» field is considered this type of field because it includes all of the fields required for the greeting line.   _____

8. Click this button in the Mailings tab to display the first record merged with the main document.   _____

9. To complete a merge, click this button in the Finish group in the Mailings tab.   _____

10. Select specific records in a data source file by inserting or removing check marks from the records in this dialog box.   _____

11. Use this field to insert variable information at the keyboard during a merge.   _____

SKILLS check

Demonstrate Your Proficiency

1 PREPARE AND MERGE LETTERS, ENVELOPES, AND LABELS

1. Look at the information shown in Figure 8.11 and Figure 8.12.
2. Use the Mail Merge feature to prepare four letters using the information shown in the figures. Name the data source file **WordL1_C8_A1_DS**, name the main document **WordL1_C8_A1_MD**, and name the merged letters document **WordL1_C8_A1_Ltrs**.
3. Print and then close **WordL1_C8_A1_Ltrs.docx**. Save and then close **WordL1_C8_A1_MD.docx**.
4. Create an envelope main document and merge it with the **WordL1_C8_A1_DS.mdb** data source file. Save the merged envelopes document and name it **WordL1_C8_A1_Envs**. Print and then close document. Close the envelope main document without saving it.
5. Use the Mail Merge feature to prepare mailing labels for the names and addresses in the **WordL1_C8_A1_DS.mdb** data source file.
6. Save the merged labels document and name it **WordL1_C8_A1_Labels**. Print and then close the document.
7. Close the labels main document without saving it.

Figure 8.11 Assessment 1

Mr. Tony Benedetti
1315 Cordova Road
Apt. 402
Santa Fe, NM 87505
Home Phone: 505-555-0489

Ms. Theresa Dusek
12044 Ridgway Drive
(leave this blank)
Santa Fe, NM 87505
Home Phone: 505-555-1120

Mrs. Mary Arguello
2554 Country Drive
#105
Santa Fe, NM 87504
Home Phone: 505-555-7663

Mr. Preston Miller
120 Second Street
(leave this blank)
Santa Fe, NM 87505
Home Phone: 505-555-3551

Figure 8.12 Assessment 1

May 6, 2010

«AddressBlock»

«GreetingLine»

The Cordova Children's Community Center is a nonprofit agency providing educational and recreational activities to children in the Cordova community. We are funded by donations from the community and rely on you and all of our volunteers to provide quality care and services to our children. As a member of our outstanding volunteer team, we are inviting you to attend our summer volunteer open house on Saturday, May 22, at the community center from 1:00 to 4:30 p.m. We want to honor you and our other volunteers for your commitment to children so please plan to attend so we can thank you in person.

The Center's summer volunteer session begins Tuesday, June 1, and continues through August 31. According to our volunteer roster, you have signed up to volunteer during the summer session. Throughout the summer we will be offering a variety of services to our children including tutoring, creative art classes, recreational activities, and a science camp. At the open house, you can sign up for the specific area or areas in which you want to volunteer. We look forward to seeing you at the open house and during the upcoming summer session.

Sincerely,

Andy Amura
Volunteer Coordinator

XX:WordL1_C8_A1_MD.docx

2 EDIT AND MERGE LETTERS

1. Open **WordL1_C8_A1_MD.docx** (at the message asking if you want to continue, click Yes) and then save the main document and name it **WordL1_C8_A2_MD**.
2. Edit the **WordL1_C8_A1_DS.mdb** data source file by making the following changes:
   a. Display the record for Ms. Theresa Dusek and then change the address from *12044 Ridgway Drive* to *1390 Fourth Avenue*.
   b. Display the record for Mr. Preston Miller and change the home phone number from *505-555-3551* to *505-555-1289*.
   c. Delete the record for Mrs. Mary Arguello.
   d. Insert a new record with the following information:
      Mr. Cesar Rivera
      3201 East Third Street
      Santa Fe, NM 87505
      505-555-6675
3. At the main document, edit the second sentence of the second paragraph so it reads as follows (insert a *Fill-in* field for the *(number of hours)* shown in the sentence below):
      According to our volunteer roster, you have signed up to volunteer for *(number of hours)* during the summer session.
4. Merge the main document with the data source file and type the following text for each of the records:
      Record 1 = four hours a week
      Record 2 = six hours a week
      Record 3 = twelve hours a week
      Record 4 = four hours a week
5. Save the merged document and name it **WordL1_C8_A2_Ltrs**.
6. Print and then close **WordL1_C8_A2_Ltrs.docx**.
7. Save and then close **WordL1_C8_A2_MD.mdb**.

CASE study

Apply Your Skills

Part 1

You are the office manager for Freestyle Extreme, a sporting goods store that specializes in snowboarding and snow skiing equipment and supplies. The store has two branches, one on the east side of town and the other on the west side. One of your job responsibilities is to send letters to customers letting them know about sales, new equipment, and upcoming events. Next month, both stores are having a sale and all snowboard and snow skiing supplies will be 15% off the regular price. Create a data source file that contains the following customer information: first name, last name, address, city, state, ZIP code, and branch. Add six customers to the data source file and indicate that three usually shop at the East branch and the other three usually shop at the West branch. Create a letter as a main document that includes information about the upcoming sale. The letter should contain at least two paragraphs and, in addition to the information on the sale, might include information about the store, snowboarding, and/or snow skiing. Save the data source file with the name **WordL1_C8_CS_DS**, save the main document with the name **WordL1_C8_CS_P1_MD**, and save the merged document with the name **WordL1_C8_CS_P1_Ltrs**. Create envelopes for the six merged letters and name the merged envelope document **WordL_C8_CS_P1_Envs**. Do not save the envelope main document. Print the merged letters document and the merged envelopes document.

Part 2

A well-known extreme snowboarder will be visiting both branches of the store to meet with customers and sign autographs. Use the Help feature to learn how to insert an If . . . Then . . . Else merge field in a document and then create a letter that includes the name of the extreme snowboarder (you determine the name), the time, which is 1:00 p.m. to 4:30 p.m., and any additional information that might interest the customer. Also include in the letter an If . . . Then . . . Else merge field that will insert *Wednesday, September 22* if the customer's Branch is *East* and will insert *Thursday, September 23* if the Branch is *West*. Add visual appeal to the letter by inserting a picture, clip art image, WordArt, or any other feature that will attract the reader's attention. Save the letter main document and name it **WordL1_C8_CS_P2_MD**. Merge the letter main document with the **WordL1_C8_CS_DS.mdb** data source. Save the merged letters document and name it **WordL1_C8_CS_P2_AnnLtrs**. Print the merged letters document.

Part 3

The store owner wants to try selling shorter skis known as "snow blades" or "skiboards." He has asked you to research the shorter skis and identify one type and model to sell only at the West branch of the store. If the model sells well, he will consider selling it at the East branch at a future time. Prepare a main document letter that describes the new snow blade or skiboard that the West branch is selling. Include information about pricing and tell customers that the new item is being offered at a 40% discount if purchased within the next week. Merge the letter main document with the **WordL1_C8_CS_DS.mdb** data source file and include only those customers that shop at the West branch. Save the merged letters document and name it **WordL1_C8_CS_P3_Ltrs**. Print the merged letters document. Save the letter main document and name it **WordL1_C8_CS_P3_MD**. Print and then close the main document

Enhancing and Customizing Documents

ASSESSING proficiency

In this unit, you have learned to format text into columns; insert, format, and customize objects to enhance the visual appeal of a document; manage files, print envelopes and labels, and create documents using templates; create and edit tables; visually represent data in SmartArt diagrams and organizational charts; and use Mail Merge to create letters, envelopes, labels, and directions.

Note: Before beginning unit assessments, copy to your storage medium the Word2007L1U2 subfolder from the Word2007L1 folder on the CD that accompanies this textbook and then make Word2007L1U2 the active folder.

Assessment 1 Format a Technology Occupations Document

1. Open **WordReport09.docx** and then save the document and name it **WordL1_U2_A1**.
2. Move the insertion point to the beginning of the heading *Telecommuting* and then insert the file named **WordDocument19.docx**.
3. Apply the Heading 1 style to the title and the Heading 2 style to the headings in the document.
4. Change the Quick Styles set to *Formal*.
5. Insert a continuous section break at the beginning of the first paragraph of text (the paragraph that begins *The march of computer technology . . .*).
6. Format the text below the section break into two newspaper columns.
7. Balance the columns on the second page.
8. Insert a pull quote of your choosing on the first page of the document that includes the text *"As the future of wireless unfolds, many new jobs will emerge as well."*
9. Create a drop cap with the first letter of the first word *The* that begins the first paragraph of text and make the drop cap two lines in height.
10. Manually hyphenate words in the document.
11. Insert page numbering that prints at the bottom of each page (you determine the page number formatting).
12. Save, print, and then close **WordL1_U2_A1.docx**.

Assessment 2 Create a Workshop Flyer

1. Create the flyer shown in Figure U2.1 with the following specifications:
   a. Insert the WordArt shape with WordArt style 15 and then customize the WordArt by changing the shadow effect to Shadow Style 1, the shape to Deflate Bottom, and increasing the width of the WordArt to 6.5″ and the height to 1″.

b. Type the text shown in the figure set in 22-point Calibri bold and center the text.

c. Insert the clip art image shown in the figure (use the keyword *buildings* to find the clip art) and then change the wrapping style to *Square*. Position and size the image as shown in the figure.

2. Save the document and name it **WordL1_U2_A2**.

3. Print and then close **WordL1_U2_A2.docx**.

Figure U2.1 Assessment 2

Assessment 3 Create a Staff Meeting Announcement

1. Create the announcement shown in Figure U2.2 with the following specifications:

a. Use the *Hexagon* shape in the *Basic Shapes* section of the Shapes drop-down list to create the shape.

b. Apply the Diagonal Gradient - Accent 5 style to the shape.

c. Apply the 3-D Style 2 located in the *Parallel* group in the 3-D Effects drop-down list.

d. Insert a text box in the shape.

e. Display the Home tab and then click the No Spacing style in the Styles group.

f. Insert the text shown in Figure U2.2. Insert the clock as a symbol (in the *Wingdings* font) and insert the *ñ* as a symbol (in the *(normal text)* font).

g. Increase the size of the shape and text so they display as shown in Figure U2.2.

2. Save the completed document and name it **WordL1_U2_A3**.

3. Print and then close **WordL1_U2_A3.docx**.

Figure U2.2 Assessment 3

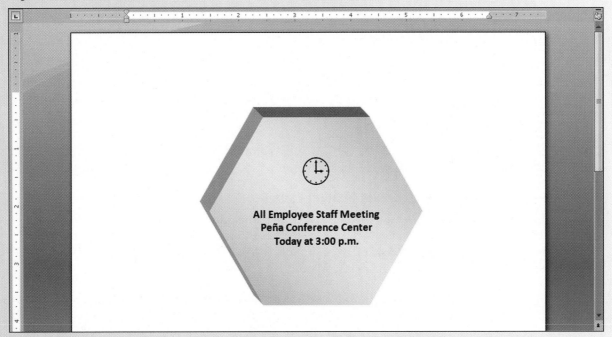

All Employee Staff Meeting
Peña Conference Center
Today at 3:00 p.m.

Assessment 4 Create a River Rafting Flyer

1. At a blank document, insert the picture named **River.jpg**. (Insert the picture using the Picture button.)
2. Crop out a portion of the trees at the left and right and a portion of the hill at the top.
3. Change the brightness to *+20%*.
4. Specify that the picture should wrap behind text.
5. Insert the text *River Rafting Adventures* on one line, *Salmon River, Idaho* on the next line, and *1-888-555-3322* on the third line.
6. Increase the size of the picture so it is easier to see and the size of the text so it is easier to read. Center the text and position it on the picture on top of the river so the text is readable.
7. Save the document and name it **WordL1_U2_A4**.
8. Print and then close **WordL1_U2_A4.docx**.

Assessment 5 Create an Envelope

1. At a blank document, create an envelope with the text shown in Figure U2.3.
2. Save the envelope document and name it **WordL1_U2_A5**.
3. Print and then close **WordL1_U2_A5.docx**.

Figure U2.3 Assessment 5

Mrs. Eileen Hebert
15205 East 42nd Street
Lake Charles, LA 71098

Mr. Earl Robicheaux
1436 North Sheldon Street
Jennings, LA 70542

Assessment 6 Create Mailing Labels

1. Create mailing labels with the name and address for Mrs. Eileen Hebert shown in Figure U2.3 using a label vendor and product of your choosing.
2. Save the document and name it **WordL1_U2_A6**.
3. Print and then close **WordL1_U2_A6.docx**.

Assessment 7 Create and Format a Table with Software Training Information

1. At a blank document, create the table shown in Figure U2.4. Format the table and the text in a manner similar to what is shown in Figure U2.4.
2. Insert a formula in B8 that totals the numbers in cells B4 through B7.
3. Insert a formula in C8 that totals the numbers in cells C4 through C7.
4. Save the document and name it **WordL1_U2_A7**.
5. Print and then close **WordL1_U2_A7.docx**.

Figure U2.4 Assessment 7

TRI-STATE PRODUCTS		
Computer Technology Department Microsoft® Office 2007 Training		
Application	**# Enrolled**	**# Completed**
Access 2007	20	15
Excel 2007	62	56
PowerPoint 2007	40	33
Word 2007	80	72
Total		

Assessment 8 Create and Format a Table Containing Training Scores

1. Open **WordTable06.docx** and then save the document and name it **WordL1_U2_A8**.
2. Insert formulas that calculate the averages in the appropriate row and column. (When writing the formulas, change the *Number format* option to *0*.)
3. Autofit the contents of the table.
4. Apply a table style of your choosing to the table.
5. Appy any other formatting to improve the visual appeal of the table.
6. Save, print, and then close **WordL1_U2_A8.docx**.

Assessment 9 Create an Organizational Chart

1. Use SmartArt to create an organizational chart for the following text (in the order displayed). Apply formatting to enhance the visual appeal of the organizational chart.
2. Save the completed document and name it **WordL1_U2_A9**.
3. Print and then close **WordL1_U2_A9.docx**.

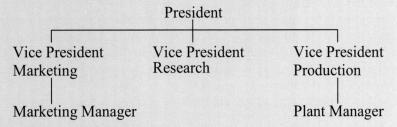

President

Vice President Marketing

Vice President Research

Vice President Production

Marketing Manager

Plant Manager

Assessment 10 Create a SmartArt Diagram

1. At a blank document, create the WordArt and diagram shown in Figure U2.5 with the following specifications:
   a. Insert the WordArt shape with WordArt style 11 and then customize the WordArt by changing the shape to Can Up and increasing the width to 6.5″ and the height to 1″.
   b. Create the diagram using the Vertical Picture Accent List diagram. Click the picture icon that displays in the top circle and then insert the picture named **Seagull.jpg** located in the Word2007L1U2 folder. Insert the same picture in the other two circles. Type the text in each rectangle shape as shown in Figure U2.5.
2. Save the document and name it **WordL1_U2_A10**.
3. Print and then close **WordL1_U2_A10.docx**.

Figure U2.5 Assessment 10

Assessment 11 Merge and Print Letters

1. Look at the information shown in Figure U2.6 and Figure U2.7. Use the Mail Merge feature to prepare six letters using the information shown in the figures. When creating the letter main document, insert Fill-in fields in place of the *(coordinator name)* and *(telephone number)* text. Create the data source file with the text shown in Figure U2.6 and name the file **WordL1_U2_DS**.
2. Create the letter main document with the information shown in Figure U2.7 and then merge the document with the **WordL1_U2_DS.mdb** data source file. When merging, enter the first name and telephone number shown below for the first three records and enter the second name and telephone number shown below for the last three records.

   Jeff Greenswald   (813) 555-9886
   Grace Ramirez   (813) 555-9807
3. Save the merged letters document and name it **WordL1_U2_Letters**. Print and then close the document.
4. Save the main document and name it **WordL1_U2_MD** and then close the document.

Figure U2.6 Assessment 11

Mrs. Antonio Mercado   Ms. Kristina Vukovich
3241 Court G   1120 South Monroe
Tampa, FL 33623   Tampa, FL 33655

Ms. Alexandria Remick   Mr. Minh Vu
909 Wheeler South   9302 Lawndale Southwest
Tampa, FL 33620   Tampa, FL 33623

Mr. Curtis Iverson   Mrs. Holly Bernard
10139 93rd Court South   8904 Emerson Road
Tampa, FL 33654   Tampa, FL 33620

Figure U2.7 Assessment 11

December 12, 2009

«AddressBlock»

«GreetingLine»

Sound Medical is switching hospital care in Tampa to St. Jude's Hospital beginning January 1, 2010. As mentioned in last month's letter, St. Jude's Hospital was selected because it meets our requirements for high-quality, customer-pleasing care that is also affordable and accessible. Our physicians look forward to caring for you in this new environment.

Over the past month, staff members at Sound Medical have been working to make this transition as smooth as possible. Surgeries planned after January 1 are being scheduled at St. Jude's Hospital. Mothers delivering babies any time after January 1 are receiving information about delivery room tours and prenatal classes available at St. Jude's. Your Sound Medical doctor will have privileges at St. Jude's and will continue to care for you if you need to be hospitalized.

You are a very important part of our patient family, «Title» «Last_Name», and we hope this information is helpful. If you have any additional questions or concerns, please call your Sound Medical health coordinator, (coordinator name), at (telephone number), between 8:00 a.m. and 4:30 p.m.

Sincerely,

Jody Tiemann
District Administrator

XX:WordL1_U2_MD.docx

Assessment 12 Merge and Print Envelopes

1. Use the Mail Merge feature to prepare envelopes for the letters created in Assessment 11.
2. Specify **WordL1_U2_DS.mdb** as the data source document.
3. Save the merged envelopes document and name the document **WordL1_U2_Envs**.
4. Print and then close **WordL1_U2_Envs.docx**.
5. Do not save the envelope main document.

WRITING activities

The following activities give you the opportunity to practice your writing skills along with demonstrating an understanding of some of the important Word features you have mastered in this unit. Use correct grammar, appropriate word choices, and clear sentence constructions.

Activity 1 Compose a Letter to Volunteers

You are an employee for the City of Greenwater and are responsible for coordinating volunteers for the city's Safe Night program. Compose a letter to the volunteers listed below and include the following information in the letter:

- Safe Night event scheduled for Saturday, June 19, 2010.
- Volunteer orientation scheduled for Thursday, May 20, 2010, at 7:30 p.m. At the orientation, participants will learn about the types of volunteer positions available and the work schedule.

Include any additional information in the letter, including a thank you to the volunteers. Use the Mail Merge feature to create a data source with the names and addresses that is attached to the main document, which is the letter to the volunteers. Save the merged letters as **WordL1_U2_Act01** and then print the letters.

Mrs. Laura Reston
376 Thompson Avenue
Greenwater, OR 99034

Mr. Matthew Klein
7408 Ryan Road
Greenwater, OR 99034

Ms. Cecilia Sykes
1430 Canyon Road
Greenwater, OR 99034

Mr. Brian McDonald
8980 Union Street
Greenwater, OR 99034

Mr. Ralph Emerson
1103 Highlands Avenue
Greenwater, OR 99034

Mrs. Nola Alverez
598 McBride Street
Greenwater, OR 99034

Activity 2 Create a Business Letterhead

You have just opened a new mailing and shipping business and need letterhead stationery. Create a letterhead for your company in a header and/or footer. Use Word's Help feature to learn about creating a header that only displays and prints on the first page. Create the letterhead in a header that displays and prints only on the first page and include *at least* one of the following: a clip art image, a picture, a shape, a text box, and/or WordArt. Include the following information in the header:

Global Mailing
4300 Jackson Avenue
Toronto, ON M4C 3X4
(416) 555-0095
www.emcp.net/globalmailing

Save the completed letterhead and name it **WordL1_U2_Act02**. Print and then close the document.

Create a Flyer on an Incentive Program

The owner of Evergreen Travel is offering an incentive to motivate travel consultants to increase travel bookings. The incentive is a sales contest with a grand prize of a one-week paid vacation to Cancun, Mexico. The owner has asked you to create a flyer that will be posted on the office bulletin board that includes information about the incentive program and some information about Cancun. Create this flyer using information about Cancun that you find on the Internet. Include a photo you find on a Web site (make sure it is not copyrighted) or include a clip art image representing travel. Include any other information or object to add visual appeal to the flyer. Save the completed flyer and name it **WordL1_U2_InternetResearch**. Print and then close the document.

Develop Recycling Program Communications

The Chief Operating Officer of Harrington Engineering has just approved your draft of the company's new recycling policy (see the file named **WordRecyclingPolicy.docx** located in the Word2007L1U2 folder) with a note that you need to add some statistics on national average costs of recycling, which you can locate on the Internet. Edit the draft and prepare a final copy of the policy along with a memorandum to all employees describing the new guidelines. To support the company's energy resources conservation effort, you will send hard copies of the new policy to the Somerset Recycling Program president and to directors of Somerset Chamber of Commerce.

Using the concepts and techniques you learned in this unit, prepare the following documents:

- Format the recycling policy manual, including a cover page, appropriate headers and footers, and page numbers. Add at least one graphic and one diagram where appropriate. Format the document using a Quick Styles set and styles. Save the manual and name it **WordL1_U2_JobStudyManual**. Print the manual.

- Download a memo template from the Microsoft Online Web site and then create a memo from Susan Gerhardt, Chief Operating Officer of Harrington Engineering to all employees introducing the new recycling program. Copy the *Procedure* section of the recycling policy manual into the memo where appropriate. Include a table listing five employees who will act as Recycling Coordinators at Harrington Engineering (make up the names). Add columns for the employees' department names and their telephone extensions. Save the memo and name it **WordL1_U2_JobStudyMemo**. Print the memo.

- Write a letter to the President of the Somerset Recycling Program, William Elizondo, enclosing a copy of the recycling policy manual. Add a notation indicating copies with enclosures were sent to all members of the Somerset Chamber of Commerce. Save the letter and name it **WordL1_U2_JobStudyLetter**. Print the letter.

- Create mailing labels (see Figure U2.8). Save the labels and name the file **WordL1_U2_JobStudyLabels**. Print the file.

Figure U2.8 Mailing Labels

William Elizondo, President
Somerset Recycling Program
700 West Brighton Road
Somerset, NJ 55123

Paul Schwartz
Somerset Chamber of Commerce
45 Wallace Road
Somerset, NJ 55123

Ashley Crighton
Somerset Chamber of Commerce
45 Wallace Road
Somerset, NJ 55123

Carol Davis
Somerset Chamber of Commerce
45 Wallace Road
Somerset, NJ 55123

Robert Knight
Somerset Chamber of Commerce
45 Wallace Road
Somerset, NJ 55123

Division: table calculations and forward slash (/) operator for, 251
Document icon, 194
Document Map feature, 103, 138, 140
    navigating in document with, 106, 107–108
Documents. *See also* Text
    active, 201–202
    arranging, 202, 220
    automatic numbering in, 71
    browsing in, 17, 18–19
    closing, 12–13, 30
    copying, 194, 197
    creating, 10, 13
    creating, with templates, 217
    customized borders and shading added to, 79–80
    deleting, 195, 196, 219
    deleting selected text from, 88
    deleting to Recycle Bin, 195
    displaying, in draft view, 104
    displaying, in Full Screen Reading view, 104–105
    drop caps in, 162
    editing, 16, 21–22
    fill-in fields in, 293
    finding text in, 130
    inserting and deleting text in, 19–20
    maintaining, 193–225
    maximizing, restoring, and minimizing, 202–203
    merging, 273–302, 280
    moving, 194, 197
    multiple, opening, 199
    naming, 12, 29
    navigating in, 106–108, 138
    opening, 13–14, 30
    paragraph symbols displayed in, 49
    predesigned headers inserted into, 122–123
    preparing, 7–34
    previewing, 206–208, 219, 220
    printing, 12, 13, 30, 194, 208
    printing, at Open dialog box, 199
    pull quotes inserted into, 175

    renaming, 194, 198
    saving, 11, 12–13, 30, 219
    saving, in different formats, 199–200
    saving, with Save As option, 15
    scrolling in, 16
    selecting, 30, 195, 196
    shapes drawn in, 177–178
    spelling and grammar checks in, 24, 25–26
    symbols and special characters in, 163–164
    template, 219
    themes applied to text in, 47
    viewing side by side, 204–205, 219, 220
    WordArt in, 184–185
.docx extension, 200
Dot leaders: setting a left tab and a right tab with, 87–88
Double spacing, 58
Draft button: in View section on Status bar, 104
Draft view, 104, 138, 140
Drawing
    arrow shapes, 178–180
    enclosed objects, 178
    shapes, 177–178
    tables, 263
    text boxes, 180–181
Drawing Tools Format tab, 177, 187
Draw Table button, 231
Drop Cap button, 162, 186, 188
Drop Cap dialog box, 162
Drop caps, 186
    creating and inserting, 162
Duplicate words, 24

E

Edit Data Source dialog box, 289, 290
Editing
    data source file, 287
    documents, 16, 21–22
    predesigned headers or footers, 125, 138
    records, 289
    records, in data source file, 290–293, 296
Edit Recipient List button, 287, 296
    in Start Mail Merge, 289

Edit WordArt text dialog box, 184
Effects theme, 46, 62
Enclosed objects: drawing, 178
End-of-cell marker: in table, 228
End-of-row marker: in table, 228
Envelope feature, 219
Envelope Options dialog box, 281, 282
Envelopes
    creating and printing, 210–212
    creating in existing document, 213
    merging, 281–282
    printing, 211–212, 219
Envelopes and Labels dialog box, 219
    with Envelopes tab selected, 210, 211, 220
    with Labels tab selected, 214, 215, 220
Envelopes main document, 297
Eraser button, 231
Excel worksheets: calculating data in, 251
Exit Word button, 15
Explain button: at Spelling & Grammar dialog box, 30

F

Feed sample box: at Envelopes and Labels dialog box, 211
Fields
    date and time inserted as, 165
    predesigned and custom, 296
    Word, 293
File names: characters not allowed in, 12
Files: inserting, 206, 220
Filing system, 193
Fill: in text boxes, 175
Fill-in fields, 293
    in main document, 294–295, 296
Fill-in merge field, 297
Find and Replace dialog box, 103, 136, 161
    expanded, 133
    expanded, options at, 134
    with Find tab selected, 130, 140